Praise for Benjamin Rachlin's

Ghost of the Innocent Man

One of the Best Books of the Year
San Francisco Chronicle, National Public Radio,
Library Journal, Shelf Awareness

"A crisply written page-turner...Rachlin painstakingly renders Grimes's life behind bars...Deploying the same precision with which he documents Grimes's prison life, Rachlin recounts the arduous and complex work to move the wheels of justice...Read *Ghost of the Innocent Man* to follow its twisted path...but don't read for the gripping story alone...The National Registry of Exonerations calculates that over eighteen thousand years have been lost by innocent people serving time...Shouldn't we be better than this?"
— Martha Anne Toll, National Public Radio

"Remarkable...A captivating, intimate profile of one man's stubbornly persistent efforts to convince others of his innocence...Rachlin is a skilled storyteller...With understatement and painstaking reporting, he fully succeeds in his rich, intimate portrait of Grimes."
— Alex Kotlowitz, *New York Times Book Review*

"Intriguing...A gripping legal-thriller mystery...This is a story that profoundly elevates good-cause advocacy to greater heights—to where innocent lives are saved...This empathetic book tells the story of the beginnings of the movement to right a national crisis of wrongful convictions—and of one of its first victories...A fine piece of investigative journalism."   —Don Oldenburg, *USA Today*

"An absorbing true-crime saga. Rachlin's debut combines a gripping legal drama with a penetrating exposé of the shoddy investigative and trial standards nationwide...His narrative offers a moving evocation of faith under duress."   —*Publishers Weekly*

"Rachlin vividly describes the anguish that would well up in Grimes again and again during his twenty-four years behind bars...In Rachlin's skilled hands, Grimes's story triggers indignation but also confers solace, Grimes being one of the solacing features."

—Dennis Drabelle, *Washington Post*

"*Ghost of the Innocent Man* is nothing less than a masterpiece of investigative reporting and virtuosic writing. It is a book that brilliantly substantiates society's elemental promise to its citizenry—that we not have our freedoms wrongly taken from us. Benjamin Rachlin's book is Greek drama brought into our own times. It will change readers' lives, I think, and inspire them. It's that good."

—Richard Ford

"Grimes's story is both compelling and enraging, and his thoughtfulness and persistence propel the story as much as the determination and passion of the lawyers working to establish the Commission...A sobering account of both a wrongful conviction and the structural impediments to fixing miscarriages of justice, with a gut punch of a closing paragraph."

—Kate Sheehan, *Library Journal*

"Dramatic and eye-opening...A hopeful story...By showing us that the specter of wrongful convictions involves flesh-and-blood human beings, *Ghost of the Innocent Man* confronts us with the cruelest injustices of the criminal justice system, even as it also holds out hope for a more humane future."

—Richard Thompson Ford, *San Francisco Chronicle*

"*Ghost of the Innocent Man* is plainspoken—frank, yes, but even more potently, unadorned—either when Grimes is speaking or Rachlin is writing...The story is clean and tight, emotionally and psychologically expressive and expressionistic, and easily visualized by the mind's eye...A fine debut effort."

—Peter Lewis, *Barnes & Noble Review*

"One of the most powerful aspects of *Ghost of the Innocent Man* is its portrait of time behind bars—the transfers, delays, and letter-writing campaigns that form the scaffolding of lives in limbo...A story so important and infuriating, it is hard to look away."

—Claudia Rowe, *Seattle Times*

"*Ghost of the Innocent Man* is deeply researched and, more important, deeply felt. For both reasons and many more, it is a profound meditation on the human condition and a vital contribution to the literature. The endurance and fortitude of Willie Grimes surpass those of any athlete or explorer. The passages in which Christine Mumma assembles lawmen and legislatures of all different creeds to help resolve an urgent national crisis should make us all consider these current times as not just toxic and tragic but filled with the possibility of hope and redemption. In the end, Benjamin Rachlin takes us through the justice system in all its immutability and shows us the light we can wield should we so choose."

—Jeff Hobbs, author of *The Short and Tragic Life of Robert Peace*

"Enraging, instructive, and profoundly moving, *Ghost of the Innocent Man* is a gripping lesson in the terrible costs of our flawed criminal justice system and the power that individuals have to change its course. The story of how a gentle soul like Willie J. Grimes received an undeserved life sentence is heartbreaking—full of human cruelty and carelessness and worse. But in the care and exactitude of Benjamin Rachlin's telling, it is also an inspiring call for readily achievable reform. With judicious compassion, he narrates the errors, omissions, and societal forces that led to this wrongful conviction, setting it all squarely in the context of a persistent national disgrace, and reminding us of our responsibility to work toward true justice. The effect is remarkable and unforgettable."

—Eli Sanders, Pulitzer Prize winner and author of *While the City Slept*

"An absorbing story...In his moving first book, Rachlin, with confidence and care, relays both the terrifying personal costs and complex legalities, so dependent on fallible humans, of wrongful conviction and imprisonment." —Annie Bostrom, *Booklist*

"In this compelling tale of crime and punishment (of the wrong person), Rachlin explores a horrible case of wrongful conviction and ultimate exoneration. Willie Grimes maintained his innocence in his 1988 trial but was convicted on flimsy evidence and served over twenty years behind bars. By twinning Grimes's story with the establishment of North Carolina's Innocence Inquiry Commission, which was responsible for overturning the conviction, Rachlin enlarges the book's scope, making it not merely a chronicle of a serious miscarriage of justice, but a broader indictment of a flawed system, and the prison industrial complex, that made it possible."
—*National Book Review*

"A chilling story of wrongful conviction, focused on one man's ordeal, and the growth of the movement to support actual innocence...Rachlin ably manages a complex narrative...A sprawling, powerful, unsettling longitudinal account of an overdue legal movement."
—*Kirkus Reviews*

GHOST

OF THE

INNOCENT MAN

A True Story *of* Trial
and Redemption

BENJAMIN RACHLIN

BACK BAY BOOKS
Little, Brown and Company
New York Boston London

Back Bay Books / Little, Brown and Company
Hachette Book Group
1290 Avenue of the Americas, New York, NY 10104
littlebrown.com

Originally published by Little, Brown and Company, August 2017
First Back Bay paperback edition, August 2018

Back Bay Books is an imprint of Little, Brown and Company, a division of Hachette Book Group, Inc. The Back Bay Books name and logo are trademarks of Hachette Book Group, Inc.

The publisher is not responsible for websites (or their content) that are not owned by the publisher.

"21,730 Days" portrait by Christer Berg.

The Hachette Speakers Bureau provides a wide range of authors for speaking events. To find out more, go to hachettespeakersbureau.com or call (866) 376-6591.

ISBN 978-0-316-31149-6 (hc) / 978-0-316-31150-2 (pb)
LCCN 2017932048

10 9 8 7 6 5 4 3 2 1

LSC-C

Printed in the United States of America

For my parents, Allan and Vicki

and for Jaclyn

Under our criminal procedure the accused has every advantage....He cannot be convicted when there is the least fair doubt in the minds of any one of the twelve....Our dangers do not lie in too little tenderness to the accused. Our procedure has been always haunted by the ghost of the innocent man convicted. It is an unreal dream.

—Judge Learned Hand (1923)

Contents

Author's Note

This is a work of nonfiction. I have changed no names or dates. Dialogue in quotation marks is drawn from trial or interview transcripts; police, hospital, or prison records; personal or legal correspondence; prepared remarks or meeting minutes; or the recollections of those present. Where a person recalled the gist of a discussion but not its particular words, I have rendered dialogue without quotation marks. Where a person's thoughts or feelings are described, these were recalled afterward in writing, testimony, or interviews. Though of course I have interpreted events, I have done so as faithfully as possible.

More detailed information appears in the Sources.

GHOST

OF THE

INNOCENT MAN

Prologue

1987

There was a knocking at her door. The sound was unmistakable on an evening so quiet, silent but for insects—a mild night for October in North Carolina, nearly sixty degrees. Must be her neighbor, Carrie thought. No one else would visit her apartment so late, a few minutes after nine o'clock. She knew the time exactly, having just taken her blood pressure pills, as every night, right at nine.

She liked Linda, her neighbor. Before Carrie's husband died, last Thanksgiving, Linda and Mason—that was Linda's boyfriend—had stopped by often to check up on him, or to bring ice cream, or to ask if Carrie needed groceries. They were so well mannered it nearly didn't matter they were black. Only Linda ever visited now, or Carrie's family, who would have called first. Otherwise Carrie never let anyone in, or even lingered outside. She was too old for public housing, sixty-nine, and ninety pounds, five feet tall if she stood up straight or wore stockings. One of the only white people around. She lived in a neighborhood they called Little Berlin, a cluster of squat, half-brick duplexes near the intersection of I-40 and US-70, an hour west of Charlotte, barely a mile from the Hickory town line. Out front lay concrete tablets for porches, nothing on them but collapsed wooden benches or classroom chairs taken from who knew where. She had disliked the place as soon as they'd moved in, two years earlier, though it was worse now that her husband was gone. On nights like these she would stay inside and cut coupons. She had a booklet of them she had collected from the supermarket that afternoon. Then to bed early. She wore a nightgown and her glasses, had already washed her hair. On her bedspread were clothes she had laid out for church the next morning.

In the porch light it was a moment before her eyes adjusted. Then she saw a man there, so near he startled her. He was a foot taller than she was, his skin as dark as the view beyond her porch. By instinct she fumbled for the handle of the storm door, but too soon it was open, its chain snapped, the hinges buckled all the way to the wall.

"I want you," the man said, licking his lips.

"You get out," Carrie gasped. She pulled for the handle of the interior door, but already his hand was inside, and the man yanked it wide.

"I'm not going anywhere," he told her. Then he was over the threshold. "I want you," he said again. He pushed Carrie across the living room, past her television set, past a potted snake plant, and onto her couch. The coupons she'd been clipping fluttered to the floor. Before she had fully registered his being inside her apartment he was lifting his shirt over his head, groping at her nightgown. She could see he was much younger than she was, and unshaven. He smelled of alcohol. "I like older women," he said. "They don't mess around."

Had Linda and Mason gone out? Linda would not be able to help — she was too small, too weak, like Carrie. But Mason. She would allow Mason inside, this one time, to help her. She thought briefly of her husband, but he was gone now, she knew. Wasn't anyone else outside? Her underwear was off. He was forcing himself into her. Her heartbeat rattled beneath his weight. She nearly screamed but chose not to. He might hurt her even more. She knew he had a knife — a switchblade, several inches long, halfway unfolded. Or he didn't. Later this would be a source of contention: whether she had actually seen the knife or if the man had simply threatened her and she had imagined one, as real as his stubbled face, as the alcohol on his breath.

He finished. Stepped back from the couch and stood there, shirtless. She hoped he might leave now, on his own, that it might be over. Her body throbbed as though from a distance.

He told her they were going to the bedroom. "Let's go," he demanded.

But he didn't know the apartment. He asked her where the bedroom was.

"I'm not going anywhere with you," Carrie told him.

This made him angry. He ordered her to the bedroom with his knife—was there a knife? Again she refused. He clutched her arm above the elbow and dragged her from the couch. Her bedroom was fifteen feet across the pockmarked linoleum floor. He found it easily. Hauled her onto the bedspread, atop the clothes she had laid out for church. Climbed over her. Forced himself again. The bedroom so narrow there was no space to run, even if she could get free, which she knew she couldn't. This man on top of her, the blood gone from her arms. The pale blue walls of the room. A box in the corner, with spare sheets. A white mug on the nightstand.

He finished again. She knew she needed to escape but lacked the strength. Her limbs pulsed when he released them. "I n-need to use the bathroom," she stammered.

He leaned away. Stumbled off the bed. "I'm hungry," he announced, then disappeared into the living room.

On the bathroom tile she knelt and prayed. The man heard this and shouted at her from the kitchen to quiet down. "I can't stand that," he told her. She could hear him opening cupboards. "What you got in your refrigerator?"

She walked to the door of the kitchen and thought of something. "My neighbors will be over soon," she told him. "They're coming over. You should leave. You won't want to be here."

The man's face was hidden inside the empty refrigerator. He was still shirtless. "Mason?" he asked, his voice muffled. Then he straightened. "I saw Mason leave," he told her. "Their apartment's empty. Nobody's here to help you." He smiled. Looked back into the refrigerator. "What have you got to eat?"

She was stunned to hear Mason's name. Were Mason and this man friends? Had this been planned? "I didn't make supper," she managed. "There isn't any other food here." She looked at the kitchen table. A box of Cheez-Its, a package of hamburger buns, a plastic bowl full of fruit. Wicker place mats.

The man tugged his shirt over his shoulders. "I never heard such screaming," he told her, nodding toward the bathroom, where she had knelt praying. Then he shook his head, as though she disappointed him. He pushed aside the hamburger buns and reached for the bowl of fruit. Took an apple, several bananas. Then he turned and the door clapped shut. He was gone.

1

Firm and Unequivocal

Just after nine thirty on Wednesday morning, July 6, 1988, as 90 percent humidity clamped down outside, Judge Kenneth Griffin settled onto his bench in the Catawba County Justice Center and brought court to session. Seen from the road, the justice center was a concrete slab of a building with asymmetrical columns, a modest parking lot, and tall, slender windows, enjambed beside a sheriff's office and detention facility. The entire complex sat shouting distance from a gas station, two fast-food restaurants, and a Speed Lube Express. All the rest was rolling farmland.

"Good morning," Judge Griffin said. Almost nine months earlier, up in Hickory, a town of fewer than thirty thousand residents, in the western third of the state, an elderly woman had been assaulted in her home. "The State of North Carolina has accused Mr. Willie James Grimes..." He paused and looked toward the defense table. "Hold up your hand, Mr. Grimes." As the man raised his arm, Griffin read the charges: two counts of first-degree rape, one count each of first-degree burglary and kidnapping. "To each of these charges, Mr. Grimes, through his attorney, Mr. de Torres, has entered pleas of not guilty," Judge Griffin told the jury. He turned the proceedings over to Bill Johnson, an assistant district attorney, who called Carrie Elliott to the stand.

What followed was unsettling testimony. Already petite, Carrie seemed even smaller on the witness stand, where she occupied barely a third of the wooden box. Beside Judge Griffin's elevated bench, she seemed a tiny fraction of his height. As apparent was her age; she was older than the judge, who himself was over sixty. It was easy to imagine her overwhelmed by an assailant. Johnson led her to recount the facts of that night in October: where Carrie lived, that she hadn't expected any visitors, her assailant's demand for something to eat. "How was the intruder dressed?"

"He had on a green shirt," Carrie remembered. "And jeans, or blue pants."

Next Johnson established the reason for having brought two separate counts of rape: the couch and the bed were distinct episodes, and he wanted Carrie to lead the jury through each of them. "Approximately how long did this intercourse on the couch last?" he asked. "Do you recall?"

Carrie didn't. "It seemed like forever to me," she said. "It was a horrible nightmare."

"And how far away was his face from yours?"

"Right up over me."

"Were you able to get a good look at this individual?"

"Yes, sir," Carrie affirmed, nodding. Had she noticed anything unusual about the man's appearance, or any identifying marks? She nodded again. She had seen a mole on his face, and that he'd needed a shave. The mole was on the right side, which Carrie recalled because she had broken a fingernail trying to scratch at it. "I fought with him the whole way," she said.

Since that night in October, Carrie added, she had seen the man again at his probable-cause hearing, and had recognized him there, too. She had also seen him in a photograph police had shown her. Johnson wanted to know more about that photograph—how had it been displayed, and how easily had she recognized Grimes in it? But Grimes's lawyer objected, and Judge Griffin sustained. Uncertain how much follow-up the judge would permit him, Johnson asked that the jury be dismissed briefly so this could be worked out in private. Once the jurors filed out, Johnson resumed his questions, knowing to proceed carefully. If the judge ruled his questions fair, Johnson would be allowed to ask them again with the jury present. Otherwise what followed would remain inadmissible.

"Mrs. Elliott, you say that you were shown photographs," he began. "And out of the photographs, picked out one of the attacker."

"Yes, sir," Carrie confirmed.

"Who showed you that photograph?"

That was Sergeant Bryant, Carrie told him, of the Hickory Police Department. Bryant had traveled to Claremont, where Carrie was staying with her sister-in-law, to show her the lineup. There Carrie had recognized Grimes's photo. "And he said, 'Are you sure?'" Carrie remembered. "And I said, 'I am positive.'"

"I'm going to show you what I am marking as State Exhibit One," Johnson advised, which was a series of photographs he expected would look familiar. Offering the lineup to her, he said, "And I ask if you recognize that."

CARRIE: No, sir.

JOHNSON: You don't recognize that?

CARRIE: No, sir.

JOHNSON: You say you made an identification of this person.

CARRIE: Yes, sir.

JOHNSON: Of the person who attacked you.

CARRIE: Yes.

JOHNSON: Do you recognize any of these pictures on State Exhibit One as the picture that you identified?

CARRIE: I saw one that looked like it.

JOHNSON: For the record—this State Exhibit One has six windows on it, with six photographs, and beneath each window is a number. Is that correct?

CARRIE: Yes, sir.

JOHNSON: Would you tell us the number of the photograph you say looks like your attacker?

CARRIE: That looks like him, over there.

JOHNSON: Do you see any of these photographs—are you able to tell from these photographs the person that attacked you?

CARRIE: They don't look like any of them now.

JOHNSON: Do any of these photographs look like the one from which you made an identification?

CARRIE: They were in little blocks like that.

JOHNSON: Are you able to tell us whether any of these is the one that you identified?

CARRIE: Hard to see any difference.

Answers like these wouldn't help before a jury. Johnson chose an easier question. "At the time of your identification," he tried, "how certain were you of this individual that you identified?"

"I knew him," Carrie answered, nodding resolutely. "I am certain that he was the one."

This was better. "Here in the courtroom," Johnson asked, "do you see the person that attacked you that night?"

"Yes, sir," Carrie said.

"Where is that person?"

"Right down there," Carrie replied, gesturing toward the defense table. "Beside the guy with the red shirt on."

Only two people sat at the defense table. Grimes, the defendant, had been allowed to change out of his prison jumpsuit for trial and now wore a red button-down shirt. Next to him sat de Torres, his lawyer. Carrie was pointing at de Torres. "I remember him," Carrie continued, not realizing her error. "I will never forget that picture of him over me. I will never be able to erase that."

Johnson was stunned. Of course Carrie meant Grimes, he knew. She had gotten confused. De Torres, who was staring in disbelief, was a white man, and he and Grimes didn't look anything alike.

To minimize her mistake, Johnson rushed for a follow-up. "When you say 'picture,' you are talking about a mental picture," he mumbled. "Not a photograph?"

"Yes," Carrie told him. "What I saw with my own eyes."

"How positive are you of your identification of him?" Johnson asked.

"I am positive."

"That is all for now," Johnson said, and sat down.

De Torres, rising shakily for cross-examination, decided he would address the photographic lineup first. Since Carrie didn't recognize any of the photographs shown to her nine months earlier by police, none of them should count as evidence, he argued. This would render Carrie's first identification of his client inadmissible in court, a ruling certain to undermine Grimes having been implicated in the first place. It would also mean Carrie's only remaining identification of Grimes was the one she could make in person. This de Torres felt sure he could discredit, having just now himself been identified wrongly as her attacker. He asked Carrie whether she recognized the lineup Johnson had held a moment earlier.

Carrie admitted she hadn't, but insisted it didn't matter. "I know the man that beat me," she told him.

"Did you recognize any of the photographs you were just shown as the same photographs you were shown by Officer Bryant?"

"Well, they look the same," Carrie said. "They were in little blocks like that." De Torres, unpersuaded, pressed for details. "If you had been through what I had been through," Carrie scolded him. "They had just brought me from the hospital."

"You said that the person who assaulted you took off a shirt," de Torres noted, changing course. "A green shirt. Did you notice any tattoos, or any marks on his body?"

"No."

"Did you notice any other marks anywhere else on him, other than the mole?"

"No."

This would be valuable later, de Torres knew. For now he had seen enough. "Your Honor," he urged, turning toward Judge Griffin, "the admission of the photographs, and her identification, should not be allowed in evidence. She does not have the ability to match any photographs with anyone that is here in the courtroom. I think that the photo lineup, and any testimony concerning that, should be suppressed. It should not be admissible in this case at all."

Judge Griffin considered this. "All right," he said. He instructed the court reporter to mark down that a full examination had been conducted, in the absence of the jury, regarding the photographic identification of Willie Grimes. "Based upon the foregoing, the court concludes State Exhibit One" — the photographic lineup — "is hereby excluded from evidence in this trial. However, the witness had ample opportunity to observe the defendant in her home on the night in question, for a considerable length of time. This was sufficient to form a reliable impression of him. The witness had a high degree of concentration, her attention was focused on him, and her observations are a reasonable and accurate description of him. Her certainty is firm and unequivocal. It is now therefore ordered that the defendant's objection to the *photograph* identification is allowed. But the identification of the defendant by the witness is competent to be received in trial."

Whether Judge Griffin had noticed Carrie's identification of the wrong man, de Torres couldn't tell.

Jurors filed back into court, where Judge Griffin decided they had seen enough for the morning session and recessed for lunch. When they reconvened at two, Johnson decided to let his co-counsel, Jay Meyers, present to Carrie their final questions. Meyers wanted to confirm the presence of a knife. Then, before the jury, he asked whether Carrie could see her assailant in the courtroom today. "Yes, sir," Carrie told him. Meyers asked that she point the man out. Carrie indicated the defense table. "Right there," she said.

"Objection," de Torres intervened.

"Overruled," Judge Griffin told him, and turned toward Carrie. "Let the record reflect that you are pointing to whom?"

"The one in the red shirt there," Carrie said.

"Let the record reflect that the witness pointed out Willie James Grimes," Judge Griffin announced.

"That is all," Meyers said, and sat down.

* * *

Officer Gary Lee, of the Hickory police, had worked the second patrol shift that Saturday in October, from early afternoon until midnight. After receiving a radio call, Officer Lee had arrived to Carrie Elliott's address at 9:22, where he and a partner first noticed the broken storm door. As his partner secured Carrie's apartment, Lee radioed patrol cars within reach to warn them of a potential suspect. To do this, he needed to ask Carrie for a description of her assailant. Later he recorded this in his initial crime report.

Johnson, the assistant district attorney, having reassumed lead responsibility from Meyers, wanted to know the details of that description. "Black male, approximately six feet tall," Officer Lee recalled. "Weighing between two hundred and two twenty-five. Approximately thirty-five years old. Dark skin and bushy hair." This amounted to nearly all he and Carrie had discussed that night, since Carrie had been "real distraught," Lee remembered, and his role was simply to learn the barest version of what had happened and whom to look for. Carrie had also told him that, once her assailant vanished from the apartment, she had crawled toward the back door, locked it, and groped for the telephone. But she couldn't think of the phone number for the police. Instead, she called her son, whose wife answered. It was she, Carrie's daughter-in-law, who phoned the police. All this Officer Lee marked in his report, as well as the fact that he'd canvassed the surroundings of Carrie's apartment and consulted with neighbors to the north and east. No one had seen or heard anything helpful. On item 34 of that report, "Can suspects be ID'ed," Lee had checked the line beside *yes*.

Secure with this timeline, Johnson turned his witness over to de Torres. De Torres asked Officer Lee whether, in Carrie's account of her assailant that night, she had described what the man was wearing. She had, Lee remembered. Jeans and a green shirt. "Did she indicate anything to you about the mole on his face?" de Torres asked.

"Not at the time," Lee answered.

"That is all," de Torres said.

* * *

While Lee was canvassing Carrie's neighborhood that night, Officer Susan Moore, also of the Hickory police, had arrived at the apartment to find Carrie agitated with "evidence of bruising that was starting to appear on her upper arms." Officer Moore proposed to drive Carrie to Catawba Memorial Hospital, but Carrie declined the offer: Carrie's son and daughter-in-law had arrived at the apartment by then, and she felt more comfortable traveling with them. Moore agreed to this, then drove behind them to the hospital, where a lengthier interview revealed further details of the assault. Because Moore had departed so soon for the hospital, she hadn't spent much time at Carrie's residence—less than five minutes, she estimated. She had barely talked with Gary Lee at all. But she remembered hearing his radioed description of the suspect: a black male, age thirty-five, six feet tall, two hundred pounds or more.

De Torres, on cross-examination, was curious; during Moore's interview with Carrie at the hospital, had Carrie mentioned her assailant having a knife? "No," Moore told him, though she thought it was possible Carrie simply hadn't thought of it. In Moore's view, Carrie had been "very distraught."

The emergency department physician that night at Catawba Memorial Hospital was Bert Crane, who confirmed the bruising on Carrie's arms and left shoulder. His records showed Carrie had arrived at the hospital at 9:51. In addition to the bruising, Crane's examination revealed a painful headache, from Carrie having been pinned during her assault, and a laceration of her posterior vaginal fourchette—a one-inch tear in the vaginal wall. The laceration was recent, Dr. Crane noticed. He agreed Carrie's injuries matched her description of the preceding hour, and conducted a formal rape examination. This involved collecting samples of Carrie's head and pubic hair, and vaginal swabs. These Crane packaged into a rape kit and turned over to the police, along with a cardboard box of clothes Carrie had worn during and after the assault. Then he stitched Carrie's tear and scheduled a follow-up for the coming Monday. By midnight Carrie was discharged, wearing fresh clothes her children had brought her and wrapped in a blanket lent by one of the nurses. Now, in court, her rape kit was introduced as State Exhibit Two. Dr. Crane recognized this as the same one from the hospital, with his signature on its label. De Torres didn't have any questions.

From the hospital, Carrie's family had driven her to the Hickory police station, where she met again with Officer Moore and her partner, Officer Jeff Blackburn. The pair of them led Carrie down the square department hallway and into a private room, to provide another full account of her assault. The details of this matched what she had shared earlier at the hospital and, before that, at the scene with Gary Lee. Officer Blackburn showed Carrie a lineup sheet with photographs of six men, but she didn't recognize any of them. Then, rising, Blackburn asked Carrie to compare the suspect's dimensions to his own. Carrie considered him for a moment, then replied that her assailant had been heavier and a little bit taller. Blackburn himself was six feet tall, a hundred and ninety-five pounds. This too was consistent with what Carrie had reported earlier. That their suspect was a little over six feet and more than two hundred pounds fit Carrie's previous assessment exactly.

De Torres wanted to know whether, during this late meeting at the police station, Carrie had mentioned any mole, or scar, on her attacker. Blackburn admitted she hadn't.

Two days after her rape, at a few minutes past noon on Monday, Carrie and her daughter-in-law returned unexpectedly to the police station to visit Sergeant Steve Bryant, supervisor of criminal investigations for the Hickory Police Department. Sergeant Bryant recognized Carrie from the previous Saturday, though he hadn't met her then, and he knew the HPD still had no suspects in her case. Carrie was visiting to share a conversation she'd had with her neighbor Linda McDowell—the same neighbor she had mistakenly guessed was knocking at her door the night of the assault. Since then Linda had stopped by Carrie's apartment to say she'd heard what had happened, and how sorry she was. The two of them got to talking. Linda thought she recognized Carrie's description of her attacker. She might know who the man was, Linda allowed, though she refused to give his name to anyone but the police, not even to Carrie herself. Carrie wanted Sergeant Bryant to know this. She also wanted to tell him two additional details she'd remembered from her assault: that the man's speech had been slurred, as though he were drunk, or spoke with a lisp, and also that he had a mole. Carrie had recalled these facts during her conversation with Linda. She was certain of them. Sergeant Bryant recorded the details in his notes and assured Carrie he would include them in his investigation.

At four that afternoon, his phone rang. It was Linda McDowell. She knew the man who had assaulted Carrie, Linda told Bryant, but she didn't want to say his name over the telephone. She also wanted to know if she would get a reward. Recently she had seen advertisements for a local program called Crime Stoppers, and she expected that, if she provided this man's name, she was entitled to a prize.

Sergeant Bryant invited Linda to the station. She was there twenty minutes later, at four thirty. Once Bryant had promised the Crime Stoppers reward, a thousand dollars, Linda revealed she knew a man who fit Carrie's description exactly. He went by either Willie Grimes or Willie Vinson. He also had a street name, Woot. He had a mole on his face—on the left side, Linda thought, though she wasn't certain. She had seen Willie on the Saturday of Carrie's rape, wearing a green shirt, in that same neighborhood, Little Berlin. She also knew his address.

At six fifteen that evening, Sergeant Bryant drove out to Claremont, twenty minutes east on I-40, where Carrie was staying with a sister-in-law. When Bryant arrived, Carrie told him she might have been wrong earlier that afternoon about the placement of her attacker's mole. It might have been on the left side of his face, not his right. In either case, it was near the corner of his mouth. She was positive. She just couldn't remember which corner. Bryant showed her a new lineup, different than the one she had seen two days earlier at the police station. In position number two, he had included a photograph of Willie Grimes. This photograph Bryant had discovered on file from a drunk-driving charge in May 1985—before now, one of Grimes's only two grazes with the law. (The other was also for driving under the influence, three years earlier, in 1982.) For fifteen seconds Carrie considered the new lineup. Then she pointed at Grimes. "This is the man," she said, and began crying. "This is the man who raped me."

Bryant asked if Carrie was certain. She was, Carrie confirmed, though in person Grimes's hair had been shorter. "I will never forget his face," she told Bryant. Then she added that Grimes had really hurt her and that, because of the way he had contorted her legs while on top of her, she was even having trouble walking. "What happened to me that night," she said, "was the worst nightmare I could imagine."

De Torres, listening to Sergeant Bryant's testimony—except for the fact of the Crime Stoppers reward, which Bryant had never been asked about, and never mentioned—realized he had forfeited a valuable argument. Because Carrie had floundered privately to recognize anyone in the photographic lineups, de Torres had succeeded in preventing their introduction to trial. But he knew that, in the lineup Sergeant Bryant had shown to Carrie in Claremont, Grimes was the only man with a mole. This was a problem. Given Carrie's gradual insistence on her assailant having had a facial mole, any lineup shown to her ought to have included several men who matched this description, or else naturally Carrie would choose the only man who did. It was important this detail be disclosed to the jury, de Torres knew, since it likely had factored into Carrie's identification of Grimes. De Torres, though, couldn't say anything about it. The district attorneys had already tried to introduce both lineups at trial, and de Torres had prevented it. Now by his own urging they were inadmissible.

Instead, jurors heard testimony by Officer Steve Hunt, a criminal investigator in his early thirties, already a thirteen-year veteran of the Hickory police. Hunt himself had grown up nearby in the projects, with eight siblings, a single mother, and his grandmother, who mostly looked after them, since his mother so often was out working one of two jobs. He still cried when he talked about that neighborhood. At five or six years old he had decided to become a police officer; just two years out of high school he'd started on patrol, one of the few black officers on the Hickory force. "I was in the projects," he would tell people, "but the projects were not in me." By 1987 he was an investigator.

Because Hunt was in the habit of switching on his radio while off duty, he heard the call about Carrie that Saturday even though he wasn't working. He decided to pass by Carrie's address.

At one o'clock Sunday morning, a few hours after the assault, Hunt steered down Center Street, perpendicular to Carrie's apartment. On the pavement he came upon an apple core. Remembering something from the radio about fruit having been taken from the scene, he doubled back to Carrie's apartment for a look around. On the grass just south of her doorstep he discovered two banana peels, ten or so feet apart. These he left untouched in the yard. The apple core he brought with him to the Hickory station, where, without examining it for fingerprints, he tossed it into the trash. To one or two of his colleagues he mentioned the banana peels he'd seen, but no one went back to retrieve them. The next day, Monday, October 26, when Carrie recognized a photograph in Sergeant Bryant's lineup, Steve Hunt was put in charge of the case.

The following day, Hunt visited Grimes's address, where he lived with a girlfriend.

Grimes wasn't home. That afternoon, though, Hunt tracked Grimes down and took him into custody. He fingerprinted Grimes and booked him. In the paperwork, Hunt marked that Grimes was six feet two inches tall, a hundred and sixty-five pounds. In the section for "Scars/Marks/Tattoos," he recorded that Grimes was missing two fingertips, from the middle and index fingers of his right hand. Especially noticeable was Grimes's middle finger, where the entire final joint was gone. Carrie had never mentioned either of these. Grimes had a mole, though, near the left side of his mouth. And he was wearing a green sweater. Hunt confiscated this sweater, along with the rest of Grimes's clothes, and replaced them with a gray jumpsuit for Grimes to wear in his cell.

De Torres, at trial, asked where Grimes's clothing had gone, because it would be valuable to test for evidence. As far as de Torres knew, this had never happened. "I have no idea," Hunt told him. That clothing had been turned over to the jailor, and no one had seen it again.

Because for nearly a decade Jack Holsclaw had served as Hickory's only evidence technician, his shifts were unusually civilian-like for a police officer: five days a week, from eight thirty to five. For the same reason, however, he remained on call at any hour. The Saturday of Carrie's assault, he had been phoned at home. When he arrived at Carrie's address, sometime after nine thirty, only Officer Blackburn was still there, everyone else having left already for the hospital or the station. By then someone had replaced the chain on Carrie's storm door.

Holsclaw's responsibility was to "process the crime scene," he explained to the court, which meant to gather any items he thought might prove relevant to the case as well as to take a series of photographs. From the kitchen table he collected two bananas and an apple, since Officer Blackburn had mentioned the attacker stealing fruit. From the bedroom he removed a pair of underwear. On the bedspread he found several hair samples; these he sealed inside a plastic bag. Holsclaw also examined the front door for fingerprints but couldn't find any. Back at the station, though, he lifted two prints from the bananas. A week later, Holsclaw was able to examine them, and to compare them with fingerprints from Willie Grimes, who by then had been arrested. The prints didn't match. Holsclaw and his colleagues guessed this meant the prints probably belonged to Carrie Elliott. Officers had never taken prints from her, though, so no one ever checked. Neither did Holsclaw think to compare the prints with those of any officer who had visited the scene. Even Steve Hunt, who had booked Grimes himself and then learned a week later of the fingerprints, never followed up to see if each set matched. It was news to him now, hearing Holsclaw testify, that the prints recovered from the scene didn't belong to Grimes.

Again de Torres found himself outside the necessary argument. This was the first he had heard of any fingerprints. No one had mentioned them during discovery, when he had requested all available evidence. For several confounded minutes he asked that Holsclaw re-explain where precisely in Carrie's apartment he had explored for evidence—the bedspread, but not the couch; the kitchen table, but not a nearby suitcase—before confirming simply that Holsclaw had recovered fingerprints from the bananas, that Holsclaw considered them valuable, and that they hadn't matched Grimes's. In what seemed like desperation, de Torres also wanted to know who exactly had been responsible for this evidence, how it had been stored, and who else could theoretically have accessed it at the station. Mostly these questions fell flat. Then he sat down.

In addition to the fingerprints, hair samples had been collected from Carrie Elliott's apartment, but it had taken Steve Hunt several months, until May of 1988, to obtain samples from Willie for comparison, and then only by Willie's own urging; he himself had filed the motion for his hair to be tested, thinking the results would exculpate him. This hadn't happened. To explain why, Johnson called Troy Hamlin, a special agent with the North Carolina State Bureau of Investigation, or SBI. For seven years Hamlin had worked as a forensic chemist, specializing in hair comparison. In his career he estimated he had compared several thousand hairs. A month after Carrie's assault, he explained to Johnson, Hamlin had received her blood, saliva, and hair samples, as well as vaginal swabs, from Jack Holsclaw, evidence technician with the Hickory police. Hamlin's colleagues at the SBI had analyzed everything except the hair samples, since hair comparison was not part of the customary protocol, and the Hickory police hadn't asked for it. Six months later, the Hickory police issued a request specifically for hair comparison. This was when the case had been assigned to Hamlin.

For hair comparison to mean anything to jurors, Johnson wanted them to understand how it worked. For fifteen minutes he asked Hamlin questions designed to illuminate the procedure. From a typical hair sample, under a microscope, a trained analyst could determine a person's race, though not gender. Technically it was impossible to deduce the source of a hair definitively, but Hamlin could get pretty close. "It is rare that you would see two individuals in the general population whose hair has the same microscopic characteristics," he explained. In May, when Officer Holsclaw mailed him the hairs from Carrie Elliott's apartment, Hamlin determined that eight of them came from a black man. Seven were fragments, inadequate for analysis. The sole remaining hair Hamlin compared with head hair from Willie Grimes. That hair "was found to be microscopically consistent," Hamlin testified. "Accordingly, it could have originated from Mr. Grimes."

"When you say 'could have,'" Johnson clarified, "can you elaborate on what you mean by that?"

"That it did originate from Willie Grimes," Hamlin said. "Or if it did not originate from him, it would have originated from an individual of the same race, whose hair had the same microscopic characteristics."

"That is all," Johnson said.

Unlike the fingerprints, de Torres had known to prepare for this. He asked Hamlin if he could be certain the single appraisable hair belonged to Willie Grimes. "It was consistent with his hair," Hamlin answered. "Hair is very specific to one individual. You cannot say, to the exclusion of all other individuals, that the particular hair came from one individual. But as I said before. In seven years of doing hair examination, it is rare that I see two individuals whose hair is the same under the microscope."

"But it does happen?" de Torres pressed.

"It does happen," Hamlin said.

Next de Torres had chain-of-custody questions. He wanted to know about the envelope in which police had stored the hairs when they weren't being tested: exactly when and how Hamlin had received that envelope, the manner in which it had been glued, whether it also had adhesive tape. When these didn't lead anywhere, he asked about DNA.

Hamlin was familiar with DNA testing, but North Carolina didn't use it, he explained. De Torres, just before trial, had read of private labs with DNA capability, and Hamlin confirmed these existed. He knew of only two such labs, and of only a couple of cases where DNA had been introduced as evidence. "But those have been on blood or semen," Hamlin cautioned. "To my knowledge, none have been tried involving a hair identification. As far as hair examination is concerned, that is a relatively new area." No one knew yet how relevant DNA was to human hair, which was the reason the SBI wasn't using it. Even if they were, Hamlin predicted, he would not feel secure relying on something so novel. He was hopeful about the technology, but it wasn't clear how well DNA testing worked.

On Friday, the final morning of trial, de Torres at last called Willie Grimes. Each session of the preceding two days, Grimes, who had close-cut hair and a light mustache, had sat at the defense table observing testimony quietly. Now, as he moved toward the witness stand, he didn't walk so much as slowly glide, as a boat under limp sails, his willowy limbs nearly like cantilevers. Nine sedentary months in prison had filled him out considerably. When he was arrested the previous October, he had weighed a hundred and sixty-five pounds. Now he was nearly two hundred. On the stand his voice emerged slowly, and with strain, as though his vocal cords lacked the necessary flexibility. For most of his life, he admitted to Johnson, he had been "tongue tied, or tied tongued," whatever that phrase was, and had trouble pronouncing certain words.

For about a year he had lived with his girlfriend, Brenda, in Hickory, Willie explained, and he owned a modest plot of land down on Friendship Road in Shelby, nearly an hour's drive south. In October, a local bank had mailed him a letter concerning eighty dollars he owed on that land in taxes. Willie had arranged to bring his payment down on Sunday, the twenty-fifth. The bank wouldn't be open on a weekend, but Willie worked two jobs during the week—one at the Hickory Country Shop, hauling furniture, and another at a textile plant—so he couldn't get down to Shelby another time. On Sunday he would bring the money to cousins who lived there and who had agreed to stop into the bank for him when it opened on Monday. Until then, Willie knew to keep his eighty dollars in a reliable place, where he wouldn't be tempted to spend it. On Friday he planned to meet friends for wine, and sometimes, when he drank socially, he spent more money than he knew he should. He didn't want to be reckless. On Friday afternoon he gave the eighty dollars to a friend named Richard to hold.

Saturday morning, the twenty-fourth, Willie shaved, as he did every morning. Other than his mustache, he liked to be clean-shaven. He dressed in a blue-and-white-striped shirt and a brown jacket, which he would wear for the rest of the day. That afternoon, he and Brenda headed to her cousin's home for dinner. On the way they stopped at Richard's house, so Willie could collect his eighty dollars. But Richard wasn't home. Instead, Willie and Brenda dropped into a supermarket for a seafood platter, to bring to Brenda's cousin, and two packages of chitlin meat, for the friends Willie planned to meet afterward. The receipts for these purchases Brenda later found in her car, time-stamped 4:14 p.m. After dinner, around eight thirty, Brenda brought Willie to the home of another friend, Rachel Wilson. Willie went inside. Brenda herself couldn't stay; she worked the third shift, from eleven at night to seven the next morning, at a local nursing home.

At nine o'clock Willie decided to try Richard again for his eighty dollars. Because Richard happened to live across the street from Rachel Wilson, Willie could walk there easily. Around this same time, Rachel Wilson's sister, Carolyn, realized she had forgotten her pocketbook outside, and returned to her car to retrieve it. Out front of her sister's house, she saw Willie cross the street to Richard's.

Richard pulled in a few moments later to find Willie had just arrived in his driveway. Richard said he was sorry for being away earlier—he had been out hunting for auto parts. The two of them vanished briefly inside, then Willie reappeared with his eighty dollars and crossed the street back to Rachel's.

In another half hour Willie was ready to return home. Because it was still before eleven, he knew Brenda hadn't yet left for work, so Willie called to ask if she could come for him. But Brenda misheard him to say *Richard* Wilson, not *Rachel* Wilson—Richard and Rachel happened to share the same last name, and Willie's speech could be hard to decipher over the phone. A few minutes later, Brenda drove the ten blocks to Richard's house, and found it empty. Deciding Willie must have made other plans, she left for work.

When Brenda didn't show up, Willie realized he would need to find another ride home. He also predicted Brenda might be exhausted the next morning, after working overnight. In case she would like to sleep in, he wanted another way of getting down to his cousins on Sunday. He called Allen Shuford, a friend with whom he often carpooled to work. Allen was the brother of Rachel Wilson, and of Carolyn, the woman who had left her pocketbook in the car and therefore had seen Willie cross the street. Theirs was a large family, all originally Shufords, though several of the sisters had changed their last names in marriage. Rachel Wilson, for one, had grown up Rachel Shuford. Another sister, Linda, had married a McDowell.

By eleven Willie realized it was getting late, and still he had no ride home. He walked to the house of another friend, where he slept on the couch. The next morning, Sunday, he woke at seven and walked back to Rachel's. Since Brenda's shift was over by then, Willie phoned to ask if she could come for him. She was there by seven thirty. She told him she was alert enough to drive, so together the pair headed down to Shelby with Willie's tax money.

The next day, Monday, Willie carpooled with Allen Shuford to work. He did the same on Tuesday. That day, Willie wore a green sweater, as he often did to work—the pullover was warm and comfortable, and wearing the same sweater whenever he moved furniture meant his other clothes wouldn't get dirty. When he returned from work in the early evening, Brenda told him the police had come looking for him.

Willie couldn't think of any reason he might interest the police. "What were they looking for me for?" he asked.

"They wouldn't tell me," Brenda replied. But she remembered the name of the officer who had come by: Steve Hunt.

"Well, I haven't done anything," Willie told her. "How about giving me a ride to the police station? So we can find out what's going on."

At the police station Willie identified himself to two officers at the front desk, and asked the reason they were looking for him. Neither officer had any idea. They consulted their records and found no warrants with his name. Willie explained that Steve Hunt had come by, so the desk officers decided they would radio Hunt to see if he knew anything. Hunt directed them to hold Willie until he got there. When he arrived, he told Willie of warrants for his arrest. Willie, mystified, asked what for. The rape of Carrie Elliott, Hunt answered.

Willie didn't know anyone by that name. "I haven't done anything," he insisted. "I don't know what you're talking about." He asked to be put through a polygraph, to show he was telling the truth.

Hunt declined. "You'd better be quiet," he warned. "You're in a lot of trouble."

As Hunt began paperwork, another officer fingerprinted Willie and photographed him. During this procedure officers noticed a large raised scar below Willie's collarbone, visible from yards away, and two missing fingertips from his right hand, both the result of accidents years earlier at a textile-manufacturing plant. That Carrie hadn't mentioned either feature was curious. The scar especially was obvious, and her assailant had spent so much time wandering her apartment shirtless. Willie's missing fingertips were also from his dominant hand, where, presumably, he would hold a knife, so Carrie likely would have noticed. Briefly, these facts gave Hunt pause. But only briefly. At five thirty in the evening that Tuesday, Willie was processed into the Catawba County jail, behind the courthouse in Newton.

HICKORY POLICE DEPT.
HICKORY, N.C.

2509 1027 87

Courtesy of the Hickory Police Department

Because of Willie's chest scar and missing fingertips, and his weight, which was thirty-five pounds too light, de Torres tried to understand why Hunt had continued anyway with Willie's arrest. He pointed out the misfortune of Willie having worn a green sweater the day he visited the police station.

"Yes, I did," Willie confirmed. "And a pair of blue jeans, and a striped shirt. And that pullover sweater."

"You had worn that to work?" de Torres asked.

"Yes," Willie agreed. "I just returned from work when Brenda told me that Steve Hunt was looking for me with some warrants. I didn't even go to the kitchen or anything to get a sandwich. I just told her to carry me up to the police station, because I was going to get this straight. Because I had not done nothing."

He hadn't gotten anything straight, though, and after the night in a cell, his preliminary court appearance was held on Wednesday before a judge and a bailiff, who brought him into an otherwise empty courtroom. All was wood-paneled and silent. There, for the first time, Willie heard the full charges against him: rape, kidnapping, and burglary. Not one of those made any sense. There had been some mix-up. Asked to enter a plea, he said not guilty. Asked if he had his own attorney, he said he didn't. He was photographed and fingerprinted again, and assigned a secured bond of twenty-five thousand dollars, a price beyond anything he could dream of affording. Then another night in jail. Steve Hunt, during Willie's arrest, had pledged to return later to hear Willie's version of Saturday night, but he never did. Willie would not see him again for another seven months.

The next morning, Thursday, a stranger wearing a suit visited Willie's cell. "I'm Ed de Torres," he told Willie. "I've been appointed as your lawyer." He asked Willie to tell him, briefly, what had happened, and Willie did, though he felt apprehensive about how young de Torres looked; this man was thirty-two or thirty-three, Willie estimated, nearly ten years his junior. Their first meeting lasted five or six minutes. De Torres promised he would come back often. But the next Willie saw him was a month later, in mid-November, at his probable-cause hearing. There the district attorneys called Carrie Elliott to testify, and asked if she could see her attacker in court.

"I don't know," Carrie told them. Then she gestured toward Willie. "That looks like him, over there." A judge asked Willie how he would plead, and again Willie said not guilty. Indictments were returned against him that December. It was much longer, though, before anyone told Willie this. From his cell he tried repeatedly to reach de Torres, but heard nothing back. It was spring before he learned the outcome of his probable-cause hearing. In the months before then, Willie couldn't understand why de Torres wasn't visiting, why they hadn't already gone to trial. No one was listening. He wanted to go *home*. He was innocent, and the trial would prove it, and until then he was locked up for a crime he hadn't committed against a woman he didn't know. The sooner he got to trial, the sooner he could return to his life.

He might have thought differently had he known Michael Lee McCormick. McCormick had been convicted that previous July, a few months before Willie's arrest, just over the border in Chattanooga, Tennessee—for a murder that he'd actually had nothing to do with. But Willie had never heard of McCormick, as almost no one outside Chattanooga had, and certainly no one outside Tennessee. So the prospect of being convicted after doing nothing wrong had never occurred to him.

Nor had it occurred to almost anyone else. It would be another twenty-five years before anyone began collecting, nationally, the names of the wrongly convicted, into a database that is still permanently growing. Until then—*even* then—the truth would remain that no one had any clue how often someone like McCormick was wrongly convicted in America, or where, or how long he spent imprisoned.

Meanwhile Richard Dziubak, in Minnesota, would be convicted of beating his mother to death. In fact she had overdosed on antidepressants, but experts misunderstood a toxicology report. Julie Baumer, outside Detroit, would be convicted of shaking her infant nephew. In fact the child had suffered an unprompted stroke. Robert Farnsworth Jr., outside Ann Arbor, would be convicted of stealing from the Wendy's restaurant he managed. In fact the cash would be found six months later wedged in a bank deposit box, exactly where he swore he'd left it. Jaime Siguenza, in Dallas, wouldn't quite be convicted, so possibly he wouldn't count; he would only be charged and deported, for planning to sell kilograms of cocaine. In fact that cocaine was powdered gypsum, an ingredient of Sheetrock, the building material.

Jerry Pacek, in Pennsylvania, would be only thirteen years old. Police would interrogate him for seventeen hours. Johnathan Adams, in Georgia, would be twelve. Police would interrogate him without his parents or a lawyer. Jeff Deskovic, in New York, would be a high-school sophomore. Police would grow suspicious of him after a class-mate was murdered, when the boy seemed "overly distraught."

Juan Rivera, in northern Illinois, would be convicted even though DNA tests before trial didn't match him. Phillip Cannon, in Oregon, would be convicted on expert testimony that bullets found in his home matched identically with bullets found at the crime scene—a type of metallurgic comparison the FBI later discontinued, as it was unreliable. William Richards, in California, would be convicted of murdering his wife—on expert testimony that bite marks on her hand were left by his teeth, a type of analysis the National Academy of Sciences later condemned for having "inherent weaknesses," since "no scientific studies support this assessment." Ernest Ray Willis, in southwest Texas, would be convicted of murder by arson and sentenced to death—five years before the National Fire Protection Association issued a report that "for the first time, applied scientific principles to the analysis of...suspicious fires," according to which principles the fire was judged an accident.

Kenneth Adams, Verneal Jimerson, Willie Rainge, and Dennis Williams, in Chicago, would be convicted of abducting and murdering a newly engaged couple, on testimony from a teenage witness with an intellectual disability. Actually the teenager witnessed nothing at all. David Ranta, in Brooklyn, would be convicted of killing a rabbi, on testimony from snitches whom police bribed with prostitutes. Curtis McCarty, in Oklahoma City, would be convicted of stabbing an acquaintance, on testimony from a forensic analyst who altered her laboratory notes to implicate him. Debra Milke, in Arizona, would be convicted of murdering her own son, on testimony from a detective who recalled that she flashed him her breasts, offered him sex, and admitted it was all for the insurance money. This detective would have a history of fabricating confessions.

But Willie Grimes, lying quietly in his jail cell in North Carolina in 1988, had heard of none of these names. Nor had he heard of so many others. Ten of the men and women in this first American accounting, from a National Registry of Exonerations, would be discovered innocent only after they'd died in prison. Still more were sentenced to be executed. All missed birthdays or weddings or funerals or graduations, or their own unraveling marriages, or the final years of their parents' lives. Several, after release, committed suicide. None of these would be the most worrisome fact. That would be a sentence on page 10 of the registry report, still twenty-five years in the future. "As best we can tell," it would read, "we have only scratched the surface."

Initially Willie's court date had been set for February 4, but for reasons he didn't understand it was postponed another five months, until July. These nearly interminable days Willie spent staring at his concrete ceiling, or through the bars of his cell, into the empty gray corridor. His girlfriend Brenda visited him once a week, when he was allowed to speak with her only by telephone, and through an inch-thick glass window. Normally a calm man, he grew obsessively, incalculably angry. At night he lurched awake to dimness so acrid and impounded he could taste it, to hallway lights thrumming outside the bars of his cell. For thirty minutes, once every two or three days, guards allowed him into a small courtyard outdoors.

The setting for these months was the county prison in Newton, though in the final week of January he was packaged over to Central Prison, just west of Raleigh, on whose twenty-nine cordoned acres no space could be made for him. After three days they shunted him to Eastern Correctional Institution, halfway to the coast, in the paltry town of Maury, which he could see from the bus ride in was really just two minimum-security prisons encompassed by farmland and housing for the prison staff. He was there hardly weeks before they trucked him back to Newton, where he stayed until his trial. Throughout, he saw de Torres once or twice a month. Each visit, Willie expected de Torres to ask further about what had happened that night in October, and that, in turn, de Torres would lay bare more evidence to support him, but this never happened. De Torres's questions seemed to Willie beside the point. Had he spoken to Brenda or Rachel about the case, once imprisoned? Did he know anyone willing to sign an affidavit? During one visit, de

Torres admitted he wasn't so familiar with criminal cases, since he worked mostly on civil suits. During another, he professed to have been working on criminal cases for several years. Willie felt uneasy. He began worrying that de Torres had chosen simply not to invest his time, having decided, for reasons Willie couldn't see, that his case was hopeless.

In fact the opposite was true. De Torres had felt confident from the start. Though he didn't specialize in criminal cases—he "dabbled," he would say, in criminal and juvenile and real estate law—he recognized a straightforward assignment when he saw one. Given Willie's avowed innocence, his nonviolent history, the consistency of his alibi, and, finally, the fact that his size, missing fingertips, and chest scar had never exactly fit Carrie's description, de Torres was skeptical the case would proceed to trial. After his first meeting with Willie, de Torres had spoken with each of the alibi witnesses: Brenda Smith, Rachel Wilson, Richard Wilson, Carolyn Shuford, and Les Robinson, another friend who had visited Rachel's house that October night, in search of a cooking pot for his wife, and seen Willie there. All their stories aligned. As important, de Torres felt, not one of those stories had altered over time. The police work, too, struck de Torres as mishandled. He couldn't believe two banana peels had been left outside Carrie's apartment; he knew those would have saliva, or fingerprints. Not to collect them seemed negligent beyond comprehension. He further knew the Hickory police had never bothered to speak to Willie or any of the alibi witnesses. Once Carrie had pointed to Willie's photograph, neither Hunt nor anyone else in the department had apparently troubled with much of an investigation. For this reason, prior to trial, de Torres had asked each alibi witness to sign an affidavit attesting to Willie's whereabouts and actions, and submitted these to the district attorney. Affidavits were unusual in this circumstance, de Torres knew, and potentially redundant, since those witnesses would testify anyway if Willie's case proceeded to trial. But the Hickory police had accomplished so little that de Torres thought it was possible the district attorneys truly hadn't realized how rickety their case was. By producing affidavits, de Torres expected that a trial might be averted altogether. Then, since it was unlikely that Willie had been Carrie's true assailant, the Hickory police might be persuaded to reopen their investigation.

In either case, de Torres needed access to discovery—any evidence the state had uncovered that might exculpate his client. A regulation called the Brady Rule, from the 1963 case *Brady v. Maryland,* required the state to disclose any such evidence to the defense. By now de Torres should have been provided with any information known to either the district attorneys or the Hickory police that suggested Willie's innocence. But de Torres wasn't finding this so simple. In March 1988, one month past Willie's original court date and five months after his arrest, there were still documents de Torres hadn't seen. Medical records from Carrie Elliott's hospital visit, including the results of her rape kit. Photographs Officer Holsclaw had captured from the scene of her apartment. The lineup in which she had recognized Willie. De Torres, citing *Brady,* requested each of these from the district attorney's office, which referred him to Steve Hunt, the lead investigator. When de Torres phoned Hunt, though, Hunt refused to provide anything, and referred de Torres back to the district attorney, to whom de Torres finally mailed a letter to ensure his request for discovery was on record.

March 30, 1988

Dear Mr. Hennigar:

Last week I attempted to secure the additional discovery you did not have from Investigator S. O. Hunt, HPD, as you had suggested previously, concerning…any fingerprints and any other physical evidence (and tests thereon) obtained at the crime scene (investigative report shows that evidence technician Jack Holsclaw processed all evidence at the scene and that evidence was found). I remind you that exculpatory evidence is to be also given to the defense.

Officer Hunt rudely informed me that he had nothing to speak to me about and if I needed any additional discovery, to get it from the District Attorney office.

Therefore, I am formally requesting the above mentioned information and discovery from you. I suppose it will be your responsibility to get this from the Hickory Police Dept. Please notify me when this will be available, as we cannot proceed to trial without this and seeing what further will be needed as a result of this discovery.

I will await your response.

Sincerely,
E. X. de Torres
Attorney at Law

Five days later, Hennigar wrote back. His office had recorded de Torres's request for discovery, he assured him, and in accordance with their open-file policy had already cooperated with each of de Torres's two requests for paperwork. But only one laboratory report appeared in Hennigar's file, dated November 1987, and Hennigar had already provided it to de Torres. Now he enclosed another copy. De Torres was welcome to review the file again, Hennigar wrote, and to request whatever copies he liked. But "we cannot furnish you material we do not have in our file. If Investigator S. O. Hunt, Hickory Police Department, has additional material, you may examine it when we receive it. If he has been rude, I suggest you take the matter up with his superiors."

Neither of these things happened. Because Hunt refused de Torres access to his file, and for months kept its full contents from the district attorney, de Torres didn't learn until trial that fingerprints had been lifted from the banana peel in Carrie's apartment. At the same time he learned the lineup in which Carrie had recognized Willie was not, in fact, the first lineup shown to her by police. There had been another lineup, at the police station, the night of the crime, before Willie had ever been considered a suspect. Because de Torres couldn't know if either of these items exculpated Willie, though, he also couldn't be certain *Brady* had been violated.

Meanwhile, in the November laboratory report Hennigar had enclosed for him, de Torres noticed the Hickory police hadn't requested hair analysis. This meant hairs recovered from the scene had never been tested. Unaware the police had sent a second request to Troy Hamlin precisely for this reason, since neither that request nor Hamlin's subsequent report had been communicated to him, de Torres assumed the responsibility to test those hairs was his. On April 6, he filed a motion for them to be examined by a private company. He was also interested in DNA. Though he'd never worked with DNA evidence before, just recently he'd happened to read of it in a magazine. The technology of the future, the article had called it. For a guilty client, if he understood correctly, he might want to avoid it. For Willie, it might clear him. Because the hairs themselves were with the Hickory police, though, de Torres would need their cooperation, and he had begun to feel pressure from the upcoming trial date. By the end of May, having still heard nothing back, he wrote to Bill Johnson, the assistant district attorney.

May 20, 1988

Dear Bill:

It's been a couple of weeks and I haven't heard anything more on the hair sample testing for Willie Grimes. Since I fully expect to try this case on July 5th, you need to arrange for this as soon as possible so the SBI can finish the hair comparison on time.

Additionally, I would also suggest that the samples undergo DNA typing as well. If the SBI can do this, it will give an almost sure identification (1 in 30 billion) to a specific person. If they cannot do this, it can be done for under $250.00 by private labs such as Cellmark Diagnostics of Germantown, MD or Life Codes Corp. of Valhalla, NY. DNA typing is a great deal more accurate than traditional hair tests, as it compares the actual genetic codes within the hair cells, with its identifying and individually unique characteristics. This will yield irrefutable evidence one way or another.

I know you're involved in the <u>Tucker</u> murder case at present, but maybe Greg, Jay, or someone else at the office can get on this right away. I enclose part of an article on DNA typing for your reference.

I await hearing from you.

> Sincerely,
> E. X. de Torres
> Attorney at Law

After more than a month came a response.

> June 28, 1988

Dear Mr. de Torres:

This is to advise you that on this date we were advised telephonically by Troy Hamlin of the North Carolina State Bureau of Investigation Lab that he had examined and compared hair samples taken from Mr. Grimes and those found at the crime scene. Mr. Hamlin advised that one of the hairs found at the crime scene matched with those samples from Mr. Grimes.

A written report should follow shortly. If you have any questions, please contact me.

> Sincerely,
> William L. Johnson, Jr.
> Assistant District Attorney

There was no response to de Torres's request for DNA analysis.

Two weeks later Willie was at trial. Eleven of the twelve jurors were white, he noticed, a proportion that mirrored very nearly the demographics of Catawba County, whose population was only 9 percent black. At least two of them he recognized as local farmers. The three elderly white ladies made him feel more hopeful; he imagined they might be skeptical about a man his age, forty-one, without any history of violent or sexual crimes, assaulting a woman as old as themselves. What the rest were thinking, he couldn't tell. He expected the sole black juror would conform to whatever the whites decided.

Also present every day of trial were Willie's cousins, to whom he had brought his eighty dollars in taxes that Sunday in October. Willie's four brothers hadn't been able to attend, nor his three sisters; not all of them lived nearby, and it was bad luck to set foot in a courtroom if you didn't need to. Besides, this was just some mistake. Their brother would be home soon. De Torres didn't think their support necessary. To the jury he pointed out that, because Willie had been present until nine o'clock that Saturday inside Rachel Wilson's house, had returned by nine thirty to phone Allen Shuford, and in between had crossed the street to Richard Wilson's house, he would not have had more than a few minutes to commit a crime even if somehow this had been in his plans. Carrie Elliott lived three miles from Rachel Wilson's house, round trip. That distance wasn't coverable by foot in the sliver of time between Rachel's and Richard's houses, and Willie couldn't have traveled by other means, since he didn't own a car. The logistics of galloping full speed to Carrie Elliott's house in order to commit a crime strained credulity even if the jury chose to disregard that Carolyn Shuford had *seen* Willie cross the street to Richard's house, where Richard confirmed having met him, and a few minutes later Willie was back at Rachel Wilson's house, calmly and unremarkably, watching television and complaining about taxes on his land.

De Torres wanted to know whether, in the nine months Willie had since been imprisoned, Officer Steve Hunt, in his capacity as lead investigator, had ever visited him to ask what had happened that night in October. "No," Willie answered, shaking his head. "He has not." Had Officer Hunt ever asked Willie where he was that night? "No. He has not." Had any of Hunt's colleagues, any police officer at all, ever spoken to Willie about the case? "Not one person at all," Willie said. "Only you."

DE TORRES: Other than these traffic offenses, have you ever been charged or convicted of any crime?

GRIMES: No, sir.

DE TORRES: Have you ever been charged with or convicted of any assault?

GRIMES: No, sir.

DE TORRES: Have you ever been charged with or convicted of any violent crime?

GRIMES: No, sir.

DE TORRES: Have you ever been charged with or convicted of breaking or entering, or burglary?

GRIMES: No, sir.

DE TORRES: Have you ever been charged with or convicted of any sex offense?

GRIMES: No, sir.

DE TORRES: And—

GRIMES: I feel like they should tell the truth. I am not saying that Mrs. Elliott lied about anything she said. She might have been raped, but it was by some other person. It was not me.

On cross-examination, Johnson asked whether Willie sometimes had trouble articulating clearly—whether, in other words, a stranger might interpret his speech as slurred. Having observed Willie for the better part of a morning, Johnson already knew this was true, and Willie agreed. To speak had always been difficult gymnastics for him, as though his throat closed and opened without notice. Johnson also wanted to know, even if Willie shaved every morning, whether he grew a five o'clock shadow by evening that a stranger might describe as stubble. Willie didn't think so, but Johnson was skeptical. He clarified the names of everyone involved—that Richard and Rachel Wilson shared the same last name, but weren't related, and that several of the women mentioned were Shuford sisters, though some had different married names. Then, without much challenge except to Willie's shaving habits, he let de Torres call more witnesses.

De Torres in turn called nearly everyone who had seen or spoken with Willie that Saturday night in October. Brenda Smith described the nine-thirty phone call wherein Willie had asked her for a ride home, and she had misheard the name Rachel Wilson as Richard Wilson. She also testified to having seen Willie shave Saturday morning. Next, Rachel remembered Willie arriving to her house at eight thirty that Saturday, and staying past midnight, save for a fifteen- or thirty-minute window around nine, when he had crossed the street. Rachel's sister Carolyn confirmed having seen Willie cross the street to Richard Wilson's around nine, when she stepped outside to retrieve her pocketbook from her car. Betty Shuford, a third sister, explained that hers was the couch Willie had slept on after leaving Rachel's so late. Lucille Shuford, the mother of Rachel, Carolyn, Betty, and Linda, confirmed that Willie had called on Saturday night to speak with her son, Allen, about a ride down to Shelby.

Richard Wilson testified that Willie had visited around nine on Saturday night, to pick up the eighty dollars Richard had been holding for him. Les Robinson, the friend who had stopped into Rachel's that night to borrow a cooking pot, found Willie there, and returned later to watch television with him, testified the pot was for his wife, who had been trying to boil a ham: "her biggest pot was too small for the ham, so she asked me to go borrow a pot from Rachel." Libby King, another friend who had been at Rachel's house, confirmed Willie had been there for nearly the entire night, and she hadn't noticed anything strange. Mary Finger, Brenda's cousin, testified that Willie had been wearing brown pants and a striped shirt, not a sweater, green or otherwise.

Alvista and Sammie Lou Vinson, Willie's cousins, both testified that they had known him since he was born, and that he was not the kind of person to commit this sort of crime. Robert Vinson, Sammie Lou's husband, testified that in the forty-odd years he'd been married to Sammie Lou, he had never known Willie to be violent.

No one who knew Willie had ever seen him express interest in older women or date one of them. De Torres asked each witness, separately, about Willie's general reputation and character:

BRENDA SMITH: He is quiet, and don't bother nobody.

RACHEL WILSON: He is a nice person, and he is no trouble to anybody. He gets along with everybody there.

CAROLYN SHUFORD: I know that he is a nice fellow.

LUCILLE SHUFORD: Well, he always come down to see me and he did not give me any trouble or nobody else any. He come down to see me and was real nice.

LIBBY KING: A real nice person, helps people whenever he can help them.

RICHARD WILSON: He is a very good person and he has never been raising any sand at me.

MARY FINGER: As far as I know, he is a nice person, and friendly.

DE TORRES: What kind of reputation does Mr. Grimes have for truthfulness, and telling the truth?

BRENDA SMITH: He will tell the truth.

RACHEL WILSON: So far as I know, he always tells the truth. He is a pretty honest man.

BETTY SHUFORD: He has been with me.

CAROLYN SHUFORD: As far as I know, he never told me or anybody else a lie.

LIBBY KING: He seems to be truthful to me.

RICHARD WILSON: As far as I know he has always been truthful.

LES ROBINSON: As far as I know, he never told me any lie.

ALVISTA VINSON: He is an honest fellow.

SAMMIE LOU VINSON: He was a truthful person, as far as I know, in my dealings with him.

ROBERT VINSON: Willie Grimes has always been honest and a good fellow as far as I know.

DE TORRES: Have you ever heard of him being violent?

BRENDA SMITH: No, sir.

RACHEL WILSON: No, sir.

CAROLYN SHUFORD: No, sir.

BETTY SHUFORD: No, sir.

LUCILLE SHUFORD: Not that I know of, no.

LIBBY KING: No, sir.

RICHARD WILSON: No.

LES ROBINSON: Well, as long as I have known him, I never known him to have been in but two fights. And he didn't start them, and he lost both of them.

On the final day of trial, Friday, July 8, at a few minutes before noon, Jay Meyers provided the first half of a closing argument for the state. He believed he and Johnson had surpassed their burden of proof, implicating Grimes "beyond a reasonable doubt." The facts in this case were "stubborn things," he reflected, "and they don't seem to go away." One, Carrie Elliott had been raped. "She told you how she fought with all her strength," he reminded jurors. "But she was not big enough, nor young enough, to defend herself against somebody that size." Moreover, Carrie had been able to describe him after-ward: "She said he talked with some impairment, and that he was like being tongue tied. You heard the defendant himself testify from the stand, and you heard his speech, you heard how he talked. There was a lot made about her description of her attacker. But she told you about a mole on the side of his face, around his mouth. She said one time it was on the right side, and then later she said on the left side, but there was a big mole and it was close to his mouth. You saw the defendant up here, and he does in fact have a mole on his face, at the corner of his mouth. It is not so important as to which side the mole is on, but that is a fact that he has a mole. That is consistent with what Mrs. Elliott testified.

"She said that she would never forget that face," Meyers contin-ued. "That face was right over her, and she had the opportunity to observe him very close up. She had her glasses on, and the lights were on. You heard the police evidence technician say that he found the lights on in the house when he arrived. She had ample opportunity to get a very good look at him. She told you she recognized him. She testified as to the clothing that he was dressed in that night, and the defendant admitted that he had on a green pullover sweater and that he did wear it frequently to work.

"Then there is one other piece of evidence in this case. That is the hair. The state submits the only place that hair could possibly come from is from the defendant, and it came from him when he was assaulting this lady."

De Torres responded with his final thoughts. A crime had been committed, he agreed, but he felt it was impossible for Willie to have committed it. Besides his alibi, which the jury had heard from every conceivable angle, Willie simply did not match the description Carrie had provided that night at her apartment, the same she had provided at the hospital, the same she had provided at the Hickory police station. Her assailant had weighed two hundred pounds; Willie was one sixty-five. Her assailant had been stubbled; Willie had shaved that morning. Her assailant had held a knife and walked shirtless in a lit room. Willie was missing two fingertips from his dominant hand, and a prominent scar was on his chest. None of these features had ever come up. Willie's mole, de Torres reminded the jury, had been mentioned only later, after Carrie had spoken with her neighbor, Linda McDowell. And Carrie had placed that mole on the wrong side of Willie's face.

Finally, de Torres addressed the imperfect science of hair comparison. He reminded the jury of what they had heard from Troy Hamlin: that it was possible for hair from two different people to look similar under a microscope. Uncommon, but possible. If a single hair was all that linked Willie to the crime, it was not enough. In this circumstance, there was only one correct choice for the jury to make. De Torres trusted jurors to make it.

At two in the afternoon, once the court returned from a lunch recess, Bill Johnson had the final word. It was important, Johnson suggested, that jurors consider the credibility of each testifying witness. Every person involved in Willie's alibi was a friend of his, or a girlfriend. Nearly half of them were siblings. Johnson didn't think these made for reliable witnesses. Willie's alibi was vague, anyway.

Richard Wilson, for example, said he'd met Willie a little before nine. "I don't know what that means," Johnson confessed. "Does that mean eight thirty? Or eight fifty-nine? Does it mean sometime in between there?" He repeated what Meyers, his co-counsel, had described: that Carrie's apartment lights had been on that night in October, and she had been wearing her glasses. "She was face to face with him not just once, but twice. If you are being sexually assaulted, where is your attention going to be directed? Are you not going to be looking at the face of the person doing that assault?" De Torres's worry about the mole, that Carrie might have been influenced by her neighbor, was misleading. "Is she the kind of person that is going to do that?" Johnson asked skeptically, gesturing toward Carrie. "Surely she wants the right person caught as much as the state does. And as much as you would, if you were in her situation." Neither did he take seriously the alleged imperfection of hair comparison. Jurors could make up their own minds about the reliability of science.

After instructions from Judge Griffin, the jury withdrew to deliberate. This took them less than ninety minutes. When they returned, their foreman was grasping three sheets of paper. At Judge Griffin's order, he handed them to a court clerk, who read them aloud. Willie Grimes was guilty of two counts of first-degree rape and one count of first-degree kidnapping. All three convictions were unanimous. De Torres, desperate now, moved to poll the jury, which meant for each juror to confirm individually that he or she agreed with the verdict. Each juror did so. Judge Griffin set a sentencing hearing for after the weekend.

Court recessed at four thirty.

STATE OF NORTH CAROLINA
COUNTY OF CATAWBA

IN THE GENERAL COURT OF JUSTICE
SUPERIOR COURT DIVISION
87 CRS 13541

STATE OF NORTH CAROLINA

VS

WILLIE JAMES GRIMES

VERDICT

WE, THE JURY, UNANIMOUSLY FIND THE DEFENDANT, WILLIE JAMES GRIMES:

_____✓_____ GUILTY OF FIRST DEGREE KIDNAPPING

OR

_____ NOT GUILTY

THIS THE __8__ DAY OF JULY, 1988.

Jack B. Kincaid
Foreperson

STATE OF NORTH CAROLINA
COUNTY OF CATAWBA

IN THE GENERAL COURT OF JUSTICE
SUPERIOR COURT DIVISION
87 CRS 13542

STATE OF NORTH CAROLINA

VS

WILLIE JAMES GRIMES

VERDICT

WE, THE JURY, UNANIMOUSLY FIND THE DEFENDANT, WILLIE JAMES GRIMES:

_____✓_____ GUILTY OF FIRST DEGREE RAPE

OR

_____ NOT GUILTY

THIS THE __8__ DAY OF JULY, 1988.

Jack B. Kincaid
Foreperson

* * *

At the sentencing hearing the following Monday, de Torres moved to dismiss the charges against Willie entirely. Judge Griffin denied this. Then de Torres moved that the verdict from the previous Friday be dismissed "as contrary to the weight of evidence presented at the trial." Griffin denied this, too.

At last Judge Griffin instructed Willie to stand. "It is ordered, adjudged, and decreed," he announced as Willie rose, that Willie "be imprisoned in the North Carolina Department of Corrections for a period of his natural life." The conviction for kidnapping carried another nine years, though credit would be subtracted to reflect the 259 days Willie had already spent in prison, awaiting trial.

De Torres said he intended to file an appeal with the North Carolina Supreme Court. Judge Griffin replied that he was allowed ninety days to do so. Then de Torres made a strange motion. He wanted access to every piece of evidence from trial, so he could submit the fingerprints from Carrie's apartment to the FBI for comparison with their database. He also wanted permission to solicit fingerprints from Carrie Elliot, so that hers could be compared with those from the banana, something the Hickory police had never done. Finally, he wanted funds for independent forensic testing, in order to pursue DNA analysis on the recovered banana, a procedure Willie would never be able to afford on his own.

Johnson objected that this was a "very unusual request." In eleven years as a prosecutor, he had never heard one like it. The FBI fingerprint database was still so new that Johnson doubted a comparison would yield anything. Anyway, a search like this required prints from all ten fingers, and only two had been lifted from that banana. Any appeal to the FBI was thus a needless expense. "Discovery and testing of evidence is a pretrial type of exercise," Johnson argued. "It's not something you do once the case is tried and the verdict's in. It just seems to me like we're kicking a dead horse here."

De Torres, though, would not be cowed. He reminded Judge Griffin about his difficulty gaining discovery prior to trial. "I would like the opportunity to see if we can discover whose fingerprints those are," he insisted.

Judge Griffin admitted he had never heard a request like this. He would take it under advisement.

But he would never rule on the forensic testing, and de Torres would never follow up. Within two years, Judge Griffin had retired.

A month and a half after Willie's conviction, on August 21, 1988, Ed de Torres sat in his kitchen reading the local newspaper, the *Hickory Daily Record*. In its pages he noticed an exposé on the new Crime Stoppers program in Catawba County. TIPS WILL AID FIGHT BY POLICE, its headline promised. Beneath a photograph of a prison guard surveying an empty cell, a caption elaborated: "Crime Stoppers Program Is Helping Put Criminals Behind Bars." Recently Crime Stoppers had led to "arrests in at least two major crimes," the article continued.

> On October 26, a confidential source telephoned HPD and pro-
> vided information that led to an arrest, and subsequent convic-
> tion, in the rape of an elderly woman. The confidential source
> had heard the description of the person being sought, and called
> HPD and directed them to Willie Grimes. He recently was sen-
> tenced to life in prison for rape, plus nine years for kidnapping.
> The confidential source was paid $1,000 for the tip.

De Torres put down his newspaper. It was the first he had heard of any tip, or informant. From the start he had been troubled by suspicion that Carrie Elliott's neighbor, Linda McDowell, had likely swayed her recollection. But he had expected Carrie's evolving memory would be enough to demonstrate this influence to the jury. No one had told him of any reward. Linda herself had never testified at trial. The district attorneys had never suggested it, and, unaware that she'd received any financial incentive, de Torres hadn't thought there was reason to call her.

Now it was too late.

2

Chris

That same summer, in Durham, North Carolina, a hundred and fifty miles east, Christine Mumma hoped to keep out of morning newspapers entirely. A pretty, blond twenty-six-year-old, just a few inches taller than five feet, she and her husband expected a daughter the coming October, and for two weeks she'd been dodging cameras, mortified that her belly might appear in news reports. She hadn't wanted to serve on jury duty at all—the company she worked for, Northern Telecom, had even made calls to get her out of it. But twice already she'd asked for excusals, so now she was out of them.

On trial that summer was James McDowell, for a murder Chris could see he'd obviously committed. On the day of the shooting he'd been carrying a gun, and boasted to friends he planned to "burn someone." The four gunshots he'd fired had followed the path of his victim's car—this was important, it showed he'd been aiming—and McDowell's own lawyer admitted he'd fired them. The woman he killed, a Sunday-school volunteer, had been on her way home from midweek service.

Whether McDowell had murdered her, it turned out, was not the variable to be solved for. The question was whether he'd been after any money. Under North Carolina law, Chris discovered, a conviction for murder alone did not guarantee the death penalty. That required an aggravating factor. McDowell's argument wasn't that he hadn't fired the gun but rather that he hadn't been trying to rob anyone. Legally, he was better off if he'd simply murdered without reason. This way he would be sentenced to life in prison.

How was it possible a decision so large depended on something so trivial? The proportions were all wrong; this felt preposterous. McDowell had fired the gun. Who cared whether he'd also been after a wallet?

McDowell himself surprised her, too. She'd imagined a murderer would repulse her. McDowell didn't. He was a skinny kid, only five years younger than she was, who'd spent most of his life in detention centers. A dozen times he'd gotten expelled from one of these to another, until he'd turned eighteen and was released. Out on his own he broke into houses and stole things. Twenty-one months later he sprayed four gunshots through some poor woman's windshield.

Looking nearly as disheveled as McDowell was his lawyer, Chris noticed, who appeared as though he were dressing on the commute in. Often he repeated himself, or shuffled papers, or abandoned his sentences mid-thought. Chris wondered how long he'd had to prepare. Then, at home, on the final night of trial, her phone rang; it was him, the lawyer. He could tell she didn't want to convict his client, he told her. She seemed nervous in her seat in the jury box, and he didn't want her feeling pressured by the others. This was why he'd called, to reassure her. How had such a nice girl wound up in a situation like this? He felt just awful about it.

Chris knew she ought to report the call to the judge, but she kept silent about it. The lawyer had been wrong about her. She wasn't nervous. She'd done the math; McDowell was guilty. It was unfortunate, the life he'd lived, and Chris felt sorry for him, though not as sorry as she felt for the woman he'd killed. And she resented his lawyer's implication that she lacked nerve, that it had anything to do with her being—what had he called her?—a *nice girl*. She wouldn't report him. She didn't need anyone's help. Instead, she would refuse his influence. She would show him precisely what he'd doubted.

Chris came from Morristown, New Jersey, a township so small that it was news when a Burger King opened, though really she'd grown up all over: in Massachusetts, in North Africa, in Rome. Her father, Ralph, had worked as an engineer for Exxon, and moved wherever they needed him. Ralph had been raised by a strict Italian family in Maryland, during the Depression, and the lessons this ingrained in him he carried through the rest of his life. His ample paychecks from Exxon made no difference; money was only paper, he knew, or numbers on a screen. Either could vanish in an instant. He'd seen it himself. He resolved to teach this lesson to his children: that the only insurance was self-reliance.

It hadn't been easy, being a teenager in Ralph Cecchetti's household, and Chris's three older siblings had very nearly avoided it: a brother moved away at sixteen, a sister went off to boarding school. Another sister was so unnaturally well behaved that, even teenage, she'd never really been a teenager. Chris was not so lucky. She lived at home and, worse, had inherited a portion of Ralph: his will, his disputatiousness, his aversion to even the appearance of following others. Both could be unforgiving. There were things around her Chris couldn't bear. Once, in Libya, at twelve years old, she saw live camels heaved like vegetables onto the beds of trucks, heavy doors slammed on their hooves. "Stop that!" she ordered tearfully, her hands clenched in tiny fists. But the men wouldn't. So she demanded that Ralph make them. But he wouldn't, either. She never forgot this: her keen, indignant sense of right and wrong, her outrage in learning that not everyone shared it.

Ninth grade she began at an all-girls school in Rome. Half of tenth grade she spent in New Jersey, the other half in Massachusetts. For twelfth grade, she was back in New Jersey—except for the two months her parents were forced to withdraw her entirely, since she'd fled on her own back to friends in Massachusetts. The other times she'd run away hadn't lasted so long: a night or two in the Port Authority, alone below moonlit glass and steel trusses; or to Duke, where a sister attended college; or for a weekend with a boy Ralph disapproved of. She was picking up broken birds, her parents told her. That was all she was doing, that was all these boys were. One bird was in trouble with the law. Chris put her babysitting income toward a lawyer.

The day after she graduated from high school, her parents boarded a plane for Saudi Arabia. Chris drove to Chapel Hill. Ralph had offered a loan to cover tuition, but Chris turned it down; she guessed he could have paid outright if he wanted, and anyway she didn't want to feel indebted to anyone, much less her father. Instead, she took a job at a bar near campus. One night, a drunken undergrad punched her in the mouth. Still it was better than repaying a loan to Ralph.

Four years later she had a degree in business administration, and soon after that was married. She'd met Mitch Mumma back in high school, during an escape to her sister at Duke, where Mitch, too, had been visiting an older sibling. She took a job with Northern Telecom. Before long, she and Mitch were expecting. Seven months after that she was summoned to jury duty, for the trial of James McDowell.

3

Only a Few Additional Weeks

No way, he thought. For a moment Willie assumed he had misheard the verdict, but then de Torres was polling the jury and the moment rushed past him. *No way.* Now de Torres was saying something about an appeal, but Willie couldn't concentrate. Guilty? He couldn't work out what had happened. Only by the knowledge that soon it would all be put behind him had he survived the long wait for trial; in exchange for a few days sitting in a courtroom he would be allowed to resume his life, move back in with Brenda, go back to work. It wouldn't look good to the boss that he'd been arrested, but he expected he could get both his jobs back, at the textile plant and loading furniture, since he hadn't done anything wrong. All this had been a mistake, and he had always been a good employee. As soon as he was acquitted he could explain and get rehired.

Now, though. Guilty. He wasn't sure he understood what this meant. Somewhere nearby a voice was murmuring; de Torres had leaned in and was saying something. "Don't worry about this," he heard. "We can beat this. They'll dismiss it in appeals court." Then a bailiff was leading him to his cell in an adjoining building. He passed the weekend in confusion. On Monday they hauled him to his sentencing hearing. There was de Torres again, assuring him a conviction meant only a few additional weeks, there was no way an appellate court would uphold any of this. The judge would rule lightly, there was so little evidence, de Torres kept saying, until the judge announced his life sentence. Still, it didn't matter, de Torres insisted. They would appeal. Until then, prison wouldn't be so bad, Willie had been there already, he could last a little longer. They had color television, remember.

For three more days he sat in his cell, trying to interpret what had happened. He knew he wouldn't be staying. From repeat offenders in Catawba County jail he'd learned all felons were processed through Central Prison, over in Raleigh, as it was centrally located and maximum security. There was no predicting how long he would be kept there before shipping someplace else, just as there was no telling where he'd eventually be shipped. If he got shipped at all. Some felons stayed at CP long term. Willie wanted to avoid this if he could, the county inmates had told him. What he wanted was a smaller prison, since those were typically quieter and more accommodating. CP held close to a thousand. And because of processing, that number included every capital criminal in the state, plus the ones on death row—the worst sorts, murderers and rapists, *actual* rapists, unlike him. It scared him to imagine what things might be like there. Would his cell be large enough to walk around in? Would he be allowed outdoors at all? He'd heard an inmate at CP got only a single phone call a year, and it could be more than this long until the prison decided what to do with him, even if de Torres was right and he could count on an appeal. How long would an appeal take? It had taken nine months to get his trial.

But now that he'd been convicted, they acted swiftly. Friday, four days after his sentencing, Willie was on a bus for Raleigh. By then his conviction had been entered into the statewide Department of Correction database, where, because of a software flaw, computers couldn't handle the numerics of a life term. Instead, the system listed his three convictions—two for rape, another for kidnapping—beside his "Term Imposed," as best the software could register it: "999 YRS. 99 MOS. 98 DAYS."

No way.

4

Lake

At Northern Telecom, Chris was promoted quickly. Soon she managed contracts. Then audits. Then budgets. Then she was finance director. But there were frustrations; one year she would overhaul the budget, then the corporation would reorganize, so she would overhaul the budget again. Then the corporation would reorganize. Her boss told her another promotion would mean her serving a rotation in Montreal, where the company was headquartered. She didn't want to move to Canada. Around the same time, she gave birth again—she took two months off to recover, longer than before, and realized she didn't look forward to returning.

She realized, too, there was other work she could imagine doing. She'd always been interested in law; at Northern Telecom what she liked most were contracts, which was basically legal work, she figured. And she'd never gotten James McDowell out of her head. Had he been executed by now? Would a better attorney have made a difference for him? How had his trial worked from the inside? Mostly, though, she knew that, if she stayed at Northern Telecom, she might wake up one morning, a frustrating career behind her, and regret not having tried something different. She had no idea how she and her husband would afford law school; she earned more than Mitch did, who'd left his job as a CPA for a career in something called venture capital, a field Chris had never previously heard of. Even Mitch wasn't sure there was a future in it. If she left Northern Telecom, it would be the second time the couple had forgone a reliable salary. Still, Chris had put herself through college, and she thought she could get herself through law school. And she'd let him pursue *his* interests, Mitch reminded her. She ought to do the same for herself.

The first thing she did when she arrived at law school in Chapel Hill was look up James McDowell, who turned out never to have been executed. He was still in prison. New lawyers had raised twenty-seven issues on appeal, one of which was that his shooting had never been part of a robbery. This time it had stuck. McDowell was still a murderer, but no longer was he a thief. "As this is the basis for the only aggravating circumstance," she read in the court's ruling, "we must also vacate the sentence of death and impose a life sentence."

She felt strangely relieved he'd never been executed. Even a criminal like McDowell deserved a better attorney than he'd had, and to fixate on the robbery as a reason for a death sentence still baffled her.

Because Mitch traveled so often for work, Chris frequently towed her three children along with her to classes. One professor saw them so many times, he inserted their names into a criminal-law exam. She drove an eight-year-old Honda whose backseat was strewn with Cheerios. Then, in her second year, a discovery: there was a future in venture capital, after all. Money ceased to be a concern. She and Mitch bought a four-million-dollar estate, flanking the sixth hole of a country club. They bought a vacation home along the shore of Lake Gaston. Chris traded her Honda for a silver Audi convertible; three different times she drove it to her own court appearances, to argue speeding tickets. She donated twenty-five thousand dollars to the law school, for a scholarship for single parents.

When she graduated, her experience at Northern Telecom attracted offers from corporate firms, but the money meant she was free to continue following her interests. She turned the corporations down to clerk in the state court of appeals. After six months, one judge recommended her to another, and she ended up with I. Beverly Lake at the state supreme court.

Lake was a square-jawed, green-eyed man in his late sixties, with a tall forehead, drooping eyelids, and wisps of hair he combed neatly horizontal. He liked to quip that his first initial stood for Integrity, or Intelligence—in fact it stood for Isaac, a biblical name. He'd sat on the bench for more than ten years, including four on the state's highest court, where his father, too, had once been chief justice. Though often he signed his name *Jr.*, after his father, actually he was Beverly the third: Lake's great-grandfather had once been colonel of a Confederate brigade from Kentucky, and had marched home from that war with its flag tucked inside his coat pocket, where it would remain with his family for the next century and a half: through his son, Beverly I, a physics professor at Wake Forest College, then through *his* son, Beverly II, a law professor and assistant attorney general of North Carolina in the difficult year of 1954, during *Brown v. Board.* That year, Beverly II had traveled north to Washington to warn that forced integration, without a period of gradual transition, might so destabilize public schools in his state as to collapse them entirely. Twice denied the job of governor, Beverly II returned instead to private practice, then was appointed to the state supreme court, and elected chief justice—like his son after him, I. Beverly Lake III, who hung on the wall of his chambers that same Confederate battle flag his great-grandfather had once marched home from a war that had already ended.

Lake himself had entered North Carolina politics as a Democrat, despite his centrist views and the fact that he got along well with Republicans. Finally he decided that Democrats as a whole had veered too far left. He registered as a Republican, thus alienating many of his closest friends, some of whom never forgave him. Elsewhere it gained him a reputation as a man who followed his principles. By the end of the decade, he was appointed a judge, then to the state supreme court. In 2000, after hiring Chris Mumma as a clerk, he was elected chief justice. He was the first Republican to hold the post in more than a decade.

Lake and Chris got along grandly—he the product of Southern gentility, she a spunky, no-nonsense thirty-something with a smile that felt like a reward, a woman who spoke "pretty normally, for a Yankee," he joked to his friends. As chief justice, Lake oversaw budgets for the state's courts, and here was a clerk with experience in finance who could help him. Before, Lake had assigned cases and then didn't see them again until the clerks had finished drafts of opinions. Now, Chris asked if, rather than everyone working in isolation, they could meet every so often for discussion of the cases. Lake agreed. Soon he found he enjoyed the camaraderie.

Still, there were frustrations. A case Chris saw on Lake's desk struck her as mishandled, like McDowell's had been. Then she saw another where her doubts were more serious. Then another. She wasn't certain these men had committed their crimes at all. It had never occurred to her that a person might wrongly be found guilty—in law school she'd learned every safeguard against this—but here they were, their files fanned out before her like a school project. She'd never been good at keeping a thought like this to herself. She wouldn't stand for it, she told Lake. She didn't think he ought to, either.

But she knew better, Lake told her. Guilt wasn't a question his court considered. That had been addressed already, at trial. Lake wasn't about to relitigate a case, and neither were his colleagues—for good reason, since none of them had been present for trial. A judge didn't overrule jurors based on his own subjective opinion. The U.S. Supreme Court had said so itself. In *Barefoot v. Estelle* it had ruled that higher courts "are not forums in which to re-litigate state trials." Lake showed this ruling to Chris, as well as *Herrera v. Collins,* where one justice had remarked that his inquiry "does not focus on whether the trier of fact made the *correct* guilt or innocence determination, but rather whether it made a *rational* decision to convict or acquit." Those italics were the court's, Lake pointed out. He could sympathize with Chris's unease, and theoretically, just as an exercise, her instincts might even be sound that a particular claimant was innocent, though it was unlikely. Either way, that was for trial courts to resolve. An appeal was only procedural. By the time a defendant reached Lake's chambers, his guilt was no longer the question.

Chris balked. Already she'd left one bureaucracy frustrated by its mismanagement. She didn't intend to join another. She felt emboldened by Lake's admission she might be onto something—it didn't matter those hadn't been his words exactly. He was wrong about this, she decided. Not about the law, but the moral logic that under-pinned it. *You might be right, but we can't do anything about it.* That was what they'd told her about the camels in Libya. Well, it wasn't good enough. She wasn't soft; if the men in these cases were guilty, she was glad they'd been convicted. She just wasn't certain they were guilty. She argued with Lake as much as she dared, and, when that went nowhere, she stalked around nearby chambers until even the other justices bristled. For one defendant she quietly filed a clemency petition with the governor. Finally, unsure what else to do, she phoned a former law professor named Rich Rosen.

5

K and O

Central Prison was a behemoth of concrete and brick and looped razor wire, all rectangles and sheer vertical faces, so cramped and monolithic that it looked from the outside like it had been modeled from toy blocks, then galvanized and blown a thousand times out of proportion. Through the iron grille shielding his bus window, Willie could make out wire fencing tipped with barbed chutes, and even taller guard towers, giant lampposts bracketing the entire campus. The prison entrance was so wide and well marked it looked like the on-ramp to a highway. After the turn, however, its pavement continued for only a stubbed hundred yards or so before the first security gate.

A new inmate began his time in K dorm, one of two floors in CP's processing wing. The other was O dorm, upstairs. Guards put him in a room the size of an elongated trailer, double bunks separated by a narrow aisle. If he rolled to one side of his mattress, not much more than a pallet, he bumped into the wall, and if he extended his arm in the other direction, across the aisle, he could touch the neighboring cot. A pair of these rooms made up K dorm, plus what looked like former social quarters. The prison had set bunks in there, too. This way it could warehouse something like eighty men, all of them dressed in identical white T-shirts and brown chino pants over white boxers and socks. Guards gave him two sets as soon as he arrived.

Prison was *loud*. From the moment they rose, inmates hollered across rooms, kicked and rattled their cell bars or metal bed frames, slapped playing cards or dominoes bricks or their open palms onto the floor and tables. They drummed with their knuckles or fingers; they "spit their lyric." Prison was bedlam. In the open cell he couldn't find anywhere that wasn't raucous. Somehow the place was both cavernous and claustrophobic. At every moment, strangers were beside or behind him; he felt exposed even under the sheets of his bed. If he lay facing the wall, he could feel attention on his back, could hear men snore along his row. He couldn't sleep this way, and, when he could, it was no more than an hour or two before he startled awake. Even then, in the artificial dusk, he could see the outlines of strangers, and couldn't trick himself into privacy.

In daylight he kept to himself, and kept quiet. This was not as easy as it sounded. A fresh inmate was an opportunity, meaning he might have funds. To find out, veteran inmates had plans. They drew pictures or their own greeting cards; did he want to buy one? They offered to wash his laundry for a dollar or two a week. Maybe he would simply loan them a little something, on faith? Another game was to offer a newcomer a cigarette, then demand it back once he'd smoked it. Not a replacement—the exact same cigarette. If he refused, he owed a favor. He had taken something without returning it, this meant he was in debt, unless he wanted trouble. Again and again Willie shook his head.

Each day that first week, a batch of inmates was transferred upstairs, to O dorm, and new felons arrived to fill the bunks they'd vacated. Willie shuffled between evaluations. First a medical screening, where staff recorded his height, weight, and blood pressure, and tested him for tuberculosis. Was he presently being treated for any health problems? He wasn't. Was he taking any medications? He wasn't. Was he thinking of harming himself? He wasn't. They wanted to know his work history, his family history, his education. How far had he gone in school? Twelfth grade. Was he married? Yes, but only technically. Had he ever held a job? Before he'd been arrested, he'd held two. They assigned him a case manager who would determine his custody level. This followed a point system. Even within any of its three levels of security—minimum, medium, and maximum, though maximum sometimes was called close custody, and minimum sometimes was called honor grade—there were steps and grades and degrees, from lockdown all the way to parole, each corresponding to various privileges. An inmate's crime equaled a predetermined number of points, as did his criminal history. It also mattered whether authorities sensed he had taken responsibility for his actions, or felt remorse. It counted in Willie's favor that he had never been arrested before, besides the drunk-driving charge. But it counted against him that he insisted he was innocent. This meant he hadn't taken responsibility, and a certain number of points. Too many points. He would remain in maximum security. In another six months, he would be eligible for reevaluation.

Until then medical staff saw no reason for mental-health intervention. "During interviewing he was polite and cooperative," a psychologist observed in his file. "Willie gave no indications to being a potential behavioral or management problem." In fact what he felt was numbness, and disorientation. Nine months earlier he had been living with Brenda, working at the textile plant and furniture shop. He couldn't believe how fast things had changed.

His family couldn't believe it, either. Back in October, when he'd been arrested, his sister Gladys, who worked as a military nurse at Brooke Army Medical Center, in San Antonio, had received a phone call from her niece, telling her Willie was in trouble. Gladys had asked what kind. "They say Woot raped a white woman in Hickory," her niece had told her.

"That isn't true."

"That's what they said," her niece insisted. So Gladys called a cousin, who confirmed what the niece had told her. At once Gladys booked a flight to Charlotte, then drove to Newton, where Willie was being held before trial. The five-hour flight was more than enough time to consider the possibilities, but when she landed she wasn't any less bewildered. Woot would know better than to mess with a white woman. And an *older* white woman? That didn't fit, either. If their mother had been firm about one rule when Gladys and Willie were kids, it was respect for their elders. One day their mother herself would grow old, she had warned them, and, because of the age gaps between her children, Gladys's and Woot's siblings would grow old not soon after, so she never wanted to hear about them causing trouble for elderly people. "I don't care how hungry you are," she had threatened. "You ever mess with an older person, you're in trouble with me." Possibly if Woot had been desperate, he might have tried to rob someone? But even this was hard to imagine, as he had always been so gentle. Now they were saying he had raped a white lady. Her cousin had told her the woman was sixty-nine years old. This couldn't be right. Their own mother had been sixty-eight when she died.

In the Newton jail Willie explained what had happened. Gladys didn't like that he had given himself to the police. "Why didn't you come here with a lawyer?" she demanded.

"Because I hadn't done anything. I wanted to know—I was told someone was looking for me. I came down to see why they were looking for me. And they arrested me."

So Gladys returned to San Antonio, where she phoned a lawyer, who charged her five hundred dollars even to look at Willie's case. "This is cut-and-dried," he promised, once she'd paid. "They don't have any evidence against him." All Gladys and her brother had to do was wait for the confusion to pass. So Gladys went back to work. A few months later she received a letter from the same niece who had phoned after Willie's arrest. "It doesn't look good for Woot," the letter read. "They have no proof, but I believe they're really going to charge him." Soon afterward, the niece phoned again, to say she'd been attending the trial and worried the jury might make a mistake. Gladys phoned Willie's lawyer, Ed de Torres, to find out what was happening. De Torres admitted it wasn't going well. In fact, he told her, Willie had just been convicted.

The news stunned her. From Silver Spring, Maryland, where recently she'd been transferred to a job at Walter Reed medical center, she drove down to see him again. This time she brought her son, David, for company, thinking it might lift both their spirits if he and Uncle Woot could see each other.

By then Willie had been shipped to Central Prison. During her first

visit to him, back in county jail, Gladys had known to expect a prohibition on physical contact, even a hug, but now that he'd been convicted she imagined that at least the logistics might be easier. They'd
already had their way with him, and in maximum security Woot
wouldn't be a flight risk. Gladys had been approved for a visit; CP
had forced her to submit an application before she'd left Silver Spring.
She assumed this meant they would allow her to sit with him.

But security at CP was tighter than she had ever imagined, startling
even to someone who worked at a military hospital. Before long she
had lost count of how many checkpoints she and David were waved
through. She checked in at a visitors' desk, where guards found her
name on a list and showed her to a waiting room: half a dozen wood-
framed couches, a dull linoleum floor, a Coca-Cola vending machine.
Obscuring a wall clock was some sort of plastic shield. A stack of
cubbyhole lockers held any belongings forbidden inside, which guards
listed as though they were annoyed she didn't already know. When
her name was called, they told her she would be seeing Willie in a visitors' booth, behind thick glass, unable to touch him. This dazed her.
David was only sixteen. She didn't want him to see his uncle like that,
even after he'd come all the way from Silver Spring with her. She told
him to stay in the waiting room. Through another doorway was a
wide, gleaming hall, lined along one side with a symmetrical row of
cinder-block booths. As soon as a guard let her inside one she began
to feel sick. The booth was airless and sweltering. Its pale walls were
barely as far apart as her arm span, and she was claustrophobic. The
window to the other side of the booth, where they would bring in
Woot, was puny, only a few feet above a grate to carry their voices.

He shuffled in wearing his prison clothes—brown pants, a white
T-shirt. He looked awful. Was it supposed to be this hot? She was too
upset to speak, even once he sat. This was so much worse than she'd
imagined. "W-Willie," she finally stammered. "What are you doing
here?"

He looked near tears. "I didn't do anything," he told her.

There was more but she struggled to follow it. She would ask a
question, then after some undefined period—she couldn't keep

track—she would notice him straining for words, and she wouldn't know what about. He was answering something, she would realize, she must have asked him a question, but she couldn't recall what it had been. The booth was suffocating. She stayed as long as she could last. When she stepped out, a guard—was it the same guard from earlier?—led her back to the holding room, where David was waiting.

Soon she was driving in her car, then she was stopped along the highway shoulder, turned toward David in the passenger seat. "You know? This is the worst thing I've ever been to in my life," she told him, weeping. "You'd better make sure you never have to deal with this." She tugged the sleeve of her shirt to dab her eyes. "And it doesn't mean you have to be guilty," she added. "Sometimes you can just be in the wrong place." People like them had to be careful; just look at their skin. Anyone might accuse them of anything, and folks would assume they had done it. What had happened to Woot was even worse. She knew that Linda McDowell, Carrie Elliott's neighbor, who had implicated Woot in the first place, was black, as was Steve Hunt, the officer who'd arrested him. *When your own people don't listen to you,* she wondered, *who do you have?*

6

Rosen

Rich Rosen, who'd recently turned fifty, was a slight man with gold wire-rim glasses whom Chris had studied under in law school. In addition to his work as a professor, Rosen was an accomplished defense attorney, so his particular goals didn't always align with Chris's; at Chapel Hill, she'd told him she wasn't sure she could represent a guilty person, and certainly wouldn't want to, since a criminal belonged in prison. Still, she and Rosen had gotten along, and because he'd made a career of representing the disenfranchised, Chris thought he might know what to do about the cases that unnerved her. Rosen agreed to meet her for lunch at a local diner. There, over sandwiches, she described her problem. Lake himself had always been generous, but she'd put her job at risk by filing the clemency petition. And there were eight other justices to think about. She'd gotten herself banned from some of their chambers, and knew other clerks had begun to resent her. But she hadn't become a lawyer only to learn that she was just as powerless as she'd been in the first place. "What else can I do?" she asked Rosen. "What haven't I thought of?"

Rosen sighed and admitted she wouldn't like his answer. "You've done everything you can," he told her. Certainly she could go on agitating, if she wanted, at the risk of alienating everyone on the court. But what Lake had told her was right; in that situation, a judge didn't reexamine innocence or guilt.

"So what am I doing here?" Chris wondered aloud. She'd turned down lucrative corporate offers in order to clerk. She didn't expect to agree with every ruling she saw, but the doubts she felt now were not over technicalities. It was ludicrous to think the courts couldn't distinguish between basic guilt and innocence. How was she supposed to work in a field like that? How, for that matter, did anyone?

Sometimes he felt the same frustration, Rosen admitted. "But listen," he added, and he leaned toward her confidentially. "We're getting something together. We'll need help."

Chris was right, Rosen agreed. Cases like these deserved attention, and there were more out there than she'd seen. Then he smiled and waved for the check. "You want to do something about it?" he asked. "Come work with us."

Rosen had begun his career as a public defender up in Washington, DC, before back problems forced him out of regular practice and he'd accepted a position on the faculty at Chapel Hill. He'd become a lawyer in the first place to represent the poor, and he soon discovered he could do this nearly as well as a professor as he had as a public defender, since his faculty salary allowed him not to charge his clients. Few lawyers in North Carolina did similar work, and quickly he earned a reputation as the person to call for free advice. In this way he'd learned of Ronald Cotton, who was serving life plus fifty-four years for two rape convictions up in Burlington. Cotton's public defender thought he'd probably committed one of those rapes, but not the other—even if the defender was right, though, he knew it wasn't enough to merit an appeal, since a convicted person couldn't just demand a new trial on the grounds his jury had gotten it wrong. To be heard at all, he had to demonstrate that his legal rights had been violated. For help with this, the defender called Rosen.

Rosen read Cotton's transcript, decided he could wring an appeal from it, then encountered an obstacle he hadn't anticipated. Cotton himself didn't *want* a simple appeal. From prison he was asking for DNA testing. He hadn't raped *anyone*, he insisted, and this DNA he was hearing about could prove it. But a DNA test was perilous, Rosen knew. Without it, he had grounds for an appeal. If they pursued DNA instead, and this turned out to match, Cotton would be hamstrung. Rosen visited the man in prison to explain the risk. "There's not a judge in the world who'll let you out, no matter how unfair your trial was, if DNA shows you've done it," he cautioned. Still Cotton insisted. So Rosen approached the local district attorney, and suggested they file jointly for testing. Legally he was entitled to pursue DNA on his own, but Rosen saw no reason to make enemies. If the results matched, he promised the DA, Rosen wouldn't file any more appeals. Cotton would be finished. He only wanted to be sure of the truth. That sounded fair, the DA agreed; the state would even pay for testing. On the minuscule chance some mistake had been made, the DA wanted to know as much as anyone. "But between you and me," he told Rosen, "you know, don't you? It's just going to show he did it."

Rosen shrugged. "If it does, it does," he said.

It didn't.

After Cotton, letters arrived by the dozens. They too had been wrongly convicted, inmates wrote Rosen, not only from North Carolina but also beyond. They had heard what he'd done for Cotton. Would he help them? But Rosen was a law professor, not a full-time attorney, and couldn't possibly accept so many cases. To one after another he wrote back that he regretted he wasn't in a position to help. Still more letters came, and he wrote still more apologies, until they haunted him. Certainly some of the letters were bogus, he knew, but if even a fraction were valid, then there were more Ronald Cottons out there, imprisoned without reason.

He was still mulling this over three long years after Cotton's exoneration, in autumn 1998, when he attended a conference at Northwestern University. There he watched more than thirty men climb onto a stage to announce their names and when exactly they'd been sentenced for crimes they had never committed. "My name is Joseph Burrows," one of them said, holding a sunflower. "The state of Illinois sought to kill me. I was put on death row in 1989, and released in 1994. If the state had its way, I'd be dead today." Then he dropped his sunflower into a vase with the others.

As he left the conference, Rosen contemplated what he'd seen. He tried to tally all the letters he'd received since Cotton, plus the sunflowers filling that vase onstage as the conference ended. If 97 or 98 percent of all cases were resolved correctly, that was pretty good, for a human endeavor, Rosen figured. But even a 2 or 3 percent failure rate—or whatever the number was, which he guessed was unknowable—over the course of years meant hundreds of Ronald Cottons, all across the country, incarcerated simply for having woken up in the morning. That was too many, Rosen decided. He had to *do* something. When he got back to Chapel Hill, he hauled a box of unopened letters into a class on criminal procedure and, before a crowded lecture hall, dumped them onto a table. "I've got all these letters," he announced. "Does anyone want to volunteer to look into these cases? And help me answer them?"

7

Some Ideas of Persecution

When Gladys was gone and his evaluations were through he was transferred upstairs to O dorm, where he waited to be shipped. By policy, an inmate was told only at the last possible moment that he was about to be transferred, and to where, partly because these were subject to change literally until he had boarded the bus, and partly as a security measure. A felon who knew his destination might also guess his route, and no one wanted him with time to confer with associates on the outside. The result was that no one in O dorm had any idea where he was bound, or how long it would be until he was sent there, which could be a few weeks or longer than a year. Nearly twice as many men hung in this suspension as were being evaluated downstairs in K dorm, and Willie couldn't sleep any better here than he had there. If anything O was worse, since its rooms were larger, meaning still more criminals whose breath he could feel, whose every movement he could measure by the squeak and shudder of a mattress, whose muttering kept him interminably conscious. Until his trial, back in Newton, Brenda had visited him weekly, on Friday afternoons, but now she stopped—not because she no longer believed him, but because CP was too far from Hickory. After one or two letters, he stopped hearing from her. By the end of his first month he was so sleep-deprived and disoriented his vision had gone blurry, and his tongue was as dry as a cotton sock. An unfamiliar pinching took hold in his forehead, then expanded, viselike; when he swung his vision to either side, he swore he could feel connective veins tugging from their anchors. Light began to chafe at him, then grew nearly blinding.

When he'd first arrived at K dorm he'd been relieved to find he was allowed outdoors onto a yard; in this small way, perversely, prison was better than county jail. But now his headaches made sunlight insufferable. He asked to stay indoors but a guard refused. Instead, he found a shaded spot and clenched his eyelids. When it was over he begged to see a nurse, who couldn't find anything wrong with him. A day later, the pain worsened into nausea, and he pleaded again for sick call, where a doctor examined him and agreed with the nurse from a day earlier—nothing was wrong. On the third day he was nearly debilitated. The prison brought in a specialist, who asked Willie to describe his symptoms. Willie did. He was having a migraine, the specialist told him. Willie didn't know what that was. A migraine, the specialist repeated. He had never had one?

No.

Well, it was a migraine, the specialist said. If he felt one coming on again, he ought to try to avoid sunlight.

The following month they brought him to the manager of psychological programs. During his initial evaluation, in July, a staff psychologist had ruled Willie an unlikely threat either to himself or to others. Now CP wanted a fuller screening. "Projection of responsibility to others and possibly some ideas of persecution are also suggested," the manager determined. "Denies any responsibility for the crime." Willie also seemed depressed, and anxious, but these appeared "situational in nature," an ordinary part of "initial adjustment reaction to prison." They also fit Willie's admission that he felt uncomfortable in crowds of strangers, and had always been something of a loner. Otherwise, the manager decided, Willie was "very soft spoken in manner" and "pleasant, responsive and cooperative." He wasn't surprised when Willie complained of insomnia. "My impression is that the sleep disturbance is due to approximately 11 months of inactivity due to housing and jail and here for processing." He predicted Willie's sleep would improve as he acclimated to life inside the walls. Until then, the manager didn't think Willie required any mental-health treatment, though he recommended Willie be assigned to some job or other, or else to classes, either of which he predicted might speed along his adjustment.

More colleagues followed up in early autumn to evaluate Willie for a job assignment. "During the interview he presented himself in a polite manner," the committee reported, and suggested Willie be assigned to work in the kitchen.

Cell and hallway lights never cut out entirely inside prison, but dimmed gloomily each night at eleven and brightened at five thirty the next morning; at six, breakfast was called, a dormitory every fifteen minutes. If Willie worked a morning shift in the kitchen he might rise as early as two or three to prepare breakfast for inmates who left before daylight on job assignments, or a transfer to another prison. Because of the early hours, most inmates avoided breakfast shifts in the kitchen, but Willie was glad for them. He often woke this early regardless, and it was better to rise and busy himself than to lie in predawn silence with time to consider his circumstances. If he helped with breakfast, usually he got to fix his own plate. Technically, this was forbidden, but guards rarely hassled an inmate on the kitchen staff, at least during that prisoner's shift, since an inmate in this position could, if he wasn't too closely supervised, make extra sandwiches, pile them with meat, and slip them into guards' hands. The better the cook, the more lenient his guards.

A good cook also had standing among fellow inmates, who often complained; meals were always too dry, or too salty, or too overdone. Most mornings Willie avoided the issue altogether and kept to oatmeal, or a banana, or eggs with juice. Then he returned to his cell block and showered, under one of three open spigots in what looked like a tiled bunker. If he wanted to shave, a guard issued him a disposable razor, then returned fifteen minutes later to collect it. Some inmates bypassed this hassle by trimming their goatees or mustaches with fingernail clippers, at least until they made minimum custody, where an inmate could buy and keep his own razors. Besides his mustache, Willie shaved every morning, as he had on the outside. Once a week he was issued identical replacements for his clothes, a single roll of toilet paper, and a bar of soap that had been stamped with the outline of North Carolina.

After he showered usually he returned to his bunk to lie down for a half hour or so; if he was lucky, he might drift off, after sleeping so little the night before. Soon guards opened the yard and blasted assignments from loudspeakers, which screeched constantly throughout the day and could be heard everywhere on the grounds: *Patty Billings, report to sick call! Les Robeson, report to your block! School call! Yard call! Work call! Chow call! Mail call! Church call!* Inmates on the yard could be overseen from inside an observation tower, and from behind the nose of a rifle, both of which conditions guards preferred. An inmate on the yard wasn't dirtying his cell block or the mess hall, or slinking through a poorly surveilled corridor. This arrangement worked fine except when it rained. Then guards corralled inmates into a particular block and kept them the entire afternoon, so the remaining blocks could be scrubbed. No one liked this—guards for security reasons, inmates because it bored them. On the yard CP had basketball, horseshoes, card tables, a volleyball net, and a weight pile. Even on a clear day, Willie touched none of these. When he wasn't suffering from a migraine he roamed huge solitary loops around the fenced perimeter, just yards inside the wire chute, five or six miles a day.

Between eleven o'clock and one the loudspeakers blared again for lunch, in the same rotating order as for breakfast. Once his block was called, an inmate had fifteen minutes to report to the mess hall and pass through a food line, then another fifteen to eat. After thirty minutes, he had to be outside again. When every block was through, the mess hall closed for cleaning, then reopened at four thirty for dinner, before another return to the yard. Throughout all this were periodic counts. These, too, were announced by loudspeaker. *Count time, count time! All inmates report to your assigned dorm! Get on your assigned bunk! Remain on your assigned bunk until the count is clear!* A count occupied thirty or forty minutes, and was called five or six times a day. Then speakers would blast *Count clear!* and Willie would return to the yard to resume his loops.

At sunset the yard closed and inmates returned inside to another count, then to church for a service, or to the dayroom to watch television, or to their bunks. As daylight contracted toward the end of the year, so did an inmate's time on the yard. For this reason an inmate who preferred to spend his time outdoors, as Willie did, preferred warmer months, despite the southern humidity, for their longer days. In December the yard closed as early as five.

Most nights he was in bed by nine thirty, more than an hour before lights dimmed. He hoped desperately to spend as much of his day as he could in solitude, in an empty room or walking a barren sweep of grass, because it was where he felt least afraid. On a lucky night he was asleep by the time other inmates retired, and didn't hear the noise they made entering. Inevitably he awoke again by midnight or one and lay there, his pulse ricocheting through his skull, staring at the mattress above him, or, if he had been assigned an upper bunk that week, at the ceiling. At night he wasn't supposed to leave his dorm—couldn't, in fact, because its doors had been locked. Even to use the bathroom he needed permission from a guard. Some guards didn't enforce this rule, but others were hardheads. If a hardhead found him out of bed he risked being charged with an infraction.

For the few hours he slept, he dreamed he was being chased by inmates in brown uniforms, their eyes widened crazily, mouths foaming like dogs'; or by guards, their batons dangling heavily from their belts, slapping their thighs as they sprinted toward him, pistols drawn. "I'm innocent!" he always screamed, and the men would smile. They never listened. Or he was pacing down a corridor, relieved at the quiet, the other inmates from his dorm off in the dayroom. Then all forty of them emerged from around the corner, carrying pistols and clubs they had robbed from the guards. They hadn't been in the dayroom after all. They had been waiting for him. Or he was back at trial, the judge was shaking his head sternly as jurors stared at Willie in horror. Then Steve Hunt showed up. When jurors saw him they all collapsed into laughter.

When he awoke his head was askew and his pillow was stuffed into a corner, his thin sheet wrapped around his leg like a telephone cord. He had sweat through his shirt and his heart was racing. His arms throbbed from clenching his fists. Often he was rigid with terror, or his knuckles were bruised from where he'd flailed against the wall. After weeks like this he came down with an illness that lasted into November. His throat burned and his appetite was gone. What little he did eat, he vomited. He put in a request for sick call, where nurses suggested a liquid diet until he could keep down solid food. They gave him cold tablets and Tylenol.

Until Steve Hunt had knocked on Brenda's door a year earlier, nothing about Willie's life had augured prison. He was the eighth of nine children; his mother, Mozella, had married four times, fully half of which ended in tragedy. At fifteen she married a man named Samuel Vinson, had her first child, and then four more. But Samuel Vinson left her, so Mozella remarried—to Cliff Grimes, with whom she bore another pair of children. One afternoon Cliff climbed atop their roof to clean it, slipped, and fell to his death. Again Mozella remarried, this time to Edgar Brooks, with whom she became pregnant with her eighth: a boy, due at the close of that summer, 1946. In July, eight months into her pregnancy, another car swerved into Edgar Brooks's, and killed him instantly. A month later Willie was born.

Most of Willie's half siblings were fully grown by then, off living with wives or husbands of their own. Only one remained from Mozella's first marriage, Robert Lee, and two from her second, Gladys and Cliff Jr. The three of them plus Willie and Mozella shared a tiny three-room, tin-roofed cottage off Route 1 in Lawndale, owned by a white family whose land Mozella sharecropped. Then Mozella remarried a final time and gave Willie a younger brother, Bobby Lewis. One of the older half siblings pinned the younger ones with nicknames whenever he visited, and each time he arrived he found Willie playing in the clay outside their cottage, rolling and digging with his bare hands. Always rooting around, his brother said, laughing at him. Always rootin'. Root. Woot.

Lawndale then was a hilly swatch of farmland midway between Asheville and Charlotte, smaller than a square mile, pocked with disrepaired barns and grass the color of copper and highways indistinguishable from back roads. Or, rather, properly this was Lawndale, though certain folks considered it nothing more than a nameless outskirt of Shelby, a town of fifteen thousand, twenty minutes south— assuming you owned a car, which many in Lawndale didn't. Others regarded both towns as the Piedmont, meaning the larger area roughly between the Blue Ridge Mountains and the Catawba River. The entire county was 460-odd square miles named for a colonel who'd helped to halt the British advance into North Carolina, and since those days it had stayed agricultural: corn, wheat, oats, and sweet potatoes, but mainly cotton. Eventually, in the 1950s, there were also dairy farms and a small handful of textile and manufacturing plants, but even then Mozella and her children knew only sharecropping, like most poor families in Lawndale. (Or Shelby, or the Piedmont.)

As early as the 1940s and '50s, blacks and whites were relatively integrated on that stretch of farmland, at least in geographical terms, since a sharecropping family occupied a fringe of the same property as the family it worked for. Besides schools, what really segregated a community like this was not race but money. A landowning family could earn income simply by sitting still. A sharecropping family, white or black, could labor from sunrise to sunset without earning a cent. (Though it was also true that most landowning families were white, and most sharecroppers black.) During cotton season, which might last three months every autumn, Willie and others like him were excused from school annually to help their parents on the farm. Even outside that season, a sharecropping child often split his day between farm and schoolhouse. A child of landowners thought only of the latter, and he kept there year-round.

Few jobs other than farming existed in Lawndale, since only a single textile mill had come to stay: Cleveland Mills, where linemen threaded yarn, dyed it, packed it into cardboard boxes, stacked those boxes onto trucks, and sent them off to warehouses. Trucks rumbled down Route 1 nearly every day, filled with yarn. If a person's future didn't include the mill or the fields, he generally headed south to Shelby, or else thirty miles north, to Hickory, where industry had taken better hold. If he had any money he could try farther still: DC, Philadelphia, New Jersey, New York.

At Vans Grove Elementary and then Douglas High, both all-black, Willie earned steady Bs. He was talented at math, and in other classes got by. He was a shy boy, and quiet; he liked school, but it was hard for him to introduce himself to strangers, and harder since he attended only two-thirds of the year, due to the sharecropping. It was obvious what a benefit education could be. A handful escaped Lawndale each year, to high schools up north or even to college. Willie tried to apply himself. He graduated from Douglas in 1964, a year before county schools integrated—though Douglas itself never would, and instead was shuttered.

Two weeks before Thanksgiving, after four months of waiting in O dorm, de Torres wrote to share that he'd filed Willie's appeal. Only now, through a fog of incomprehension, did Willie begin to absorb what had happened: unless an appeal succeeded, the prison would keep him, though he had committed no crime. All through his nine months in county jail and the four days of trial, literally until the moment of the jury verdict, he'd assumed the truth would come out. Of course it would. He had waited so long to go home. In all that time he hadn't seen a single piece of real evidence against him. The fingerprints hadn't matched, the hair had been uncertain, and Carrie Elliott—couldn't anyone see that she hadn't truly recognized him? Now he saw the facts had never mattered. That was the explanation. Everyone at his trial must have known he was innocent. There had been a decision to convict him anyway. Had Miss Elliott really even been raped? Possibly she and Linda McDowell had invented this fiction, as they had the others.

Regardless, de Torres should still have gotten him off—he seemed like a good man, de Torres did, but where had he been during the long wait for trial? Willie didn't know how many hours de Torres had invested in his case, but it hadn't felt like enough. Then Steve Hunt, and the Catawba County prosecutors, had denied him any chance by refusing to turn over evidence. He hadn't done a single thing wrong, and these people had thrown him in prison anyway. Why had they told those lies? Linda must have grown jealous. That was what all this was about. He'd never been as close with Linda as he had with her sisters; as far as he could remember, they'd never had problems, but that must have been it. What about the others—the Hickory police, and the district attorneys? He wondered this constantly.

When he shuddered awake at two in the morning he was aglow, he was seething. His every filament vibrated hideously. Against the walls of his lungs roiled gales of pressure, as though his entire chest had been cauterized. He sensed he might be corroding internally, like a battery. He felt equally likely to explode, like gunpowder, or cave in, like sand. He was livid. He was incandescent. The blood in his veins was spoiling. For entire days his own limbs felt prosthetic.

He held no hope for de Torres's appeal, because he knew direct appeals were ruled on locally, meaning the people who considered them were the same goddamn people who had sent him here. It didn't surprise him when de Torres's appeal was denied. Legally the next step was the court of appeals, but Willie didn't want to waste his time. He wrote directly to the state supreme court. This was denied, too.

8

Newman, Coleman, and Weitzel

Around the same time that Rich Rosen asked his law students for help reading letters from inmates, a separate group of students, at Duke University, just ten miles southwest of where Rosen worked at Chapel Hill, were volunteering to read letters of their own. None of the Duke students knew Rosen personally, but they'd heard of Ronald Cotton, the man he'd freed, and resolved to do something to help. Because they weren't yet licensed to practice law, they couldn't formally accept clients, but they could respond to inmates who wrote them for help, and mail police or prosecutorial files, which inmates usually couldn't access on their own. Students hadn't been at this for long before they heard from two professors up in New York, at the Cardozo School of Law, who'd founded a nonprofit called the Innocence Project, aimed at solving the same problem. Appeals for help had overwhelmed them, too, so they were putting out word to a handful of top law schools across the country, hoping to plant seeds for a national network of satellite programs. The Duke students agreed to convert their volunteer group to an innocence project. For that, however, they needed faculty advisers.

They chose Theresa Newman and Jim Coleman, two well-liked, left-leaning professors they guessed would be receptive to the idea. Polite and self-effacing, Newman looked precisely the scholar she was, with short, no-fuss hair and the demeanor of someone who spent considerable time in libraries. Her colleague Jim Coleman, one of the few influential lawyers in North Carolina who also happened to be black, wore horn-rim glasses and a trim gray beard, his hair as short as moss. The effect was of a kind, oval face, ringed by gray fuzz.

"Seventy to seventy-five percent of people in prison today went to trial with a court-appointed attorney," Coleman once bemoaned to *Duke Magazine*. Pay for such work was low, which meant that many court-appointed attorneys in North Carolina were not in fact professional public defenders. "Instead they are attorneys who take the cases because they are just starting in practice, and need the work. Or they don't have other work, because they are not very good at what they do...Judges are satisfied to appoint a lawyer who is breathing."

Newman and Coleman both agreed to serve as faculty advisers for the new Duke Innocence Project. This required they attend a training session up in New York. There they met Rich Rosen, who had come to explore the same possibility for Chapel Hill. All three lawyers had never been in the same place before, and now they got to talking. Their two campuses were only twenty minutes apart, they realized. It made sense to work together.

Not everyone agreed their work was worth doing. To many of Rosen's and Newman's and Coleman's colleagues, in North Carolina and across the country, the letters they were reading were no more than acts of desperation; there was zero chance these inmates were innocent, only that they had nothing to lose by filing paperwork. The American criminal justice system had always trivialized the chances of wrongful conviction, feeling certain—as Chris Mumma no longer could—that protections at trial made that outcome impossible. A series of reforms in the 1950s and '60s had bolstered this attitude still further. In *Mapp v. Ohio,* the U.S. Supreme Court clamped down on unlawful searches and seizures, and in *Gideon v. Wainwright* it extended the right to an attorney to those defendants unable to pay for one. After *Miranda v. Arizona,* anyone who was arrested had to be informed of his rights; after *United States v. Wade,* he was entitled to his lawyer during most lineups.

Quickly these reforms proved controversial, publicly as well as on the court itself, since, by design, in addition to protecting defendants, they provided new hurdles for conviction. One justice, dissenting from *Miranda,* warned that "the rule announced today will measurably weaken the ability of the criminal law to perform [its] tasks":

> I have no desire whatsoever to share the responsibility for any such impact on the present criminal process. In some unknown number of cases, the Court's rule will return a killer, a rapist or other criminal to the streets and to the environment which produced him, to repeat his crime whenever it pleases him. As a consequence, there will be not a gain, but a loss, in human dignity.

Over the next two decades the court reeled back several of these reforms, narrowing what precisely it had promised and in which circumstances those promises applied. First it ruled that poor defendants, though entitled to a lawyer, were not entitled to choose which particular lawyer they liked. Then it defined *counsel* only modestly, as "reasonably effective assistance given the totality of the circumstances." Other reforms required legislative follow-up that had never come to pass. The courts already were getting it right—why reshape them? "Our society has a high degree of confidence in its trials," wrote Justice Sandra Day O'Connor, in 1993, "because the Constitution offers unparalleled protections against convicting the innocent." That sentiment had prevailed for seventy years. "Under our criminal procedure, the accused has every advantage," a court of appeals judge, Learned Hand, had remarked in 1923. "Our dangers do not lie in too little tenderness to the accused. Our procedure has been always haunted by the ghost of the innocent man convicted. It is an unreal dream."

At last that ghost would appear, however—on October 26, 1987, one day before Willie Grimes's arrest in North Carolina, in an article in *Newsweek* magazine. Over in Britain, *Newsweek* relayed, a geneticist had discovered a technique for comparing human DNA. Already the technique had been used "to resolve a handful of paternity and immigration cases," as well as, "more dramatically, to link a twenty-seven-year-old man...to the rape-murders of two teenage girls near the English village of Enderby."

One reader of that issue of *Newsweek* happened to be an American lawyer whose client had been incarcerated for a decade, for a rape outside Chicago. From *Newsweek* the lawyer understood that DNA might implicate a person, but now he wondered if it had ever been used for the reverse: not to implicate someone, but to exculpate him. It hadn't. In January 1988, he filed a motion to try.

The result made his client, Gary Dotson, the first person in United States history to be exonerated by DNA testing.

It didn't stop, though, at Dotson. Over the next half decade came nearly thirty more DNA exonerations, so many that in 1996 the National Institute of Justice chose the subject for its annual report. Of twenty-eight convictions the report examined, every one had relied on eyewitness testimony at trial. Seven had relied on hair analysis. Four had relied on "expert scientific testimony" by a man who'd worked as a forensic serologist, and then a medical examiner, in two different states before being charged with fraud. On average, the exonerated men had spent seven years in prison, though eight had served a decade or more. One had served nine and a half years for the rape of a woman on whom sperm had been found—despite the fact that he'd previously undergone a vasectomy, so couldn't have produced sperm if he'd wanted to.

In response to that NIJ report, the U.S. attorney general, Janet Reno, formed the National Commission on the Future of DNA Evidence, which in turn produced a document called *Eyewitness Evidence: A Guide for Law Enforcement*. "Recent cases in which DNA evidence has been used to exonerate individuals have shown us that eyewitness evidence is not infallible," the guide warned. "Even the most honest and objective people can make mistakes in recalling and interpreting a witnessed event; it is the nature of human memory. This issue has been at the heart of a growing body of research." Nonetheless, the guide offered no enforceable rules, only a "consensus of recommended practices."

Still, the cumulative effect of each commission and report was plain. DNA testing had provided the equivalent of a random audit of trial verdicts, which in turn had laid bare a vulnerability no one foresaw. In 2001, a national poll found that 73 percent of U.S. adults believed an innocent person had been executed within the past decade. "If statistics are any indication, the system may well be allowing some innocent defendants to be executed," Sandra Day O'Connor admitted that July, before an association of women lawyers in Minnesota. O'Connor had changed her mind from eight years earlier. Within another year, in *Atkins v. Virginia,* five of her colleagues had, too. Read their majority decision: "We cannot ignore the fact that in recent years a disturbing number of inmates on death row have been exonerated."

A few weeks after Rosen, Newman, and Coleman returned to North Carolina from their Innocence Project training in New York, Pete Weitzel read in the local *News and Observer* that Duke and Chapel Hill law schools hoped to merge their respective innocence programs. Weitzel was a lanky, rheumy-eyed man in his sixties whose ruddy complexion resembled a carpenter's on some cold-weather job. In fact he'd spent forty years with the *Miami Herald* before retiring and moving to North Carolina, where his wife took a position at Duke as an associate dean. Since then he'd been teaching journalism part-time, and looking for something else to do. He'd never reported much on law at the *Herald,* but this idea of an innocence project intrigued him. He imagined it might feel satisfying to help investigate cases, uncover where the law had been misapplied, and repair its abuses, if he could. He also happened to live down the street from Jim Coleman. That afternoon he laid down the newspaper, strode across his yard, and knocked on Coleman's door.

Coleman was relieved for the help. Neither he nor Newman had any clue about administration, he admitted to Weitzel. The pair of them wanted to collaborate with Rich Rosen, but law school hadn't taught them a thing about how to go about it. Weitzel, an editor, knew how to get disparate parts working together. He drove to Chapel Hill to introduce himself to Rosen, where he recognized in Rosen's office several of the same cases from Coleman's files. This wouldn't do, he chided. The two campuses weren't in competition, and both had complained of being submerged in paperwork. Why were they fielding letters from the same inmates? What they really ought to do was incorporate as a nonprofit. Some sort of umbrella organization, even staffed modestly, could screen letters from prospective clients, forward those with promise along to Rosen at Chapel Hill, or Newman and Coleman at Duke, and help to avoid duplicates.

That arrangement sounded perfect, the lawyers told Weitzel. But none of them knew how to organize it.

Weitzel did. In 2000, he helped them found a nonprofit called the North Carolina Center on Actual Innocence, "to identify, investigate, and advance credible claims of innocence made by inmates convicted of felonies in North Carolina," its mission pledged. Their center would accept nearly any case of wrongful conviction, the four agreed—not only capital cases, or cases where DNA was available, as the original Innocence Project did. "What DNA investigations illustrate is just how wrong the system can be in normal circumstances," Weitzel told *Duke Magazine*. "Whether you have the conclusive proof—the silver bullet of DNA—or not."

Without any budget, Newman and Coleman persuaded Duke to donate the center office space, and Rosen borrowed resources from Chapel Hill, mostly funds the law school had set aside for pro bono projects, assuming that, since he was a professor, no one would ask him many questions. Then he persuaded a dean to fund a research assistant. A proper nonprofit also needed a board of directors, Weitzel insisted. Since there were only the four of them, this would have to be themselves. He personally would be executive director; Rosen could be president. Newman agreed to be vice president. She didn't know what this entailed, exactly, except that whenever Rosen got his wish and stepped down, Newman would replace him as president. Besides Weitzel, none of them knew exactly what that entailed, either.

The center made everyone's job easier except for Weitzel's. Of the four, only he had never worked on wrongful convictions before, or, for that matter, gone to law school. He'd imagined he understood criminal justice in America, at least broadly; he was a journalist, after all, he wasn't naive. He knew that not everyone could be relied on. As he read through cases, however, what surprised him was the reverse; not how often there were villains, but how often there weren't. He'd assumed that any false outcome would be traceable to misbehavior at trial: a biased judge, a negligent lawyer, a witness who'd lied on the stand. Sometimes this prediction held up. Other times it didn't. The cases that unnerved him most had been tried precisely as they ought to have been, and still had turned out all wrong. One small error, somewhere down the line, then bad luck to compound it—that was all it took, especially for a defendant without money or influence. A defendant like this couldn't afford his own lawyer, so the state appointed him one, and now Weitzel saw the sheer volume most court-appointed lawyers carried; even if they were conscientious, which of course most of them were, their workload was just unsustainable. Others, it was true, weren't any good. Once Weitzel phoned a lawyer whose client was serving a life term in prison. "I don't remember much about it," the lawyer confessed, "that was my first-ever case." Another time Weitzel asked if he might photocopy a particular file. "Oh, I didn't keep them," the lawyer told him. "I don't keep any files." Weitzel hadn't foreseen cases like these, and now they were piled all around him; packed into boxes at Chapel Hill, stacked atop conference tables at Duke, stuffed inside envelopes at the center, spread across the carpet in his home.

To help screen these cases, the center relied on law students, but now Weitzel wondered about recruiting journalism students for the same job. He knocked on the dean's office at Chapel Hill: what if he taught a course in investigative reporting? The dean was intrigued, but listed a handful of concerns. Then Weitzel added that, since he was retired, he didn't need any salary. He would teach the course for free. The dean forgot his concerns.

The next semester, under Weitzel's guidance, student journalists began combing through center cases. There they discovered James Bernard Parker. Parker was serving a life term for child abuse in Monroe, a growing Charlotte suburb. Nearly fifteen years earlier, in 1990, an elementary-school counselor there had learned that several students were being "bothered" in their neighborhood, a vague claim she'd shared with police, to whom several of the boys admitted having been abused, and pointed toward Parker. Parker was tall, ebony-skinned, and easy to recognize; he lived in a housing project near the school. Four of the accusations against him had held up in court.

Weitzel's journalism students, however, had questions about the case. More than four boys had claimed abuse. Why only this many charges? What evidence had counted against Parker, besides the testimony of schoolchildren? They drove up to Monroe to ask for Parker's files, where a desk sergeant told them he didn't think his department had kept any. But he remembered the officer who'd originally investigated the case; that officer had since retired, but maybe, if students got lucky, he'd kept a few files from his time on the force somewhere around his house. The sergeant gave an address.

"I don't have them," the retired officer answered, scratching his chin, when students showed up at his door. "But I know where they are. Want me to get them for you?" Together they all drove back to the station, where the officer disappeared inside, then reappeared minutes later with a cardboard box so large he could barely wrap his arms around it. "Here you are," he said.

Students hauled this box back to campus, where Weitzel's entire class helped pore through it. Lying flat on the very bottom, beneath what might have been forty pounds of paper, were the elementary-school counselor's original reports. According to those, two of the schoolboys had never mentioned the race of their assailant at all. Two others had been abused by "a light-skinned negro." Six had been abused by a white man.

IS THE WRONG MAN BEHIND BARS? read a *Charlotte Observer* headline the following December. After reading the article, a local attorney agreed to represent Parker pro bono. The DA, however, was reluctant to reopen the case—Parker's original prosecutor had since become a chief circuit judge, and the political implications of this were unappealing. Instead, he offered a deal: if Parker pleaded guilty to a lesser offense, the DA would settle for time served. Parker did, and was released. Still, the conditions of his deal didn't sit well with Rich Rosen, who told the *Observer* he thought it was "a great accomplishment" that Parker had been freed. "But I think the system didn't work for James Parker," he added. "It didn't work at the time of trial. And frankly it didn't work at the end, when he was pressured to plead guilty to a crime he didn't do."

Around the same time Weitzel began teaching free journalism courses at Chapel Hill, Chris Mumma, disillusioned by those cases she'd seen under Beverly Lake at the state supreme court, phoned Rosen to ask for guidance. She didn't much need a salary, Chris admitted, over their lunch at the local diner. She only wanted meaningful work, and the feeling that she was empowered to achieve something. To Rosen those terms sounded like a bargain, since meaningful work was precisely what he could offer, and a salary was precisely what he couldn't. Their center needed a staff attorney. He and Newman and Coleman were lawyers, but all three of them held faculty jobs, so lacked the flexibility to add full-time nonprofit work.

Chris accepted.

To keep one another abreast of cases, the center's original four board members—Rosen, Newman, Coleman, and Weitzel—had gotten into a habit of lunch every so often at the Weathervane, a Southern-themed restaurant just a few minutes north of the Chapel Hill campus. Now Chris joined them. Over cornmeal-crusted catfish and coastal shrimp and grits, the five shared their recent cases and what they imagined was next for the center. It was satisfying to work so directly on the issues—an unfamiliar sensation for Chris, who'd felt so disempowered as a clerk. She still shared Weitzel's surprise that cases like these existed in the first place. Without DNA testing, or a cooperative prosecutor, many couldn't be relitigated. That was the most discouraging scenario: a wrongful conviction, and nothing they could do about it.

Rosen had learned, from his experience with Ronald Cotton, how the process could work when everyone collaborated. But he also knew how rare that was. A prosecutor had no incentive to reexamine a closed case; at best this meant more labor for him, and, at worst, a discovery that he or someone in his office had made a mistake. It was extraordinary the DA in Cotton's case had been so amenable. Rosen, too, had helped the process along, by risking his client's fortunes simply to find the truth.

That was what they needed in a case like that. Some way to find the truth—the nonpartisan, supralegal *truth*. But such a model was hard to envision. Of the lawyers they knew, how many would risk their own interests to learn whether they personally had gotten a case wrong? For that even to be possible would require conversation with DAs, and also with sheriffs and police, who had something at stake, too. And who was supposed to bring all those parties to the table? Rosen, Newman, and Coleman were all outspoken, anti-death-penalty liberals. Weitzel was a journalist from out of town. Say one of them went ahead and organized a statewide meeting, a summit, of sorts, on the issues. A roomful of defense attorneys would show up, and no one else. They'd be preaching to no one but themselves.

Chris set down her fork to contemplate what she was hearing. How seriously were they considering this? she asked the others. This idea of a summit?

Newman shrugged. They were serious, she answered, if only it would happen.

What if they had a person like Beverly Lake? Chris asked. The pair had a good relationship. What if she were to approach him with their idea?

The others regarded her skeptically. Wasn't Beverly Lake a Republican? An old-fashioned, law-and-order conservative?

He was, Chris confirmed. For that matter, so was she. But Lake was also fair-minded, and Chris had grown close with him over the three years of her clerkship. Plus, he had something personally at stake, she happened to know. Public trust in the courts had long been Lake's signature issue. Every false verdict left that trust more brittle, and Lake knew it. Chris had made *sure* he knew it, had hassled him about those cases in his chambers. What she'd wanted from him then was for him to intervene single-handedly, and he'd declined to. This was different. They weren't proposing that Lake overturn any verdicts, only that he lend his reputation to a dialogue about them. What if Chris could persuade him to lead the discussion they were imagining?

Rosen, Newman, Coleman, and Weitzel all glanced at one another. Then, in unison, they looked at Chris.

Yes, they told her. Try.

9

The Benefit of Every Reasonable Inference

There were only so many ways for a man to occupy his time in prison, and he saw every one of them. The value of a job was not that it paid but that it passed hours. When he wasn't eating, working, reading, sleeping, or exercising, chances were good an inmate was gambling—on cards, on televised football or basketball or NASCAR, on footraces or on duels between insects captured from the yard. Technically gambling was prohibited, but a rule in prison meant only as much as guards' enforcement of it, and guards had larger concerns than petty gambling.

Because de Torres had told him to be a model prisoner, and a crowd of inmates unsettled him anyway, Willie rarely gambled. If he happened to win he walked away before the stakes rose too high, to avoid any trouble. Or he gave away his winnings. Money had never made any difference to him; he'd lived forty-one years without it, expected nothing different of his future, and didn't see the value of money in prison anyway, except at the canteen, the prison store.

For his work in the kitchen, and how cooperative he'd been, he was promoted that first winter to medium security, allowing him more hours in the yard. A week later the promotion was nearly rescinded. After a breakfast shift that Monday, he and two other assistant cooks discovered a jug of buck the head cook had brewed, nearly a gallon and a half. Buck was a sort of homemade wine, from fruit juices and sugar yeast; Willie had never tried it, but now he and the others were alone in the kitchen, and the head cook said they were welcome to it as long as they saved him a gallon. An hour later, a guard was drawn by their voices. What was all the noise? he wanted to know, and looked Willie over. "You don't usually talk like that."

Willie shrugged. "I guess I'm feeling good," he said.

"What got you feeling good?"

"I don't know." He considered the others. "I guess we been drinking. Whatever we been drinking, we feeling good."

The guard hauled them to his lieutenant, who suggested all three inmates be returned to their bunks until they settled down. That afternoon a sergeant showed up to charge Willie with substance possession, worth thirty days in segregation. Entering the infraction into Willie's file, though, he noticed Willie's promotion to medium custody had been only ten days earlier. In the eight months Willie had been at CP, he hadn't caused any other trouble. To keep from reversing his promotion, the sergeant decided to cut him a break. He reduced the thirty days to three.

A segregated cell was roughly the same as any other, only filthier, and located in an entirely different wing, a distance from general population. Bolted to the wall was a low steel bed and a combination toilet-and-sink joined into one dull metal skeleton. Through a slat in his door, meals appeared, along with paper and a pencil for one letter a week. For an hour each day, guards let him outdoors, not into the main yard but a solitary eight-by-ten cube where he could hardly feel a breeze. Otherwise what defined segregation was absence: no job or canteen or radio, no gambling or television or cards.

In short, segregation held nothing but his own interior, which had turned against him. In the semidarkness of his cell he could think only of his case, and of his molten anger at the fraud of his trial. The conspiracy he was now certain of tormented him. He was awfully, throbbingly lonely. Brenda was out there, somewhere, he knew, moving about in the winter chill. It'd been weeks since he'd heard from her. He missed her. He missed his family.

He missed Thomas Hill. His closest friend since childhood, Thomas had been a shy, self-conscious boy, too, with eight siblings, just like Willie, but few intimate friends. They'd taken to each other immediately. It hadn't mattered that Thomas's family had moved often, to sharecrop different land, so long as he kept within the same five-mile radius, since anything less than this counted as walking distance. Whenever they weren't in the fields, Thomas and Woot had played checkers, or cards—gin rummy and spades, the only two games whose rules they understood. Often Thomas stayed the night. He graduated from Douglas High in '64, in the same class as Woot, then after six months studying auto mechanics at Catawba Tech, up in Hickory, a U.S. Air Force recruiter promised him the same training in the military, tuition-free. In fact, the air force would pay *him,* the recruiter said. He enlisted six months later.

Besides Thomas, Willie's closest friend in school had been Louie Ross—a less likely match, since Louie was extroverted and boisterous. After graduation, Willie's income from a textile plant, and help from his sister Gladys, had allowed him to scrape together enough for a secondhand car, which he had used on Friday or Saturday nights to drive Louie the ten miles down to Shelby, where Louie's girlfriend lived. Then at ten thirty Willie would reappear to bring Louie home. What had his friend been up to while he'd waited? Louie would ask. Didn't Woot have plans? Did he want to see a girlfriend of his own? But Willie had only hung around a nearby pool hall—he didn't mind. When he refused Louie's offer of gas money, Louie would decide he was hungry, ask to pass by a fast-food joint, and buy the pair of them hamburgers.

After that summer Louie left for college down at Fayetteville State, where a brother was enrolled. In the summers that followed he would return for seasonal jobs; since there was no work in Lawndale, he often landed at Pittsburgh Plate Glass, down in Shelby, or at Ace Springs, up in Hickory, assembling chairs or the internal springs for mattresses. On weekends he phoned Willie to spend a day or two together. Then Louie would mention he'd like to see his girlfriend before returning to Fayetteville. "Just tell me what day you want to go, what time you want to go, and what time you want to come back," Willie would promise, "and I'll bring you."

When he finished college and saw that he was about to be drafted into the Marines and sent to Vietnam, Louie chose to join the air force instead. By 1987, almost twenty years later, he'd been discharged and was working as a high-school counselor in Raleigh. In his apartment one evening that autumn, he got a phone call from Willie's cousin, who told him Woot was in prison for rape, on a life sentence. Louie was dumbfounded. Woot? For rape? This wasn't possible. He reached out to other friends from Douglas, every one of whom agreed the news made no sense. The Woot they knew was nothing like that. At once Louie regretted having lost touch; he arranged a visit and drove to Central Prison, to let Willie know that his friends believed him.

Thomas Hill, meanwhile, who had also enlisted in the air force, was discharged in '69 and found work at Cleveland Mills, there in Lawndale. He had also reconnected with Willie, who by then was living up in Hickory. That same autumn, Thomas heard from Willie's nephew about the arrest. Like Louie, Thomas felt certain Woot hadn't raped anyone. *Wrong place, wrong time,* he assumed. Once police figured out who had really done it, he predicted, Woot would be released.

But they never figured it out.

When guards led him from segregation back to his block, he turned his attention to getting out entirely. If he cut short his walks around the yard, he found he could visit the prison library, which opened between breakfast and lunch, then again from one until four in the afternoon. Using the law volumes he found there, he tried appealing again to the North Carolina Supreme Court, hoping it would reconsider its earlier refusal even to read his case. When he didn't hear back, he learned that, in addition to books, the library often held inmates who knew more about appellate procedure than he did. Some had even taken law classes offered in prison.

One inmate named Terry had studied law on the outside, at an actual law school, before he'd gotten arrested—he had been sentenced to something like six hundred years, but all on his own had reduced this sentence by two-thirds. Willie tracked him down to ask if he would read his trial transcript. Terry agreed. But Willie's appellate deadline was only a few days away, and his case manager told him he was about to ship to another prison. Terry drafted a rapid appeal, and Willie sent it off to Ed de Torres, who agreed that Terry had actually done a pretty good job. Because de Torres was listed as the attorney of record, though, he couldn't very well submit a brief someone else had written. Instead he drafted his own, then decided to submit them both. In March, eight months after the conviction, he filed the pair of them with the court of appeals.

A month later Willie received a letter from the attorney general, but as far as he could tell it didn't include a ruling. "Due to administrative oversight, counsel for the State has not yet received the verbatim transcript of the trial proceedings as requested, and is therefore unable to complete the brief for the State within the time prescribed by rule," the letter read. Willie didn't understand what this meant. He wrote again to de Torres: "My caseworker and lawyer aid have look over all my papers and told me that the state have not got anything against me to hold me and their is some type of motion that you could be filing to help get me out of here. So I am asking you what are you going to do now and will be hoping to hear from you soon."

Around the same time, his sister Gladys, whom Willie had told by phone how confused he was about the attorney general letter, wrote to de Torres as well. "I would like to ask you what you think is going on? Do you feel that Willie will get a new trial? If so when and can family be present? My brother says that he cannot understand why they are seeking more time, when they seemingly had no problems convicting him. Please let him know what is going on."

Finally, in late August, three months after Willie had written, de Torres replied that he was preparing to argue Willie's appeal the coming Thursday—a week from then. This meant a thirty-minute oral presentation, after which the court was entitled to ask questions. If it granted his appeal, the court could order either a resentencing or a new trial. De Torres expected a decision sometime in October. "I trust this will answer your questions about what is going on."

As he had waited, meanwhile, Willie had been transferred. One Friday that spring, guards rounded up a few dozen inmates from O dorm, announced they were shipping, and loaded them onto a long, slate-colored bus. Inmates called it the Gray Goose. Because the Gray Goose visited four or five prisons each haul, and always varied its order and route, there was no predicting how long the trip might take; an inmate simply stayed in its cabin until a guard told him he was up. They were lucky to be transferred on a cool afternoon, someone mentioned. The Goose had no air conditioning, and its windows were sealed shut; come July, with fifty men on board, the cabin temperature wouldn't rise so much as thicken, so that the bus felt like a kiln.

When the Goose arrived at a prison it backed into a fenced chute and a handful of unfamiliar guards emerged to meet it. Names were called for who ought to climb out, and however many this was trekked out the rear hatch, beyond a set of gates, and through the door of an intake room, its benches soldered to the walls. A sergeant gave orientation, which was a list of rules, while guards sifted through every scrap of property an inmate had stored in the Goose's lower compartment, and determined what he could keep. A particular prison might or might not allow pencils, pens, books, magazines, photographs, or radios, depending on the rules and the mood of the guards, and regardless of the rules at whatever prison the inmate had arrived from. Anything else was confiscated or trashed. Then guards brought him to a nurse. Was he presently being treated for any health problems? He wasn't, except for migraines. Was he on any medications? He wasn't. Was he thinking of harming himself? He wasn't. They brought him to the clothes house to collect white and brown clothes for the week. Within a few days they assigned him a new case manager, who repeated the rules the sergeant had listed in orientation.

He told his new case manager that he had worked in the kitchen back at CP, and was willing to do this at Harnett Correctional, too, if there was an opening, but that really he wanted laundry duty. He'd heard Harnett lacked its own laundry facility, despite housing nearly a thousand inmates, in medium security, in the same layout of open dorms; the nearest facilities were back at CP, or down at Sampson, or over at Chase. All those were nearly an hour's drive, meaning an inmate on laundry duty took regular day trips. And, like other jobs, it paid. Depending on the position, Correction Enterprises, the company that operated laundry services, offered wages of forty cents, seventy cents, or a dollar a day. In prison this was a lot of money. At different locations Correction Enterprises ran different operations: over at Johnston County it managed an enormous paint plant, where inmates mixed gallon after gallon of white and yellow paint that Correction Enterprises then sold to the state, for marking roads. At Nash it managed a printing plant, where inmates copied forms for the DMV, public schools, and post offices. At other prisons it managed plants for sewing, canning, or making road signs. Harnett held soap- and meat-processing plants, but neither of those required travel. He wanted laundry.

While he waited for assignment, and for de Torres to share the outcome of his appeal, he wrote more letters. From the library he filed a motion for appropriate relief, asking for either a new trial or the dismissal of all his charges. Again he heard nothing back. Then he wrote to North Carolina Prisoner Legal Services to ask for help. Within two weeks he received a reply from a staff attorney, Phillip Griffin, who had read Willie's questionnaire and felt interested in his case, but didn't want to act until Willie's appeal had been ruled on. He asked Willie to have de Torres forward a copy of his trial transcript and appellate briefs. Willie forwarded the request to de Torres, but it was another six weeks before de Torres replied with an update: he was still waiting for a decision from the court of appeals.

He didn't have to wait much longer. The appeal was denied in early December. At trial, the court reasoned, de Torres had raised various objections to Carrie Elliott's identification, and the judge had ruled on them; de Torres had also motioned to dismiss the verdict, and the judge had ruled on that, too. The court didn't intend to overrule either decision. Once Willie had been convicted, the ruling explained, he was no longer innocent until proven guilty. Now that burden was reversed: "The evidence is to be considered in the light more favorable to the State, giving the State the benefit of every reasonable inference to be drawn therefrom. Contradictions and discrepancies are for the jury to resolve and do not warrant dismissal." Its finding: "No error."

Nearly a year and a half had passed since Willie's conviction.

Because the court had forwarded its ruling only to de Torres, de Torres wrote to Willie, at Harnett, to share the news:

December 12, 1989

Dear Mr. Grimes:

I would advise you that now is the time to re-contact Mr. Griffin at N.C. Prisoner Legal Services for any additional post-conviction assistance they can offer. If he needs any copies of the transcript, briefs, etc., please let me know or have him to contact me. I will be happy to send it to him upon request.

This will officially terminate my representation of you under my appointment by the Court, as there is no court appointed counsel rights beyond the initial appeal. I sincerely wish that the outcome was different, <u>as I am still convinced of your innocence.</u>

Good luck to you in the future.

Sincerely,
E. X. de Torres
Attorney at Law

10

A Problem for Everyone

They pulled up to Chris Mumma's house at a few minutes after eleven, on a cool, overcast Friday morning in late November. For days Chris had felt self-conscious about welcoming so many strangers to her home, but finally she'd been forced to admit that it made more sense than anyplace else. She and Beverly Lake had both wanted neutral ground; they couldn't ask prosecutors to come to a liberal university campus, or defense attorneys to go to a sheriff's department. Lake had hoped for a private home, but whose might comfortably hold fifteen? Her own, Chris offered grudgingly, where she and Mitch had moved after his breakthrough in venture capital—Mitch's choice, she insisted, not her own. The two of them and all three kids had once lived in a modest A-frame. Now they owned a ten-thousand-square-foot Georgian Revival, with charcoal shutters and a winding, iron-railed front entrance, whose pillared balcony overlooked a golf course. Between its guesthouse and expansively landscaped lawn unspooled a stone-lined driveway large enough for the dozen-plus cars Chris and Lake expected.

Besides Rosen, Newman, Coleman, and Weitzel, from the center, and one or two colleagues of Lake's, none of the invitees had any idea who she was, Chris knew. They'd come not because they recognized the address on Lake's invitation but because the chief justice of the North Carolina Supreme Court had invited them, and now here was some stranger at her porticoed mansion, welcoming the attorney general inside. Chris worried about impressions. She wondered if some of them presumed she and Lake were having an affair. She'd borne that sort of suspicion before, though it had been wrong then, too; as a young, blond executive at Northern Telecom, more than once she'd considered cutting her hair, or wearing glasses, to downplay the effect of her looks. Finally she'd decided not to. Today she was nearly forty, old enough to be taken seriously. The best way she knew to prove others wrong was to be undeniably good at her job. If for the next thirty minutes or so a handful of police chiefs and district attorneys mistook her for some restless trophy wife, with some sequined childhood, and this some hobby luncheon, they would learn quickly enough. The meeting had been her damn idea in the first place.

Not that persuading Lake had been any chore. All she'd done was bring him the idea her center colleagues had dreamed up at the Weathervane, knowing Lake harbored sympathy for their cause already. The pair of them had read identical cases during Chris's clerkship; she suspected those had unsettled him, the same as they had her, despite their disagreeing about how empowered Lake and his court were to respond. "I *know* these matter to you," she finally told him. "I *know* you agree we should be doing better." Every wrongful conviction dumped an actual perpetrator back onto the streets, meaning reforms would help to catch *more* criminals, not fewer—this was harder on crime, not easier on it. In addition to that were the potential exonerees themselves, whose names Chris saw as a call to action. Listed on a notepad she'd begun carrying in her purse were the names of incarcerated men she believed were innocent. To help them all would require more than the center alone, and *that* would require someone like Lake, to bring deal-makers to the table.

And Lake no longer intended to evade the issue, which he regarded as obvious. Every exoneration dented public trust in his courts, and trust was necessary for those courts to function at all. When Chris had approached him during her clerkship years earlier, with cases she suspected were flawed, and Lake had demurred, it wasn't because he felt indifferent toward the problem. It was because he was chief justice. He didn't make policy. He oversaw the courts. Now Lake recognized a way he might address the issue without violating the boundaries of his chambers—not by dictating change, but by fostering its conditions.

At Chris's urging he wrote to fifteen of his colleagues, including a pair each of judges and district attorneys, the attorney general, and the deputy chief of the Charlotte-Mecklenburg Police Department, the largest in the state. He felt "growing concern" in the recent number of exonerations arising from wrongful convictions, Lake shared. Collectively these had forced him to consider whether anything could be done about them, to "minimize future convictions of the innocent, without jeopardizing the conviction of the guilty." Along with his letter he enclosed a list of everyone he was inviting: "a forum of representatives of our justice system," he explained, "including police, prosecutors, defense attorneys, and judges."

Now Chris welcomed the invitees into her hardwood and marble and bronze-chandeliered living room, where the previous week she'd dragged aside two embroidered couches and unfolded a rented conference table. Mitch was at work; all three kids were at school; Zeus, their hundred-pound Bernese mountain dog, she'd put in the yard. She'd also paid more than four hundred dollars to a private caterer, guessing that men might stay longer if she fed them, and that if they stayed they might as well choose to talk with one another. Then she'd looked around her house, seen her new friends Theresa Newman and Jim Coleman, and inhaled deeply. She'd gotten all these people in a room. It was impossible to predict what happened next.

As the invitees settled around the table, Lake thanked them all for coming. He wanted to begin by reiterating something many of them had heard from him before, that he was certain their criminal justice system in North Carolina ranked among the strongest in the country. Wrongful conviction was a national problem, however, and he felt it ought to concern everyone, Republican or Democrat, prosecution or defense, pro- or anti–death penalty, police or academics. Every one of those ought to be pursuing the same aim, Lake believed: to decrease the number of wrongful convictions, *without* decreasing, or, better, even *increasing,* the number of *rightful* convictions. The issue concerned him personally, since he oversaw the state's courts, and he didn't see how a democracy could function without courts its citizens trusted. Counterintuitively, an exoneration usually led to a pair of conflicting consequences, he pointed out. On the one hand, it brought justice to the exoneree. On the other hand, it exposed the initial error, thereby undermining confidence in the system even as it actually made the system more just. The longer an innocent person's incarceration, the more dramatic the breach in confidence, and the more harmful its backlash. Within their own state Lake had observed this phenomenon a handful of times already: after Ronald Cotton, who'd been exonerated seven years earlier, after spending more than a decade in prison. Again after Lesly Jean, Terence Garner, Charles Munsey. Technically Munsey had never been exonerated, but the verdict against him had been based largely on his confession to a cell mate at Central Prison. Records later proved this supposed cell mate had never been interned at CP at all. Munsey had died awaiting a decision from prosecutors.

More than five hundred more men and women like these had been exonerated over the previous decade, all around the country: thirty or so per year throughout the early 1990s, up to fifty in 1997. And almost ninety just last year, in 2001.

"Look," Lake finished, "I'm a law-and-order person. I think my reputation bears that out. But we need to be sure we're doing this the best we can. And we need to be sure we have the public's trust." He gestured around the table. "You're all here because you're respected representatives of every branch of the law. What we want to find out is whether you all are interested in participating in something like this. An honest evaluation of the issues. Some research and brainstorming of solutions, some discussion of potential changes. No one's asking anyone to commit to any particular action just yet. But we want to know if this is a conversation we can have."

There Lake paused to consider the room. When no one volunteered anything, he nodded toward Rosen. "Now Rich is going to say a few words," he said.

"Thank you, Mr. Chief Justice," Rosen began, and leaned forward. "I think I have about twenty minutes to talk about the problem of convicting innocent people, and what we do about it." He smiled briefly. "No easy task. There are really two major issues in front of us today. The first is whether we believe there is a problem with our justice system convicting innocent people. The second is, if we *do* believe there is a problem, whether there is anything we could, or should, be doing about it.

"I think all of us here, if we were asked this fifteen years ago, we would have said conviction of an innocent person wasn't a serious problem. That's what I would have said. Technically, sure, it might happen — in a big city, maybe, where you had some sort of corruption. But I think all of us felt pretty comfortable with the job we were doing. That comfort level has changed. Not only here, but all over the country. Today we know, from DNA testing, that in some indefinable number of cases, we convict the innocent. So far, nationally, at least one hundred and sixteen of them. That we know of."

Here Rosen rested for a moment, to watch his colleagues. "This is a nationwide phenomenon," he repeated, "but North Carolina isn't exempt. The most famous case here, probably, has been Ronald Cotton, which, I think you all know, touched a number of us here directly." He gestured to three other men around the table: "Rob Johnson was then an assistant DA in Alamance County. Mike Gauldin was the investigating detective. Tye Hunter represented Ronald in one of his earlier appeals."

Several lessons had stayed with him from that case, Rosen continued. One was that an innocent person could be convicted even when no official did anything wrong. Gauldin and Johnson were both professionals, good at their jobs, and had acted honestly. So had Jennifer Thompson, the victim, who'd felt convinced that Cotton was the man who'd raped her. Sure, Cotton himself had always claimed he was innocent — but so what? Many defendants claimed the same thing.

"Honestly, I've gotten a lot of pats on the back for my work on that case," Rosen admitted. "But the real credit goes to Mike and Rob.

Those two guys are what was unique about that case. We all know nobody likes to see an old case reopened, especially prosecutors or police. But Mike was completely willing to work with us." And Rosen had never forgotten how Rob had answered, when he'd asked him to cooperate on DNA testing. "The state has no interest in keeping an innocent man in prison." In retrospect, that was what struck Rosen most about that case, that everyone had stepped outside their usual roles. "That's why Ronald is free right now. We tested DNA in conjunction with Rob, and Mike spent an afternoon with us at the Burlington station, going through old evidence, until we found the one envelope with test tubes." When the results came back, neither man had thought once to argue. Instead, they'd driven straight to the prison, for the culprit DNA had implicated, who'd then confessed.

"If it weren't for all that—if Mike hadn't kept the rape kit evidence, if we hadn't had DNA testing—Ronald would still be in prison right now, and he'd be there for the rest of his life. And we have to admit we don't know how many more Ronald Cottons are out there, sitting in North Carolina prisons, in cases without evidence, or where the evidence was lost. Ronald isn't even the only case we know about."

Which brought Rosen to the second issue facing them today: whether the people in this room could, or should, do something about it. He motioned toward Newman and Coleman. "Several years ago, partly because of Cotton, partly in connection with a national trend, Duke and UNC joined to form an innocence project, where law and journalism students investigate innocence claims by inmates." That work was coordinated by the Center on Actual Innocence, he explained, a nonprofit whose legal counsel was Chris Mumma—the woman in whose house they were sitting. "It is a slow, frustrating, laborious process. Those students sort through hundreds of letters, and everyone involved is doing this on a volunteer basis. We are not interested in technicalities. We don't even look at procedural claims. We are looking for cases with a claim of actual innocence. That's all." Some of those cases the center lawyers assumed they would carry through themselves, while others they hoped would be brought to court by fellow attorneys, or else be directed to the governor for clemency consideration.

"I'll be honest, though. This is not a problem to be handled by law students or a few volunteers. If we are truly looking to meet this, every part of the criminal justice system will need to be involved. I really mean all parts. The innocent are being convicted, and that isn't a problem only for the defense bar. It's a problem for everyone with a stake in the system. As the public comes to believe we convict innocent people, as recent polls show they are, the entire system is going to suffer. And for every innocent person convicted, some guilty person is still at large."

He wasn't asking anyone to abandon what he or she did in the courtroom, or on the streets, Rosen clarified. "We need police officers to find criminals, and solve crimes; we need prosecutors to bring charges; we need judges to instruct juries, and review cases. But we think it's time to consider whether, collectively, we can do something about these wrongful convictions, and about correcting them, when they occur. Not *if*. We *know* they do occur."

Certainly it was time for him to stop talking now, Rosen finished, smiling again. He thanked Lake for organizing the afternoon, and everyone else for attending. "I hope you'll join in this discussion and that the discussion will be ongoing. I'm not here to suggest any particular solution. We're only asking to look at the problem, and to consider whether we can make things better."

As he spoke, Rosen had been watching for clues from around the table, any body language, especially from prosecutors or police, that might hint at what they were thinking. He'd made this argument before, but never to an audience whose politics were so varied, or whose every member had a career in the law. Everyone in the room had arrived with lessons from his own experience and, thus, with his own bias, Rosen knew—his own idea of how the law worked, or ought to. He could sense the danger in alienating them. He'd meant what he said about breaking down conventional roles, was willing to do this himself. One idea he'd had was for completely open discovery—an agreement by defense and prosecutors to share all evidence that either side uncovered in preparation for trial. The potential benefits of this were obvious. So were its pitfalls. That was the catch. For a defense attorney, who was interested in competitive advantage, open discovery posed a risk, Rosen knew. For more accurate outcomes, however, it posed none. For that reason he thought he could be open to it. Rosen didn't know if the other side could be persuaded to think like this. He waited for some clue.

Then Don Stephens spoke up. One of the few Republicans in the room, Stephens had been a conservative superior court judge for more than two decades. Before that he'd headed what Rosen called the death squad, the division of the attorney general's office that handled capital cases. In that role he and Rosen had clashed on opposite sides of Rosen's first death-penalty case. "If we're going to do this, we'll need something that isn't adversarial," Stephens said.

Rosen perked up.

"Look, I'm a judge," Stephens continued. "We see motions all the time—many, many, many of them." This deluge of postconviction appeals was a problem for everyone, he added. A convicted felon, with nothing to lose, might file every motion he could get his hands on, and many of them did. The result was an ocean of claims, many of them without merit, impossible to differentiate from shore. The sheer labor of evaluating these fell to judges and DAs especially. "I can't possibly read them all closely enough to determine which have merit, and which don't." Stephens swiveled toward Rosen. "If what we're saying is that some of these are serious, then the fact is, I need help. We'll need some nonadversarial context to hear these things. If there's a serious claim, we can't be invoking procedures and doctrine to keep from determining what the truth is."

From across the room, Rosen looked to Tye Hunter, the friend who'd handled one of Ronald Cotton's appeals and who now directed the state office of indigent defense. Hunter's eyes had widened. Then Rosen looked to Coleman, who was staring back at him, astonished. *The nonpartisan, supralegal truth.* Rosen himself was stunned.

Stephens had spoken nearly the same words Rosen had to his center colleagues, back at the Weathervane.

Theresa Newman felt her expectations rise suddenly. She'd never heard a judge speak the way Stephens just had. She knew that judges and prosecutors both were vulnerable in a way she wasn't personally, since professors like her didn't need to be elected. Anyone whose livelihood depended on votes was vulnerable to misinterpretation, and partisan blitzes, she understood. She'd never considered that those on the other side of the issues might feel the system wasn't working for them, either. Now, behind closed doors, those people spoke up. Lake and Stephens had given them permission.

Law enforcement, it turned out, didn't like what DNA testing had done to recast the public's view of its investigative work. On the surface, new technology ought to have buoyed that view, as DNA provided a more reliable form of evidence. Instead, the reverse had happened. Because DNA was available in only a portion of cases, suddenly the remainder had become vulnerable. Once the public knew what DNA testing was, it might mistrust arrests achieved without it. Worse, that mistrust might prove valid—of the exonerees that Rosen had mentioned, several had pleaded guilty, having been counseled that doing so would lighten their sentence. Even after a confession, or testimony by an eyewitness, now a person could still be innocent. Evidence that yesterday had stood as solid as granite today was disintegrating into fog.

Prosecutors had felt this shift as acutely as law enforcement, partly because they relied on the same evidence at trial, and partly because their job was also to find jurors who felt willing to convict. The more kinds of evidence that DNA testing undermined, the more skittish those jurors might grow. It was possible that DNA testing might accomplish the reverse of what one would expect—not increase convictions, but reduce them.

In addition to all that, sometimes things happened at trial that were manifestly unjust. As Rosen had said, this could happen even if no one did anything wrong. The resources allotted to each side might simply be uneven. Or a lawyer might know something he was prevented from sharing, since professionally he was obligated to win cases. Or a lawyer might simply be unqualified—even his opponent might recognize this, and regret it.

Another problem was existential, Lake pointed out. Most exonerations over the previous decade had come not from any court's initiative but from media pressure. Munsey and Garner, for example, had been cleared only after investigative reporting by local newspapers. Only after prodding had the courts self-corrected. They ought to have done this sooner, before the press forced them, Lake knew. It was bad enough for the public to distrust its legal system. It was worse to think that it ought to.

The agreement Chris was hearing amazed her. She'd expected that the invitees would need persuading that the postconviction process didn't work. Now she realized they *knew* it didn't work, that the fact of it not working had for many of them become a part of their daily lives. Soon everyone was speaking at once, and she was forced to type rapidly to record minutes. By early afternoon she had recorded a list of every topic that anyone in the room had suggested for study.

Lower barriers to DNA testing / backlog
False accusations / false confessions
Defense attorney competency
Modify eyewitness identification process
Ban snitch testimony—at minimum, require corroborating
    evidence
Eliminate or suspend "junk science"—microscopic hair
    comparison, handwriting analysis, fiber techniques
Avoid tunnel vision; continuous investigation of suspects
Postconviction, nonadversarial process for innocence review

When conversation lulled after nearly three hours, Lake announced a proposal. He had in mind a special commission, including everyone in the room, that would meet every month or two to continue the discussion they'd begun today. Would others join him?

All fifteen around the table agreed. They liked this idea, they remarked. An unusual forum for an unusually important issue, and one that was more complicated than most people imagined — distinguishing the guilty from the actually innocent. That was what they should name it, someone suggested. The Actual Innocence Commission.

They agreed to meet again in February.

11

One of Those Cases

When he learned the court of appeals had denied him, he petitioned the state supreme court a third time, hoping it would reconsider now that his options were narrowing. Then he wrote again to Phillip Griffin, at Prisoner Legal Services, to share the outcome of his appeal: "Of course I expected this but I still know that my trial was not a fair one." Could Griffin get him another?

But the reply he received three weeks later only confused him. "Our office is not able to handle direct appeals from convictions," Griffin's letter read. "Thus I cannot take over your case from Mr. de Torres. Please communicate directly with your appellate attorney." Whatever logic this was, Willie couldn't follow it, since Griffin had already expressed interest in his case, had asked specifically that Willie let him know the outcome of his appeal. De Torres had been his appeal attorney as well as his trial attorney, and de Torres could no longer help, so Willie couldn't see what other lawyer Griffin was referring to. Who else would help him, if Griffin wouldn't? He wrote again: "I would again like to respectfully request that you please consider accepting my case," he repeated, and enclosed a copy of de Torres's final correspondence. "As you see...he does in fact feel that I am not guilty of the offense of which I was charged, but for reasons I also don't understand he's unable to push my case to another level in the judicial system."

When he received this second letter, Griffin wrote in turn to de

Torres, asking for Willie's trial transcript and the briefs from his appeal. "I am not sure whether we will be able to help him, but I will be happy to review the record." De Torres replied within the week, with copies of every transcript and appellate brief and opinion he had. "I hope that there is something that can be done, as I strongly feel that this is one of those cases where justice was cheated and an innocent man wrongly convicted," he confided. "In case that you can offer no assistance to Mr. Grimes, I would appreciate forwarding the materials to Mr. Grimes should he have need of them in the future with another source. If I can assist in any way please contact me."

But neither of them mentioned this to Willie, who didn't realize Griffin and de Torres had spoken at all, and so still didn't know whether either lawyer could help him. Instead he felt bewildered and angry and sleepless. Several times a month he was incapacitated by migraines. He couldn't shake a cold, which might have been the flu. Until now nurses had continually tossed him over-the-counter cold medications, but that winter they stopped. "Note—inmate has been taking entirely too much cold meds," read an entry in his medical chart. "Advised to stop all meds. Throat lozenges only." Since medication hadn't seemed to help, anyway, they suggested he try drinking more liquids. Soon he was so miserable he filled out a form for psychological services, to ask for an appointment. Under "Why do you want to see a psychologist (be specific)?" he wrote that he was depressed, nauseous, tense, upset, and couldn't sleep. Then he filled out a page-long questionnaire.

Information Questions:	Yes	No
1. Have you ever heard voices talking in your head when no one was around?	✓	—
2. Is your imagination very active?	✓	—
3. Do you dream while you are awake?	✓	—
4. Do you have difficulty concentrating?	✓	—

5. Are you confused at times? ✓ ___

6. Do you experience racing thoughts? ✓ ___

7. Does anyone talk about you? ✓ ___

8. Do you feel that others are out to get you? ✓ ___

9. Are you being watched? ✓ ___

10. Are you anxious or tense? ✓ ___

11. Do you have crying spells? ✓ ___

12. Do you feel excited or high without reason? ✓ ___

13. Have you ever attempted to harm yourself? ___ ✓

14. Do you have any special powers? ✓ ___

15. Subtract 7 from 100 _92_. Subtract 7 from 93 _88_.

16. a. How are an apple and an orange alike? _Both are round_.

    b. How are a radio and newspaper alike? _News._

17. What is today's date? Month _1_ Day _28_ Year _90_.

18. When were you born? _44_.

19. Who is the President? _Ragaun_.

20. Who is the Vice-President? _Bush._

21. Can you name the Governor of N.C.? _No_.

22. Where is the capital of N.C.? _Charlotte_.

23. How many miles is it from here to California? _2000_.

24. If you were walking down the street and saw an addressed and stamped envelope on the sidewalk which had fallen out of someone's pocket, what would you do? _Open it see if any money is in it, and then through it away_.

25. If you were in the back of a movie theatre, saw a fire break out, and were the only one to see it, what would you do? _Get out_.

26. How would you describe your:

	BELOW AVERAGE	AVERAGE	ABOVE AVERAGE
Appetite	✓	——	——
Sleep	✓	——	——
Energy Level	✓	——	——
Sex Drive	——	——	✓

Willie Grimes

Inmate's Signature

Soon after, he met with a staff psychologist named Buck Thomas. "Mr. Grimes maintains he is innocent of his charge," Thomas recorded in his notes. "His incarceration despite his innocence has resulted in considerable distress." Still, he saw no evidence Willie was a risk either to himself or others, and concluded Willie was simply "adjusting to his lengthy prison sentence." He diagnosed an "adjustment disorder with mixed emotional features" and offered ongoing counseling, which Willie declined. Then he referred Willie to a consulting staff psychiatrist, who found Willie "polite and friendly," with "no signs of overt psychosis," though he agreed Willie did "appear to be somewhat depressed." He prescribed an antidepressant called Sinequan, for Willie to take before bed.

Before long, Willie found the Sinequan helping—it lowered a sort of dampener over him, so peaks of his anguish no longer broke the surface. Where previously live flames had engulfed him, now he only simmered. But still he couldn't sleep past one or two in the morning, so the psychiatrist increased his dosage. His cold worsened, though, and he went on sleeping fitfully. Finally nurses relented and prescribed more cough syrup. This didn't help, either. Since he'd been ill for longer than two months, nurses tested him for anything serious: bronchitis, tuberculosis, pneumonitis. All negative. Then nurses x-rayed his chest, for signs the blood test might have missed. This was negative, too.

* * *

Mozella as a child had suffered from rheumatic fever, and had never fully recovered from the damage this had done to her heart. Eventually she'd also developed chronic bronchitis. Bearing nine children had not helped either condition. She'd come to Lawndale from Jasper County, Georgia, and, once her first husband left, had taken on work as a maid in white folks' homes, in addition to the sharecropping, while concealing her poverty from her children as best she could; when one of them needed shoes, it wasn't that Mozella didn't have the money, only that she didn't have it *right now,* the implication being it was merely a difficult week. For her girls she could afford only two slips each, to wear under dresses, and for her boys only a few changes of clothes, which was why Willie's rooting in the clay was such an amusement to his brothers. At the end of a long day in the fields she found a chicken or potatoes and stretched it for supper; then she cleaned and folded and dusted, not only in her own tiny cottage but for white families down the way. This meant she often was gone, so it was mainly Gladys who raised Willie, though she was only five years older than him. A bright student, Gladys realized early that her own future wasn't in cotton, couldn't stand the labor or see how a sharecropping family would ever get ahead. A half sister, Roberta, from Mozella's first marriage, lived up in Pittsburgh, where the schools were said to be better. Mozella made arrangements for Gladys to go there.

Willie was nine years old by then, and every so often he sent Gladys trinkets in the mail, scrawling notes and stuffing tiny gifts into the envelope — a plastic ring, a dollar wallet he'd made himself. On a visit home she noticed for the first time the separate drinking fountains for white and black folks, which she'd never registered as a child. When she mentioned this to her mother, Mozella nodded sadly. "I never said it, because I didn't want you to grow up with it. But there's a separation between blacks and whites." Suddenly Gladys recalled a mystery that had tugged at her as a child: whenever Mozella fell ill and phoned a doctor, he had always taken so long to come. Gladys had never understood it; no matter how early Mozella called, she always seemed to be last in line. Now at once Gladys saw why. His other patients had been white; the doctor had gone to them first. Mozella simply had never mentioned it, so Gladys had never asked.

When Gladys finished high school she enrolled at Hunter College, in New York, the first—and, it would turn out, the only—member of her immediate family to attend a university. To cover tuition she found work at a cleaner's, making thirty-five dollars a week, and when this proved too little she took a job at a bank. After graduating she joined the U.S. Public Health Service, as a nurse; for the next several years she was stationed throughout New England, "a fly in buttermilk," she joked to friends. Then she was transferred to Brooke Army Medical Center, in San Antonio. She was still living there in 1987 when her niece Shirley called, to tell her Woot was in trouble.

When Willie was through at Douglas High he landed a factory job up in Hickory, molding steel and rubber, and for extra income he added a second job at a textile factory. Then he was drafted into the army, stationed mostly at Fort Bragg, over in Fayetteville. After two years of bouncing around stateside he was slated for Vietnam. Then his brother Bobby Lewis was killed.

The circumstances of this weren't clear. Bobby Lewis had volunteered for the air force after graduating from high school in '66, two years behind Willie. He'd been on a base in Thailand, on R and R, so Willie knew he hadn't been killed in action, but the military provided no specifics. *Drowning*, their paperwork read. Willie traveled home for the funeral carrying in his pocket the orders commanding him to Vietnam. But in Lawndale he learned Mozella had listed him on some form as her only unmarried son, now that Bobby Lewis was gone, which by army formula put Willie in line to care for her. As long as he stayed in the reserves, they agreed to discharge him, rather than send him overseas.

So he went back to work at the textile factory, and at the manufacturing plant, operating a hydraulic press that punched holes into bed rails. For a second too long during one afternoon shift he was distracted; in that second his hand strayed, there was a disorienting shock of pain, and when he looked again the knuckle had vanished from his middle finger, along with the tip from his pointer.

After two years in Hickory he left for Pittsburgh, where he'd heard steelworkers had unionized and there were opportunities. His half sister Roberta still lived there, and he slept on her couch. A union job required certain paperwork: his birth certificate, his high-school diploma, his DD214 from the army proving he'd been honorably discharged. The second and third of these were no problem. But on his birth certificate he saw his own name was wrong: he was listed as Willie James Vinson. His diploma and DD214 both named Willie James Grimes. The unions couldn't accept conflicting forms. They denied Willie a job.

When his father died, it turned out, still a month before Willie was born, Mozella had been worse off than Willie was ever told. She had barely recovered from the death of Cliff Grimes Sr., who had fallen from the roof. The loss of Willie's father—her third husband, Edgar Brooks—by another random tragedy proved nearly too much for her to bear. She'd expected her grief might literally be the end of her, and if that happened, Willie would be orphaned; both his parents would be gone, and no one would share his last name. Really that name ought to have been Brooks, after his father, but Edgar had died in that car wreck, and Mozella couldn't make him a Grimes, either, because Cliff had died, too. So on his birth certificate she chose the name of her first husband, Samuel Vinson. Samuel had divorced her more than a decade earlier. She had no illusions that, if she did die, he would suddenly appear to care for infant Willie. But the first five of her children, Willie's half siblings, all shared the name Vinson, and four of them were older and married; if Mozella was gone, a sibling could pass Willie off as his or her own child. He would avoid being an orphan.

But Mozella had survived, and no one had ever told Willie about his birth certificate. He had passed through school and jobs and the army all with a misconception of his own last name. He'd known he wasn't a Brooks, since he'd never known his father, but he'd assumed he was a Grimes, the same as Gladys and Cliff Jr. He'd been a Vinson the whole time.

* * *

When the unions turned him away, after six months in Pittsburgh, he returned to another textile plant in Hickory, loading barrels of cotton onto the sharp pin of a drawing machine, which spun the cotton into yarn. One shift he bent to retrieve a roll of thread and lost track of where he was; the machine's pin stuck him in the chest. The scar it left would last his lifetime. He added another job, moving furniture, then walked to the nearest Social Security office and changed his last name to Grimes.

Mozella by now was traveling seasonally between Lawndale and New York, a schedule she'd begun as soon as Willie finished high school. Half the year she lived up north with Gladys, then left before winter, as her bronchitis worsened in the cold. Back in Lawndale, she normally rotated a week or two with each son, but now she asked Willie if he would mind her staying with him permanently. He didn't. But the extended arrangement let him notice how badly her health had declined, and because he worked two jobs he worried he was gone too often, meaning Mozella spent most days alone. As long as she'd been healthy and self-sufficient, she had liked this privacy, but now he saw she was neither. Willie was dating a woman named Towana, and it occurred to him that, if they married, Towana could move in and help care for his mother. He proposed, and they married.

A year later Mozella died.

After that, a curious thing happened: Willie fell in love with his wife. He'd always cared for Towana, but he'd also been so preoccupied with his mother that he'd never regarded Towana without her. He saw now that he had married for the wrong reason—but, fortunately, had married the right person. The problem was his two jobs. Now that Mozella was gone, Towana had long days and evenings home by herself, and she began to date other men. Willie was crestfallen. But he also remembered that Towana had sacrificed for him when his mother had been ill. He told her, reluctantly, that she could leave if she wanted; he would give her the money she needed. It *was* what she wanted, Towana told him, and took off for DC.

Within weeks he regretted letting her go. He quit the textile mill and furniture shop and followed her to DC, where the two reconciled. For nearly three months he kept afloat on temporary jobs. Then a week came when he could find no work. For the short term he drove back down to Lawndale, where promptly his car was stolen. Then he got a phone call from DC, where another job had opened up. Without his car, though, Willie couldn't make it north again, and he couldn't afford to buy a replacement. It was the end of his relationship with Towana.

Instead he headed back up to Hickory, where the work was.

At Harnett Correctional a letter arrived for him from Brenda, his girlfriend in Hickory, saying that she was moving to a new apartment, would forward her new address and phone number to him in prison as soon as she arrived. But weeks passed and he didn't hear anything. He'd hoped they could write more frequently again. If she forgot to forward her new address, he knew, he would have a hard time locating her from inside the Harnett walls. Just as likely, Brenda had already sent her letter, but the postal service had lost it or, more maddeningly, Harnett had refused or neglected to deliver it: he knew guards intercepted inmates' mail, to screen for drugs or pornography, and sometimes a letter disappeared this way even if it contained neither.

To distract himself from worrying, he asked again to be assigned to a laundry job. Again the psychiatrist increased his antidepressant, Sinequan. Then his cold medication ran out. The next day he checked himself into the nurses' station. "Stated he felt like he needed to be by himself for a while," a nurse entered in his chart. "Feels like everyone is messing with him and can't sleep. Inmate remains in OR and will be referred to psychologist." The psychologist referred him back to the psychiatrist, who suspected Willie's cold medications, along with the Sinequan, had combined to disrupt his system, and guessed Willie would do better in a different housing arrangement. He recommended Willie be allowed to stay a few nights in a quieter annex, rather than in the open dorms, "so that he might get some rest away from the stress of the general population." Again he increased Willie's dose of Sinequan.

* * *

Two months had passed since Phillip Griffin's promise to read Willie's case and report back, but Willie hadn't heard anything, so in spring he wrote again: Had Griffin ever received his files from de Torres? "I understand you have many cases that your firm is presently investigating, however I do ask that you please understand my position." Would Griffin please let him know whether he'd received anything? "I pray there will be meritable issues found that can provide relief in my case."

Griffin confirmed he had received Willie's file, though he hadn't had time to read it. He pledged to be in touch once he had.

Another two months passed, however, making a year and a half since his failed appeal, and still Willie didn't hear anything. He met another inmate who doubled as a jailhouse lawyer and agreed to write to Phillip Griffin on Willie's behalf. "Inmate Grimes has ask me to find out what I can and see if there is anything that I can do to help in the process," he offered. So he had read Willie's file three times. "Each time that I do so I become more amazed. I will not sit at this typewriter and tell you how much of a miscarriage of justice I see when I read these papers, nor will I say that this man is innocent. But I will say that he has not had a fair much less impartial trial. As an inmate I see this on a daily basis, but not quit in this manner." He himself wasn't an attorney, the inmate admitted, but he had earned a master's degree from Chapel Hill, "and I am far from stupid. This guy does not belong here." He wanted to file an appeal on Willie's behalf to the state supreme court, but felt uncertain which of the legal problems he'd discovered in Willie's paperwork was weightiest, and didn't want Griffin to think he was so presumptuous that he would tell a professional lawyer how to do his job. "All he wants me to do is help if there is some way that I can. I told Willie that I would do what I could."

None of which struck Griffin as a good idea. Allowing a fellow inmate to file anything could be "very detrimental," Griffin replied, harming Willie's chances at both of the two appellate procedures available to him—the motion for appropriate relief, for which he could apply to the state, and habeas corpus, for which he could apply federally. "If a petition does not raise an issue, it can be foreclosed from future litigation," Griffin warned. "Therefore an inexpertly drawn petition can ruin a good issue." Griffin himself intended to visit Newton, the town where Willie had been tried, and meet with Ed de Torres. Once he had done this he would let Willie know what he determined to be the wisest course of action. "In the meantime, please do not allow any non-attorney to file any papers on your behalf. I appreciate your patience while I investigate your case."

But Willie *wasn't* patient. When precisely would Griffin be visiting Newton, and what did he expect to find there that wasn't already included in Willie's file? Four months had passed since Griffin had received his documentation, and Willie couldn't see what Griffin had accomplished. From inside prison, he had watched other inmates' appeals proceed to the state supreme court; he couldn't understand why his own hadn't. "I want you to know that I'm not trying to be hard, I'm only trying to do the right thing and I feel enough time has elasped now and something should already been done," he insisted. "Though I've been very patient and enduring, Im looking foward to hearing from you within three weeks from todays date."

While he waited, he met again with the psychiatrist and asked for more Sinequan. Again his dosage was increased. His three-week deadline for Griffin passed in silence. After two more months, when he still hadn't heard anything, he wrote to the court of appeals, the attorney general, and again to Ed de Torres, all to beg for help. The next day he wrote again to Phillip Griffin, and to a man named Marvin Sparrow, whose name he had found on Prisoner Legal Services letterhead, above *Executive Director*. He assumed this meant Sparrow was Griffin's boss.

Dear Gentlemen,

This letter is to be read and answered by the both of you. I am very destrissed by the fact that since Mr. Griffin has taken over my case I have not been able to make any headway in getting out. I feel that it is past the time when some answers should be given. I am not a guilty man and there has to be something that you can do to prove this to the courts.

Mr. Sparrow, I know that your office has been over worked and that most cases are back logged for months at the time. But after speaking with numerous inmates about the progress that your office has been able to make with their cases, I feel that I may very well be spending the rest of my natural life in prison. As harsh as that my sound, it is what I see from my end of things. Mr. Griffin has had plenty of time to prepare a defense on my behalf. He has had plenty of time to notify me of the progress that he has made.

I would like for you gentlemen to understand the position that I am in. I am serving life plus nine years for something that I did not do. Just because your office has control of my case does not mean that it makes everything right. I want some action and some answers. It took the state of North Carolina much less time to put me into prison than it is takeing your office to process an appeal.

I would like to know what progress has been made. I have asked this same question before and have received little to no answers. So, now I am asking the director of North Carolina Prisoner's Legal Services. If you are having problems, notify me and maybe I can help or maybe I can be more patient at the least.

> Respectfully,
> Willie James Grimes

Again he waited.

12

*N*obody Could Be Against *This*

When it reconvened at Chris's house after the New Year, the Actual Innocence Commission had grown by seven members, including the director of the North Carolina Victim Assistance Network, the secretary of the Department of Crime Control and Public Safety, and attorneys or staff members from the governor's office, the Wake County sheriff's department, and the State Bureau of Investigation—each of whom promptly sat with fellow prosecutors or police officers. No one sat near the defense attorneys.

Like a middle-school dance, Lake thought. "Fellas, this won't work. We've got to mix this up." He watched patiently as everyone rearranged chairs.

Since their last meeting, each commissioner knew, the risks of their endeavor had grown politically—not due to events in North Carolina, as they might have predicted, but rather thanks to news up in Illinois. Since the death penalty had been reinstated there, twenty-five years earlier, in 1977, twelve inmates in Illinois had been executed. During the same period, thirteen *other* inmates, awaiting the same end, on the same death row, had been exonerated by new evidence. Finally this worsening ratio unnerved even the governor, a Republican who not only favored the death penalty but had been among those legislators who'd voted to reinstate it. His position hadn't changed: he still supported the death penalty. But for the guilty. Not the innocent. He'd begun to doubt that courtrooms in his state were distinguishing one from the other. So on a chilly, blustery day up in Chicago, around the same time Chris Mumma was hauling boxes into her new basement office at Duke, he'd appointed a study group to examine what was happening. "I have grave concerns about our state's shameful record of convicting innocent people," he announced in a press release. Until he could be certain that everyone sentenced to lethal injection in Illinois was truly guilty, he was halting the practice entirely.

What followed was dysfunction on a scale that every commissioner sitting in Chris's living room hoped to avoid. It had taken two long years for that Illinois study group to issue its report, a nearly three-hundred-page catalog of policy recommendations whose upshot was a single sentence from its introduction: "Achieving a higher degree of confidence in outcomes will require a significant increase in public funding at virtually every level." Ten months later, though, the state legislature had neglected to adopt even one reform. So, forty-eight hours before the end of his term—barely a month ago, in mid-January 2003—the governor had commuted the sentence of every death row inmate in Illinois, all 171 of them, replacing their execution dates with life terms in prison.

And the news had gone national. The *New York Times* named it the largest emptying of death row in U.S. history; the governor himself acknowledged it was likely to "draw ridicule, scorn and anger." At home, he admitted, even his wife was disappointed in him. But what choice did he have? He had witnessed in Illinois a "spectacular failure to reform the system," he bemoaned. "The Legislature couldn't reform it, lawmakers won't repeal it, and I won't stand for it. Our study has found only more questions."

Quickly, he was proven correct—about the ridicule and anger, at least. His successor to the governorship called the mass commutation "a big mistake." A local firefighter, whose brother's murderer was among those inmates removed from death row, hoped publicly the outgoing governor would be charged with corruption and imprisoned. "How can one person have all this authority and power?" he demanded of reporters. "It's making a mockery and a farce out of our legal system."

* * *

Today at Chris's house, before commissioners could begin on any of the concerns they'd assembled the previous November, Don Stephens, the superior court judge who'd spoken up at that meeting, believed they should settle on a mission statement. They ought to proceed cautiously, Stephens said, since it would be difficult to find language that everyone agreed on. But he didn't like the prospect of moving forward without one. From a folder, Chris withdrew five neat pages she'd drafted on her own, including a list of procedural rules and a statement of purpose. " 'The primary objective of the North Carolina Actual Innocence Commission is to make recommendations which reduce or eliminate the possibility of the wrongful conviction of an innocent person,' " she read aloud.

Neither Stephens nor anyone else could think of any objection to this. "I can't believe you were able to do that," he admitted ruefully to Chris, who smiled at him politely. *See?* she thought. *Not a restless trophy wife.*

Across the room, Rosen grinned.

The problem to address first, commissioners agreed, was eyewitness identification, a matter that appealed to them for several reasons. First, it was preventive, not retrospective—targeted future verdicts, in other words, not past ones, so it posed no risk to closed cases, a prospect that made some commissioners squeamish. And eyewitness ID was so obviously a problem that everyone in the room could imagine agreeing on it. This meant Chris and Lake could use the issue as something of a trial balloon for the commission's influence. Four hundred and seventy-five different law enforcement agencies operated in North Carolina, each of whose criminal procedures depended further on district attorneys, trial judges, and the state legislature. None of those bodies was certain to follow suggestions by a volunteer commission, Chris and Lake knew. They might as well use eyewitness ID to find out.

To show commissioners the scope of the problem, Chris invited Jennifer Thompson, who lived in Chapel Hill. Thompson was a blond, vibrant, sharp-featured woman, as pert and compact as a gymnast, with the charisma of someone who'd been popular in high school. Her expertise with eyewitness identification was personal: Thompson was the victim who'd wrongly identified Ronald Cotton as her rapist eighteen years earlier.

In late March, at the state bar association headquarters in Cary, a colonnaded brick and concrete building where the growing commission had migrated from Chris's house, Thompson shared what it had felt like. That July night in 1984, up in Elon, barely an hour northwest from where they sat today, she'd awoken in her apartment at three a.m. to a gloved hand clamped over her mouth, an unfamiliar man in her bedroom. He could have her car, her credit card, everything in her wallet, Thompson had begged him; if only he didn't hurt her, she promised not to call the police. "I don't want your money," the man said, and at once Thompson realized what would happen. Telling this part to commissioners now, her eyes welled.

Think, she had told herself that night, lying still in her bed. *Think, Jennifer. How will you get through this?* She remembered having read that a person who remained calm had the best chance of surviving an assault. If she did survive, she would need to remember details for the police. How tall was her rapist, and how old? "I tried to memorize the things about his face I thought would be important," she recalled for commissioners, literally during the assault. Did he speak with an accent? Was he missing any teeth? *If I survive this and make it to the police,* she thought, *I will give them what they need to get you.* Finally she escaped to the kitchen, on the excuse that she was thirsty. Then she bolted through her back door, toward a neighbor, who phoned the police. Soon men in uniform were asking whether she'd gotten a good look at her rapist. Yes, she had, Jennifer told them: about six feet tall, twenty-one or twenty-two, maybe twenty-four at the oldest. An African American man with a light complexion. Short-cropped hair and a pencil-thin mustache. He had worn dark pants, canvas shoes, and a navy shirt with white stripes on the sleeves.

Jennifer's memory had impressed the police, and over the following days they assembled a lineup. "It was my job to find him," she remembered, "and I found him. He was number five. Ronald Cotton.

I *knew* it." She had felt proud to be so reliable a witness. She hated Cotton, and would make sure he was convicted. "I thought about it every moment," she told commissioners. "I wanted him caught, I wanted him tried, I wanted him convicted, and had the state of North Carolina had the death penalty for rape, I would have wanted him dead."

Cotton was sentenced to life plus fifty-four years.

Three years later, in 1987, an appellate court granted Cotton a retrial based on two facts his original jury had never been told. That same night as Jennifer, another woman had also been raped, likely by the same attacker. The second woman didn't recognize Cotton. Together these facts might have influenced a jury's thinking; if the other woman wasn't sure about Cotton, how could Jennifer be? Jennifer herself resented this implication. During her assault, Cotton's face had hovered four inches from her own, so close she'd seen her own reflection in his pupils. Where else would she have been looking, if not at him? She knew what she had seen. Again Cotton was tried, again Jennifer testified. This time Cotton's lawyers argued that, during the three years he'd been incarcerated, another inmate had boasted that Cotton was serving time for a crime he himself had committed. Lawyers dragged this man to trial so Jennifer could look at him. His name was Bobby Poole. Jennifer had never seen him before in her life. "Are you sure?" a judge asked.

"I'm positive," Jennifer told him.

Again Cotton was convicted.

Over the following years, Jennifer married, and mothered triplets. In March 1995, more than a decade after her rape, Mike Gauldin — the lead detective on her case, who'd since been promoted to captain, and now sat in the conference room as a commissioner, listening to Jennifer speak — came to visit, along with an assistant district attorney. There was something new called DNA, the pair told her, and Cotton had asked that his be tested. The man had never stopped protesting his innocence. Gauldin and the DA and Jennifer all knew he was lying, and Gauldin didn't think Jennifer should have to submit to any test she didn't want to. But the blood sample that police had kept on file had deteriorated since 1984, and Gauldin wanted her to know that a court might order her to provide more.

Jennifer rolled up her sleeve and offered her arm. "Let's do it," she said. She saw no reason to wait for a court order. She had never doubted who'd raped her. Cotton's face still appeared in her nightmares. If DNA would prove finally that he was the monster she knew he was, she would call her doctor right then, drive to his office to give a blood sample. "But after this, don't ever talk to me about Ronald Cotton again," she warned Gauldin. "It's been eleven years. I'm the mother of three five-year-old children. Okay? I'm raising children now."

Three months later Gauldin called again, wanting to know if he could come see her. "We were wrong," he told Jennifer, standing sadly in her kitchen. "It wasn't Ronald Cotton who raped you. It was Bobby Poole." Already Gauldin had tracked down Poole in prison, to confront him with the DNA results. There Poole had confessed.

"Everyone likes to ask me, 'Well, dang, Jennifer, how did that make you feel?'" she told commissioners now, in the bar center. "'What did you do? What did you say? Did you scream? Did you faint?'" She shook her head. "No. I just thanked him for the information. And wished him a good day. Because: What. Do. You. Do? With that kind of information?" She felt like a figurine inside a snow globe that someone had lifted and throttled. There in the conference room she raised her arms and quaked them, to show what she meant. "You believe something *so strongly*. So strongly that you put your hand on the Bible, and you testify. You swear to tell the whole truth and nothing but the truth." She shook her head again. "I *told* the truth. And it was *wrong*."

The discovery of her error felt entirely different than the aftermath of her rape. *That* she had never experienced shame or guilt over, had understood was not her own fault. But this? Unwittingly she'd robbed some stranger of ten years of his life. Those years were *gone*. She pinched her fingertips before her face, then opened them suddenly, spreading her hands as wide as her shoulders. "Just *gone*," she repeated. "I can't give them back." And who was this man, this Ronald Cotton, if not a rapist? Certainly he hated her now, wanted revenge. He was out of prison. He was going to come for her or, worse, for her children. For two more years she'd lived in persistent dread, before finally deciding the only way past it was to meet him.

This she had done in February 1997, in her pastor's study. When Cotton pulled up, Jennifer, watching him through the church window, was stunned; this man was taller than she remembered, taller than her rapist. How hadn't she noticed that before? She'd planned to stand to meet him, but now her limbs went leaden and she spilled into tears. "If I spent every second of every minute of every hour of every day for the rest of my life telling you how sorry I am for what happened to you," she pleaded, "it wouldn't come close to how I feel."

But Cotton had knelt to take her hand. Had offered his forgiveness. "I've never been angry at you," he told her. "You don't need to be afraid of me."

From that meeting had bloomed an unexpected friendship. Today, six years later, Jennifer and Ronald traveled the country together, to share what had happened and to speak out for reform. The courts needed to do more about postconviction DNA, she declared. They needed to do more about forensic science in general. And they needed to do more about eyewitness identification. Often, when she gave talks like this, a person would raise his hand and confess not to understand how Jennifer could have made her mistake. Not that she was a bad person, but how could she have made an error like this? For more than twenty minutes she had stared into the face of her rapist, had memorized his nose, his chin, his eyebrows. How could she do that, and then choose Ronald Cotton?

Here's what she told that person, Jennifer said. She gestured with her arm across the conference room. "How many of you have a mother?"

The roomful of lawyers raised their hands.

"How many millions of times have you looked at your mother's face?" Jennifer asked. "Millions, right? Billions. But if you sat down with a police artist, if you sat down with an identity kit, you *cannot* do a composite sketch of her. Because your mom's nose isn't in the kit! Her ears aren't there, her hairline's not there. You'll come up with a *likeness* of your mom, but you won't come up with your mom.

And as soon as you have a likeness, that's your new image. Your memory is contaminated. There's no way to *de*contaminate it." She shook her head. "You can't peel back the wrong layers." All you could do was to prevent wrong layers from collecting in the first place. In fact this was possible, she had learned in the decade since her own error had come to light. And this was what she had come to talk about. "You know, this is 2003. If you went into a hospital and you needed open-heart surgery, and somebody said, 'We do it this new, better way, where you can heal quicker and cleaner, and avoid infections, and your recovery time's shorter, but we think we might want to do it the old way,' would you opt for that? No! You wouldn't. Well, it's the same thing in law. Science tells us here's a new, better way, which reduces the risk for an innocent person. Why wouldn't we do it this way?" While her friend Ronald Cotton was incarcerated, she pointed out, Bobby Poole had raped other women. Convicting the wrong person did nothing to reduce crime.

Aside from Mike Gauldin, who had experienced Jennifer's story firsthand, only a few commissioners had met Jennifer before, including Chris Mumma, who'd invited her today, and Theresa Newman. Newman had always thought Jennifer a dynamo; impassioned, unafraid of eye contact, one of the most arresting speakers she'd ever seen. At events where she knew Jennifer would be presenting, Newman had gotten into the habit of watching the audience, rather than Jennifer, to see people's reactions as they listened. Today at the bar center she saw tilted heads, and tears, and flushed, dumbfounded expressions. One of these belonged to Rich Rosen. Because he'd represented Cotton during his DNA appeal, Rosen had met Jennifer before, but he'd never heard her entire version of the story. *No wonder Cotton was convicted*, he thought now. *Against a witness this persuasive, the poor man didn't stand a chance.*

Even those commissioners whose work often brought them into contact with crime victims, like police officers, had never heard directly from someone in whose case a verdict was reversed. Not one of them envied Mike Gauldin, whose job it had been to tell Jennifer of the mistake. The prospect of doing this themselves filled them with dread. Other commissioners, like Bob Orr, a colleague of Lake's on the state supreme court, rarely met victims at all—not out of personal aversion, but simply because their portion of the law distanced them from the people whose cases they ruled on. Orr had never met someone like Jennifer. *Oh God,* he thought. *So this is who I read about in the newspaper.* It made him uneasy to think a defendant in a case he'd reviewed might one day turn out to be innocent. Might Orr himself have sentenced that man to prison, or even to be executed? He couldn't imagine this was possible, though he knew, theoretically, it was. And if *that* was true, the imperative was obvious, he decided. If anything could be done to prevent another person from repeating either Jennifer's or Cotton's experience, then clearly the commission ought to do it.

Which of course had been Chris's strategy.

To the next commission meeting, in May, Chris summoned Gary Wells, a psychologist and national expert on eyewitness identification. Wells, using a PowerPoint presentation, explained the science of Jennifer's experience—data proved the accuracy of an ID diminished when it was cross-racial, and diminished, too, if a weapon was present. Identifications by the elderly were notoriously unreliable; so were identifications by the very young. More problems emerged from lineups themselves, where a witness typically viewed six or eight suspects simultaneously. In this case a witness usually compared each suspect to the image in her memory, and chose the suspect who seemed nearest, a tactic called relative judgment. A witness in this scenario was answering the wrong question—not whether a particular suspect *was* the criminal, but whether he looked *similar* to him. To avoid this impulse, it was smarter to show one suspect photograph at a time, so a witness could compare him not to the others but discretely to her memory of the criminal.

The person administering the lineup also mattered, Wells explained. The best lineups were double-blind, for the same reason any good clinical study was: an officer with preconceptions could sway the proceeding in all sorts of ways, even unintentionally. When Jennifer had pegged Ronald Cotton, the officer running the lineup had told her, "That's who we thought it was." The effect of this on Jennifer was obvious.

Here was the thing, though, Wells finished. Research showed that all these problems could be solved—with double-blind lineups, shown consecutively rather than simultaneously—*without* decreasing accurate identifications. That was the genius in all this. None of these methods made recognition any less likely, as long as the recognition was genuine. Reform would allow police to reduce mistaken IDs while preserving real ones.

Across the conference room, an unlikely pair had gotten into the habit of sitting next to each other: Rich Rosen, the defense attorney, and Don Stephens, the conservative judge who'd once specialized in prosecuting death-penalty cases. Stephens's early openness to discussion had impressed Rosen, and the two had grown to like each other, even as they'd built careers on opposite sides of the issues. In an earlier commission meeting the pair had joked that, if they ever came to agree on any particular issue, they could be certain something had gone wrong. Now Stephens leaned toward Rosen, and shook his head helplessly. "Well," he said. "Nobody could be against *this*."

After Wells's visit, Chris reached out to the deputy attorney general of New Jersey, the only state in the country where eyewitness-ID reform had already been implemented, and invited her to a commission meeting, too. Then she packaged video recordings of both presentations, along with copies of New Jersey's guidelines and computer software and a report from the Department of Justice, and forwarded the entire bundle to various associations of North Carolina sheriffs, police executives, and chiefs of police. Meanwhile, to find out how lineups were currently being handled, she distributed a survey to police officers statewide, and cajoled a third of them into responding. Every one gave lineups simultaneously. Nobody administered them double-blind. Less than half routinely warned a witness that the suspect might not appear in a particular lineup—a finding that dismayed Chris, since a rule about this already existed.

In June the commission resolved to draft its own reforms. To encourage them along, Chris continued paying out of her pocket for private catering services, the bill from which regularly topped five hundred dollars: chipotle-rubbed flank steak with red pepper aioli; tomato, mozzarella, and avocado napoleons; mixed greens with balsamic vinaigrette. By September a well-fed commission had adopted reforms unanimously. A month later, Chris submitted them to relevant organizations statewide, including law bars for both defense and prosecution and every police figure she'd reached out to four months earlier. Accompanying the recommendations was as gentle an explanation as Chris could stomach: "Although it is believed that the risk of conviction of an innocent person in North Carolina is small, it is the obligation of the justice system to identify the cause of even one innocent conviction and correct it if possible."

By January, state associations of both district and police attorneys offered endorsements. Commissioners, assuming their efforts on eyewitness ID complete, began to consider which issue they would address next.

Before they could, however, they heard from Winston-Salem.

Back in October, when it received the commission's recommendations, the Winston-Salem police department had appointed a four-person committee—two detectives, a sergeant, and a crime scene technician—who had read the commission's proposal skeptically and replied with a memorandum of its own. Their concerns were many. After noticing the commission had relied heavily on the research of a Dr. Gary Wells, the department had begun with a background investigation of him, and determined that "while he is in-fact a highly regarded research scientist and educator, his own curriculum vitae makes no mention whatsoever of any form of practical work experience in law enforcement." Wells's research was based on controlled laboratory experiments, not actual policing, and Winston-Salem doubted that findings from either of these applied to the other. They didn't see why this Actual Innocence Commission had fixated suddenly and arbitrarily on eyewitness identification as its "entire concern," especially given that the commission's proposal had offered "no supporting statistical basis about how many such wrongful convictions have occurred in North Carolina, and more specifically in the 21st Prosecutorial District, in comparison to the number of correct convictions."

What followed was a line-by-line rebuttal to many of the commission's twenty-seven recommendations. Four of these the committee agreed with; another seven were already policy. Three more it already followed informally, and now agreed to codify. One it remained undecided about. Eleven others it rejected. The last it declined to comment on at all.

This twenty-four-page reply the Winston-Salem committee then submitted to its captain, who scrawled across the front page: *Concur! Excellent work done by the committee!* On January 30, 2004, the department distributed its memorandum statewide, to what looked like every jurisdiction it could think of. Except the commission itself, which learned of the document only secondhand, when it blindsided them near the end of February.

13

In Favorable Times and Difficult Times

As early as the Catawba County jail, where they'd sent him after his arrest, he had prayed every night for the chance to go home, for the truth to come out, for God to offer him peace of mind. When none of these happened he began to consider the possibilities. Maybe the trouble was in his prayers; maybe he was doing it wrong. Mozella had raised him Baptist, though she had rarely brought him or his siblings to church, and now he worried he had never absorbed the proper method. The act felt clumsy. He clasped his hands and knelt, but even these he wasn't certain about; as a boy he'd seen Mozella pray simply while she walked around the house. When he'd fretted aloud that God might not hear her, as she wasn't in the correct position, Mozella had smiled. "Think about when you sitting at the table, saying grace before you eat. Are you going to get onto your knees?" This was right, Willie realized, no one knelt at the dinner table. That was sensible before bed, since a person was about to lie down anyway, Mozella assured him. "But God gonna hear your prayers if you're praying right." *Right* depended not on posture but on frame of mind.

So in prison he tried every way he could think of — before eating in the mess hall, while walking his loops in the yard, at the foot of his bunk before bed. His lips moved, but he had no idea what to say beyond the obvious. "Let me go home," he tried. "I haven't done anything wrong." Aloud he realized how selfish this sounded, but it was the truth. He really *did* want to go home, he really *had* done nothing wrong. It didn't work; he remained in prison. At CP and again at Harnett he saw a preacher who visited weekly to lead inmates through church services; with his own prayers foundering, Willie decided to try someone else's. There the preacher told him that to pray meant to let go, and to give to the Lord. Willie had no idea what this meant. "There isn't any one way to pray," the preacher promised. "You've just got to go to the Lord with honesty."

But Willie had gone to the Lord with honesty.

"Man accomplishes nothing on his own," the preacher told him.

That much, at least, was right. Filing appeals by himself had proved pointless. It ought to be enough that he was innocent; he ought to be able to put that in a letter. But he'd tried, and nothing had come of it. This preacher was right—a man accomplished nothing on his own. Man had to reach out to others. So Willie had changed his prayers, had asked God not to get him out of prison but simply to lead him toward someone who could. This was how he'd landed on jailhouse lawyers inside the prison library. But courts had denied their letters, just as they had his. What he needed was help from outside the prison, but who on the outside would hear him? This was how he'd reached Phillip Griffin, at Prisoner Legal Services.

But Griffin had dragged his feet, if he'd done anything at all, and again Willie considered the trouble might lie in his own prayers. Maybe still he was doing it wrong. A pastor on the outside had mailed a Bible to him in prison, and now Willie began to study it, to learn for himself how he might convince God to help him. He read every day, when he wasn't walking loops or on a work assignment. One afternoon he sat on a bench in the yard, reading, when another inmate approached and nodded toward the open Bible in his lap. "You ever think about where you'll go when you die?" the inmate asked. He was a slender man with skin as black as his pupils, a thin mustache, broad eyes, and a long, oval face. Willie didn't recognize him, but he was smiling widely.

"Well, from my understanding, I'm going back to the dirt," Willie answered cautiously.

"You don't feel like you're going to heaven?"

"I don't know much about heaven yet," Willie admitted. He still had a lot to read. "I think it depends on what type of person you are."

But Willie was in prison—certainly he'd done something to be in here, the inmate pointed out. "So do you think *you're* going to heaven?"

"Well, the Bible ain't told me," Willie answered. And wasn't everyone a sinner, inside prison or out? "If God don't forgive me, I suppose I'm going to hell."

"Suppose I told you there is no such thing as hell."

"There's always been heaven and hell," Willie insisted, lifting his Bible.

The inmate shook his head. "That's what they've *taught* you," he said. "You don't *know* that. What you've *learned* is, be a good person, you'll go to heaven. But also, you'll live forever here on earth."

"The Bible says, once you die, you go back to where you come from," Willie said. "That's the dirt."

The inmate gestured around their prison yard. "Isn't this dirt?"

"I ain't listening to this shit," Willie told him, and rose and walked away.

But every day for two weeks the same inmate returned to his bench, and there Willie was, squinting at pages in his Bible. Always he had more questions. One night Willie tracked him down inside his block to show him a passage he'd discovered in Psalms: "The wicked shall be turned into hell." There, Willie said. See? He pointed toward the page. A sinner went to hell.

And what exactly was hell? the inmate wanted to know. Did the Bible say?

As Willie considered this, the inmate produced his own Bible and turned to Matthew. " 'For the one who has died has been acquitted from his sin,' " he read. He looked at Willie. If a man was acquitted from sin, he asked, why would God continue to punish him?

Willie couldn't answer.

The inmate with the questions was named Bryan Garner, and he was a Jehovah's Witness, he told Willie, unlike the Baptists who visited weekly. He hadn't always been this way; twenty-five years ago, on the outside, Bryan had been a different man, one with a drug habit, until he'd gotten picked up for speeding, assault, and armed robbery. After more than a decade he'd grown frustrated he still wasn't up for parole, so one summer morning in 1985 he'd gotten a jump on guards and fled from minimum security. For the next three years he'd lived normally on the outside—changed his name, gotten married, and first learned about Jehovah. It was this last that had proven to be a problem. If the Bible had taught him only one thing, it was to live honestly, to devote himself to the Truth. And there he was, a fugitive who rightly belonged in prison. He was a hypocrite, he realized gradually, not only in his own eyes but in Jehovah's, which was worse. He'd had no choice but to do what he did next. In March of 1989 he'd walked into a lawyer's office and then to the gates at Central Prison, to turn himself in for the remainder of his sentence. After processing through CP he'd been transferred to Harnett, same as Willie.

Since then Bryan had continued studying Scripture with a Bible teacher who visited Harnett on Wednesdays. The next week, Bryan brought Willie to meet him. The pair gave Willie a copy of their Bible, the New World Translation; this was the basis of their faith, Bryan explained, the literal words of Scripture. Anything he said he encouraged Willie to trace back in the text. Constantly Bryan and his teacher were leafing through passages for the particular words and sentences that answered Willie's questions. The teacher had volunteered to come to prison because this was a place he felt he was needed. " 'Preach the word,' " he quoted from Timothy. " 'Be at it urgently in favorable times and difficult times. Do the work of an evangelizer.' "

Willie felt skeptical. Every religion he'd seen kept its own version of the Bible, and he knew a person could translate a text to support whatever he wanted. He kept both Bibles, the New World Translation and his own King James, to compare them. Mostly the two books aligned, he found, but the words of the New World Translation were simpler, more direct. From King James he had managed to decipher generalities, but often its language was dense and unfamiliar:

Wherefore, my beloved brethren, let every man be swift to hear, slow to speak, slow to wrath: For the wrath of man worketh not the righteousness of God. Wherefore lay apart all filthiness and superfluity of naughtiness, and receive with meekness the engrafted word, which is able to save your souls.

In the New World Translation Bryan gave him, he found the same message, put more clearly:

Know this, my beloved brothers: Everyone must be quick to listen, slow to speak, slow to anger, for man's anger does not bring about God's righteousness. Therefore, put away all filthiness and every trace of badness, and accept with mildness the implanting of the word that is able to save you.

The effect was more than convenience, Willie saw. The more cryptic a language, the more one person relied on another to interpret it for him. This in turn propelled him not toward the Bible but toward his fellow men, who were unevenly faithful and unevenly qualified, whom Witnesses mistrusted. Whenever Willie arrived at a word or phrase he didn't recognize, Bryan suggested he look for it in a dictionary, to find for himself what it meant. No preacher Willie knew had ever done that. Others had simply furnished an answer and expected him to accept it. There was no hierarchy among Witnesses, no ministers or reverends or priests; Bryan's teacher was no nearer to God than Bryan was, and Bryan was no nearer than Willie. On the outside, Jehovah's Witness congregations had elders, but these were only men who'd been practicing longer. It didn't make them any holier. Nearly anyone could observe the Truth for him- or herself, directly in Scripture, and could share it with others who hadn't. Could serve as a witness on behalf of Jehovah. Thus Jehovah's Witnesses.

Willie wasn't certain. But none of his own prayers had worked. He didn't see what he had to lose.

* * *

In autumn, after a year and a half at Harnett, he was transferred again, to Sampson Correctional. A laundry job had opened up there on the hangarlike floor of a warehouse, nearly a third of the camp's four hundred or so inmates hauling white socks and underwear and T-shirts from the washing machines to the dryers, or peeling brown chino pants and shirt jackets from heaping plastic bins. That was what inmates called a smaller prison—a camp, like they were on vacation.

A week after he arrived, his sister Gladys wrote to Prisoner Legal Services, just as Willie had, preferring it over some jailhouse lawyer her brother could find in a prison library. Because the attorney she'd asked initially, down in San Antonio, had told her not to bother attending Woot's trial, she still only barely understood what had occurred there. Would someone at PLS please look into her brother's case? "Raised as we were by our mother, I cannot see any of her sons doing such crimes, because they were taught to respect women, and to treat women as they would want their mother and sisters to be treated," she wrote. "It is because of our upbringing that I am becoming gravely concerned that my brother may indeed be serving [for] a crime that he did not commit. I do not know any place else to turn."

In response, Prisoner Legal Services forwarded Willie a generic request form for postconviction assistance. He'd already filled this out, more than a year earlier.

Less than two weeks later the state supreme court denied Willie's latest petition to hear his case. When he heard the news he wrote again to Phillip Griffin; after Willie's long complaint to him and his boss, Griffin had promised answers within a week, but since then Willie hadn't heard anything. "I would greatly appreciate if you would let me no what you have done in my case," he pleaded. "By the way it look you have not done anything. I am looking to hear from you soon and would appreciates any answer that you could give me."

A week before Halloween he finally heard back. The news wasn't good. "I appreciate your impatience," Griffin wrote. "Unfortunately, I am unable to provide you with the answers you want." He had read

Willie's transcript and appellate briefs "several times" through, and also examined the law concerning witness identification, hoping to find precedent for appeal. And come up empty. "Thus far, I have not been able to solve the basic problem in your case," Griffin explained: "The jury believed the victim's identification of you, supported by the hair found at the scene. While I personally believe that you are innocent, that does not mean that I can get you a trial." If Willie could afford private counsel, or a private investigator, to persist where Griffin himself had failed, he recommended Willie try this. "Because I believe you are innocent, I have not yet closed your case but continue to explore various avenues. I will let you know when I have given up."

Louie Ross, from high school, learned the prison phone schedule and began sending Willie money, then waiting by the phone in his apartment, so Willie could call him collect. But insomnia and colds plagued Willie into winter. Now when he blew his nose the tissue turned bloodstained. Nurses prescribed him Tylenol, Robitussin, and Drixoral, sometimes two at a time; they screened his blood and put him through another X-ray, for pneumonia. All negative. Shortly after Thanksgiving, the head psychologist at Sampson summoned him for a meeting. "He was soft-spoken and he talked at length about his despair about being involved in a life sentence in the prison," the psychologist observed. "He also talked a lot about his mother who had passed away." His conclusion: "I think Willie enjoys talking. I also think that he is experiencing continued depression."

Upset the state supreme court continually refused to hear his case, he appealed its latest denial to the nearest district court, in Raleigh—on his own, since he no longer had any lawyer, as de Torres's appointment had expired, he couldn't afford another, and Prisoner Legal Services had declined to help him. Then he wrote again to de Torres, to ask for the documentation he needed for another motion. "I hope you will be able to assist me with this as I have no other way to obtain this much needed material," he begged. By January de Torres hadn't replied, so Willie found another jailhouse lawyer. But he still needed his own complete case file. He wrote again to de Torres, then to Griffin, back at PLS, with the same request.

Replies from both lawyers arrived on the same day. Each had enclosed a photocopy of the brief Willie had asked for, and de Torres had added further paperwork he expected Willie might not have. "Hope this helps," he wrote.

With this new plan in mind he met again with the prison psychologist, for a checkup. "Willie seemed to be in good spirit," the psychologist observed. "He talked about focusing his attention on getting a re-trial and his desire to keep his mind off of the fact that he has such a long sentence." The psychologist himself was skeptical further appeals would lead anywhere, but still privately believed they were valuable, "as a means of diverting [Willie's] attention." He also noticed Willie was "investing himself a good deal into religious activities and he finds that helpful. He can see that the medication is helping with the depression. He seems to enjoy our conversation and appreciates the contact."

His depression aside, something about Willie struck the psychologist as unlike other inmates he had seen. He couldn't quite articulate what it was. "In general Mr. Grimes appears to be a man who has less of the overall characterological elements to his personality of many other inmates," he noted. Why this was, he wasn't certain.

District court in Raleigh denied his appeal, on the ground that it lacked jurisdiction over state supreme court decisions. Phillip Griffin visited him in prison, which turned out not to matter, since Griffin could do no more in person than he had in his letters. He still believed Willie's transcripts suggested his innocence, but this alone still wasn't enough for an appeal. With some luck, another attorney, or a hired detective, might turn up something more—Griffin himself worked for the state, however, and PLS didn't conduct those sorts of investigations. They received letters from as many as twelve thousand inmates a year. There was nothing more he could offer.

Willie couldn't afford another attorney, or a detective. He realized he needed someone who could take his case on for free, someone with influence. He wrote to Oprah Winfrey to explain who he was and what had happened to him. He wrote to Montel Williams. He wrote to the Legal Defense Fund at the NAACP. He wrote to the clerk's office back at Catawba County, to ask after his evidence. He didn't know that Ed de Torres had tried this already; a couple of months earlier, in January, around the same time Willie had mailed his latest appeal to Raleigh, de Torres had phoned the clerk to ask for the same thing. The rape kit that doctors had conducted on Carrie Elliott, the hair that police had recovered from her robe and bedspread, the fingerprints they'd lifted from the banana in her kitchen—the DNA tests he'd asked for at sentencing had never been conducted on any of these, de Torres knew, and they remained Willie's best—only—chance for appeal.

When the clerk's office phoned him back at ten thirty the following morning, however, de Torres was out of the office, and his secretary had taken a message: "Evidence has been destroyed."

To __Ed__
Date __1-24__ Time __10:35__ ☐ AM ☐ PM

WHILE YOU WERE OUT

M __Ann Lemons__

of _____

Phone (___)

Area Code		Number	Extension
TELEPHONED	✓	PLEASE CALL	
CALLED TO SEE YOU		WILL CALL AGAIN	
WANTS TO SEE YOU		URGENT	
	RETURNED YOUR CALL		

Message __evidence has been destroyed__
__12-13-90__

Operator _____

♻ Benchmark   DISTRIBUTED BY STATIONERS DISTRIBUTING CO., INC.
P.O. BOX 11320 FT. WORTH, TX 76109   62-272

* * *

The town of Hickory, though only thirty miles north of Lawndale, was another country. After his car was stolen, unable to make it back up to Towana in DC, he decided to try there because, unlike Lawndale, over the past several decades Hickory had industrialized, so that, also unlike Lawndale, it was hiring—at its furniture plants, its textile and hosiery mills, even its fiber optics and telecommunications companies.

But the end of farming in Hickory, though it had brought jobs, had also ended the only incentive for black and white families to occupy the same land, and the town had had a difficult time integrating its schools, which was another way of saying it had done its very best not to. After the decision of *Brown v. Board* in 1954, wherein the U.S. Supreme Court, partly at the urging of Beverly Lake's father, had ordered that southern schools integrate not at once but rather with "all deliberate speed"—a phrase North Carolina interpreted to mean its different towns could proceed however they liked—the Hickory school board had formed a committee to study how *Brown* applied within its jurisdiction and concluded more or less that it didn't.

In a radio address at the start of that academic year, the governor urged black families statewide to "take pride in your own race by attending your own schools." If his state could no longer segregate by law, he figured, then its students and parents must assume that responsibility themselves. Just in case, he helped enact the Pupil Assignment Act of 1955, and a year later the Pearsall Plan, each intended to delay integration. Both the state's senators, and eight of its twelve representatives, signed the Declaration of Constitutional Principles, also called the Southern Manifesto, denouncing *Brown* as "a clear abuse of judicial power...with no legal basis," whose consequences they predicted to be "explosive and dangerous." Integration was "certain to destroy the system of public education in some of the states," the manifesto argued, or at least cause "hatred and suspicion where there has been heretofore friendship and understanding." And anyway, it was "contrary to the Constitution," whose principle of segregation was "founded on elemental humanity and common sense," and North Carolina didn't intend to fool with.

For the next nine years Hickory proceeded as though *Brown* had never happened. Then came the Civil Rights Act of 1964, banning the use of federal funds for any discriminatory purpose. The following year, the Department of Education withheld ninety thousand dollars from Hickory public schools for noncompliance, and soon the Pupil Assignment Act and the Pearsall Plan were both underneath too many lawsuits and desegregation orders for North Carolina to sustain them. Finally, in 1966, the Hickory board developed a plan "intended to prevent or eliminate any and all possible discrimination." Among its provisions was the closure of two all-black schools—soon it would close four more—as well as townwide redistricting and the end of "race, color, or national origin" as considerations "in the hiring or assignment...of teachers and other professional staff."

It was an imperfect solution. In fact, several of those all-black schools had been symbols of pride and identity for their communities, especially one, Ridgeview High, which held only two hundred and fifty students but nonetheless had reason to boast: in the thirty-five years Ridgeview had fielded a football team, it had lost eleven games—total. Local families had tagged the team the Untouchables. A surprising number of its alumni had gone on to play sports professionally, for the Buffalo Bills and Washington Redskins and for several teams in the NBA.

All this vanished when Ridgeview was shuttered. "When the school [moved] across the tracks, people who didn't have transportation couldn't see a game," Sam Davis, coach of the Ridgeview Panthers for their final fourteen years, recalled a decade later. "And in the winter, it would be too cold to walk. When you move a school like that, some people lost interest." Administrators at the newly integrated Hickory High, uneasy at the prospect of a black man coaching its varsity team, named Davis an assistant to the ninth-grader team at a nearby middle school. His own assistant, who had coached for more than three decades, was asked to take the eighth grade.

White Hickory families, meanwhile, displeased at black children attending classes alongside their own, began to transfer out of Hickory High and into North State Academy, an all-white private school that had opened, conspicuously, only one year after the Civil Rights Act. By the end of 1976, so many had transferred that Hickory High lost state allocation for three full teacher salaries. Within another decade, public-school enrollment had dropped by nearly three hundred.

Black families were leaving Hickory, too. Those students who at Ridgeview had been star athletes or cheerleaders or members of student government now found themselves outsiders at Hickory High — stark alienation for a community whose pillars had long been its schools and churches. Like white families, able black families got out entirely, a pattern that mirrored what was unfolding miles south in Lawndale — for different reasons, since in Hickory the flight was from discord and in Lawndale it was from joblessness.

The escape of wealthier citizens meant decay to their former neighborhoods. VIOLENT CRIMES INCREASE 67% IN COUNTY, read a July 1978 headline in the *Observer-News-Enterprise,* out of Newton, just twelve miles southeast, where a decade later Willie would be tried. From February 1981: "Report shows crime rate soaring in Newton...Crime in Newton increased by a staggering 22.7 percent during 1980. Aggravated assaults alone increased by 80 percent. The amount of burglaries, and breaking and enterings are up 52 percent." To improve its most blighted neighborhoods, the town of Hickory installed several low-income housing complexes, including one near where Ridgeview High had once stood, a sorely needed project that also had the effect of wiping out any sense of community that had persisted there. The complex was named Hillside Gardens, though people also called it Little Berlin, and it was where Carrie Elliott lived.

When Willie arrived in Hickory, in 1978, he met a friend named Rachel Wilson. Rachel had siblings — Betty, Carolyn, and Allen Shuford, plus Linda McDowell — and most of them had children of their own, but because the Shufords were poorer even than Willie, their entire family occupied the same two-bedroom house. This meant eight to ten bodies, depending on how many were home at once. So when he and Betty began dating, and Betty asked if she and her two young children, a boy and a girl, could come stay with him in his apartment on Third Avenue, Willie agreed.

By 1986 the romance between him and Betty had cooled, though the pair stayed friendly, and there was no reason for either to leave the apartment. Then Betty met another man she was serious about. Willie noticed the new boyfriend had no place of his own; if Willie stayed in the apartment, he saw, he might be in the way. He wanted his friend Betty with a place for herself, and for her children. He volunteered to move out. Then he met and began dating a woman named Brenda Smith. Brenda and Betty got along just fine, since Betty too was now dating someone else, so Brenda didn't mind him keeping Betty as a friend, or looking after her kids, or, once or twice, if he couldn't find a ride, passing the night at Betty's apartment, so long as he passed it on the couch. It had once been his couch, after all. After four months on his own in a temporary apartment, he was invited by Brenda to move in with her.

They'd been dating for a year or so when Steve Hunt of the Hickory Police Department knocked on her door.

14

Their Different Individual Viewpoints

When she learned of the memorandum from the Winston-Salem police, Chris was furious. At the computer keyboard in her home office, she punched out a withering seven-page, single-spaced response, divided into ten sections and nine subsections, replete with italics and bold print, each forwarding a counterargument. While the memorandum had not been addressed to the commission, she felt "compelled to respond," she began irately. "I hope this response will be circulated to as many agencies as have received copies of the committee's memorandum."

She resented the implication that she or the commission had relied on only one source for their research into eyewitness ID. In fact they'd consulted with five nationally recognized experts and had reviewed publications or materials from the National Institute of Justice and police jurisdictions in both Illinois and New Jersey. They'd further solicited input from nearly every major law enforcement agency and association in North Carolina. These Chris listed in an enormous paragraph. "I'm sure the committee did not mean to suggest that there is an acceptable percentage of wrongful convictions," she added, in reply to the complaint that the commission had offered no statistics. Another complaint she considered "dramatic." A third she dismissed as "humorous." "If Winston-Salem can not *understand how to interpret and apply this recommendation,* it is not surprising that the committee has adopted an overall 'it can't be done' approach."

Even as she banged at her keyboard, though, Chris knew she could never send the letter. It would only alienate police, whose support she needed for the reform she was after. So she kept her seven-page screed private. In its place, she drafted a simple three-page summary of Winston-Salem's complaints, brought this to the commission for discussion, and scheduled a meeting with the Winston-Salem police for the final week of May.

Then she recruited allies on the commission. She began with Mike Gauldin, the detective from the Ronald Cotton case. Gauldin was a matter-of-fact man with the build and mountainous jaw of a wrestling coach; Ronald Cotton had changed his life entirely. "I never imagined that I would be involved in a case like that," he'd once told the *Raleigh News and Observer*. "It's caused me a lot of soul searching." Gauldin had realized immediately that he could never restore the decade Cotton had wrongly spent in prison, so had done the next best thing, which was to place himself and his department, up in Burlington, at the forefront of every possible reform. At times this put him at odds with fellow police, but Gauldin didn't care. Fellow police hadn't lived through Cotton.

Next Chris enlisted Tom Ross. Today Ross directed the Z. Smith Reynolds Foundation, the largest nonprofit in the state, but before that he'd been a superior court judge and had led the Sentencing and Policy Advisory Commission, the body that recommended sentencing guidelines to the North Carolina General Assembly. Because he had served under chief justices from both parties, his reputation was nearly apolitical. Tall and watchful-eyed, Ross had businesslike reserve—like Beverly Lake, he'd once been an Eagle Scout, though the two men's relationship had sometimes been strained. Ross had long been close friends with Henry Frye, the first black chief justice in North Carolina history; when Ross was appointed to the bench, it was Frye he'd chosen to administer the oath for his swearing-in. And it was Frye whom Beverly Lake had campaigned against for chief justice. Ross didn't have anything against Lake personally, but he hadn't liked Lake's decision to run.

But Ross had come independently to the same concerns as Lake about the credibility of the courts. As a postconviction judge, Ross had been the one to rescind the conviction of Charles Munsey, the inmate whose confession at Central Prison turned out to have been fabricated—the first death sentence in state history overturned on grounds that the convict was innocent, as far as Ross knew. (Across the country, there had been forty or so others.) Munsey had been so polarizing that Ross had decided to write that opinion himself, rather than delegate it to his clerks, and then, even rarer, to read it aloud in open court. He felt determined to get this one right. Years later he still remembered walking down the long hallway from his chambers to the courtroom, past guards and officers who knew the case he was about to rule on. "You got to keep him in jail, Judge," they whispered as he passed. "If he didn't kill that woman, I'll bet he killed somebody else." At the end of the hallway Ross swept into his courtroom, settled on his bench, and ordered a retrial.

Since then Ross had won the William H. Rehnquist Award, a national honor bestowed each year at the U.S. Supreme Court, in Washington, DC. There he decided his speech would concern public trust in the courts. Almost two years later, Ross had received a letter from Beverly Lake, expressing identical concerns. He'd arrived to that first meeting skeptical it would lead anywhere; as far as Ross knew, Lake had never been a reformist. And he'd never heard of this Chris Mumma woman. Politically, Ross knew that reform was risky territory. A person couldn't whisper the word *reform* in North Carolina, in connection with criminal justice, without everyone assuming he meant the death penalty. The baggage of that could define a person politically, and Ross wasn't sure what Lake was up to. But it impressed him that Chris had only been a clerk when Lake met her, since he knew this meant Lake could have easily patted her on the head and ignored her. *Aw, Chris, I know you believe in that, but you're barely out of law school, you really aren't sophisticated enough to know.* Instead, Lake had seen precisely what Ross had, planning that speech two years earlier. The concern Chris raised was valid. Someone credible needed to address it, even at risk to his own reputation. This was what Lake was trying to do, Ross realized. He pledged to help however he could.

Coincidentally, the Z. Smith Reynolds Foundation, the nonprofit Ross now led, was based in Winston-Salem. Chris decided his office would make a good location for a meeting.

In May, Winston-Salem's district attorney and police chief arrived to Ross's office with the same concerns their colleagues had laid out months earlier. Reforms would make it harder to catch criminals, and harder to put them in prison. They doubted the commission knew about either of these things.

"Look," Chris argued, once pleasantries were through, "we've got five representatives from law enforcement on the commission, including Chief Gauldin here. We've also got nine prosecutors. We are *not* lacking input from those with practical work experience."

Nor was the commission focused solely on eyewitness ID, Gauldin added. They'd simply chosen to address this first, because research proved it was the single largest factor in wrongful convictions. The commission wasn't *fixated* on ID, as Winston-Salem had charged. They'd only prioritized it.

Ross allowed that the department's memorandum had raised a few valid concerns. One had to do with staffing: it was true that double-blind lineups generally required more officers, and in smaller jurisdictions, he knew, these could be hard to come by. But police in New Jersey, where all lineups were administered this way, had faced the same challenges, and had found ways around them, partly by using particular software and partly by sharing resources among adjacent counties. If those weren't enough, the commission understood, Ross offered. Maybe, in a few exceptional cases, lineups *couldn't* be double-blind, because the necessary staffing wasn't available. Ross could live with that, as long as the other reforms were implemented—if suspect photographs were still shown one at a time, for example, rather than all at once. These weren't laws the commission had proposed, only best practices. The idea was to follow them as closely as a department was able.

The idea was also to *improve* their chances of getting the bad guy, Chris added. Not to make it harder. This was the whole point.

Studies proved that ID reform would help Winston-Salem catch the criminal, rather than some guy who *looked like* the criminal. A lineup run this way also held up better in court, and provoked fewer legal challenges. This was important, because the issue was coming, whether Winston-Salem liked it or not. As long as the department insisted on keeping its outdated procedures, any smart defense attorney would pounce on them at trial. Didn't police want to stay ahead?

The DA and police chief both paused. This seemed reasonable. They still weren't thrilled with the software costs, but reforms sounded better in person than they'd looked on paper. They agreed to take these back to their department, where the chief, Pat Norris, pledged to begin implementing them. Norris liked this idea of finding the correct suspect, and of fewer objections in court. If *that* was what the commission was up to, she offered, she was interested in helping out.

A month later Chief Norris joined the commission.

The Winston-Salem endorsement Chris brought with her on a tour around the state—first to a meeting with two dozen police chiefs, then to another with the North Carolina Justice Academy. More departments wrote to her for training materials, so Chris forwarded every document she'd bundled together a year earlier. Then she visited the police chiefs association and the police executives association. Then the Criminal Justice Education and Training Standards Commission.

A year after that, in 2005, the commission's reforms were finally added to North Carolina's basic law enforcement training.

As Chris wrangled over eyewitness-ID reform, meanwhile, the commission at large had moved on. Or tried to. From the outset, commissioners had agreed not to discuss the death penalty; consensus on that issue was clearly beyond hope, so rather than risk derailing the whole enterprise, commissioners had pledged not to touch it. Since then the issue had hung on the horizon, like storm clouds. And every so often winds blew from that direction.

Usually this had to do with Jim Coleman. Long before Lake had invited him onto the commission, Coleman had chaired a section of the American Bar Association calling for a moratorium on the death penalty, and also served on the board of North Carolina's Center for Death Penalty Litigation. Now he testified on the issue before the general assembly. Coleman saw his participation in the two movements as unrelated, but prosecutors in the commission didn't. Coleman was dragging them into an argument they'd promised to avoid, DAs complained; they'd never intended to join a group opposing the death penalty, and resented any appearance that they had. Then the state senate passed Bill 972, a two-year moratorium on executions—a bill that, in its preamble, referenced the commission specifically.

Coleman hadn't been involved with the legislation, but it didn't look that way. He knew DAs were threatening to leave the commission unless he abandoned his work against the death penalty, so privately he went to Beverly Lake and offered to resign. The DAs were necessary for the commission to function, he admitted to Lake. He himself wasn't. If anyone was leaving, it should be him.

Lake refused. Like the DAs, he personally believed in the death penalty, he told Coleman. But he'd also grown to like Coleman, despite the conflict in their politics, and felt Coleman was valuable to the commission. "Listen, I don't think anything you're doing is affecting what we're doing," Lake assured him. It was probably true that public attention had conflated the commission with the death penalty, but this wasn't Coleman's doing. So Lake wasn't having anyone resign.

Instead, Lake drafted an open letter to the two state senators who had sponsored the moratorium. "The Commission is made up of members who support capital punishment and of members who do not," he clarified. "Their different individual viewpoints regarding capital punishment and a moratorium are irrelevant." Bill 972 hadn't explicitly claimed the commission's support, he admitted, but he didn't like that it referenced the commission at all, as this could easily be misinterpreted. "I respectfully request, to avoid any inference that the Commission endorses or takes a position on the moratorium or the bill and out of respect for the important work of the Commission, that any reference to the North Carolina Actual Innocence Commission in Senate Bill 972 (H1199) be removed."

The amended moratorium bill didn't fully stamp out DAs' irritation toward Coleman, but soon something else did. In one of Coleman's classes that semester at Duke, a student spoke up to share an experience from the previous summer, when he'd interned with Ben David, the district attorney down in Wilmington. Over the course of that internship, the student recalled, two capital cases had crossed David's desk. The defendant in one of these cases had been black. The other had been a Lumbee American Indian, though he was so light-skinned that strangers usually assumed he was white. Ben David, in his office, had been describing to interns the political realities of being a prosecutor in the South. If he sought the death penalty against one of these men but not the other, or even in a particular order, he might be accused of racism, he predicted offhandedly. Not that he would make any decision for this reason—it was just that he was an experienced prosecutor, and he recognized the discomforts of his job.

Coleman didn't give the story a second thought. At the end of that week, he left for vacation with his wife. But a colleague, a Duke staffer, had been in the room. When Coleman left, that colleague filed affidavits alleging that David's remarks proved he'd pursued the death penalty on racial grounds. She wanted a conviction and death sentence both vacated.

When Coleman learned what his colleague had done, he felt bewildered. And livid. He'd never met Ben David—as far as he knew, neither had his colleague—but he remembered his student's recounting of the internship, and it hadn't been anything close to this. He e-mailed his entire class, commanding them not to say a word until he got every one of them a lawyer. Then he phoned Ben David's office to explain who he was. "I was there," he insisted. "It was in my class. And that's not what happened. That's not what the student said." He volunteered an affidavit of his own, and to testify on David's behalf.

David was cleared, and Coleman's colleague was fired—an outcome that displeased the Center for Death Penalty Litigation, who now felt Coleman had betrayed their cause, even as he sat on its board. Coleman didn't care. He'd told the truth. "Look, there are enough racial issues that actually *do* affect the death penalty," he assured Ben David. "We don't need to make them up."

That Coleman, a black defense attorney, had voluntarily come to the aid of a white prosecutor, especially on an issue of race, impressed DAs in the state who heard about it. At the next commission meeting they regarded Coleman with new, grudging respect. "I see you gave one for the good guys," one said.

Coleman shrugged. *He's a tree-hugging, anti-death-penalty hippie,* he could see them thinking. *But he has his principles.*

Now that commissioners had settled eyewitness-ID rules, and reconciled—disagreeably—on the death penalty, together they turned to a different problem. Since the commission's earliest meeting, back at Chris's house, one obvious question had overshadowed all others, even as they'd pursued ID reform. That issue commissioners had taken to calling a front-end solution, but logically the one term raised another. What about *back-end* solutions? It was fine to try to prevent a wrongful conviction from happening again in the future. But what were they going to do about those that already had happened?

That, Bob Orr had thought for months, *is the elephant in the room.*

15

We Must Use Our Judgment

To serve a long term in prison was to stay at a permanent, insulated distance from all that had comprised the first forty-one years of his life. His friends and siblings, the fence posts and grassy acreage of Lawndale, his jobs at the textile plant and furniture shop, even his old apartment and clothes. Every one of them was gone. Week after week, his memories strained an inch further—their colors bleached a shade paler, their voices calling a decibel softer—until he had worn them nearly threadbare. In the other direction expanded one long, sluggish afternoon into another, lined as far as he could see.

An inmate in this position controlled whatever he could. He turned the knob of his shower at precisely the same minute each morning, stored his toothbrush on precisely the same square inch of shelf in his locker. On the yard he lifted a particular weight a particular number of times. In the mess hall he ate precisely the same foods, or else deliberately did the reverse, never repeated a meal on consecutive days, simply to show that he could. He stuffed crumbs into his pockets and snuck them into his cell, to draw out mice, which he kept as pets. He collected books or photographs or letters or radios, and he protected his collections, sometimes ferociously. If he worked in a sewing plant he tailored his own clothes, or stitched them with his initials, out of view of the guards. Now he no longer borrowed those clothes; now those clothes belonged to him.

Or an inmate serving a long term might disengage entirely, might flee, as far as he could, his own senses. He might regiment his day, his month, his year, his decade, so as to automate them. He might rise at a certain time, engage in certain physical actions, and rest at a certain time, as an engine idling at low speed. He ignored Christmas and Passover and his birthday and the New Year, same as the old year, all holidays that no longer existed. An inmate like this never got his hopes up and thus never felt disappointed. He took naps. If he was lucky he realized it was four in the afternoon and the morning had already passed. He'd barely noticed.

Or an inmate might make the best of his time. He might be gregarious. He might play cards and checkers and dominoes; if he had money, he might gamble. He might run errands for guards, to curry favors, or join a gang.

Or an inmate might pursue his education, spend his hours at the library or in classes. He might read thrillers or mysteries or literature or philosophy. He might read the Bible. If he was optimistic, or enterprising, he might read law.

Three suffocating years Willie had spent mired in anger so liquid and churning it had nearly choked him. Now, in moments of calm, he began to recognize certain facts. Obviously it did not matter that he had committed no crime. This was irrelevant. As soon as police had arrested him, nothing he said about his own innocence counted. That was the reason they'd denied his appeals, and it meant they might not ever release him. He'd believed all this amounted to one long delay, but now he saw this might not be true. Possibly their convicting him had been no procedural error, to be corrected later, but an actual outcome. Possibly his imprisonment would be no exception to his life but its defining condition.

The thought devastated him. And it meant he'd trusted wrongly in the Hickory police, the Newton judge, the guards he saw making their rounds. These were not people who, in the long run, got things right. These were not professionals. There was no such thing as professionals. These smartly uniformed guards, with their desks and nameplates and badges, their rifled towers, their Gray Goose buses, acted not out of power but out of fantasy. They reeked of falseness.

For every rule they'd invented, he saw an inmate who flouted it; to every law in North Carolina, there had to be an exception, as he himself was. Any guard, like any judge or any lawyer in any courtroom, was worthless. What power they imagined they held amounted to nothing at all. That so-called power was uncivilized and conditional. It was puny; it was hollow; it was an illusion. He had been foolish not to realize this. It made no difference for a prison to be built of brick or concrete or razor wire because in fact it was built of smoke.

Nothing in a world like this could be relied on; it was all only chance. He grasped now he had been wrong to think some influential person might help him. There *was* no such person, there *was* no such influence. He could trust no one and nothing but himself. Prison had stripped him to his elements. His mind alone he knew was not a fraud. He recognized the irony in this. Inmates complained they owned so little when prison only laid bare what had always been their condition: they had never owned anything more. Prison had simply released them from the delusion. A man's true circumstances came not from his environment but from his knowledge that environment was trivial, and from the weight of his principles. To discover he owned no more than his own mind was to discover not that he lacked authority but that he commanded it. "Stop being molded by this system of things, but be transformed by making your mind over," he read in Romans.

When he wasn't working he carried two Bibles, the King James Version of his childhood and the New World Translation the Jehovah's Witnesses had given him. God, like anyone else, had a name, the Witnesses taught him, and it appeared in the original Hebrew Scriptures. But ancient Hebrew lacked vowels, so His name was spelled YHWH, and translation into Greek and then Latin had complicated the issue. Latin lacked a letter *W*, and its *Y* was closer to the *J* of English. In this way, YHWH had become JHVH, had become Jehovah.

Not to everyone. There were those who had kept the *Y* and *W* of Hebrew and pronounced it "Yahweh"; there were those who avoided saying God's name at all, and replaced YHWH entirely in their translations with a different Hebrew word, *Adonai*, meaning "Lord" or "My Lord," deferring to the commandment not to take His name in vain. This allowed a reader of Scripture to avoid speaking His name aloud, out of respect.

Witnesses believed this an important mistake. Lord was Jehovah's title, not His given name, and censoring it had rendered Him distant and impersonal. Everywhere the Bible exhorted them toward intimacy — toward "close friendship with Jehovah," according to the Psalms. A person rightly called his friend by his name. "This is My name forever, and this is how I am to be remembered from generation to generation," Jehovah had told Moses. Jehovah *wanted* them to use His name. This was a fact they had witnessed.

In this way Willie read Job and marveled at what trials a man could bear. He read Jeremiah. He read Joseph, who was betrayed and sold off to Egypt. "But Jehovah was with Joseph," Scripture promised, even in Egypt, where Joseph was betrayed once more — falsely accused of rape. Now Joseph was thrown into prison. "But Jehovah continued with Joseph and kept showing loyal love to him," Scripture promised again. At last word of Joseph was carried to the pharaoh, who recognized his wisdom, freed him from prison, and took him as an adviser. Now Joseph's brothers, the same men who had conspired against him, came for Joseph's help. "I am Joseph your brother, whom you sold into Egypt," he reminded them. Still, he obliged. "Do not be upset and do not reproach one another because you sold me here," he said. They had not sold him there at all; "God sent me ahead of you."

Like Joseph, Willie was being tested. The task was to retain his faith, whose value was more than gold — since faith, unlike gold, could withstand fire. Jehovah cared for him, he read in Scripture, would absorb his suffering if Willie in turn would stand against the devil, who "walks about like a roaring lion, seeking to devour someone." This was what his anger felt like exactly. "Take your stand against him, firm in the faith," he read in Peter. "After you have suffered a little while, the God of all undeserved kindness, who called you to His everlasting glory in union with Christ, will himself finish your training." At last Willie might be freed, despite the walls of prison—despite the sham of his Newton trial and Prisoner Legal Services. "For Jehovah loves justice," the Psalms promised. "And He will not abandon His loyal ones."

The smaller a camp, the more lenient its guards, generally speaking, though of course this was relative in prison. On a large camp, with hundreds or even a thousand inmates, a guard had to oversee so many things he couldn't afford exceptions. A smaller camp was easier on him to supervise, its relationships easier to manage. Usually this relaxed him. Most of the camps out west were trouble; word was that guards in the mountains could be rednecks, and hostile. A camp that recently had been built or renovated was cleaner, which often meant it was safer. Old, decrepit buildings were depressing, and sent a message to inmates about how little they mattered. This in turn influenced their behavior. A camp with jobs, or a school, was more likely to draw a certain type of inmate, and this, too, could make things more tolerable. The same applied on a smaller scale. A cell block that housed mostly working or student inmates generally was safer than a block that didn't. On a block like this an inmate could expect less violence, and fewer drugs, though still he knew to expect violence and drugs.

Drugs could be smuggled inside packages, which was difficult, or body cavities, which was worse. By far it was easier for guards to bring them in, which was what happened. Willie saw more drugs in prison than he had seen in his life—marijuana, crack, heroin, cocaine, morphine, Dilaudid, Demerol. A guard who smuggled or sold drugs earned extra income this way, and developed influence among the mobs. So did an inmate, for whom drugs also simply passed the time, same as a job with Correction Enterprises. Given the choice, an inmate who used drugs preferred a single cell, where guards couldn't watch his every movement, but it wasn't much harder to use them out on the yard or anyplace a guard wasn't, or even where a guard *was,* so long as he and the inmate had an arrangement. Every so often inmates were drug-tested; the penalty for failure was points on the inmate's record, or a stint in segregation, or both, depending on the mood and allegiance of the guard. A clever inmate in this position simply refused to urinate into his cup. This counted as disobedience of a direct order. Disobedience carried fewer points than a positive test. Eventually even the slowest inmates caught on to this, so the prison changed its policy. Now failure and refusal counted the same.

A mob was a clique of inmates; a gang, more or less, though not every one was violent. This too depended on the camp, and on the guards, and on the level of custody. A mob usually aligned itself with one guard or another, whom its members could rely on for drugs or favors. A dispute between rival mobs could be dangerous, though it depended on the mob and the situation. By far violence was likeliest in maximum security, but it could happen in medium, too, on a camp that was especially hostile or where guards were especially compromised. Or if you were simply unlucky. Violence could be indiscriminate or it could be particular, could target crackers or niggers or fags. A camp like that could be a source of terror. An inmate could make a weapon out of nearly anything, and often he did. A combination lock purchased from the canteen, slung into the toe of a sock. A toilet brush with a filed wooden handle. A broken lawn-mower blade recovered from the yard, sharpened on a grinder in the woodshop, wrapped around one end with an Ace bandage.

"If you're one of us, we've got ways of showing it," the mobs had promised Willie as soon as he'd arrived in prison. "We'll get you on your feet." Instead he avoided them. He was shy, and he sensed their danger. Joining a mob meant declaring allegiance, which he didn't have; accepting favors meant becoming indebted, which he didn't want.

To pass the time he began making small loans. Jobs in the kitchen and laundry had provided him income, which he felt indifferent toward; he didn't use drugs and rarely bought anything from the canteen, so couldn't see what he would spend it on. If he made two and a half dollars in a week he loaned it to another inmate for the price of fifty cents in interest. The resulting three dollars he loaned to someone else for a full dollar in interest. Every so often an inmate didn't repay him, which didn't matter. He wasn't pursuing a business model. He was only occupying his afternoons. He learned to be careful of the mobs, which loaned money themselves and didn't like him encroaching, especially if his interest rate was lower. But the mobs figured out he worked alone, not for any rival, so they tolerated him. The risk was in crossing their path accidentally. He tried not to loan to anyone who already owed someone else. If he noticed a dispute between rival mobs, for a while he stopped loaning altogether.

Other times he stopped loaning because he felt too ill to keep it up. His colds worsened into the flu, and he asked to see a doctor. But nurses misunderstood and sent him to the dentist, where recently he'd had a tooth filled. A day later they realized their error. A day after that he was prescribed more Robitussin and Drixoral, and something called Theo-Dur, for bronchitis, which no one was sure he had. In case this was wrong they also prescribed him an antibiotic.

The following week he was up for custody review, an evaluation by prison administrators. "His work performance has been rated as excellent by his work supervisors," his case manager wrote. "Willie has gotten along well with other inmates and the staff as well. He has not been a management problem here at Sampson." To be promoted to minimum custody, however, he needed to be within five years of eligibility for parole. He was nowhere close.

That same week he met again with a psychiatrist, who thought him "friendly" and "talkative." In Willie's medical chart, under "Comments/Progress/Explanation," the psychiatrist wrote, "Denies guilt."

After a month or so of mostly restful nights, his trouble sleeping returned. Nervous that all his medications were agitating his symptoms, rather than helping them, he asked to stop his antidepressant; before prison he'd never taken a single medication, and he'd heard of inmates growing addicted. He also suspected they were causing his nightmares. But he didn't know how else to soothe his colds. His psychiatrist replaced his Sinequan with Trazodone. He petitioned again for habeas corpus—this time in district court, rather than the state supreme court, which had already denied him. A few weeks later he received an unexpected letter from Phillip Griffin's boss at

Prisoner Legal Services, Marvin Sparrow. Sparrow too had reviewed Willie's entire file, he wrote, and come to the same conclusion as Griffin. "Unfortunately, I don't think there is any way of attacking your conviction that has any reasonable chance of success," he admitted. He and Griffin had spoken several times about Willie's case over the previous year. "He has said that you are an innocent man and he wanted to find some way to prove that," Sparrow relayed. Both men initially had hoped to challenge Carrie Elliott's ID of Willie at trial, which they agreed was suspect. "The problem is, that, at least by the time she got to court, the victim was convinced that you were the person who attacked her. As unlikely and unbelievable as that identification was, the jury believed it." Sparrow was forced to agree with Griffin, though it unsettled him; without any new evidence, Prisoner Legal Services simply had no grounds for overturning Willie's conviction. "As a man in prison due to mistaken identification, you are naturally angry at our failure to try anything, no matter how slim the chance, that might get your case reversed. But we must use our judgment and take only cases which stand some chance of accomplishing something. Because there seems to be no promising way to attack your conviction, I find that Mr. Griffin was correct in not filing any petition or motion in your behalf. I understand that you have now asked for documents back and that you intend to file your own motion. Good luck. We are closing your case file in our office."

At the end of summer he was transferred again—to Vance Correctional, near the Virginia border, where he took a job as an assistant cook. In the fall he came up again for custody review. "Willie is presently working in the kitchen, and gets good reports from his supervisor," his case manager noted. "Has caused no problems since his assignment to this center."

Three months after his latest petition for habeas corpus, he began worrying the court might not respond to him at all, in which case he would need to refile with another circuit. He wrote to a lawyer he found in Charlotte, who agreed to help him draft another petition for a fee of four thousand dollars. He wrote to a cousin in Lawndale, who found a different lawyer, who made the same offer, for the same fee. Even if he found someone to help him for free, he realized, another petition required a form he didn't have, so he wrote to a third lawyer, at the Department of Justice, to ask if she would send it to him. While he waited, he used the prison phone to call his niece Shirley collect, hoping he might feel better if he heard a voice from home. "I hate to be the one to tell you this," Shirley told him, "but Brenda died two weeks ago. Then her mama died last week."

For a long moment he was disoriented. "W-what?" he finally stammered. Until Brenda had moved to a different apartment, and Willie had lost track of her, the pair had written letters. Not as often as he would have liked, and she hadn't visited him after his trial, but he knew how far he was from Hickory, and the long hours she worked at the nursing home. They had dated just a year before his arrest, and he didn't expect she would wait for him forever. Still, he counted her a friend. He didn't see how she could possibly have died. She was only forty-one years old. He hadn't even known she was sick.

Almost no one had known, Shirley told him. But Brenda and her mother had both had breast cancer.

It pained him that Brenda had not reached out with this news. Had she purposely not told him? Or had her illness moved so quickly she'd had no chance? He knew almost nothing about how cancer worked. Possibly she'd been driving to and from her doctor for months, in the same car they'd once driven together down to Shelby, to collect his tax money. Now she was gone. He felt a surge of loneliness—no longer a temporary feeling, but now a constant in his life. He told his case manager he wanted to be transferred to a camp nearer Lawndale. Maybe, if he had been housed closer to her, Brenda could have visited. His case manager referred his request on, where it was approved. But two months later he was transferred instead to Central Prison, and a week after that back to Vance, where he'd been in the first place. No one explained why. Reluctantly he wrote again to Phillip Griffin, with a copy of the habeas corpus petition he'd filed in district court and still hadn't heard any result from. A month later

Griffin replied that he didn't see how he could help, for the reasons he and Marvin Sparrow had explained previously.

On a good night that winter he slept five hours, rarely straight through. In his medical chart someone entered "Major depression in full remission." His psychologist crossed a line through "full remission" and, in its place, wrote "partial remission."

There were a number of reasons an inmate might be transferred between prisons, including a custody change or a job or a class or a rehabilitation program that one camp offered but not another. If an inmate caused trouble on a particular camp, he might be transferred. If he sensed he was in danger, or might get along better elsewhere, he could request this himself. The reverse was also possible; if administrators noticed an inmate growing too close to his guards, they were likely to transfer him, since the friendlier that relationship, the likelier a guard was to give favors or skirt rules, and the simplest way to halt this was to remove one of them. If an inmate had been shipped especially far from his family, he could request a transfer nearer his home, to facilitate visits. Sometimes this was granted; sometimes it wasn't. Or he might be transferred simply for processing reasons. For every new batch of inmates shipped from O dorm, back at CP, beds had to be cleared to receive them, which meant other inmates had to be moved, either to another prison or to a different bunk in the same facility. At Vance, Willie kept being reassigned to a new cell block, as he had continually at Harnett and Sampson. This was one reason he had such trouble sleeping. Each reassignment dropped him into another unfamiliar environment, where he was surrounded anew by strangers.

During a work shift in the kitchen, he mentioned his failed transfer request to his supervisor, a sergeant. He *had* to get back to Cleveland County, he insisted. It was the only way anyone could visit him. He didn't see why the prison had promised this only to send him back to Vance.

Personally, she was glad Willie hadn't been transferred, the sergeant admitted. Since he was a good worker, it would be hard to replace him. Then she realized how upset he was.

The next day she pulled him aside. "I'll tell you the best way to get there, if you really want," she whispered, glancing around. "But it's possible it could hurt your record, down the line."

Willie didn't care about down the line.

Here's what you do, the sergeant told him.

That Sunday evening he retired to his bunk early, before others on his block. After only a few hours he woke to a crowd of inmates staring at him. "We're going to fuck you up," one said.

He cried out and a guard appeared. "They're going to attack me!" he shouted, gesturing toward the crowd. "They're going to attack any minute!"

The guard looked around. He saw no one. Willie lay alone on his bunk.

Again the guard asked what the trouble was. Again Willie pointed toward empty space. His eyes darted and he startled at nothing. He rubbed his palms as though washing his hands. "I'll hurt them before they can hurt me," he warned.

The guard didn't follow.

"Get me out!" Willie hissed. "Get me away from them!"

The guard rushed him to the nurses' station, where Willie was placed in an observation cell—"for his protection," nurses wrote. In the morning they transferred him to Central Prison's mental-health clinic for evaluation, where Willie explained what had happened the night before. "He is paranoid, feeling others may harm him and that he may harm others, feeling he needs to protect himself," a psychiatrist observed. In addition to the voices he was hearing, Willie "appeared jumpy and nervous," and was "physically shaking and obviously anxious...Inmate Grimes stated that he was ready to go off." In Willie's chart the psychiatrist read he was being treated for depression but also that he'd never had any episode like this—according to his file, Willie met with a prison psychiatrist only once a month, on an outpatient basis, and had responded just fine to treatment. Under "Relations with Other Inmates," some staffer had written, "No problems. Stays to himself most of the time."

Until he deciphered what had gone wrong, the psychiatrist was taking no chances. As a suicide precaution and "to protect staff and other inmates from the threat of harm," he placed Willie in another observation cell.

When he returned the next morning, however, whatever had happened appeared to be over. Willie seemed fine. "The patient cleared quickly from this acute psychotic episode and was tolerant to his medications and his treatment plan," the psychiatrist wrote. Besides the initial alarm, Willie hadn't presented any problems. Now he told the psychiatrist he felt much better, didn't think he needed any more treatment, and was willing to go back to Vance. The psychiatrist agreed. "This hospitalization was unremarkable," he recorded. To Willie's medical chart he added a diagnosis of "schizoid personality disorder," though a note revealed his uncertainty: "? Psychotic (doesn't seem so)." He prescribed Elavil, another antidepressant, in addition to the Prozac and Trazodone. Then he discharged Willie back to Vance.

As soon as he returned there, Willie applied again for a transfer. If he wanted to be shipped to a particular camp, the trick was in not asking for it, the sergeant had told him. Administrators were reluctant to accommodate a request so specific, since they didn't like an inmate thinking he ran the place. Instead, she had told him to find the next closest prison to the one he wanted, and ask for transfer there; administrators likely would send him to the other one. Because he had already been denied Cleveland County, this time he chose Lincoln, twenty miles northeast. He told his case manager he suspected his recent incident had to do with being kept so far from home, without any visits. This time his transfer was approved. But only partially, administrators told him. They couldn't send him to Lincoln.

By June he was at Cleveland County Correctional.

For the first time this was near enough to home for visitors. Twice that year his sister Gladys drove down from Silver Spring, and his brothers Samuel Lee and Cliff Jr. from Lawndale. A friend from high school came, too. It had taken nearly five years, but he felt more like himself than he had since being arrested. Finally he was sleeping entire nights through. He told a psychologist he didn't think he needed any more monthly therapy. In his medical records his diagnosis was changed from depression to dysthymic disorder. "Friendly and cooperative, rather subdued," the psychologist noted in Willie's chart. "He explained that he is actually feeling better now that he is housed at a camp near his family."

A month later Willie learned that district court had finally denied his petition for habeas corpus. It had taken them twenty months.

Soon his colds returned. Nurses prescribed him Robitussin. When this didn't help they put him on amoxicillin, and also theophylline, in case it was bronchitis. Then they put him on Rhinatate, for cold and flu symptoms. Then Organidin, a decongestant; then Drixoral, in case it was allergies. In May they ordered a chest X-ray, which turned up normal. Whatever illness he had lasted into winter, when finally Cleveland County placed him under medical observation. But after twenty-eight hours there he'd neither improved nor worsened, so nurses returned him to his block. From there he asked them for a spare pair of thermal underwear; he owned only one, and when he removed it to wash laundry he often got chills and was overcome by coughing fits. Would nurses write him a note for another?

Despite the illness he took a job as a library clerk. From eight to eleven in the morning, then again after lunch, he restocked books, signed them in and out to inmates, dusted shelves and tables. He discovered he liked this better even than breakfast shifts in the kitchen, because it was so quiet. Often he had the library to himself, his favorite part of the job. Besides medical observation, and the one time he'd been placed in segregation, for drinking buck, he'd never been apart from other inmates like this, hadn't found anyplace in prison so peaceful and still.

Now that every court he knew had denied his petitions for habeas corpus, he turned his attention elsewhere. If no one would grant his appeals, he wanted the next best thing, which was minimum custody. From there he knew he might be paroled. In the solitude of the library he reread his conviction and sentence, and realized one had been filed incorrectly. He'd been convicted of first-degree rape, which corresponded to a class B life sentence. But for some reason the judge had assigned him a class A life sentence, normally reserved for capital murder cases. This made him forever ineligible for parole. He wrote to the Newton courthouse, where he'd been tried, to find out why and whether they could fix it, but Newton wrote back to tell him they couldn't. Even more confused, he wrote to the parole commission. "If its not supose to be a class A why can't the court change it," he wanted to know. "They tell me here the Clerk of Court should be able to change it since it supose to be a class B anyway." The parole commission lacked authority to change or commute his sentence, they replied. Exasperated, he found another jailhouse lawyer, who told him the only way to amend a sentence was through the governor. Then he asked his case manager, who suggested he try writing to Ed de Torres. Like Willie, his case manager didn't fully understand the distinction between class A and class B sentences, but he agreed it looked like Willie had been assigned the wrong one. He helped Willie draft a letter to the governor and enclosed it in a note to de Torres.

When he received Willie's letter, de Torres reexamined his case file, and saw that Willie was right. Back in 1988, when Judge Kenneth Griffin had consolidated Willie's two sentences, he'd made a clerical error. Today Griffin no longer served on the bench, so de Torres phoned the clerk of court to learn how the error could be amended. The clerk told him he needed something called a motion to amend the judgment and commitment order, signed by a superior court judge in Catawba County. This didn't need to be the same judge who had made the error. So de Torres drafted the motion and mailed it, along with an explanation and a stamped, self-addressed envelope, so the judge simply could sign the order and return it. As soon as the judge had done this, de Torres would forward it to the Department of Correction, he promised Willie, so the DOC could update its records and Willie would recover his chance at parole. "I will do this at no charge to you. If I can help you on any further appeals, let me know. Good luck."

In early January 1994, the same day nurses released Willie from medical observation, a superior court judge approved de Torres's motion, and ordered that Willie's sentence be amended.

Willie, meanwhile, wrote to the governor, to ask that he be considered for clemency. "I am not guilty of these crimes," he promised. "The fingerprints did not match my prints...Sir the Due Process forbids the judge from relying on materially false or unreliable information." In the same envelope he enclosed copies of the 1988 affidavits de Torres had gotten from Betty and Carolyn Shuford, Rachel and Richard Wilson, Les Robinson, and Brenda Smith.

To help Willie's chances, de Torres agreed to add a letter on his behalf, free of charge, to accompany Willie's own.

> Dear Governor Hunt,
>
> I was the attorney who represented Mr. Grimes. Throughout his trial, Mr. Grimes maintained his innocence of this crime. I am convinced that Mr. Grimes is innocent of the charges against him, and that he was convicted only because of the nature of the crime of rape and the sympathy towards an aged victim.
>
> Mr. Grimes is a gentle, mild-mannered and soft-spoken older man, and his character does not represent him as a man who is capable of such a crime as rape. It is clear to all who know him that he just could not have committed this crime, and had no previous record for violence.

In fact, "the trial disclosed no physical evidence that directly tied Mr. Grimes to this crime," de Torres pointed out, and "witness affidavits and testimony at trial clearly show that Mr. Grimes was at the home of Rachel Wilson during the hour in question."

> In this case justice and fairness failed, and an innocent man was wrongfully convicted. Mr. Willie James Grimes has been incarcerated since October 28, 1987 and I urge you to take a close look at this case and grant the petition for clemency on

behalf of Mr. Grimes in the interest of justice. I wholeheartedly feel that the State of North Carolina has nothing to fear from the release of Mr. Grimes, and that it can gain by correcting this injustice after nearly seven years of incarceration.

Sincerely,
E. X. de Torres
Attorney at Law

In summer Willie's clemency petition was denied. He wrote to the ACLU, to ask if they could do anything at all to help him. "Unfortunately, the American Civil Liberties Union of North Carolina Legal Foundation is not able to assist you with this matter," read their reply. "We have only one attorney and one paralegal." Because of its "very small budget," the ACLU only considered cases referred to them by a lawyer, or by another organization. Instead, the ACLU suggested Willie try Prisoner Legal Services, which had a larger staff, and whose "primary purpose is to represent prisoners with legal claims," the ACLU promised. It hoped Willie would have better luck there.

16

The Elephant in the Room

No one knew what a back-end solution might look like. It had been hard enough persuading the relevant authorities to adopt ID reform. Now to revisit convictions? This would be worse. At least they had air conditioning, one commissioner joked; it was barely eleven in the morning on a Friday in May 2004, and the temperature outside the bar center already soared near eighty.

Different states offered different procedures, but an inmate in North Carolina had four available routes out of prison, and there were problems with all of them. First was a direct appeal, which didn't consider new evidence and, even if it succeeded, provided only a retrial. Second was habeas corpus, in federal court, which didn't consider new evidence, either, since it was designed to remedy constitutional violations. Third was clemency from the governor, which, for political reasons, was granted rarely. Fourth, and by far the most common, was a motion for appropriate relief.

MARs considered a wider range of conditions than any other appeal, including certain bureaucratic errors—if "the trial court lacked jurisdiction," for example—as well as a discovery of new evidence. It also offered a wider array of potential outcomes: a new sentence, a new trial, even a dismissal of charges. But all this had caused a different problem. Nearly every inmate statewide filed at least one MAR claim, so the courts were inundated with them. Even a well-meaning judge could read only so many before he grew skeptical and cursory. And the huge majority of MARs were easy for him to deny, since, despite the range of grievances MARs considered, the burden for proving any one of them was steep. To count as new evidence, for example, a particular fact had to be "unknown or unavailable to the defendant at the time of trial." If a fact *had* been available at trial, then it did not count as new evidence, even if jurors had never seen it. If the fact passed this hurdle, an inmate still had to prove that his new evidence demonstrated "prejudice...by a preponderance of the evidence," or that rejecting his claim would "result in a fundamental miscarriage of justice." This meant a situation where "no reasonable juror would have found the defendant guilty." It was a high standard. Terence Garner had filed three MARs before he was finally exonerated, in 2002; Charles Munsey had filed four before his death in 1999. An exoneree from 2004, Darryl Hunt, had filed eleven.

Even if an MAR succeeded, the most it could offer an inmate was acquittal, another commissioner mentioned. This was a court's way of saying, *We no longer find you guilty of the crime we once found you guilty of.* If commissioners were acknowledging this was possible, for an inmate to be wrongly convicted, wasn't that a paltry gesture? The inmate's guilt had been a finding of law. It wasn't enough to now find him *not guilty.* The law ought to find him *innocent.* Those were different, both legally and in principle.

Which meant an overhaul of the MAR statute, nearly everyone agreed. But how to do *that?* They'd just said the problem was twofold. On the one hand, an MAR's criteria were too narrow. There were too many circumstances it didn't account for. On the other hand, its criteria were also too broad. It allowed too many nonsense claims. The process had to be quicker, but it also had to be more sensitive. No one saw a way to do this. How was it possible to rule on motions both faster *and* more carefully?

Were they pursuing the wrong strategy? one commissioner wondered. The fact was, MARs were procedural. They'd never been designed for innocence claims. Maybe what they were trying *was* impossible. Maybe what they needed was some new, separate process—not to replace the MAR but to function alongside it, for innocence claims exclusively.

* * *

To learn about the possibilities, in June Chris invited David Kyle to join the commission at the bar center in Cary, a considerable trip from where Kyle lived in England. A former British prosecutor, Kyle now worked at something called the Criminal Cases Review Commission, an independent body in the United Kingdom that reviewed and investigated potential wrongful verdicts. Established by Parliament a decade earlier, today the CCRC had its own budget and fourteen salaried members, all of whom had been recommended by the prime minister, then appointed by the queen, to staggered three-year terms. There they could subpoena police or prosecutorial files in cases where new evidence had emerged, or where attorneys intended a new argument. The CCRC could then refer valid claims to nearby appeals courts, which, given enough evidence, could overturn convictions.

Kyle spoke to a full room. By now the commission roster had swelled to more than thirty invited members, each of whom saw plainly what Kyle was proposing: an independent body, separate from MARs, grounded in inquisitorial rather than adversarial review— a collaborative model, not a competitive one, a philosophy more common in Europe than here.

But how would a model like this work in North Carolina? Over four hours that day, then three more in August, commissioners listed every concern and question they could think of. Frivolous claims had flooded the MAR process; what made anyone think they wouldn't flood some new process, too? And who would serve on an American version of the CCRC? Who would appoint these people, and for how long? What guarantee did anyone have that such an appointment process would work fairly?

Each constituency could appoint its own representative, someone suggested.

But how would people appointed this way behave once they got there? Wouldn't they feel beholden to whoever had sent them? Wouldn't someone who represented prosecutors feel pressure to uphold convictions? Wouldn't someone who represented defense attorneys feel similar pressure to topple them?

Representative was the wrong word entirely, another commissioner offered. As soon as she arrived, a person in this position would need to be loyal to the facts, not to her colleagues. If she couldn't evaluate a verdict empirically, there was no reason for her to be there.

Perhaps members could be appointed by an independent third party, rather than by constituencies, another commissioner proposed.

But who would *that* be? The governor? The Speaker of the House? And once members were appointed, what would qualify a case for review? How, for that matter, would investigators review it? To review the wrong cases was a waste of resources, but it was also a problem for another reason: appeals were important, but so was closure. The courts couldn't be endlessly recursive. At some point, a verdict had to be final. "A system of justice is about resolving disputes," Tom Ross, the former superior court judge, pointed out. "If there's no end to those disputes, then we're not doing our jobs." A typewritten list of this and other obstacles ran for twelve single-spaced pages, in ten-point font, until, halfway down the last page, someone finally wrote, "Enough, already!"

To regard a CCRC model seriously, commissioners needed two things, the group decided at last. The first was a high threshold for what counted as a credible claim. A felon had to provide more than his word. He needed additional evidence, beyond what had been presented at trial. Second, his claim had to be for complete, literal innocence, not just for reduced culpability or a lesser sentence.

To guarantee both of these, commissioners invented a pair of novel requirements. To apply to this new body in the first place, an inmate had to agree to absolute transparency. This meant waiving every one of his constitutional protections and privileges, including his Fifth Amendment right against self-incrimination, his attorney-client privilege, and the privacy of anything relevant he'd ever told his doctor, priest, or spouse. Second, any evidence at all that investigators uncovered, they would be entitled to act on—no matter what it proved, no matter what case it related to. If an inmate was claiming he was innocent of murder, he'd better not have confessed otherwise to his therapist. And he'd better not have committed any *other* crimes. If he'd done either, investigators would learn of it and, because it counted as new evidence, would forward the information to police.

Neither requirement thrilled defense attorneys, who nonetheless agreed both were necessary. "Look, we're creating something new," Rosen later told colleagues who phoned him to complain. "*Completely* new. We can't do that and also keep all the rules from before. We'd just have another MAR." Besides, the commission hadn't been founded on behalf of the guilty. Rosen's job wasn't to shield clients like that, at least not during commission meetings. He and Newman and Coleman were focused on *innocent* clients.

Once investigators accepted a claim, they would be uniquely empowered to pursue it, commissioners decided. If they were going to reopen cases, they would need the authority to do this correctly—to subpoena witnesses and evidence, to direct forensic tests and searches, to petition for affidavits and court orders, to administer their own oaths. After all that, if investigators still believed an inmate credible, they would bring his case to a hearing. Some verdict would be necessary, and then it would proceed to a panel of judges. There the entire case, including all its new evidence, would be argued anew, and judges would render a final decision.

No one knew exactly how a case would proceed from the hearing to the panel. Clearly some threshold would need to be met, but commissioners couldn't agree on what it was. That an inmate was "more likely innocent than not"? That he was innocent "beyond a reasonable doubt"? And what about the panel of judges? What requirements would need to be met *there*? For that matter, how many judges were they talking about? And how many of these would need to agree the threshold had been met? Every one of them? A majority? Would their votes be public or confidential?

Unable to agree, they tabled these questions for later. Still, after a year discussing back-end solutions, look how far they'd come, commissioners murmured. Already they'd invented an entirely new model. In a few more meetings, it would be simple enough to complete. This wouldn't be so hard, commissioners didn't think, compared to what they'd accomplished already. The most challenging obstacles were behind them. All that remained were details.

They were wrong.

Two years earlier, shortly after Beverly Lake had summoned fifteen of his colleagues to the first meeting of his tentative commission, Chris had made a phone call of her own—to Donna Pygott, of the North Carolina Victim Assistance Network. NCVAN was the state's largest advocacy organization for crime victims, an influential group in local politics that had long opposed any legal reforms that, interpreted narrowly, made criminals any harder to catch or punish. It was easy to predict what NCVAN would think of the commission's proposal to revisit convictions, so Chris wanted to soften the ground before Pygott heard about the plan elsewhere. She invited Pygott to lunch. Both women happened to share backgrounds in accounting—Chris at Northern Telecom, and Pygott at various nonprofits—so for several minutes, the two swapped industry stories. Then Chris broached why she had phoned. How did Pygott think NCVAN would respond to the commission's efforts?

Not at all well, Pygott answered. The people she represented had been victims of crimes. Some of those crimes were unspeakable; Pygott still shuddered when she thought about them. The point of NCVAN was to support people like these, to walk them through the court process and help them heal in the aftermath of tragedy. The courts as they stood were often the only thing a victim felt he or she could rely on. And NCVAN was often the only access victims had to someone who understood them, as well as their only advocate with lawyers or police or in the legislature. In certain jurisdictions, no one even kept a crime victim informed about his or her assailant's trial. Could Chris believe that? Pygott was wary of any legislation that trampled on people like these, or that made convicting perpetrators any harder. The last thing a crime victim wanted to hear was that the person who'd caused such harm would never be brought to justice.

"I understand all that," Chris told her, nodding. "But I need you to consider something. Let's think about death row. Those people are scheduled to be executed. Do you believe it's possible that one of them, a person on death row, could be innocent?"

Pygott hadn't thought much about this.

She wasn't asking rhetorically, Chris insisted. She really wanted to know. "Is it possible?"

On her fingers, Pygott ticked off every stage a felon had to pass through before he was convicted. A police investigation; formal charges; a preliminary hearing and indictment; a jury trial, where he had a lawyer; appeals. To be found guilty at each of these hurdles, and still be innocent? "It would have to be near impossible," she told Chris.

"Define *near impossible*," Chris urged. "Because *near impossible* means *someone* on death row *could* be innocent. The only way we know *nobody* there is innocent is if it's fully, literally impossible."

Pygott considered this. "Well, no," she finally conceded. She couldn't say it was *literally* impossible.

Chris nodded again. "That's all we're saying."

When she left lunch, Pygott phoned the board of directors at NCVAN to let them know what was happening. Not one of them was pleased. The very existence of Lake's commission sent a message they opposed: that the criminal justice system in North Carolina was flawed. This was the system their constituents relied on! Why had Pygott afforded Chris Mumma any credibility at all? Why had she agreed to lunch, and, once she did, why hadn't she answered *yes*? Yes, it *was* impossible for a person on death row to be innocent. The courts hardly rushed to verdicts. More than one NCVAN board member had experienced firsthand all their bureaucratic foot-dragging. A person didn't make it through that entire process and end up on death row accidentally. It happened because he was guilty.

Nevertheless, if the commission was going to exist—and Lake had gone ahead and formed it, without their blessing—then NCVAN wanted someone at all its meetings, to report back and make sure the group didn't do anything reckless.

After her lunch with Chris, Donna Pygott thus began attending commission meetings, often bringing a crime victim along to sit quietly with her in the rear. Personally, she felt ambivalent. She had a responsibility to NCVAN, whose mission she believed in. Victims were the only ones in a criminal situation who'd gotten there involuntarily, Pygott knew. Everyone else had come by choice: the criminal, the police officer, the lawyer, the judge. Only victims had been put there without any say.

But the question Chris had asked still tugged at her. Was it literally impossible that a convict might be innocent? *No,* she still thought. *It isn't impossible.*

NCVAN had never been thrilled with the commission's eye-witness-ID reforms, but this proposal to revisit trial verdicts distressed them even more. The commission was hoping to free criminals. It planned to return felons to the streets. And it was reneging on the promise of closure that courts made to victims. Pygott's home phone began ringing: Why was she wasting taxpayer dollars to scuttle their own judicial system? How many of those same dollars was anyone spending on victims? Didn't Pygott understand why trials existed, and what harm this could do to them? How had she allowed any of this?

To all these complaints, commissioners themselves felt sympathetic. To a point. Beneath NCVAN's valid concerns lay another, subtler reason for its opposition, more than one commissioner suspected: not only anxiety that closure might unravel, or that criminals might be freed, but also an unspoken defensiveness. Say a felon turned out to be innocent. What did that *mean?* Suddenly there were *two* victims, weren't there? And what if one had testified against the other? What did *that* mean? Didn't it blemish her? Didn't it change things?

The psychology of all this was complicated. No one wanted to trivialize the experience of victims, many of whom had lived through horror. But NCVAN had chosen an unnuanced view toward an issue that was provably nuanced. And Chris could extend only so much sympathy toward a person who refused to extend sympathy toward others.

No one exemplified this more vividly than Jennifer Thompson. After Ronald Cotton was exonerated, Jennifer, obviously still a victim, had instantly become something else, too. It was her, wasn't it, who'd put Cotton behind bars? Wasn't that her fault? Strangers on the Internet had sent her death threats. In a sense, this made her precisely the sort of victim NCVAN existed to support. Except that Jennifer had begun advocating for reform, which placed her counter to NCVAN's interests, so that many in that group felt she'd effectively changed sides. Now Jennifer worked for defense attorneys; now Jennifer was shielding criminals. And, more simply, now Jennifer symbolized what many at NCVAN continued denying categorically. Many victims still insisted what Donna Pygott had never felt able to, that the chances any convict was innocent were zero. But it was harder to insist on this when Jennifer was around, harder to square one of these facts with the other. Though she was a gifted public speaker, Jennifer had never once been invited to present to a victims' organization. One time she'd been heckled from the audience: "Do you have any idea what you're doing to the victims?" In more than a year of commission meetings, she and Pygott had barely said a word to each other. Pygott's colleagues, seated with her in the rear, hadn't acknowledged Jennifer at all.

Friction between victims and the commissioners had menaced from the start, but finally Dick Adams had heard enough. It was Adams who had founded NCVAN, two decades earlier, after his own son was murdered during a robbery. Periodically he'd spoken up at commission meetings to protest what he regarded as its abandonment of victims. This prospect of reopening cases exasperated him. Now he stood up. The commission had forgotten why the courts were even in place, he nearly shouted. Didn't they know? The courts existed to provide justice for victims—

Before he could finish, Beverly Lake interrupted him. "An innocent person who is in prison *is* a victim," Lake said.

17

Does Not Admit to Crime

Late one afternoon in February 1995, a guard approached him in the yard at Cleveland County Correctional. It had been a mild day but now the temperature was falling. Behind the guard trailed three inmates, and abruptly Willie realized that each owed him repayment on a loan. What were they doing with Sergeant Orsky? He never collected more than a single loan at a time—this was too risky, since camp rules forbade inmates to hold more than thirty dollars, and multiple loans would put him over.

But now Orsky ordered all three inmates to pay him. Reluctantly, each man handed Willie his twenty-five dollars. Then Orsky, looking on, announced he had no choice but to search Willie. In addition to the seventy-five dollars, he found eighty-eight cents in Willie's pockets. This meant he had no choice but to search Willie's locker, Orsky said. There he found another three dollars and twenty-three cents. "Inmate Willie Grimes is in violation of DOC prison policy of possessing funds in a form other than authorized," he scolded in a note in Willie's file. "Due to the amount of funds involved staff feels subject should be removed from his assignment pending disciplinary action."

Because of the violation—D10, unauthorized fund—administrators removed him from his job in the library. Then they transferred him to Craggy Correctional, out in Asheville, eighty miles west. A month later, without explanation, he was transferred to Central; three days after that, he was transferred back to Craggy. There he came down with the first of two ear infections. The entire right half of his skull throbbed, and he had trouble eating. "My ear infection is hurting real bad like I have not took any thing for it," he wrote on a sick-call request, though he'd tried eardrops and an antibiotic. Now he was out of both. "I think that I needs to see the doctor! I am <u>hurting</u>."

Near the end of his first summer at Craggy he volunteered for DART, a drug and alcohol recovery treatment program; he'd never used drugs, but his case manager had told him the more programs he completed, the more likely he was to be promoted to minimum custody. In a brochure he read the goals of DART were "breaking through denial and admission and ownership of the problem" and "transition from treatment to recovery." Willie signed up. In his final report the following autumn, his DART counselor remarked that Willie had "done very well," and invited him to serve as a peer counselor in the future. Willie declined. Three days earlier he'd asked for a transfer back to Shelby, and since the request had been approved, he doubted he'd remain at Craggy long enough to be a counselor. He turned out to be wrong about this; it would be more than a year before he was transferred. While he waited, he took a job in the laundry, then as a janitor.

In spring he was promoted to canteen operator. This ranked among the most important jobs on any camp, along with head cook. The canteen was part supermarket, part drugstore, and only a single inmate operated its window, meaning others had to go through him for noodles or cough drops or Diet Coke. But in the middle of a shift that June, loudspeakers ordered Willie to the guards' office. There had been a tragedy in his family, the sergeant told him, and he ought to call his sister Gladys. His brother John Thomas—the oldest of his half siblings, from Mozella's first marriage—had died.

JT had lived to seventy-one. His funeral was planned for First Baptist Church, in Lawndale, this coming Wednesday, Gladys told him over the phone. Because this was an hour and twenty minutes east of Craggy, she'd lobbied prison administrators for six hours of temporary leave, beginning that noon. The form they'd signed to grant his leave also listed his conditions: "Inmate will be accompanied by two (2) armed correctional officers and will be restrained to one officer at any time outside the security vehicle."

First Baptist Church sat in a mostly black section of Lawndale, but the guards Craggy assigned were both white. To transport him they put Willie in handcuffs and leg shackles, each threaded heavily to a waist chain. He wore an ill-fitting navy suit and black loafers the prison had lent him from its donated collection. After parking their cruiser, the guards escorted him by his elbows into the church, to sit in a rear pew. Up front stood his remaining siblings—Robert Lee, Samuel Lee, Gladys, and Cliff Jr.—who stepped as near as they dared to say hello. He saw his childhood friend Thomas Hill, too, beside other familiar faces from Lawndale, but guards let him speak with no one but family. To see everyone like this felt better than a prison visit, and also worse—to be so near them, so many at once, and still feel so distant. As soon as the service ended guards led him back to their cruiser and set off back for Craggy.

A few days later he was closing the canteen window at the end of a shift when one of Craggy's administrators, its head programmer, appeared at the counter.

Fetch me something, will you? the programmer asked, reaching for his wallet.

Willie shook his head apologetically. The canteen had already closed, so he wasn't allowed to wait on anyone.

Don't worry about that.

He was sorry, Willie repeated. His supervisor had just told him not to wait on anyone once the window was closed. He couldn't.

The programmer stared at him incredulously. Then he spun and marched away.

Later that week Willie's bunk was chosen for a shakedown. This was an excuse for guards to upturn all an inmate's belongings—supposedly in search of drugs or weapons, though they rarely found either. Normally a shakedown exposed nothing more than paper clips, rubber bands, or hardcover books. Depending on the guard, any of these could be violations. In Willie's bunk a guard found a spare radio, in addition to the one Willie carried around with him. He'd brought this spare from Cleveland County, where inmates had been allowed two. Here at Craggy, inmates were allowed only one, the guard announced. A spare radio was a violation. He flipped open its battery cover and then a wad of bills was in his hands.

What's this? he demanded. You hiding fifty dollars?

Willie shook his head, startled. He had no idea where the bills had come from.

You been hiding money?

I never saw that fifty dollars before, Willie insisted.

Arms wide, the guard commanded him. He patted Willie down and discovered eight more dollars in his pockets.

That was his, Willie agreed. He was allowed to have eight dollars. But he'd never put anything inside his radio.

Can't be hiding money, the guard scolded him. Hide money, you lose privileges. He pocketed the fifty-eight dollars and snatched the spare radio, leaving the rest of Willie's things strewn across the floor. Then he revoked Willie's phone privileges for two weeks and assigned him fifteen hours of extra duty. These Willie could work off by washing dishes.

He was demoted from canteen operator back to assistant cook, then to baker. When he came up again for custody review, his case manager noticed the violation had added five points to his record; this made him ineligible for minimum custody, even if he were within sixty months of his release date, which he still wasn't.

When he completed the extra duty hours he asked again to be transferred nearer to Lawndale. More than a year had passed after his first request, which had been approved, but he'd been backlogged ever since. Two weeks before Thanksgiving, the request was approved again. As he gathered his few belongings that morning to bring with him on the Goose, the head programmer appeared suddenly at his bunk. "A lot of jobs, they go to a man's head," he remarked, peering around Willie's cell. This was too bad, he added. "Makes them do crazy things." He stared at Willie. Then he turned and was gone.

By the afternoon Willie was at Marion Correctional, nearly forty miles east.

"I have had long johns on every camp I been on to keep me from getting sick," he wrote on a sick call request five days after arriving, "plus I don't have a jacket or cap here; they took them." Over the next six weeks Marion pinballed him between five different bunks. Then, the day before New Year's Eve, less than two months since he'd arrived, he was transferred right back to Craggy.

Since meeting Bryan Garner on the benches on the yard at Harnett, each time Willie was transferred from one prison to another, the former congregation phoned ahead to the next, so a new Bible teacher could visit him as soon as he arrived. In all the transfers he'd lost track of Bryan, whom he'd heard had been paroled early for good behavior. Still, at Sampson and Vance, then Cleveland County and Craggy and Marion, there were always new Witnesses to teach him, in addition to the Scripture he was reading on his own. Otherwise he noticed that guards and inmates regarded him with vague suspicion. He was part of a cult, they told him, and tried to talk him out of it. They'd heard Witnesses didn't salute the flag, which meant they were Communists. They'd heard Witnesses didn't celebrate Christmas.

No one he'd met was a Communist. It was true they didn't celebrate Christmas, but for good reason—according to Scripture, the day men had assigned the holiday was all wrong. The Bible itself provided no date for Jesus's birth, but it *did* mention that, during the same season, "there were also in the same region shepherds living out of doors and keeping watch in the night over their flocks." Did this make any sense in the cold of a Bethlehem winter? No. So Witnesses had chosen to ignore it.

Nonetheless, there *were* reasons that Witnesses could be hard to get along with, even for Willie, and these saddened him. The removal of Jehovah's name from Scripture they saw as one instance of a broader, hazardous migration away from the literal truth of the Bible, a migration they took seriously. Other religions had strayed, they believed, and it was up to Witnesses to correct them. They disapproved of preachers, ministers, rabbis, monks, all titles men had invented to govern who could be nearest to God. They disapproved of a religion like Lutheranism, named literally after a man. Who were Lutherans really worshipping? In His very first commandment, Jehovah had said to worship no god but Him.

For these reasons, a Witness's faith meant to some degree his opposition to any other. Theoretically this principle applied to most anyone, but it applied to Witnesses more literally than most. It was even how a Witness asked whether a stranger shared his religion: Not "Are you a Jehovah's Witness?" but "Do you know the Truth?" Different Witnesses practiced this habit with varying amounts of humility and tact. Willie understood how, in the wrong combination, it might turn a stranger away.

Privately he doubted one or two of his teachers' lessons. Most Witnesses resisted close friendships with those outside the religion, but Willie couldn't see any sense in this. How could a Witness share Jehovah's word, as He had bid them, without interacting daily with nonbelievers? Jesus Himself had been kind to prostitutes and criminals. To spurn another person conflicted with everything Jehovah had taught him. The less judgmental his thoughts, the more faithful he felt. So many of the people who'd been good to him in his life—his friends from Douglas High, most of the Shufords—weren't Witnesses. Neither was Mozella or any of his siblings.

Witnesses had simply gotten that part wrong, Willie decided. A good person was a good person, regardless of what he called Jehovah. Scripture said so. No one would persuade him otherwise.

He began struggling to urinate. Often he felt the urge to go but couldn't, for as long as ten minutes. Nurses examined his prostate and found it tender and enlarged; a screen for prostate cancer returned negative. During a follow-up a few weeks later, a doctor decided he had prostatitis, a type of inflammation. He prescribed Willie an antibiotic, and something else called Hytrin. He lost more

than ten pounds in two weeks. Nurses prescribed him another antibiotic. In late summer they transferred him to Central Prison, for
further examination; by then he'd lost another fifteen pounds.

A week before the start of autumn he was transferred back to
Craggy. By October he'd gained back the weight he'd lost, but now
his recovered health allowed him time to think, which was a problem. He could while away only so many hours walking loops around
the Craggy yard, and the remainder he inevitably filled by ruminat-
ing on his case. He simply had no idea what to do. The realization
made him tremble. If his appeals were used up, and he was never
promoted to minimum security, and he never got work release or
parole, then he was certain to die in prison. His siblings and a few
close friends knew the truth, but otherwise that would die with him.
No one else would remember him at all, and if they did, they would
remember him a rapist.

His sleep was fitful, then ceased almost altogether. At least once a
week, exhausted and despondent, he was moved suddenly to tears.
One afternoon another inmate asked to borrow his headphones,
which Willie had purchased from the canteen, and Willie agreed.
Then the inmate turned unexpectedly and jogged away. When Willie
caught up, the inmate insisted the headphones were his.

But I just lent you those, Willie protested.

Nope, the inmate replied. These headphones always been mine.

Sputtering, Willie complained to a guard, who returned the headphones to him. The following afternoon, though, a different guard
appeared and snatched them from him again. Heard you tried to
steal these, he told Willie.

Again he asked for a transfer nearer to Lawndale, and was denied.
To keep himself occupied, and to prevent the piling up of empty
hours, he volunteered for double shifts at the canteen, where Craggy
had reinstalled him after his brief stay at Marion. But the job was
harder than he remembered. Inmates often made rude customers; in
the past this had never bothered him, but now he grew instantly, con-
vulsively angry. Sometimes he boiled over even before registering

why. Afterward he felt overcome with guilt. He'd invested so much in becoming a new kind of person, and now he could feel himself unspooling, like yarn. He knew Jehovah would consider him a failure. He asked to leave his position at the canteen window and take a job in the warehouse instead, loading and unloading merchandise out back. There he wouldn't need to interact with other inmates. Then he filled out a request for mental-health services.

The psychologist he met noticed Willie made "poor eye contact," and seemed to hold a "low self image." His trouble sleeping the psychologist attributed to "anxiety regarding his placement in the center of the prison dormitory. He tells me that he has always been most comfortable in prison either in a cell or at the corners of the dormitory where he is not surrounded by others. He has asked to be moved to a corner bed assignment...A related factor is that he has been losing weight and nursing staff have ruled out any medical reason for this." He referred Willie to a psychiatrist.

"Willie continues to be slow and deliberate in his movements, speech, and he shows poor eye contact," the psychiatrist observed after Thanksgiving. "I suspect he is a quiet, shy person and he displays this, but I also detect the presence of a depressed mood." Willie still wasn't sleeping well, but a new antidepressant, Paxil, had calmed him. "Overall, he seems to be doing better. He has decided that he does not want to be at the window at the canteen. He feels that it is less stressful working in the back."

He made it off the backlog to Cleveland County, but stayed there less than a week before being shipped to Lincoln, twenty miles northeast. He didn't understand this; after being the last to arrive at Cleveland County, then he'd been the first to leave. He asked his new case manager why this had happened, but his case manager had no idea. Still, Lincoln was an improvement, Willie decided—only a thirty-minute drive from Lawndale, a third of what Craggy had been. He asked for a job in either the rear of the canteen or the kitchen. "Appears to be easygoing and presented good attitude," the case manager wrote in his file.

He met with a psychologist, who determined he was doing better now that he was nearer his home, and could receive visits. "He presented w/ a broad affect + spontaneous smiling."

In 1997 his sister Gladys found a lawyer out of Greensboro, who agreed to look over Willie's case for a fee of $1,400. So she paid him and forwarded her brother's transcript, which the lawyer read before agreeing to take on the case for another $2,800. Again she paid. Now every time she called she got his receptionist, who told her the lawyer couldn't discuss the case with anyone but Willie, since Willie was his client. From her brother's letters, however, Gladys knew the lawyer wasn't discussing the case with him, either. For months the two of them waited, into the new year. Then Gladys got a letter from the firm with news that the lawyer had been disbarred. Another partner in his office was willing to take on Willie's case, for a new fee. Gladys refused. The lawyer hadn't accomplished a thing, so she wasn't about to pay some partner of his simply so *he* wouldn't accomplish a thing, either. More than four thousand dollars was gone, and her brother was back to where he'd started.

In fact, this wasn't quite true. Before the lawyer was disbarred, he'd filed a motion for appropriate relief on Willie's behalf, alleging ineffective assistance of counsel. He simply had never told Willie or Gladys about the filing. This oversight turned out not to matter. In July 1998, the MAR was denied.

Willie had spent a decade in prison.

His case manager asked him once more if he wanted to serve as a peer counselor in the DART program. This time he agreed. Since now he was near Lawndale again, he hoped to remain at Lincoln for as long as he could, and he liked the idea of helping other inmates even a fraction as much as Jehovah had helped him. A DART classroom held twenty or so students, two teachers, and two inmate counselors, who passed around handouts and shared their own experiences. Willie guessed inmates might listen to him before some teacher coming in from the outside, so in class he explained as best he could how drugs harmed a person's body and how he personally had learned to avoid them. When the program was through he met again with his case manager, who decided Willie had done so well in DART he would refer him to a second program, called SOAR, specifically for sex offenders. Enrolling was the first step toward promotion to minimum custody, then parole. To be eligible, however, Willie needed to show he had taken responsibility for his crime, which he could do by signing a form expressing remorse for the rape he'd committed. Willie declined. He hadn't committed any rape, he pointed out. A staff psychologist in turn filled out a form rejecting Willie from the program.

SEX OFFENDER ACCOUNTABILITY AND RESPONSIBILITY PROGRAM CLINICAL ASSESSMENT REPORT

Directions: This report is to be completed by a designated member of the referring area/Institution's mental health staff after interviewing the inmate being referred.

Inmate's Name: _Willie Grimes_   Inmate #: _0158046_
Location: _Lincoln_   Date of Report: _5 – 29 – 98_
Report Completed By: _Melanie Morgan, MA_

1. Desire to Participate: ✓ Low ___ Moderate ___ High
2. Intellectual level: ___ MR ✓ Borderline ___ Normal ___ Above Normal
3. History of psychosis: ___ Yes ✓ No
   Admits to crime: ___ Yes ✓ No
4. Accepts personal responsibility for crime: ___ Yes ✓ No
5. Empathy for victim: ✓ Low ___ Moderate ___ High

6. Has received treatment for sexual offense in the past.
   ____ Yes   ✓ No   Comments: _____
   _____

7. Is currently participating in treatment for sex offense.
   ____ Yes   ✓ No   Comments: —————————————————
   _____

8. Has participated in mental health treatment or counseling in
   the past.
   ____ Yes   ✓ No   Comments: —————————————
   _____

9. Is this person sufficiently stable to handle an intensive confron-
   tational program?
   ✓ Yes   ____ No

10. Do you recommend this inmate be accepted in the SOAR program?
    ✓ No   ____ Some Misgivings
    ____ Recommended ____ Strongly Recommended
    Comments: _____ *Does not admit to crime.* _____
    _____

Release: I do not wish to be considered for treatment in the
SOAR Program at this time. If I wish to be considered in the
future, I understand that I can contact any mental health staff
with that request.

Inmate Signature: _*Willie j. Grimes*_ Date: _5/29/98_

18

An Extraordinary Procedure

Before and after meetings, splitting her time between the center and her home office, Chris wrote a preliminary draft of legislation, anticipating the commission would spend the next several months amending it. She e-mailed her draft to fellow commissioners and arrived optimistically at the bar center in January 2005, with spare copies in her briefcase.

But she never had a chance to bring them out. Instead, Colon Willoughby spoke up. For more than twenty years, Willoughby, a Democrat, had been the district attorney there in Wake County; before that, he'd served as president of its local Academy of Criminal Trial Lawyers, then as president of the statewide conference of DAs, and then on the board of directors of the National District Attorneys Association. Meanwhile he'd been a member of the commission from its very beginning at Chris's house. Already the law provided safeguards against wrongful convictions, Willoughby pointed out. He agreed with the others that MARs were flawed. He just didn't see how this premise had led them to abandon the process entirely. Why hadn't the commission tried at all to *improve* MARs, if everyone agreed they needed to be? Wasn't that a better idea?

Anyway, commissioners had never voted on this, Willoughby added. They'd voted initially only on whether to take up the issue at all, not on this new model, which undermined the whole nature of their adversarial system—the premise, he reminded them, of American jurisprudence in the first place. Consider the message that would send. They might as well hang a banner saying the justice system couldn't be trusted.

Mel Chilton agreed with Willoughby. Chilton had replaced Donna Pygott as the newest director of NCVAN. Revisiting jury verdicts would do nothing but cast doubt on the system, thereby crippling it, Chilton remarked. Eventually this would make it impossible to convict anyone.

Willoughby and Chilton were right, some commissioners murmured. In fact, their new model might be a terrible idea. Why *hadn't* they discussed MARs more seriously? They all knew what a mess it was to start rethinking jury verdicts, and yet here the commission was, rethinking them. Whose idea had it been to invent a totally foreign procedure? How exactly had they ended up here?

Chris felt dumbfounded. How had they ended up here? *Read the fucking minutes*, she thought. At every meeting she recorded these minutes herself, then e-mailed them to everyone afterward. They'd *had* this conversation, two months earlier, in this exact same room, while seated at these exact same conference tables. *If you people are against revisiting verdicts*, she thought, *let's not revisit this one*.

She felt a flush of anger toward Willoughby, who she believed had opposed this idea from the start, for the same reasons most prosecutors did. A DA's job was to seek convictions, and now he was supposed to help overturn them? That verdict had been his own work, or his colleague's, or his predecessor's. The harm this could do to his reputation was obvious.

In addition to that, DAs, perhaps more than defense attorneys, who regularly filed appeals, were trained to defer to a jury's decision. If twelve men and women had been presented evidence at trial, and determined a man was guilty, then who was anyone to overrule them? The prospect made DAs uneasy. So did calling a man *innocent*, as a finding in a court of law. The term hadn't come up in law school; it didn't appear in their vocabulary. A trial found someone either guilty or not guilty. It didn't find anyone innocent.

Still, all these were poor excuses for protecting a wrong verdict, Chris felt. And even among DAs, Willoughby from the beginning had been most outspoken. Now he was staging a coup, she thought.

While Chris fumed, her colleagues spoke up. No one had thrown this model together hastily, over cocktails, Newman insisted. The commission had been discussing it for months, as everyone in the room well knew. They'd all been present the entire time.

MARs were *not* isolating valid claims of innocence, Coleman added. They'd grown into a bureaucratic nightmare. Commissioners could spend a lifetime disentangling that process, or they could form something better.

If the others wanted, they could put aside the moral argument, Rosen offered. If that didn't compel them enough—and it disappointed him to consider it might not, he admitted—then what about the financial problem? Wrongful convictions, combined with a dysfunctional appeals process, was reckless moral policy, and reckless legal policy, but it was also reckless fiscal policy. Needless prison time, plus needless appeals, plus needless compensation once the inmate was exonerated—all three of those cost taxpayers more than this review model they were proposing.

Finally, Beverly Lake had heard enough. Often Lake was content simply to listen at commission meetings, and sometimes he even let Chris shepherd the proceedings. No longer. "This isn't your meeting to run," he told Willoughby. Then he addressed the room.

It was a mistake to cite the public's trust as a reason to do nothing, Lake declared. That trust had already been harmed; the problem was out there, people knew of it. He didn't see how responsible legislation would make anyone trust the courts less.

That problem was twofold, Lake continued. He hadn't formed the commission solely to free the wrongly convicted. He had also formed it to convict the wrongly free. Every mistaken verdict meant a criminal remained on the streets. A broken appeals process meant he stayed there. This needed to change, and MARs weren't getting it done. *That* was why the review model had gained traction. *That* was how they'd ended up here.

Privately, Lake had been dealing with criticism from Willoughby and others for as long as the commission had existed—not just against its policies but against himself personally, and not only from commissioners but among his closest friends. Those who knew him had once considered him a reliable conservative. Now they felt he'd betrayed them. What was Lake doing, leading a bunch of liberals? For months between meetings, he'd also been phoning reluctant commissioners, persuading them not to abandon the effort. Not once had he asked anyone to temper where he or she stood. He knew this strategy might lead to friction during meetings, but he also believed it was the only way that meetings would continue at all.

And he'd had an especially difficult time with Colon Willoughby. The two men knew each other, but only barely. Nearly from the start, Lake felt he had watched Willoughby obstruct the commission from within, at every opportunity. Even when consensus finally emerged, Willoughby's tactics meant this always took longer. And now Lake himself was under time pressure. By North Carolina law, he faced mandatory retirement at the age of seventy-two. He was seventy-one. His birthday was in eleven months; if he wanted legislation on this new appeals model, that was how long he had to propose it.

Willoughby was right about one thing, Lake granted him; they'd never voted. It was time they did, at least on the concept. If commissioners agreed this model was worth doing, they would know what they had to work on. If not, they would find something else.

One commissioner, from the attorney general's office, voted nay. Three others abstained, among them Mel Chilton from NCVAN.

Everyone else voted yea. Including Colon Willoughby.

The January vote was the turning point Chris had hoped for. For more than seven hours that February, over two separate meetings, commissioners negotiated final details—the first time they'd met more than once in the same month. Because the review body would be essentially judicial, they agreed that the chief justice would appoint its members. It would include seven positions, representing every conceivable perspective on the law, including a prosecutor, a defense attorney, a victims' advocate, at least one judge, and a regular citizen. In a private hearing, this body would determine whether a particular case included "sufficient evidence of factual innocence to merit judicial review." If it did, the case would be forwarded to a panel of judges, who would decide whether there was "clear and convincing evidence of innocence." *That* proceeding would be public, and amounted nearly to a new trial, though with a pair of important differences. At trial, the burden of proof ordinarily fell on the state; a defendant was innocent until proven guilty. At the panel, this would be reversed. The inmate would be guilty until proven innocent. And at trial, obviously, this decision came to a jury. At the panel, three judges would make this decision themselves.

It had taken weeks to agree on language— "sufficient evidence of factual innocence to merit judicial review," "clear and convincing evidence of innocence"—and on a name for the review body: the North Carolina Innocence Inquiry Commission. A synopsis of its purpose had come more easily: "This Article establishes an extraordinary procedure to investigate and determine credible claims of factual innocence," the proposed statute read.

Soon, more compromises. For a case to proceed to the three-judge panel, five of seven IIC members would need to vote this way at a hearing. Then, for an inmate to be exonerated, all three judges on the panel would need to agree.

At last, in March 2005, the commission voted on whether to submit its bill to the general assembly. Two commissioners abstained. Twelve voted nay.

Beverly Lake, Chris Mumma, Rich Rosen, Theresa Newman, Jim Coleman, Jennifer Thompson, Mike Gauldin, Tom Ross, Don Stephens, Bob Orr, and six others voted yea.

"I think whatever we got is going to the General Assembly without any broad base of support from victims, law enforcement, or the district attorneys," Colon Willoughby told the *Raleigh News and Observer* that spring. "Should we be trying to do this fast or should we be trying to do this right?"

Obviously no one opposed justice for the wrongly convicted, unnamed "law enforcement officials" promised the newspaper. Their concern was only that they hadn't been allowed enough time to discuss the issue. "When we introduce this bill, let's make sure we have the support we need," cautioned a representative from the state's bureau of investigation. "I'm afraid at this point we don't."

Other police officials responded more warmly. "I can hold my head up and say I've done what I think is right," Chief Mike Gauldin told reporters.

"It's the right thing to do," added Tom Ross.

Another commissioner, Bill Hart, who worked in the attorney general's office, wrote Chris and the commission an eleven-page open letter explaining his reasons for opposing the IIC bill. When he didn't hear back, he sent a seven-page follow-up. Obviously he was in favor of an improved justice system, and of the improved public trust that would be its result, he wrote. But he didn't see how the IIC would lead to either. A defendant deserved an "open, public trial," which the IIC did not provide. Also, he had financial concerns. Already the courts offered plenty of avenues for someone who'd been wrongly convicted, without some brand-new agency. "In fact, the cases often cited as examples of innocent people wrongly convicted have had their convictions set aside and have been granted new trials or have had their cases dismissed based on claims contained in motions for appropriate relief." Ronald Cotton, Darryl Hunt, Charles Munsey, Terence Garner, James Bernard Parker—all these men had ultimately been freed, or at least offered new trials. Didn't this show the system was working?

"I am in receipt of your memorandum of March 3, 2005, much of which seems to be taken directly from your memorandum of February 17, 2005," Chris finally replied. "I can only assume that you did not think Commission members read or understood your previous memo." In fact, she'd chosen not to respond for the simple reason that several of Hart's concerns had been addressed already at commission meetings, and because she'd noticed that both his letters had been shared publicly, rather than with the commission alone. "Perhaps your most recent memo was actually written for the benefit of a different audience," she suggested. Or perhaps Hart failed to understand what had occurred at the commission's many meetings and votes. As for his suggestion that innocence claims were being handled properly, she found this hard to take seriously. Hunt, Garner, and Munsey had combined for eighteen MARs. Parker had been freed not by court initiative but by investigative reporting by journalists. And to hold up Ronald Cotton as an example of the courts functioning as they were meant to—well, this was hard to fathom. "The distribution of your memorandum to non-members of the Commission has called into question your motivations and your commitment to being a member," Chris wrote in closing. "I would appreciate an explanation."

It never came.

"The bill's prospects are uncertain," read another *News and Observer* article, in April. "Crime victims are opposed and want to study the idea further. Prosecutors support the concept but want changes. Law enforcement officials appear undecided and are conferring with the district attorneys."

That summer, however, at nearly nine on a Thursday evening, the bill passed the House of Representatives, 80 to 23.

The victory had required further compromise: the addition of an eighth position on the IIC, to be held by a county sheriff, and a decision that the chief judge of the court of appeals, not only the chief justice, could appoint its members. The legislature also wanted annual reports, so that representatives could keep abreast of the IIC's progress.

Chris and Lake could live with those concessions, they decided, as long as they meant the bill now could be forwarded on to the state senate, which in turn could codify it into law. This needed to happen by the earliest hours of 2006. By the close of that January, Lake would turn seventy-two. Without him in office, Chris couldn't predict what might happen. The longer the bill remained in limbo, the longer its opponents would have to organize. Chris and Lake needed the legislature to act now, while they had momentum.

The problem was political. Democrats owned a majority in the state senate—and Democrats, Chris knew, were unhappy with Lake. Three years earlier they'd tried remapping local voting districts, a ploy Republicans had challenged, and the case had made it to the state supreme court, which had ruled the plan unconstitutional. The controversy this provoked had ensnared nearly the entire court. In 2001, the state's Academy of Trial Lawyers had named Bob Orr, one of Lake's fellow justices, its appellate judge of the year. In 2002 the same group had refused to endorse him at all.

But it was Lake who had authored the opinion, and Democrats had resented him ever since. Now, three years later, they saw a chance for reprisal. The IIC legislation amounted to Lake's twilight achievement. They refused to consider it at all. Instead, they put the bill on hold until next session, when Lake would no longer be in office.

They also wanted a promise from Chris. Back in 2004, around the same time the commission had finished with eyewitness ID, Chris herself had campaigned for a seat in the state senate, and lost. Now Democrats wanted a promise that she wouldn't try again. Otherwise they'd prevent the IIC bill from ever appearing on their senate floor — even once Lake was gone.

The threat made Chris livid, and she considered taking her chances. But she also knew something Democrats didn't. She'd spent more than three hundred thousand dollars on her failed campaign, so much money that afterward she'd wondered whether she had broken some record. A Republican like her stood no chance in Durham, she'd finally realized. To be elected, she would need to run as a Democrat, or move elsewhere. Neither was in her plans. This meant she didn't intend to run again, anyway. What harm was there in letting Democrats think they'd made the choice for her?

19

A Situation Not of His Making

He checked the activities board at Lincoln Correctional and found a notice for meetings of Jehovah's Witnesses: six o'clock on Thursdays. He met his new teachers that same week. "You must be Willie Grimes," the two men told him, shaking his hand.

He was, Willie agreed.

How were the guards treating him? How long had he been at Cleveland County before his transfer? Where was his family from? Tom and Eddie were both elders in the local congregation, they explained. Tom himself had first visited Lincoln to meet with a particular inmate, discovered unexpectedly that he liked it, felt he could do good there, so he had asked the warden for permission to visit regularly. From then on he'd come every Thursday evening to host a Bible discussion or just sit with any inmate who wanted to chat. Often this meant he sat there alone, so Eddie, a friend, had offered to come along for company. The pair had been visiting Lincoln together for several months before a call had come from down in Cleveland County, about Willie.

From that Thursday on, Willie met with Tom and Eddie each week. With Eddie especially he felt a nearly instant friendship. A trim, shy white man, with a soft voice and a neat snowy mustache, Eddie smiled so often that Willie wondered if his mouth simply rested that way. For how much Eddie knew about Scripture, Willie had assumed Eddie was older than him, but it turned out both men were nearly the same age. Eddie had been a Witness his entire life, he explained, like his parents and even his grandparents, who'd once offered Bible classes out of their home up in Statesville. After high school, in place of college, Eddie had studied at Watchtower Farms, a kind of seminary for Witnesses up in New York. Now he lived nearby in Cherryville and worked as a site superintendent for a construction company. His cell phone's ringtone was a car engine revving.

Because Eddie had been visiting prison for only a few months, he hadn't met as many inmates as his friend Tom had, and privately he felt sure he'd never met one like Willie. The others were boisterous, and didn't always listen; he couldn't help suspecting they cared more about visitors than they did about Jehovah. But Willie preferred quiet, like Eddie. When the men read Scripture, he sat as still as a monument. No one concentrated this way unless he was sincere, Eddie knew. The two got along so well that Eddie began mentioning Willie to his wife, who startled him one day by announcing she'd like to meet this Willie in person. Virginia had never visited the prison before, but Eddie wasn't about to tell her she couldn't, so she joined him at Lincoln the following Thursday, and took to Willie at once. He was so *gentle,* she told Eddie on the drive home, so *kind,* she could just *tell.* The couple gave Willie their home number, and encouraged him to phone whenever the prison would let him. Virginia began writing him letters.

He asked his case manager about returning to his job at the canteen, thinking he could handle the service window again. Until then, he went to work as a baker. He met with a psychiatrist, who scheduled a follow-up in twelve weeks. But Willie wouldn't remain long enough to keep the appointment; five days later, he was transferred back to Craggy.

Through the summer and early fall he avoided the head programmer who he remembered had schemed against him. Eddie and Virginia, when they could, drove the ninety miles from Cherryville to visit, but they couldn't make this distance every week, as they had at Lincoln. In November he met with another psychiatrist. "During the interview, Mr. Grimes was pleasant and cooperative," the psychiatrist noted. "Appeared mildly depressed but was not all that remarkable." Together the pair filled out a worksheet called "Measurable Goals," to help Willie guide his own treatment. To monitor his progress, they planned to meet every three months. Before the chance for their second meeting, however, Willie was transferred again, back to Lincoln.

Lincoln reinstated him as canteen operator, but he was on the job barely a month before trouble struck. In December a supervisor noticed conflicting invoices and ordered one of the guards, Officer Mull, to close the canteen and verify his math. On a table beside the register, Mull discovered two five-dollar bills and a little over eight dollars in coins, which he noticed didn't appear in any receipts. He asked Willie what had happened. Those five-dollar bills weren't being hidden, Willie answered—he'd simply placed them aside until he had twenty of them, to make a neat hundred-dollar bundle. He always did this, to keep revenue organized; it was why the bills were so near the register. The eight dollars and eight cents in spare change was from tips other inmates had given him. Often, when an inmate bought something, he let the canteen operator keep a spare nickel or dime or even a quarter, and in a good month, these tips added up.

Mull was skeptical. The following day, under orders to conduct a full inventory, he marked a total shortage of $141.20. Willie must have stashed this amount in his pockets, or in his bunk, Mull decided. Neither he nor other guards could find it in either place, but he ordered Willie to segregation.

When his case manager visited on his second day in segregation, to ask what he'd done, Willie still didn't know what he was being charged with. No one had explained to him exactly what had happened. All he knew was that it had something to do with the canteen.

More than a hundred dollars was missing, his case manager told him. Did he have any idea where the money might have gone?

Willie, bewildered, shook his head. Then he remembered something. Part of his job was to help open and stack large boxes of merchandise, and his last time in the warehouse, he'd seen a shipment of coffee sitting uncounted. A day later it was gone. A full shipment of coffee equaled about the amount that was missing.

Did Willie have any idea where that coffee had gone?

The only person he'd seen nearby was Officer Mull.

But it was Mull who'd been put in charge of the investigation, and Mull had blamed Willie. He spent two more days in segregation. When he was released, he discovered he'd also been assigned ten hours of extra duty, and been suspended for half a month from organized yard sports, which he didn't play anyway. And he'd been demoted from canteen operator back to assistant cook. He asked his case manager for a transfer away from Lincoln, so was added to the backlog. "Feel inmate got caught up in situation already existing in the canteen," his case manager noted, pointing out that it had been two years since Willie was charged with any infraction. That same afternoon Willie filled out a sick-call request, asking to see the psychologist. "I am having problems," he wrote. "He ask me to fill this out if I need to see him."

"He had been doing well until an incident which had upset him," the psychologist observed, when they met the following week. "He feels that he has been treated unfairly. This has caused an increase in some tension and anxiety and depressive feeling. He, however, anticipated that if he is transferred to another unit, he would do much better, and he has requested a transfer." He scheduled a follow-up in another month, and told Willie he agreed it would be good for him if he were removed from the environment that had caused the problem. This Willie relayed to his case manager, who agreed to look into a transfer again. "Inmate is no problem," the case manager reiterated in Willie's file. "Simply got caught up in situation not of his making."

The following day he was transferred. Instead of Cleveland County, he landed at Pasquotank, out in Elizabeth City, in the northeast corner of the state—nearly four hundred miles from Lawndale, so he knew at once he had no hope of any visits. Before long his insomnia returned. He was referred for a mental-health assessment, which began poorly; a psychologist asked whether Willie was married, and Willie replied that he wasn't sure. He hadn't seen or heard from Towana in two decades.

The psychologist referred him to psychiatric services. "Lately he had been down because he was transferred farther from his home," a psychiatrist observed. She admitted she didn't fully understand why; Willie claimed there had been "some problems coming up short with money in the canteen," but also that his own name had been cleared, which she didn't entirely follow. She also noted Willie's expansive medical history. In his file, nurses had written *asthma*, but Willie himself doubted that diagnosis, since nurses had also told him variously that he had COPD, for which he was taking theophylline, or allergies, for which he was taking an antihistamine. For an inflamed prostate he was taking Cardura and Bactrim. He also suffered from stomach problems, which seemed distinct from the prostate problem, and for which he periodically took Tagamet, in case it was acid reflux, or tetracycline and Flagyl, in case it was an infection. "He is a quiet man," the psychiatrist observed. "He is cooperative. He is depressed about being far from family." She diagnosed him with "major depressive disorder, recurrent and moderate," as well as a list of other maladies: alcohol dependence ("in remission"), prostatitis, possible benign hypertrophy of his prostate, migraine headaches, history of peptic ulcer disease, history of asthma or perhaps COPD. Possibly all the medication he was on was only making things worse, she wrote. Under a column for additional problems, she added, "Poor coping mechanisms."

He asked for a transfer back to Lincoln, or, if there were no beds there, even to Craggy, but since he'd just been transferred his case manager told him it would be at least six months before he was eligible again. Instead, he was assigned to work as a janitor. In August he met another psychiatrist. The pair of them agreed to meet twice monthly. At the end of that week, however, he was transferred back to Lincoln.

As soon as he arrived, he told his case manager he hoped to stay this time. "Always has a pleasant demeanor," she noted in his file. But seven months later, in spring, without explanation, he was transferred to Craggy.

He asked his new case manager there what had happened, since he'd expected to stay at Lincoln, but his case manager didn't know, and listed what jobs and classes Craggy offered, which Willie knew already from having been shipped there several times. The case manager also suggested Willie think about what his goals were. He already knew his goals, Willie replied. As he listed them, his case manager wrote them down: "1. Get his medical condition straightened out. 2. Transfer back to Lincoln to continue working in the kitchen there. 3. Attend Jehovah Witness service weekly. 4. Get out of prison."

Even when Willie was at far-off Pasquotank, Virginia Moose had continued writing him letters, and now she and Eddie drove Route 40 out to Craggy as often as they could. Most Saturdays Willie still phoned them collect, though the prison cut off their calls after fifteen minutes. She and Eddie had never had children of their own, Virginia confided, but she imagined this was what it felt like to be a mother. "I've got a son now," she told him, and this settled things.

He hung up the phone each week feeling uplifted. He saw clearly that Jehovah had put Eddie and Virginia in his life, and felt grateful, only now it occurred to him they still didn't know his entire story. Neither had asked what he'd done to end up in prison, and Willie had never offered to tell them. Eddie was visiting to teach the Bible, he knew, not to listen to Willie's legal problems. And, in the past, when he'd tried telling guards he didn't belong there, they had laughed in his face. "Right," they'd scoffed. "No one in prison really belongs here." That, plus his natural shyness, had taught him quickly to keep his mouth shut, except rarely with his case manager or a psychologist.

But it also meant withholding from Eddie and Virginia, something he knew friends didn't do. Over the phone one Saturday, Virginia asked how he'd spent his afternoon, and he told her he'd been studying law books, as he usually did on Saturdays.

"Oh? What are you studying for?" Virginia asked.

"I have been in here for something I didn't do," Willie admitted. "I'm trying to learn law, to try to help myself."

Virginia believed him. Since Willie's first transfer between Cleveland County and Lincoln, meanwhile, word of him had spread across several congregations, and Eddie had met others who knew him, including a friend of Willie's from Douglas High who had known him before his arrest. Today that friend happened to be a Witness, and she told Virginia that she, too, felt certain Willie was really innocent, as did everyone she still knew from Douglas High. Eddie asked around, and everyone he knew in the friend's congregation agreed that the friend was trustworthy. He told Virginia that he believed Willie, too.

That winter he was transferred back to Lincoln once more, and once more his case manager tried persuading him to attend SOAR, the rehabilitation program for sex offenders.

I thought I wouldn't have to go to SOAR, if I didn't want to? Willie pressed her.

That was true, his case manager granted, since SOAR was elective. But she wanted Willie to understand what he was turning down. SOAR was his best chance at release, since it led to a custody promotion and then to parole, and if he enrolled, he increased his chance at certain privileges. In minimum custody, an inmate with a good record could go out to lunch with his family, as long as the restaurant was nearby and they signed him in and out of prison. Eventually he could wear his own clothes and apply for a work-release job on the outside. All Willie had to do was sign a form, admitting responsibility for his crime, and sit through a course.

He was willing to do one of those, but not the other. It was fine with him to sit through a course. But since he'd never raped anyone, signing the form amounted to lying, and he couldn't do that—it was against Jehovah, which He would see, as He saw everything. Prison was nothing compared to His blessing. For thirteen years, Willie had held on to his word. He could see what he'd be left with if he gave that away. As a liar he'd be nothing on the outside, even if it worked and the prison released him, a promise he distrusted anyway. He'd watched other inmates take deals with the DOC, for a reduced sentence or to avoid incarceration at all. Sometimes it worked, but other times it didn't, and either way now his guilt would be stamped on him forever. He would die there in prison before signing some form, pretending he was someone he wasn't.

That spring he decided he felt ready to be baptized. By custom, Witnesses didn't baptize infants, since they regarded this rite as a freely chosen thing and a child, obviously, wasn't equipped to choose it. Instead, a Witness simply chose to be baptized, once he or she grasped what the ceremony represented. Willie told Eddie he did. Normally this meant a ceremony at Kingdom Hall, but Willie couldn't leave Lincoln Correctional, so instead Eddie and Tom found a third elder from their congregation, then gathered in one of the prison's visiting rooms, the four men their own audience.

Eddie didn't see how the logistics would work; how were they going to submerge Willie in water? But guards, when he asked, told him they kept a folding tub for this purpose exactly. They unfolded it and helped Eddie fill it halfway with water. Eddie asked Willie again if he felt ready. He was. He stripped to his underwear, climbed in, and laid himself back.

And Eddie saw a problem. His friend had gained back the weight he'd once lost, so when Willie lay back, a dry island of his belly protruded. Witnesses believed in full submersion. "We're going to have to try this again," Eddie observed. "We need more water."

Guards helped Eddie haul more water from a bathroom sink, filling five-gallon plastic buckets, topping each load to the brim. After each trip Willie tried reclining again, and slowly the island of his belly sank below the surface. Finally it disappeared entirely, water splashing over the edges of the tub. When he rose again Eddie was standing beside him, water sloshing onto his sneakers, smiling broadly and welcoming him to Jehovah's family.

Midway through June 2001, an inmate named John Minton begged guards for protective custody, complaining that Willie had struck him in the face while the two worked in the kitchen and threatened his life. "If you tell anyone, I will hurt you," he recalled Willie threatening. But neither guards nor nurses could find any marks on Minton's face. They asked Willie for a statement, or any witnesses he wanted to gather on his own behalf. "I don't have any statement, because I don't know what's going on," he told them. A guard wrote this into his report. A brief investigation revealed that a separate pair of inmates had recently borrowed money from Willie, then hadn't wanted to repay, so instead they'd paid Minton a smaller amount to try framing him, hoping this would shunt Willie off to segregation or, better, a different camp, where the two inmates couldn't be expected to repay him. Minton's charges were dismissed for lack of evidence. Two weeks later Willie met with his case manager. "He as always had no complaints," he wrote in Willie's file.

One morning that autumn an inmate rushed hysterically into the kitchen, interrupting Willie on a breakfast shift. "They bombed New York!" the man shouted. "They're gonna kill a whole bunch of people."

Willie followed him into the dayroom, where on a television monitor he saw two buildings were aflame. He'd never seen buildings so tall, or so much smoke, billowing like thunderheads. A caption read "New York City." Inmates overcrowded the dayroom, panicking about where might be next, after New York, but the thought hadn't crossed Willie's mind. A place like New York City was a geography he could no longer imagine. Thirteen years in prison had shrunk his frame of reference to the scale of a pinhead. He recalled a joke he'd heard once: no one ever heard of terrorists attacking a prison, just like no one ever heard of an earthquake striking one. *Doesn't matter what goes on in the world,* a saying went. *You don't exist out there anymore.*

He was transferred to Piedmont Correctional, an hour northeast, where after a month he learned that his brother Samuel Lee had died. Prostate cancer. Gladys wanted him at Samuel Lee's funeral, but when she phoned Piedmont, a receptionist told her it was a bad idea. "He'll be in shackles," he kept repeating, and it was so much paperwork to get a day pass.

She'd gotten Willie out on a day pass once before, Gladys insisted.

Wherever she'd gotten that, it was someplace other than Piedmont, the receptionist told her. He doubted she realized how much paperwork this required.

Even if she got her brother a day pass, Gladys knew, he'd be chained to guards for the entire service. Seeing him like that had been so awful the last time, worse even than the funeral, and she didn't know if Willie wanted to go through it again, either. Finally she gave up.

A new case manager identified four goals he wanted Willie to achieve while at Piedmont. He wrote these into Willie's file: "1. Attend vocation schools 2. Enroll in the S.O.A.R. program 3. Attend the N/A [Narcotics Anonymous] program 4. Remain infraction free." He was transferred back to Lincoln, but as soon as he arrived a guard told him he was backlogged for Piedmont. He'd just *come* from Piedmont, Willie complained; he didn't understand why he kept being shipped back and forth. Not every inmate was tossed about this way. Some stayed on one camp for a dozen years at a stretch. The determination seemed random. A new psychologist confessed he had no idea about Willie's transfer schedule, and promised his health care and records would follow him wherever he went. Willie knew this wasn't true; several times already his prescriptions had gotten lost in transfer, and he'd had to find a new doctor to prescribe them. If only for the autonomy, he decided to stop his antidepressants. Then, clearheaded, he decided he would divorce Towana.

He'd lost touch with Towana years earlier; as far as he knew, she was still in DC, where he'd always assumed news of what happened to him must have traveled. But Towana had never reached out, so he wasn't certain. For a long time he'd hoped they might reconcile one day, but now reality had sunk in—as long as he continued refusing SOAR, he didn't expect ever to get out, and this guaranteed he'd never see Towana again. As long as their marriage was still valid, it prevented her from marrying anyone else, he realized. This was selfish of him. Wherever Towana was, probably she wanted to get on with her life. Legally, a divorce required that Towana sign papers, but Willie didn't know where to find her. All he remembered was her mother's address. He signed the relevant forms, had them notarized, and mailed them off, hoping eventually they would find Towana.

Virginia Moose learned that Willie had been offered parole and had refused, so she shared this with her husband Eddie, who got to thinking. For a while now Eddie had believed Willie was telling the truth, but to hear he had turned down a chance at freedom, if only he admitted guilt...that was something else, Eddie thought. He got his hands on a copy of the transcript from Willie's trial, decided to read it for himself. And was astonished. Other than the hair comparison and Carrie Elliott's ID, both of which seemed awfully flimsy, he couldn't see a single thing that tied his friend to the rape. *How could they have proven this?* he thought. He mentioned his impression to Virginia, who urged him to do something about it. But what? Carrie Elliott had passed away, meaning her testimony could never be recanted.

He resolved to find a lawyer. In the newspaper recently he'd read of one over in Charlotte winning some high-profile case, and he recalled the lawyer's name, Noell Tin. For a second opinion, he called a friend who lived over that way and happened to work in the district attorney's office. Did his friend know any particularly good lawyer? Noell Tin, the friend answered, unprompted. This was enough for Eddie. He called Tin's firm, made an appointment, and drove to Charlotte.

Tin didn't fully understand why Eddie was interested in the case—was Willie Grimes a relative?—so Eddie explained he was a Jehovah's Witness and about the prison ministry. He wasn't any legal advocate, trying to free someone, he promised. "It just seems to me, reading his case, there was no evidence to support his conviction. But I don't have any legal training. So I just wanted a professional to look at it." Neither he nor Virginia had any idea what it would cost for Tin to do what they were asking, but Virginia had vowed to Willie they would find a good lawyer to at least read his transcript, even if it meant taking out another mortgage on their house.

That wasn't necessary, Tin assured Eddie. He'd visited enough prisons to know what Witnesses did there. He offered to read Willie's transcript for three hundred dollars.

A week later Tin phoned and invited Eddie back to Charlotte. He shared Eddie's view, he agreed; Willie seemed to have been convicted without much evidence, so Tin thought the case was worth pursuing. That was the good news. The bad news was that Tin doubted Willie or even Eddie could afford his rate. Tin's schedule was filled with other clients, and the cost of taking on another might be prohibitive. Still, there was another option. Tin knew of an organization out of Duke Law School that worked on cases like this one, and for free. Tin sometimes referred clients there. If Eddie was interested, this was what he wanted to do for Willie.

Eddie agreed.

That winter Tin phoned the director of the organization he'd mentioned, Pete Weitzel, to share he had a case he thought Weitzel might be interested in. Weitzel invited Tin to send it along, so a few days later Tin did, with an explanation: "I have done a preliminary review of the transcript, and concluded the case may have merit but requires further investigation." Because he personally was at work on other cases, Tin couldn't take this one on, too, so he hoped Weitzel might offer the transcript to "those energetic law and journalism students" he knew Weitzel worked with, "to see if anyone is interested in looking into this matter." Finally he passed along contact information for Eddie Moose.

Tin had warned Eddie it might be a long while before the center responded, so he and Virginia waited for news. Then, in May, Willie received an envelope from a name he didn't recognize, the North Carolina Center on Actual Innocence. The letter inside had also been copied to Eddie Moose and Noell Tin. Included was a nineteen-page questionnaire, and a release form. Near the bottom of the letter was a disclaimer:

Proving innocence is never easy; it becomes more difficult with each subsequent year. There's also a great deal of luck involved in any successful challenge. In most cases, because of these difficulties, we will have no course of action available to us once we have concluded our initial investigation. In only a few instances will we be able to pursue our investigation to the point where the inmate will benefit. We know you recognize these difficulties; we ask only that you have patience and understand the odds that are facing us—and you—in pursuing this inquiry.

During visiting hours, with Eddie's help, Willie filled out the center's questionnaire and signed and dated it: June 9, 2003. Then he dropped it in the mail.

20

We Recommend the Closing of This File

Most of the time she wasn't at a commission meeting Chris spent at her center office in the lonely basement of Duke Law School, a narrow, windowless room with two desks and a file cabinet. Besides Mitch and the kids, she didn't have much of a social life; occasionally she met colleagues for dinner or coffee, but for as long as she remembered her closest friend had been her own sister, who threatened an intervention every so often, since she worried Chris worked too much. In spring and summer Chris liked pruning roses in her garden, but she didn't enjoy just lying about, since that never felt restorative, only tormented her. One friend she did have, who lived down in Florida, had once bought her a gift, a T-shirt that read RELAXING STRESSES ME OUT. If she left her center desk even for lunch, new e-mails always filled her in-box when she returned, so she often stayed awake until midnight or later, sending replies. "Are you really that altruistic, or do you just have a rich husband?" someone had asked her recently, during a ceremony at the local bar association. "Both," Chris had answered.

One of those e-mails was from Pete Weitzel. A lawyer over in Charlotte had forwarded Weitzel a letter about a potential client, so Weitzel in turn had forwarded this to Chris. Before piling it onto a stack with the others, Chris asked a staffer for a preliminary read; this meant a search of the Department of Correction database, then tracking down the inmate's trial transcript, appellate opinions that were public record, and any newspaper articles that could be found on the Internet. By the time the staffer had finished, a complete questionnaire had arrived from the inmate himself, so Chris opened a new folder and labeled it with the man's name: *Willie Grimes.*

Next Chris asked one of the center's volunteers, a law student from Chapel Hill named Nadia Konstantinova, to begin a formal summary of the case. This included a synopsis of the initial crime, police investigation, and trial, plus a list of everyone who'd been subpoenaed and outlined arguments from both the prosecution and defense, and what Konstantinova regarded as weakness in each. Among these was the hair sample that police had recovered from the victim's apartment. That hair had never undergone DNA analysis, Konstantinova realized, but an SBI technician had testified that, in his experience, distinct people almost never had microscopically identical hair.

Bull, Chris wrote next to this line in Konstantinova's report.

Other than that hair, Grimes's case had mostly come down to the victim's identification, Konstantinova concluded. This "seemed to fade in and out. Her reports to the police were not consistent and became a lot more detailed once she spoke with Ms. McDowell," the victim's neighbor. Other evidence "was minimal," which on the one hand cast the trial's outcome under suspicion, but on the other hand meant Konstantinova wasn't certain how to proceed. "While innocence issues exist, actual innocence may be difficult to prove due to the lack of collected evidence and the age of the case."

So she met again with Chris, who suggested that Konstantinova reach out to the sheriff's department, to see whether it held on to what little evidence it had collected. Konstantinova did. Within a month she had "reached a road block," she e-mailed Chris; no one with the Hickory police was able to match the inmate's report number to anything in their evidence room. When that hadn't worked, Konstantinova had gotten in touch with Ed de Torres, the inmate's original defense attorney. "While he strongly believes in Mr. Grimes's innocence, he said that he is not sure whether anything can be done for him. He said that various groups have looked at this case and have not been able to do anything about it." De Torres had suggested that Konstantinova try the Catawba County clerk's office, since evidence typically was kept there after it had been introduced at trial, so Konstantinova had done this, but the clerk had checked her evidence room and found records only as far back as 1991. Grimes had been convicted in 1988. "She told me that I can come look myself if I want to. I'm not sure what to do next. It seems that everyone believes in his innocence. If he is innocent, it's pretty horrible that he has to spend the rest of his life in prison. Please let me know if there is anything else I can do."

Take the clerk up on her offer, Chris replied. "It sounds like the evidence should either be there, or there should be an order for it to be destroyed. Hopefully you can find one or the other."

So Konstantinova drove the hundred and forty miles to Catawba County Superior Court, where she sifted through evidence logs only to confirm what the clerk had told her by phone: there was no reference at all to Willie Grimes. Somehow the evidence had been destroyed, without any order to do so or any formal record that it had been done. For Chris she drafted a fresh synopsis of the case, including her failure to track down any evidence or even a reliable clue for where it had been moved and why. "His defense counsel, prison ministries volunteer, and various other people who have looked at the case strongly believe in his innocence," Konstantinova wrote. Which was sad, but, legally speaking, she didn't see what else there was to do. "If there are any additional avenues to pursue, I will be glad to continue working on the case."

Chris assigned three more student volunteers, each of whom read Grimes's entire file and met a week later to match it with Konstantinova's synopsis. They couldn't find any discrepancies. "All of us agreed that we believed in Willie Grimes's innocence," they reported to Chris. One of the students had even phoned Ed de Torres to ask for his thoughts: "He immediately told me that he believed in Willie Grimes's innocence, but he was not sure that there was any legal recourse left to free him. He believed that there was no bad faith on the part of the victim." The student had also asked de Torres whether he knew where the rape kit was (de Torres didn't) and whether, theoretically, de Torres would mind someone filing an MAR on Grimes's behalf, alleging ineffective assistance of counsel. If it would help Willie, de Torres answered, they had his blessing to do anything they could think of. "He basically informed us that there was no real help that he could provide us with this case, but that he wishes us the best of luck."

Several more times the students phoned the Catawba County clerk's office to confirm that neither the rape kit nor the hair evidence still existed. Then they persuaded the clerk to phone colleagues in Raleigh, on the unlikely chance that somehow his records had been forwarded there. They hadn't. "The three of us believe in Willie Grimes's innocence," they concluded in their final report. "Unfortunately, it will be difficult if not impossible to secure his release." Willie had been convicted on two pieces of evidence: testimony from Carrie Elliott, and a hair recovered from the scene. "Both are unobtainable for review now, as the victim is dead and the hair is no longer with the Clerk of Courts. There are no samples on which to run DNA tests. All of Willie's avenues for appeals have been exhausted. No suitable grounds for a Motion for Appropriate Relief exists." So they didn't see what more anyone could do. "We recommend the closing of this file."

But Chris, who'd been anxiously reading each student report, couldn't swallow this prospect. Closing a file meant archiving it into a cabinet that stretched nearly an entire wall of the center office, and then, eventually, since they'd run out of space there, into a box in the attic at Chris's house, where she'd taken to storing overflow. Once she relegated a case to her attic, she'd never brought it out again. It was plain what this would mean for Grimes.

But she couldn't justify keeping Grimes's file in the cabinet she wanted, with the center's active cases. Short of somehow finding new evidence, the center would never be able to move forward with it, she knew. Grimes's file would only sit there, robbing space from others.

She settled on a lukewarm compromise. From her purse she drew out a sheet of paper where inmates' names were listed in two columns: *Cases of Innocence Still Open* and *Cases with No Avenues to Pursue*. Reluctantly she scratched out Grimes's name in the first column and wrote it in the second. Then she gathered together his file. Most center cases fit neatly into folders, but for this one she and her volunteers had collected enough documents to fill a short stack of purple binders. Rather than drop these into a drawer, she simply placed them atop the office file cabinet, spread alone across several feet, and labeled them each with a handwritten sticky note: *Willie Grimes*. The case was no longer active, exactly. But she wasn't closing it, either.

On the opposite side of the country, a district attorney in Oregon named Joshua Marquis, who also served as a vice president of the National District Attorneys Association, wrote an op-ed, published January 26, 2006, in the *New York Times*. Recently he'd seen previews for a new television show on ABC called *In Justice*, a drama that followed a fictional organization as it freed the wrongly convicted. A person who watched this "popular culture" or listened to its "conventional wisdom" must believe "that our prisons are chock-full of doe-eyed innocents," he complained. That was "a misconception," since "the hordes of Americans wrongfully convicted exist primarily on Planet Hollywood." Marquis cited a study from a year earlier, in the *Journal of Criminal Law and Criminology*, that had named three hundred and forty exonerees from thirty-eight different states who averaged more than ten years each wrongly imprisoned. Authors of the study estimated those numbers made up only a portion of a larger, unknowable total.

Even if their estimate was right, Marquis argued, those wrongful convictions amounted to a tiny fraction of the million-odd felony verdicts that American courts rendered accurately every year. An error rate of several hundred, even several thousand, per decade or so was a proportion worth admiring. "Most industries would like to claim such a record of efficiency." True, human lives were "more important than widgets." That was what appeals were for.

Still, journalists and entertainers, in their "thirst for drama," focused on "the rare case in which an innocent man or woman is sent to prison." Their audience read books like *To Kill a Mockingbird,* watched off-Broadway plays like *The Exonerated,* and believed those cases were a majority. In real life, the criminal justice system was "a work in progress," Marquis agreed. "But nothing is gained by deluding the public…Americans should be far more worried about the wrongfully freed than the wrongfully convicted."

The same week of that op-ed, Beverly Lake retired, and nearly a year after Democrats' stalling, the state senate finally took up his IIC bill—and passed it, without much suspense, 48 to 1. Now the senate bill just had to be reconciled with the version the house had approved a year earlier. Then it could be voted on again in both chambers. "I have no doubt that we'll resolve the differences and there will be an innocence commission by the end of the session," Rick Glazier, a local Democrat who'd sponsored the legislation in the house, told reporters. "It's already in the budget, and I think both sides have indicated by their overwhelming votes it's a high priority." Only one senator disagreed—Hugh Webster, from Burlington, incidentally the same town where Ronald Cotton had been convicted. It was Webster who had cast the senate's single dissenting vote. "I would much prefer that we fix what's wrong with the system," he complained to WRAL, a local TV news outlet. He disliked the notion of creating something new rather than reforming what they already had, as he worried about the message this sent. "We're saying it's not working. So we have to have this commission to catch and correct errors."

"We have flotation devices on airplanes," Chris retorted, when WRAL phoned her to ask for comment. "We have seat belts in cars. We have built-in protections. The justice system should not be the exception."

By month's end, the North Carolina house and senate had reconciled. Until now, no one had been able to settle on how many judges would need to agree in order to exonerate someone—two of the panel, or all three?—nor had anyone answered whether an inmate who'd initially pleaded guilty should be entitled to apply to the IIC at all. Finally legisla-tors compromised: The judges' decision would need to be unanimous. In exchange, however, an inmate who'd pleaded guilty could still apply.

The deal also inserted a further wrinkle. This was a sunset provi-sion; unless the legislature voted to renew it, the IIC would dissolve at the close of December 2010—four years from now.

On the final Wednesday in July 2006, the house passed this newest version of the bill 86 to 28. On Thursday, the Senate followed, 46 to 2. A week later the governor signed it into law. "Its creation gives our crimi-nal justice system yet another safeguard by helping ensure that the peo-ple in our prisons in fact belong there," he announced in a statement.

"It's a whole different kind of animal," he added to WRAL.

Passage of the law made news as far away as California. NORTH CAR-OLINA TO WEIGH CLAIMS OF INNOCENCE, read a headline in the *Los Angeles Times*. Because of the sunset provision, several news outlets described the agency as a "four-year pilot program," though still the first of its kind in the country. Two days after the *Times* article, National Public Radio ran a feature on *All Things Considered* describing the IIC as a statewide agency "to review the cases of inmates who say they can prove they were wrongfully convicted." For balance, producers also reached out to opponents of the idea, including the newest director of NCVAN, Mel Chilton. "No one wants an innocent person to serve one minute in jail," Chilton agreed on air. "But we do not feel that there are these numbers of people that are wrongfully convicted. And this just undermines the whole system that we have lived under for two hundred years." Chilton worried that her state had simply added more bureaucracy, and more protections for criminals, both of which meant "a step backward for victim's rights," all because of what she regarded as "disproportion-ate focus" on a tiny number of wrongful convictions. "It's very con-cerning to those of us who have experienced a very violent crime, and fear that our safety is going to be jeopardized, that someone will get out on some technicality, and we will not be safe in our homes."

Chilton wasn't the only one who thought so. The courts already worked, one local DA complained to the *Winston-Salem Journal.* "It is not necessary to create another level of red tape and bureaucracy such that victims will never get closure now."

Even defense attorneys weren't uniformly enthusiastic about the new agency, though for the opposite reason—not because they predicted it would be too disruptive, but because they predicted it wouldn't be disruptive enough. "I don't know who's going to get relief," one told reporters. "I hope to be proven wrong, but I'm afraid that the innocence commission is more symbolic than practical."

It didn't take long for Chris, who was reading the deluge of columns from her nearby home in Durham, to exhaust her limited patience. She penned an incensed letter to the editor of Raleigh's *News and Observer.* "It mystifies me when people take the time to compose a written uninformed opinion. Why not make a phone call or send an e-mail to those who are informed on a subject and ask a question or two before expressing an opinion? And, in this case, why not read the Bill establishing the Commission?" She listed several of the complaints she'd seen in recent weeks—that the new agency would be flooded with meritless claims (in fact claims would be "heavily screened," and the IIC would turn any evidence of guilt over to police, thus providing a disincentive for guilty inmates to apply) and that DAs across the state had uniformly opposed the idea (in fact the conference of district attorneys had publicly endorsed it). Then she named personally two critics whose letters she'd read, including a local judge who'd claimed the agency would "abrogate the responsibility of the judiciary" (the reverse was true) and a local radio host who'd made so many bogus claims that Chris had space to respond to "just a few." One of these was "laughable," and another was answered already in the legislation itself. "Reading the Bill would have shown you that," she pointed out. If the radio host was interested in the truth, Chris invited him to phone her—"which is what you should have done in the first place."

Then she opened a bottle of wine.

She didn't rest for long. Those purple binders she'd stacked atop the center file cabinet still nauseated her each time she walked past them.

She'd read Willie Grimes's file enough times to believe he was innocent, to feel exasperated that evidence in his case had simply been trashed. How could that possibly be an office's policy? So, back while the IIC legislation had slogged through the general assembly, she'd begun phoning and writing restless letters to the offices of clerks and DAs and sheriffs around the state, asking how they stored their evidence, hoping Catawba County was an exception. It wasn't. None of the hundred counties in North Carolina had been appropriated much of a budget, or enough storage space, and each followed its own distinct policies. Some didn't even have log-in or log-out forms for evidence.

Which seemed to Chris like a task for the commission. To its next meeting she invited clerks from eight different counties, all of whom agreed they'd never been trained to preserve evidence and that no one had given them the time, space, or resources to be "evidence police," as they called it. All eight were open to reform, since it didn't do them any good, either, when things went missing.

The problem was Beverly Lake—or, rather, the absence of him, following his retirement. Now the few commissioners who'd always bristled at their work recognized an opportunity. With Lake gone, maybe it was wisest to disband, these commissioners suggested. The IIC was about to become law—once that happened, what was left for their commission to accomplish?

Plenty, Chris snapped. Even once it passed, the IIC didn't study legal issues, or recommend policy, either. She didn't see what one had to do with the other.

But that same month, half a year after Lake had retired, the IIC did become law, and even Chris could see the commission sputtering. To avoid confusion with the new IIC, commissioners decided they needed a new name; it took them three separate meetings, over five months, to agree on one. Uneasy still with that term *innocence,* several commissioners hoped to avoid it in their title entirely. But the next most sensible word, *reliability,* as in the Commission on Reliability in Criminal Procedure, didn't work either, as this suggested the criminal justice system wasn't fully reliable already. At last they settled on the North Carolina Chief Justice's Criminal Justice Study Commission.

But the truth was, the commission's energy had dissipated. The IIC fight had been its apex—or, to some, its nadir—and with Lake gone, it was now under his successor, Chief Justice Sarah Parker, who had never shared Lake's enthusiasm. Technically the commission had been established by court order, meaning a court order was necessary to end it. But by the end of 2006 it had ceased meeting at all.

By January 2007 all eight positions on the new IIC had been filled, though still the organization lacked any staff; those eight commissioners would hear cases that proceeded to a hearing, but employees were necessary to screen and investigate claims in the first place, and to determine which would make it to a hearing. As soon as the director position opened, Chris Mumma had applied, but the IIC hadn't given her the job—a choice that initially rankled but that she finally admitted made sense. For an agency she'd championed to make her its director looked too much like a conflict of interest. And to be credible the IIC had to be neutral. Politically, Chris's loyalties were too obvious.

Who, though, if not Chris? The agency's initial proposal had asked for an annual budget of nearly five hundred thousand dollars, but the legislature had appropriated less than half; combined with the fact of the sunset provision, this had made the position less appealing for prospective candidates. What attorney wanted to uproot himself and move to Raleigh for a job that might vanish in four years? And if she couldn't be director herself, Chris wanted someone she approved of. She recalled a law student she'd worked with at Duke, a protégée of Newman and Coleman's who'd helped run the Innocence Project there, Kendra Montgomery-Blinn. Chris had been impressed with her. Better still, Chris thought she remembered that, after Duke, Kendra had gone to work as a prosecutor, at the DA's office there in Wake County. A prosecutor would be perfect, Chris realized, in terms of credibility—the same way it had been useful that Beverly Lake was a Republican.

She looked up the number for the Wake County DA's office and phoned. Was Kendra interested? She understood the risk to a recent graduate in leaving her steady job, Chris allowed. But she and Newman and Coleman and Rosen all were committed to the IIC becoming permanent. Together they would see it didn't vanish after four years. Ignore the sunset provision, she urged.

By spring Kendra was hired. By summer she'd designed a suite of rules and procedures for the new agency, with the help of her eight commissioners but otherwise nearly from scratch; legislation had established what the IIC could do, but given no particular method for how to do it, so her first two months Kendra had spent turning a vague statute into material policies, all without the luxury of an office. Since the building that legislators had planned for her agency was still being renovated, Kendra had been forced to rent two empty rooms in a local judge's office until autumn. Fortunately she hadn't needed much space, just one desk for herself and another for a case coordinator, the only two positions that anyone had hired for.

The bylaws she designed looked sensible enough on paper, her eight commissioners agreed. But no one had tried anything like them before, one pointed out—they couldn't be certain before seeing them in action. Why not practice them on a mock case, in a sort of dress rehearsal?

Kendra liked the idea. Without a full staff, however, she hadn't yet begun processing claims, so she didn't have one ready. She phoned to ask if Chris had a case available. To avoid any conflict of interest, she wanted one the IIC was unlikely to see down the road in an actual referral, ideally a known dead end, where Chris suspected an inmate innocent but it was impossible to know. Kendra could even mask names. Did Chris have one like that?

Willie Grimes, Chris answered without hesitation. Then she paused to reconsider. *Is the Grimes case too obvious?* The point was to challenge Kendra's procedure with a claim that included some doubt— Willie might be too obviously innocent to make for great training, she realized. *No, that will be good. They'll see how clear a case can be.* She brought his purple binders to Kendra's rented office and laid out the facts and names.

Soon Kendra summoned her eight commissioners to an empty conference room near Greensboro, where a community college had agreed to lend her more space. They were there to consider the case of Billy Times, she explained.

Kendra had grown up Kendra Ashcroft Montgomery, a tall, gangly, chestnut-haired girl from Indiana. In high school she'd watched a favorite teacher be fired for trivial reasons—he'd taught summer-school classes, then neglected to fill out some form. In fact, school administrators only wanted to cut their agriculture program, which her teacher directed, young Kendra realized. This was wrong. She organized fellow students to protest, which caught the attention of the Indiana teachers' union, and finally a hearing was held. Kendra was called to testify. He was a good teacher, she promised nervously; he ran the ecology club, had begun the school's recycling program, and periodically took students on field trips, camping. Who cared about some form? He hadn't done a thing to get fired.

In the end it made no difference; his firing stood. Still, the impression the hearing made on her lasted. *Look at this one person up against a giant school district,* she'd thought. *The hearing gave him a chance to be heard.* She decided then and there to become a lawyer.

But first she'd gone to Purdue and graduated as a member of Phi Beta Kappa; the following summer she'd gotten married and became Kendra Montgomery-Blinn. Then she'd continued straight on to Duke Law School, where her very first week she volunteered for the Innocence Project. It was there she met Theresa Newman and Jim Coleman and, eventually, Chris Mumma. Here were people who got it—one defendant, up against a system, with a chance to be heard. Everything else about the law she found tedious. Who *cared* how much money one company made by merging with some other company? That wasn't why she'd wanted to become a lawyer.

By her third year she was student director of Duke's Innocence Project. When she graduated cum laude in 2003 she applied to be an assistant DA there in Durham. She saw no conflict at all between this and what she'd done at the Innocence Project. A good DA looked not to convict, but rather to do justice. Sometimes this meant dismissing a case that lacked evidence. Sometimes it meant negotiating a plea deal, so a defendant could get medical treatment. Sometimes, yes, it meant prosecuting for as long a sentence as possible.

For three years she worked mostly on child abuse and domestic violence cases, and meanwhile she kept in touch with Newman and Coleman and Chris, following the IIC battle excitedly in newspapers, hoping their legislation would pass. Criminal justice was an evolving field, whose culture and technology both developed over time, Kendra knew. This meant even smart, ethical lawyers were necessarily imperfect, and judges too, since the context they worked in was. DAs like her had once believed that hair comparison, and eyewitness testimony, and blood-spatter evidence were each infallible. Now they knew better. That wasn't anyone's fault, since you couldn't blame a person for not predicting the science of a decade later. But it meant that, over time, mistakes happened, even with a good DA, even with a good defense attorney, even if everyone everywhere was perfectly competent and principled. It was a human system that convicted defendants, and humans were constantly learning. So it seemed obvious that *someone* ought to be able to review old cases, and the appeals process wasn't built for that. Nothing was, until the IIC.

When she saw the IIC had finally succeeded into law, she wondered who would lead the agency. Then her phone rang. It was Chris. "You should apply for this," Chris told her.

"Me?" Kendra asked, startled. She was twenty-eight, she protested, only three years out of law school. She wasn't qualified to be anyone's executive director. Besides, she liked her job as a DA.

"Think about this," Chris insisted. "It would be good for everyone."

So Kendra hung up and thought about it. Then she phoned Jim Coleman, her mentor from Duke. "You should really do this," Coleman told her. She phoned Chris back, to ask what the job entailed. No one was certain, Chris admitted, since there had never been anything like it.

The sunset provision made her nervous. Wasn't it reckless to abandon a steady job for some experiment? But she was making only thirty-something-thousand a year as an assistant DA, and, even working weekends, could barely repay her student loans. She and her husband had adopted a son, and now they couldn't afford day care. And, intimidating as it was, the prospect of being director thrilled her to imagine. She had assumed the job would naturally go to someone experienced, who would get things in order — maybe by the time that person stepped down, Kendra would be better qualified, and would dare apply. Now she recalled what Chris had told her on the phone: no one was certain what the job entailed, because there had never been anything like it. If she applied now, *she* could be the person who got things in order. She could help build the agency from scratch.

She submitted her application and interviewed with the eight new commissioners. In March, they told her she was hired. "It's clear from both her work history and our discussions with her, Ms. Montgomery-Blinn has neither a political agenda nor an axe to grind," one of them, a superior court judge up in Nash County, announced in a press release. "She's seen and experienced how criminal law works from both sides of the fence."

21

Some Concerns About His Medical Condition

He decided to enroll in a computer class. On the outside, before his arrest, no one he knew had owned a computer, but now he kept hearing about them—word among inmates was that everyone out there owned one, and he knew that even the DOC had digitized its records. On the activities board he found an announcement for a class called Computer Applications, up at Mountain View, so he signed his name and asked his case manager for a transfer there. A few days later a guard told him to expect his transfer the coming Thursday. But that same afternoon his case manager called him over the loudspeakers to share conflicting news: Willie was backlogged.

As he waited for transfer, a letter arrived from the North Carolina Center on Actual Innocence, confirming it had received his questionnaire and assigned his case "to a team for an in-depth review." Because the center was inundated with requests, its review might not begin for more than a year, the letter warned, and limited staff meant the center couldn't provide regular updates on its progress. "We will be in touch when a decision has been made on your case."

Soon he passed a milestone. By DOC rules, an inmate qualified for promotion to minimum custody exactly five years before his parole eligibility date—according to Willie's sentence, December 2, 2008. As of the previous Tuesday, he was four years and three hundred and sixty-four days out. For the first time, he was formally eligible for promotion. After fifteen years in prison. "Inmate has remained infraction free since 12-2-98," his case manager praised, when he next was up for custody review. "He continues his assignment in the kitchen receiving excellent evaluations." Nonetheless, she and her colleagues agreed he was too early in his eligibility. They issued an override, to keep him in medium.

He was shipped to Craggy, which made no sense, since he'd asked for Mountain View—luckily Craggy turned out to offer Computer Applications, too, though here the class didn't begin until spring. When finally it came around, he liked it so much—the way it hastened his afternoon, the orderliness of tapping a button and seeing its result on the screen—he signed up for another once the first eight weeks were finished. When this second one ended he asked for a transfer back to Lincoln, since the classes were the only reason he'd come to Craggy. That same month he came up again for custody review. "Inmate's aggressive behavior shows that he could/would pose a threat to the community if promoted at this time," a supervisor wrote in his file.

He was transferred to Caledonia, all the way out in Tillery, three hundred miles east of Lincoln. "He wants to transfer to another facility," his new case manager wrote, nearly as soon as Willie arrived. "He does not like it here." Before he could be moved, a guard roused him in the middle of the night for a drug test. Every so often guards announced these unexpectedly, usually at midnight or later, when inmates were unlikely to be prepared for them. He corralled Willie and five others from their cells into the gymnasium, then handed each a clear plastic cup. Once they pissed, the guard told them, they could return to their bunks.

He couldn't urinate on command, Willie admitted sheepishly.

The guard shrugged and handed him a cup of water. He had two hours.

That wasn't what he meant, Willie explained. He was on medication to help him with problems urinating. He promised he'd never taken drugs, but two hours might not be enough.

The guard only glared at him, so Willie gulped his water and waited. He tried again. Two hours passed. This counted as refusal of a direct order, the guard decided, at two a.m. He charged Willie with an infraction: A14, refusal to submit to a drug test. A sergeant arrived and asked Willie to sign a form. Willie signed. Did he want to make any statement on his own behalf?

He'd already told all he had to say.

Rather than taking him to his bunk, the guard marched him to segregation, where Willie spent the rest of the night. In the morning he asked for a sick-call request, scribbled on the form what had happened, and asked a different guard to carry it to the nurses' station. Another day and night passed before a nurse responded with a copy of his prescription. Willie had been telling the truth, she verified; he was on Cardura, 4 milligrams a day, for trouble urinating.

Another guard revised the infraction note in Willie's file. "It is recommended that his charge be dismissed and that inmate Grimes is tested at a later date." He released Willie back to his bunk.

His heartburn flared suddenly, then light-headedness, then a thudding, bone-deep fatigue, as though his limbs had been replaced with sandbags. When he used the bathroom, he noticed blood. Nurses referred him to a doctor—the first black physician Willie had seen on any camp, Dr. Land, who visited twice weekly. Land asked how recently Willie had had his prostate examined, and Willie told him it had been a couple of years. Would Willie mind if Dr. Land performed an exam now? Willie didn't, so Land snapped on a latex glove. When he finished, he regarded Willie seriously. "I can tell you right now," he said, "you've got prostate cancer. And you've had it for years."

Willie felt dazed. How could Land know?

"The first couple years, cancerous tissue will feel bumpy, like a bunch of blisters," Land explained. He held his thumb and forefinger a centimeter apart and squinted at the gap to demonstrate. Then he drew both hands into a circle, and held this before his chest. "Your prostate is hard as a rock, all the way around. That tells you how long it's progressed. You know, prostate cancer—you can have it for twenty years, and if there aren't any symptoms, and no one checks for it? You wouldn't have known."

But the prison checked him almost annually. His urinating problems had been happening for years, and they'd even put him on pills for an enlarged prostate. No one had said anything about cancer.

Land shrugged. He couldn't be certain when the inflammation had turned cancerous, but the blisters he was describing usually were a year or two before they hardened around the edges. Willie's might have been cancerous for a decade or more. Of course he'd refer Willie out for formal tests, he promised. But he had no doubt—Willie had prostate cancer.

Land made an appointment for him at a nearby urology clinic, and two months later, in January, a specialist conducted the same exam, and then a biopsy. Of the six samples the urologist tested, five were positive for adenocarcinoma. He estimated this meant 30 to 35 percent of the organ was cancerous. "His cancer is really bad," he wrote in Willie's medical file. Then he wrote to Dr. Land, back at Caledonia. "I think he has an aggressive cancer. So I think he needs some aggressive treatment." Before that began, he wanted a CT and a bone scan, to rule out metastases.

Depending on the scan results, they had a decision to make, the urologist explained to Willie in his office after the biopsy. He could remove the prostate altogether. Or radiation might work, though it carried certain risks, mainly permanent bladder or bowel problems. Theoretically, Willie was a candidate for cryotherapy—this meant freezing the cancerous cells with liquid nitrogen—or even hormone therapy, but the urologist didn't recommend either, given how far along Willie's prostate was. A final option, watchful waiting, meant exactly what it sounded like: punting the decision for later, and observing how the cancer behaved. He didn't think this was a good idea either, for the same reason.

How would each treatment affect his life span?

That was the right question, the urologist agreed—unfortunately, it was also impossible to answer. Willie's cancer didn't look to have spread from his prostate, so guessing his life span even if they did nothing was hazy enough. Predicting it after each hypothetical treatment? That was even hazier.

Willie considered this. From his early despair in prison, two lessons had stayed with him. First, from his slew of failed appeals, that whatever control he felt was largely an illusion. Second, from Scripture, that Jehovah helped only those who helped themselves. Neither of these facts conflicted with the other. "All the things you ask in prayer, having faith, you will receive," Jesus had told His disciples in Jerusalem. But: "If I am not doing the works of My Father, do not believe Me," He had told the Pharisees. A man was responsible for himself, for laboring on his own behalf, *and* he needed help. It was Jehovah, after all, who'd brought Willie to doctors, he realized.

"It's up to you," the urologist said. But personally he recommended surgery.

Willie agreed.

A scan of his pelvis two weeks later confirmed what doctors already knew: a calcification, measuring seven millimeters. There was no evidence of metastasis. Next his chest was x-rayed, which came back normal, then his abdomen, which came back normal, too. More doctors examined him at UNC Health Care, the state hospital over in Chapel Hill. In Willie's medical chart, under "Physical Examination," one wrote, "Pleasant black man…in shackles." He agreed Willie's prostate was inflamed, and noticed that Willie's prostate-specific antigen—a protein that oncologists used as a marker for prostate cancer—measured 8.5 nanograms per milliliter. A normal PSA was under 4. He diagnosed Willie with prostate cancer, stage 2, and explained the same options Willie already had discussed with Dr. Land, at Caledonia, and the urologist, at the clinic. He offered a consult with a radiologist, which Willie declined; he'd made up his mind for surgery.

Finally, doctors recorded a complete inventory of all his medications, and wrote up the plan everyone agreed on in Willie's medical chart. "The patient would like to pursue surgical intervention and will undergo radical retropubic prostatectomy in the near future. We need to get Department of Corrections' approval...and we are working on this currently."

"Based on his age, management feels that he can be managed in a less secure environment," a supervisor decided. He referred Willie to a psychiatrist for a DOC-mandated risk assessment, which included a review of his "social, criminal and mental health history data," plus a psychological examination and a recidivism worksheet. Had he ever had sexual intercourse with his own mother? He checked *No.* What about his siblings? *No.* What about another man? *No.*

Based on confidential findings, however, kept even from Willie, the psychiatrist assigned him a failing score. "Promotion [to minimum custody] not recommended due to unacceptable risk assessment," an assistant superintendent wrote in June.

That same afternoon Willie met again with the urologist. "I told him that with God's grace I have never had any major complications," the urologist entered in his notes. "I discussed with him for a long time, even though he was an inmate, he had a lot of questions and I answered them all patiently."

Two weeks later, Willie returned for surgery.

Three days after his surgery he was transferred back to the inmate hospital at Central Prison. He still wore a catheter, and knifelike pain still quivered through his abdomen, but soon he was able to stand on his own and shuffle gingerly down the widely tiled corridors. The urologist had told him to expect the catheter for at least two weeks, after which he could turn to adult diapers. How long he would need those was harder to estimate. Midway through July, at his first follow-up, he appeared to be recovering on schedule; the urologist removed his catheter and cleared him for discharge back to Caledonia.

A week later he was shipped. He met a new case manager, whose notes on him were straightforward: "Inmate stated that he had some concerns about his medical condition. I informed the unit manager."

* * *

A bladder sonogram six months after surgery showed a normally healing abdomen. Because the pain was still worst when he sat or lay down, he asked for a spare pad to soften his mattress. Then he came up again for custody review. "Willie is a sex offender and has not participated in any program to address this during his incarceration," his case manager wrote. "Staff feel that Willie should participate/complete a SOAR program prior to custody promotion. The recommendation is to retain in medium custody with an override." Three days later, a supervisor added: "Inmate has not been a management problem but states that he refuses to participate in recommended SOAR program because he's not going to admit something that he did not do. Therefore retention in medium custody is recommended."

Loudspeakers summoned him that autumn to the guards' office, where a sergeant told him his brother Cliff Jr. had died. From the office he phoned Gladys, who told him that Cliff had been on dialysis, awaiting a kidney transplant that had never come. Despite the distance, she wanted to get Willie to Lawndale for the funeral. But she'd run into a problem. A recent law in North Carolina forbade carrying firearms in any funeral procession. This turned out to apply even to prison guards, who couldn't escort an inmate without their guns, and also couldn't allow Willie anywhere unescorted.

Cliff's funeral proceeded without him.

After a loop around the yard, he rested on a bench to watch a game of horseshoes, as other inmates milled about loosely in groups. From the game came periodic *thump*s and *clang*s. Then shouting, a commotion. He looked up and saw an inmate's arm raised—was he celebrating?—but now the arm blurred downward, it was up and down again, Willie saw blood, he realized there was a knife. By then another inmate had spun and crumpled to his knees, gasping. Something was impaled in his chest, a stain spread down his shirt and into his pants. The horseshoes game had ceased and there was an unfamiliar silence. *Where are the guards?* A crowd blocked Willie's view and abruptly there was noise again, then the crowd opened and one inmate was striding away, and the crowd closed again behind him. *Where are the guards?* At that moment guards appeared and Willie worried he'd accidentally spoken aloud. A guard was demanding to know what happened, but no one would answer. "What happened here?" he shouted, into downcast faces. Inmates began drifting away. Nothing good would come of answering, Willie knew. He rose from the bench and walked off.

He was given a pad for his mattress, five months after he'd requested it. He wrote another letter to the Center on Actual Innocence: "They is trying to get me to sign papers saying that I'm guilty and go to the SOAR program before giving me any type of help," he protested. "I can't sign papers saying I did some thing that I didn't do just to get some help."

A letter arrived with news the center had been contacted by the *Denver Post,* which was running a story on cases where evidence had been destroyed or gone missing. Now a reporter wanted to visit him in prison for an interview, and there was a consent form. Willie didn't follow; had the center sent him this letter, or had the *Post?* Was he supposed to consent? He wrote the center again. "I'm asking you this because I have not heard from you all or been told if I have a lawyer in my case. I would appreciate if you could answer me and let me know if you all ask them to interview me or should I talk to them. I would like to thank you for your time and patience for any kind of information you can help with."

22

Any Cases Where Evidence
Had Gone Missing

At her desk at the center, around the time she phoned Kendra Montgomery-Blinn at the Wake County DA's office, Chris got an e-mail from a reporter at the *Denver Post,* which was planning a feature series on the problem of criminal-evidence storage—how much of it vanished or was destroyed, not only in Colorado but nationally. For leads, the *Post* had reached out to the original Innocence Project, up in New York, where someone had shared Chris's e-mail address. The reporter, Susan Greene, wanted to know if Chris had any cases where evidence had gone missing, evidence that, theoretically, could have proved someone innocent. A case like that would help dramatize their series, Greene and her editors predicted. Did Chris know of one like that?

She did.

Greene wanted to visit Willie in prison, so Chris mailed a consent form to him at Caledonia Correctional, since she needed his signature to bring a reporter. Then Greene flew in from Denver, and Chris drove with her the hundred miles up to Halifax County.

23

In Three Dimensions

The letter had come from them, the center confirmed, so Willie agreed to sign. On a humid, overcast Wednesday two weeks later, February 21, 2007, a pair of women showed up wearing gray and black suits and dress heels, each carrying a notepad. A photographer trailed in jeans and a T-shirt. Willie and the two women sat at an outdoor table under cloudy skies while the photographer hovered, snapping photos.

In Willie's own words, how had he gotten here? the *Post* reporter wanted to know. Where had he been that October night in 1987? What had he thought of Ed de Torres, his lawyer? How many appeals had he tried? How was he spending his time in prison, how long had it taken for him to adjust there, and how did he feel about his prospects?

Steve Hunt, of the Hickory police, knew he was innocent, Willie replied. He saw no other reason Hunt would have arrested him so quickly, without evidence. This had to have been on purpose. But he had no idea why. He did know the solution: from trial he remembered that several fingerprints had been lifted from bananas on Carrie Elliott's kitchen table, and that, back in 1988, police had compared those to his own, found they didn't match, and guessed they must be Carrie Elliott's. As far as he knew, though, no one had ever bothered to check. They weren't his, and, if they weren't hers, then they had to be her rapist's, Willie knew. Someone had to find those prints and compare them to Carrie's. At last Willie could go home.

But those fingerprints had been destroyed, the reporter pointed out. This was the reason she was writing about Willie's case in the first place. She'd seen for herself a photocopy of the county clerk's 1991 message for de Torres—those fingerprints, along with the hair samples and both rape kits, were gone.

Willie shook his head. He didn't believe that, he told her. No one had found a paper trail showing they'd been destroyed. He couldn't see a clerk destroying evidence without recording the action somehow— anyone on staff would know better than that. Until someone found a paper trail, there was no proof those fingerprints or anything else had been trashed, only that they had gone missing.

But hadn't people looked? she asked. If the fingerprints were out there, where did Willie believe they were?

He didn't know, Willie admitted. But everyone who'd looked had been searching in his file. Why would the fingerprints be in his file? If he'd actually raped Carrie Elliott, or even been inside her apartment, it would follow they'd have been put there. But he'd never done either of those things. Why put fingerprints in the file of a man you knew they didn't match? He didn't know whose file they'd been added to, but obviously it wouldn't be his. That explained why no one had found them there. Until someone proved otherwise, he believed the evidence was still *somewhere*. He just didn't know where.

Privately Chris had dreaded the entire afternoon nearly since Greene had proposed it. She hated meeting clients in person, had learned to avoid it as long as she possibly could. It was hard enough to deal with paper files, to know the letters in print corresponded to a real person and that he was imprisoned. To see him in three dimensions, to hear his voice and touch his hands—it was all too much, it haunted her.

From the mug shot in his file she recognized Willie instantly. Mentally she'd tried to age his photograph, to predict what he would look like today, but too late she realized she hadn't accounted for how sick he was. She knew of the prostate cancer; he'd written of it in his letters. The man she met at Caledonia was the height she'd expected, he had the right mustache, the short, graying Afro—but he was gaunter than she'd foreseen, feebler, nearly waxen. *Of course,* she berated herself.

Willie moved and spoke slowly, as though his words were viscous. As Greene asked him questions Chris could see him considering his every sentence. She noticed his hand, which he'd injured in those factory accidents. "Willie's deformed fingers on his left hand are very obvious," she wrote on her notepad. "It is surprising that the victim did not mention them." She listened to him answer Greene. "Willie thinks detective Steve Hunt knows he's not guilty," she added.

When Greene had gotten what she'd come for and her photographer was satisfied, Chris hugged Willie and the two women wished him good-bye, then returned to the parking lot. Greene opened her car door to leave, but Chris raised a hand, *Hold on,* leaned against the hood. Began crying. She hated this part.

"Are you going to be okay?" Greene asked.

Chris nodded, trembling. She lifted a finger—*Just give me a moment*—and then rocked forward, gripped her knees, crouched over the pavement. She was going to vomit, she realized. She reached a hand to the car bumper to steady herself. A wave of nausea rippled over her; she opened her mouth, but nothing emerged. Another ripple. Then it was gone.

She regained her balance, looked at Greene, nodded, opened her car door. "Okay," she said.

24

I Can Tell That This Lady Have Went Over My Case

A month after the *Denver Post* meeting, Willie wrote to the reporter, whose address was listed on a business card she'd given him. When she'd come for his interview, another woman had been there, too, he described—at first he'd thought this was a second reporter, but then she'd mentioned working at Duke Law School. "I don't know any one at Duke Law School or any one that teach there but I can tell that this lady have went over my case a few times or talk to some one that know about my case because she ask about things that were not in court and I think she will do a good job because she is concern about the truth." But Willie hadn't thought to write her name down, and now he'd forgotten it. "Is this lady a professor or a lawyer," he wondered—could she let him know? "I do want to thank you for all you doing or will do to get the truth out."

The answer came a week later.

March 29, 2007

Dear Mr. Grimes,

I was disappointed to hear from Susan Greene that you apparently had not received my letter which I sent shortly after our visit with you. I hope you will receive this one and it will help to answer any questions you have.

It was a pleasure to meet you during my visit with the reporter from the *Denver Post*. I sincerely apologize that someone from the Center had not been to see you sooner and that you were not receiving communication from the Center that you were entitled to. I think part of the reason for our limited communication is that your case is very difficult for the Center staff. There is very strong support for your innocence and there is very high frustration that our options for presenting evidence to support your claim in a court of law are very limited. I am hopeful that including the story of your case in the *Denver Post*'s series will help.

Mr. Grimes, the rape victim in your case is deceased and the clerk's office claims that all of the evidence collected after the rape, including the rape kit and the hair evidence, has been destroyed. Without the witness and without the physical evidence, there are limited avenues for the Center to pursue to prove innocence in your case. It is our hope that the publication of your story in the *Denver Post* will heighten interest in your case enough that if there is any evidence left in your case, it will be uncovered. We will keep you informed of our progress.

Again, I sincerely apologize for the delay in communications. Our office is a volunteer office with limited resources and we never seem to have the time to communicate with our inmates to the level we would like or they deserve.

I wish you well.

Sincerely yours,
Chris Mumma
Executive Director
NC Center on Actual Innocence

"I know that if we had that hair we could [prove] that I'm innocence," he wrote back. "The only reason the jury found me guilty is because the doctor told them the one hair they had were in fact my hair." If not the hair, Willie wanted the fingerprints: "If we had the fingerprints we might find who did this rape." He and his lawyer Ed de Torres had learned of those fingerprints only at trial, he repeated, and he expected the Hickory police deliberately hadn't compared them to other suspects', because that would have proved Willie innocent, which for some reason they hadn't wanted. "They knew I were innocence the whole time." Had anyone contacted Linda McDowell, to ask why she'd given the police his name in the first place? "I think she were the one trying to tell Mrs. Elliott what to say."

Chris had visited the Catawba County clerk's office herself, she wrote back. Neither the hair nor the fingerprints were there.

He wrote to Chris again, to share some advice a jailhouse lawyer had given him in the prison library. She probably needed to file a motion with the attorney general to learn when exactly the evidence in his case had been destroyed, who had authorized its destruction, and why. Since he was skeptical the evidence had been destroyed at all, he predicted the Hickory police, unable to answer those questions, would be forced to turn over what they'd been holding this whole time, and, because the fingerprints didn't match him, they would turn out to match someone else, a fact that would prove he'd been telling the truth. "They know this," he insisted. "That is why they didn't tell us about them." Still, he would trust whatever Chris chose to do. "I'm going along with what you decide to do until you give up, because I believe Jehovah, who is my God is going to help us and I don't believe He is going to let me die in here."

"States he would like to attend the SOAR program, but will not admit guilt," a new case manager noted in his file. "Therefore he will not be admitted. He showed me paperwork from Duke Law School and the Innocence Project, that are supposedly working on his case." The following month he was switched to a different case manager, so he asked for SOAR again. "We discussed his plan and he again states that he will not admit guilt. Therefore he can not attend the SOAR program."

The next day he was up again for custody review. "Inmate Grimes has attended no sex offender treatment programs. He has refused to attend the SOAR program, and it is felt retention in medium custody is warranted at this time."

25

Everybody Knows He Didn't Do It

Susan Greene e-mailed Chris from Denver with a question that had occurred to her while writing her feature for the *Post*. She didn't have a law degree, Greene admitted, but she'd been looking into hair analysis and discovered it had been "discredited, even by the FBI, as somewhat of a pseudo-science based on the faulty assumption that no two specimens are alike." The police in Hickory who'd worked on Grimes's case had recovered one hundred hairs from Carrie Elliott's bedspread, sent eight to the crime lab, and analyzed just one. "That was the only physical evidence against him," Greene pointed out. "Also, it seems that using only one hair specimen, as in Grimes's case, goes against accepted practice. Can you do anything for him on those grounds?"

She wished, Chris replied. She'd considered this already. Greene was right; at trial, a so-called expert had suggested the one recovered hair belonged to Willie. But the expert had only hinted that; he'd never said it outright. This was the worst of both worlds, as Chris saw it. The flimsy comparison had certainly influenced the jury, and prosecutors had certainly relied on it, but the expert had never said anything explicitly false, so Chris didn't have anything to challenge. That one hair comparison hadn't been the only evidence, either—Greene had left out Carrie Elliott's ID of Willie. That ID had been "incredibly weak," Chris admitted, but jurors had believed it, which was all that mattered. Even if Chris tried appealing the hair comparison, a judge would simply cite the ID. As far as the court was concerned, Willie's case hadn't depended on hair comparison alone. "This case just sucks more and more every time we touch it," Chris wrote.

"Got it," Greene replied. "That does suck."

A week later Greene e-mailed again. She wanted Chris to know that she'd reached out to a captain in the Catawba County sheriff's department, who'd told her he "liked old cases" and would look personally for Grimes's evidence. The captain himself had gone on to search three different evidence rooms, including one that held everything for cases that never proceeded to trial, just in case something had been misfiled there. But he hadn't found anything.

The *Post* feature ran that summer of 2007, in a four-part series called "Trashing the Truth" that Greene had written with a colleague. "In some evidence rooms, chaos and disorganization makes searches futile," a caption read. "Others are purged of valuable DNA samples, leaving cases unsolvable." The problems with storage that had once alarmed Chris turned out to exist nearly everywhere: "In a country whose prime-time TV lineup glorifies DNA forensics, many real-life evidence vaults are underfunded and mismanaged," the *Post* reported. In certain counties it had found bicycles, lawn mowers, car parts, computers, rifles, tree branches, and six-packs of beer piled atop rape kits, test tubes, and bloody T-shirts, all logged haphazardly in incomplete, handwritten catalogs. One district, in Florida, had taken to storing overflow evidence in a men's bathroom. Another, in Louisiana, used the attic of a local courthouse, where marijuana leaves scattered on the floor were marked with tiny perforations—these turned out to be the bite marks of rats, which clerks had laid traps for. "The system is almost foolproof," another clerk promised. "I've got a photographic mind, see. I know from memory where almost everything is."

In ten different states, the *Post* had discovered evidence rooms so overburdened that clerks had finally decided simply to purge them, intending to begin fresh. Instead, this had compounded the problem. The *Post* had found 141 inmates, across twenty-eight states, whose innocence claims had been collapsed by lost or destroyed evidence. "You can't keep everything," one clerk, in New Orleans, told reporters.

The problem, clerks agreed, was that no policies prioritized evidence from felonies over evidence from misdemeanors, and since a car bumper from a hit-and-run typically occupied more space than a DNA swab from a sexual assault, evidence rooms had gotten organized this way. Or that was one problem. Another was jurisdiction. To avoid politics and confusion about who held authority over what, federal and state governments often left the handling of evidence to local courts, or to police, both of whom had less training and fewer resources. In 2004, Congress had passed something called the Justice for All Act, requiring that all biological evidence be preserved in federal cases, but no equivalent mandate existed for local or state cases, which were far more common. And some officials still weren't sure what biological evidence even was. "That would include tree bark, right?" one courthouse official, in Houston, had asked a *Post* reporter.

"Nobody has stepped up to the plate and said, 'This is the way it has to be,'" one expert told the *Post,* and in all the patched-together confusion, many districts weren't sure themselves of what evidence they had, so inmates in those districts who might truly be innocent had absolutely no way to prove it. "To give the public the impression that the bad guy will be caught and the good guy will be exonerated based on DNA evidence is a fraud," a defense attorney in Southern California remarked. "Because more likely than not, the evidence is in the trash can, and that trash was taken out years ago."

The *Post*'s feature on Willie ran July 24. APPLE TOSSED IN GARBAGE MAY HAVE CLEARED MAN, its headline read. In addition to Chris, Susan Greene had interviewed the Catawba County clerk, Al Jean Bogle. "In an evidence room packed to its brim, Bogle was flummoxed to discover that her predecessor had destroyed the only DNA samples that could have freed Willie Grimes before he dies in prison." It was a mystery to Bogle why that had happened: "I've been clerk for almost eight years. We've got four truck tires in the evidence room. We've got bales of marijuana that have been in there since I became clerk. And Mr. Grimes's evidence, evidence in a life case, is gone. I hate it."

Grimes would become eligible for parole in another year, but he was unlikely to get it, Greene's feature continued, because he refused to join a program that would require him to admit guilt. "Whether I ever get out or not, I'll never sign papers saying I'm guilty of something I didn't do," she quoted Willie, from her visit to Caledonia. "I'll spend the rest of my life in here before I do that." Greene had followed up with Betty Shuford, Willie's onetime girlfriend, who also happened to be the sister of Linda McDowell, the neighbor who'd implicated him. "She just got the wrong person, mixed up," Betty had said. "She's my sister, so it's hard. But everybody knows he didn't do it." Finally Greene tracked down Linda herself, who hadn't recalled the details of Willie's case. "All I know is he went away. It's over and done with now."

"He says he hopes he won't die behind bars," Greene's feature closed. "But without any evidence, he knows it's likely that he will. He struggles to find meaning in his disappointment." Its final page included a photograph from Greene's visit: Willie, his face tilted slightly upward, flecks of white in his mustache and hair, fluorescent ceiling lights reflected in his bulky, prison-issue glasses.

Chris hoped the *Post* series would attract new scrutiny to Willie's case, or pressure officials to look once more for his evidence. Now that it had run, she listened for her office phone neurotically, pleading for it to ring, or stared at her computer screen, hoping for a promising e-mail to appear.

And waited.

"As you know, it was my hope that the *Denver Post* series would heighten the interest in your case and perhaps result in some additional searches for evidence," Chris wrote him. "Unfortunately, I do not know of any new developments at this time." She folded a copy of the *Post* article into her letter so Willie could read it. "My plan now is to go to Catawba county to go to the Sheriff's Department and Police Department to go through the evidence rooms one more time. There is a very good chance that everything has been destroyed, Willie, but we will keep pressing until we are 100% sure."

"I would like to take this opportunity to thank you for all your time and effort that you have exerted on my behalf," Willie replied. "I am truly grateful."

"I know you have been waiting for an update on your case," Chris wrote him some weeks later. "I wish I had better news for you." She'd searched all three evidence rooms at the Catawba sheriff's office, but turned up nothing. "It continues to look like the rape kit was destroyed in 1990 as part of normal operating procedure...The victim is deceased, Linda McDowell stands by her story, and it is becoming certain that the biological evidence has been destroyed." Their only remaining option was a clemency petition to the governor. Chris knew Willie had applied for this once before, a decade earlier, but she expected she could file a better petition than he had managed on his own. "We have not given up on looking for evidence in your case," she promised. "We think about your case constantly. Rely on your faith and continue to be strong."

A week later, he sat down with a pencil to write back.

11-09-07

Dear Mrs. Mumma

I do hope that this letter will find you and family in the best of health and I were glad to hear from you.

I do want you to do what you think is the best thing to do, so if you think petition for Clemency is the best, I agree with you and it's been on my mind too, plus I know you can have it done better than myself. And I didn't have any one behind me when I did it.

Respectfully
Willie J. Grimes

26

The First Real Test

Now that she was executive director, Kendra embarked on a campaign to promote the IIC to nearby law schools and police and attorney organizations, especially those she predicted might be skeptical, hoping to make herself and the organization seem as transparent and unthreatening as she could. "We do not advocate for inmates," she repeated to anyone who would listen. "We try to find out what the truth is about a crime, and a conviction, in order to achieve justice." The IIC wasn't on one particular side or the other; the cases that interested her involved an element of doubt, and Kendra intended to put that doubt to rest. If she could do this by establishing guilt *or* innocence, then as far as Kendra was concerned, justice had been done.

By the close of that first year, 2007, she'd received more than two hundred and fifty claims from North Carolina inmates. A portion of these she had rejected outright; another hundred and fifty she was currently screening. On three, she'd begun formal investigations. Seven others were bottlenecked. Her agency lacked the staff to probe multiple cases at once, something it would need to do, given the volume of its claims, Kendra knew. For now, with only herself and an administrative assistant, she relied on Chris and student volunteers at the center to screen the majority of IIC cases—an arrangement that had begun before Kendra was hired, and that Chris envisioned as permanent, but that Kendra wanted to change as soon as she

244 • BENJAMIN RACHLIN

could. For the IIC to be fully neutral, it also had to be fully independent, Kendra believed. She liked Chris, but Chris represented individual clients. Someone in that position couldn't also be vetting cases. Obviously this was a conflict of interest.

Chris bristled at that idea. But all eight commissioners agreed with Kendra.

So Kendra requested funds from the general assembly for two additional positions, a secretary and another investigator. Meanwhile, she made do with what she had. In December 2007, her agency's first case proceeded to a hearing; that of Hank Reeves, a former police officer up in Pitt County who'd been convicted of child abuse. Today that child was fifteen and had recanted, claiming she'd been coerced into testifying.

Rather than alienate the Pitt County authorities who'd convicted Reeves in the first place, however, Kendra went out of her way to praise them. "They were extremely helpful and cooperative with our investigation," she announced in a press release. "The new evidence in the case was not available to them at the time of trial and this was the first they had heard of it." At a hearing in mid-December, commissioners agreed that Reeves's case included "sufficient evidence of factual innocence to merit judicial review," and voted it forward to a three-judge panel. "It's a landmark case no matter how it's resolved," a local defense attorney told newspapers. "It's a unique proceeding in American jurisprudence."

But nine months later, the three judges at Reeves's panel determined he had not presented "clear and convincing evidence" of his innocence. Reeves remained in prison.

Still, Kendra felt proud of what had happened. She personally had never offered whether she believed Reeves innocent, and never planned to; no one at the IIC had asked her opinion, and from reporters she kept this private, knowing it irrelevant. The rest of the criminal justice system could choose one side or another, she thought. Her own job was not to. She knew that Reeves himself was unhappy with the outcome, and also that she might encounter skepticism in newspapers, since, at the end of it all, judges had simply found a convict guilty again. But the proceeding had functioned exactly as she'd hoped. Attorneys for each side had done a good job, behaved fairly. New evidence had been introduced and considered, and the judges had ruled how the judges had ruled. What else did she want? "The parties should be commended for the way they handled this case," she wrote in a report to the general assembly. "The judges heard every piece of evidence and not a single objection was made during the entire hearing. The Commission is proud of the work they have done and this hearing has been fair and thorough."

She felt the same about Terry Lee McNeil, she insisted, whose case the IIC heard the following January. McNeil had been convicted of armed robbery and kidnapping down in the town of Apex. Again the IIC turned up new evidence, though again it would not be enough; this evidence was insufficient to merit judicial review, commissioners ruled, and declined to forward it to a three-judge panel.

Which was fine with her, Kendra repeated. She was no attorney for McNeil, just as she had been no attorney for Reeves. Both men had gotten fair investigations.

Not everyone shared Kendra's enthusiasm. Chris felt unhappy that McNeil in particular had proceeded to a hearing at all. "If you're presenting a case to the commission, it should be because you believe that person is innocent," she protested.

"No, I don't think so," Kendra answered. "The statute says, if there's new evidence of innocence, and it's credible and reliable." The question wasn't what she believed personally, she pointed out. Her eight appointed commissioners got to make those judgments. She and her staffers only followed statutes.

Chris, though, had good reason to be anxious. Looming in 2010 was the IIC's sunset provision. Already it was 2009; in two years, the agency had accomplished two hearings, one three-judge panel, and zero exonerations. If all the IIC was going to do was reconfirm prior convictions, then it was hard to see the legislature keeping it alive. For the agency to endure, Chris saw, it needed a case it could point toward to justify its own existence. It needed to show what it was capable of.

Then Kendra learned of Greg Taylor.

Taylor was a goateed, bespectacled, sandy-haired man from Raleigh who, back in 1991, had gotten his Nissan Pathfinder trapped in the mud in an unlit cul-de-sac. So he'd abandoned the car and returned the next morning—to find the entire area roped off by police, who'd discovered a woman's body in the same cul-de-sac.

By sunset, police had charged Taylor with murder. He offered his clothes, hair, saliva, and blood, and to undergo a polygraph or hypnosis. Twice he declined a plea deal. His reason for getting his car trapped wasn't ideal, he admitted; he'd found the secluded spot to use drugs. But he'd never killed anyone.

To prove it, Taylor's parents found a lawyer, Jim Blackburn, and took out a second mortgage on their home. Three months before trial, though, Blackburn resigned—a development Taylor learned not from Blackburn but from one of his partners, who confessed the firm had no record of how much Taylor's parents had paid or what, if anything, Blackburn had accomplished on his case. (Within a year Blackburn would plead guilty to fraud, embezzlement, forgery, and obstruction of justice, and surrender his license.)

At trial, police testified that blood had been recovered from the fender of Taylor's Pathfinder, and that a police dog, provided with the victim's scent, had jumped against the car's exterior, indicating the victim had been inside it. A local prostitute, in exchange for her own sentence being halved, testified that she'd seen Taylor that autumn night in the same neighborhood as the murder. A cell mate of Taylor's testified that, while they'd been incarcerated together in jail, awaiting trial, Taylor had privately confessed the entire crime. This cell mate was serving time for embezzlement, though previously he'd also been convicted of forgery, writing worthless checks, and obtaining property by false pretenses. He himself had already been sentenced, he explained to jurors, so his testimony couldn't help to reduce his own time, though he admitted that "it would look good for parole purposes."

Taylor was convicted in April.

Since then Taylor had appealed unsuccessfully to the state supreme court and the U.S. Court of Appeals; he'd tried a federal Petition for habeas corpus and two different motions for appropriate relief. One of these had asked that evidence from his case be DNA-tested, which Taylor offered to pay for himself. All were denied. From their home in Raleigh, Taylor's family had followed the politics of the IIC debate as closely as anyone, and his father, Ed, had even attended committee hearings as the bill foundered in the general assembly. To those hearings, Ed brought handouts of his son's story and distributed them to legislators, hoping to persuade them to pass the bill, since his son's case proved the need for this sort of agency. Eventually a copy of that handout made its way to someone who happened to have dinner plans with Chris Mumma and Beverly Lake.

Chris had taken the handout home with her from dinner and, intrigued, reached out to Taylor, though without any promises. "We're going to try to prove you guilty," she warned. "Then, if we can't prove you guilty, we'll try to prove you innocent." Eventually she'd been unable to prove either. Because the center was a nonprofit, and therefore limited in what it could demand, she couldn't get the access she needed to Taylor's records. Instead she forwarded Taylor's case to Kendra, at the IIC. "They had subpoena power," she later explained to CNN. "They could get access to all the prosecution's records, all the police records, everything that the defense never had access to. And we couldn't get access to. They could order DNA testing that Greg was denied previously."

That autumn Kendra began a full investigation. She and her staffers compiled a 438-page brief and presented this to commissioners at the IIC's third hearing, alongside testimony by three SBI agents, a forensic biologist and pathologist, and an expert each on confessions and crime scene reconstruction. Both the state's original witnesses, the prostitute and the jail informant, now recanted their testimony, and the police dog that had tracked the victim's scent to Taylor's truck turned out never to have been trained to track scents this way.

Commissioners voted Taylor's case forward to a three-judge panel.

When that happened, IIC statute entitled the inmate to choose a lawyer. Taylor chose Chris Mumma, who agreed to represent him for free, as she represented everyone. Then, also by statute, Kendra notified the DA in the case's original jurisdiction, so that he, too, could prepare for the three-judge panel. Greg Taylor had been convicted in Raleigh, so jurisdiction fell to the DA for Wake County.

Colon Willoughby.

Willoughby in turn asked his assistant DA, Tom Ford, to review what new evidence the IIC had uncovered. Ford had been on the job a good while—long enough, in fact, that it was he who had prosecuted Taylor in the first place, back in 1991. It was also Ford who had persuaded a judge to deny Taylor's later motion for DNA tests. Now Willoughby wanted Ford to review the IIC's new evidence and share what he thought.

Because the IIC had subpoenaed every record in the case, it now turned these over to both sides, and, on a single page of a single folder in a single cardboard carton, Chris and her colleagues noticed something. Among the records were personal notes from Duane Deaver, the SBI agent who'd testified about the blood on Taylor's Pathfinder. According to his own notes, however, Deaver had told only a fraction of the truth. A preliminary test *had* turned up positive for blood. Because that test was inclined toward false positives, though, Deaver, per SBI policy, had conducted another, confirmatory, test. Which had turned up negative. But Deaver had never reported this second result to prosecutors, who therefore continued to believe the substance was blood, and presented it as such repeatedly to jurors.

The panel lasted six days. On the second, the *News and Observer* ran a profile of Beverly Lake, who was attending each session, in the front row. "Sitting quietly, a trench coat folded neatly under his feet,

I. Beverly Lake Jr., former chief justice of the state supreme court, is not on one side or the other in the case," the profile read. "But he has plenty at stake. This is the first real test of Lake's idea for a truth-finding agency to right the wrongs of the state's justice system."

The blood evidence was "a red herring," Willoughby argued, "to try to make you forget about the other information." Greg Taylor had committed murder, then tried the next morning to retrieve his car without drawing any attention to himself. Why Taylor had left his car there overnight if he had just committed murder, Willoughby didn't address. And he was willing to forget the whole thing, he offered privately to Chris, if they dropped the appeal. Willoughby would settle for time served; Taylor could walk away from prison.

Taylor refused.

The following week, on Wednesday, as the three judges deliberated, bailiffs led Taylor back to a holding room, where soon they realized they hadn't any clue what to do next. "What happens if they find him innocent?" one bailiff asked the other, in front of Taylor. Neither had ever seen a proceeding like this, and no one had told them the rules.

The second bailiff considered this. "I guess we just do it like at the courthouse," he finally answered. "And carry him back to the jail, to let him get his stuff."

But neither bailiff felt certain, so finally they asked Chris Mumma. "If those judges vote him innocent, you release him *then*," Chris ordered. If Taylor wanted his belongings from prison, he'd be retrieving them voluntarily, and on his own.

All three judges voted that afternoon that Taylor had proved his innocence by clear and convincing evidence. It was the first such verdict in United States history. Upon hearing it, Taylor half stood, disoriented, his mouth hanging open in disbelief, as his family, in the audience, started shrieking. Chris wandered the courtroom in shock, touching her hands repeatedly to her cheeks, as though checking her own temperature. Colon Willoughby stepped toward Taylor and shook his hand, a moment cameras caught on film. "I told him I'm very sorry he was convicted," Willoughby later told the Associated Press, when asked what he had said. "I wish we had had all of this evidence back in 1991."

A string of news articles appeared over the rest of that week in outlets from the *News and Observer* to the *New York Times,* recounting not only Taylor's exoneration but the unusual process that had led to it.

"Gregory Taylor's victory points to the wisdom of the state's process of pursuing claims of innocence," praised the *News and Observer.*

INNOCENCE COMMISSION IS LAKE'S LEGACY ran a headline on WRAL.

The IIC represented "a new standard of jurisprudence in America," read a statement from the governor. "I believe in this Innocence Commission. I believe the ruling today shows bad things can happen, even in the finest of systems."

"If I was in any other state, I would still be in prison for the rest of my life," Taylor himself told the *Boston Review.*

Kendra shied away from reporters, though she admitted feeling glad the agency at last was finding broader attention. "This just shows the process the state created works," she said.

Other state processes had stalled, however. The Raleigh Police Department reopened its investigation into the murder that Taylor had wrongly been convicted of, but by 2014 neither it nor Willoughby had found any leads. "Too many years have passed, and now we hear nothing," Yolanda Littlejohn, the victim's sister, told WRAL that autumn. "I don't want my sister's case to be forgotten, because her murder hasn't been solved."

Obviously it exhilarated her that they'd proven him innocent, but it was a mistake to regard Greg Taylor as her agency's only success story, Kendra felt privately. Sometimes the IIC did the reverse, and those were successes, too. Sometimes it found and tested a DNA sample that in fact matched the inmate, proving him guilty, information that Kendra turned over to authorities. A case like this often had dragged through motion after petition after MAR, and now the IIC had provided closure, had ended the loop of meaningless, expensive appeals. Where once there had been doubt, now there wasn't. After a finding like this, Kendra sometimes received angry letters from the inmate, but that was fine—it was what she'd signed up for, she'd done her job well, justice had been served. This portion of her work never made headlines, and usually Kendra was prohibited even from talking about it, for confidentiality reasons. Still, she cared about those cases, they satisfied her. A question had been answered; the truth had been shown; the correct person was incarcerated.

Or, other times, inexplicable things happened. An inmate wrote to the IIC that he honestly didn't know whether he'd committed the crime he'd been convicted of. That wasn't glamorous, either. "If you're in this because you want your name attached to cases, or you want personal credit, or you want to make money off lawsuits, this is not where you're going to be," she'd gotten in the habit of telling candidates for jobs on the IIC staff. She knew some of these applicants had seen photographs of a lawyer clasping his exonerated client's hand, raising it triumphantly overhead like a boxer's, accompanying national headlines. Nonprofits, or private attorneys, could do that—it was exciting, Kendra didn't have anything against it—but the IIC was different, was a state agency, didn't choose sides, didn't boast. "We're never going to represent an inmate in a civil lawsuit," she reminded her staffers periodically. "We're never going to go around and do press junkets with them to say, 'I found this case, I did it.' The *Commission* found it, the *Commission* did it."

In July 2010, five months after Taylor's exoneration and five months before the IIC was set to expire, a bill was proposed to the general assembly that would remove the sunset provision, installing the IIC as a permanent agency rather than a temporary experiment. Three state senators and one representative voted no. The other hundred and fifty-two voted yes.

27

They Will Try to Get Me to Sign Papers

Guards chose his cell for another shakedown and found a handheld radio Willie had painted; when its plastic cover had chipped, for a dollar Willie had asked an inmate who worked in maintenance to gloss it black again. This turned out to be a violation. They also found two handmade wallets Willie had sewn from discarded leather—a hobby he'd picked up during idle afternoons, and a way to recycle old boots. "These items have been bagged and tagged and placed in the evidence locker," a guard reported. "The inmate is being charged with a D03 for nonthreatening contraband." He sentenced Willie to ten days in segregation and suspended his visitation privileges for four weeks.

He was sent to an unfamiliar clinic for a prostate checkup. For the first time since his surgery, the news wasn't good. His physical exam was normal, but Willie's PSA, the protein marker, had risen, a clue his cancer might be returning. If they waited too long to address it, they might miss their chance entirely, a new urologist told him. He referred Willie to a radiation oncologist, who agreed and prescribed a course of radiation: five times a week until he'd completed thirty-eight treatments. A staffer abbreviated this prescription to "38 daily radiation treatments (5 weeks)" for his own shorthand notes, which a prison nurse further garbled, adding it to Willie's medical chart as "5 x wk x 38 weeks," or fully five times the radiation his doctor intended. Fortunately the error was caught before Willie left in early spring for Alexander Correctional. This sat only fifteen minutes from Catawba Valley Medical Center, where for the next seven weeks guards shuttled him each morning in the rear of a police cruiser. There the radiation machine was a huge white plastic-and-metal arm, like a massively oversize faucet. Doctors laid him on a cot, wheeled him under the spout, and told him to lie still. Two or three hours later, guards put him in their cruiser again and drove him back to Alexander.

The radiation exhausted him, and several times a week he felt nauseated, but now blood tests showed his PSA dropping. When his treatments were through he expected another transfer, since he'd been told he would stay at Alexander only as long as his health required, but now a case manager told him the opposite: he wasn't listed on any backlog. In that case, Willie decided, he might as well enroll in a behavior course. He found one in character education and signed up. Before it began, though, he was transferred back to Mountain View.

"Inmate stated that he was not willing to admit guilt in his crime," a case manager wrote in his file. "Stated that he did not do the crime that he was incarcerated for. No other issues were addressed."

February 4, 2008

Dear Mr. Grimes,

Once again, I apologize for taking so long to respond to your letter. I always hope that if I wait a little longer to write, I might have something hopeful to share with you. I'm sorry that I don't. I know it probably is not much comfort, but I want you to know that I, and others at the Center, think about your case constantly. It is one of our most heartbreaking cases. We believe in you. Edwin Moose believes in you too. I spoke with him the other day about the steps we are taking in your case.

First, I want to answer some questions you asked. I know it is very difficult to understand how it can be proper for departments to destroy evidence in a case. The importance of preserving evidence didn't really catch on with law enforcement until the mid to late 90's when more was learned about the power of DNA. In North Carolina, the law requiring the preservation of evidence was not passed until 2001. Even now, few departments follow that law because there is no funding for storage space/proper conditions and the law does not provide for consequences if evidence is destroyed contrary to the law. We are working on changing the law, but it is not easy.

As I mentioned in my last letter, we are working on a clemency petition in your case. Our hope is to submit the petition to Governor Easley before he leaves office and, if he does not grant clemency, to resubmit it to the next governor who comes into office January 2009.

I wish I could somehow provide you with better news/any news, Willie. I really wish I could. I hope knowing that there are people who believe in you provides you with some comfort.

Take good care.

Chris Mumma

Every few weeks that summer he rode in a police cruiser down to Wake Medical Center, in Raleigh, then over to Catawba Valley or Frye Regional Medical Center for checkups, and each time the news was a little better. "Mr. Grimes is doing well and has had a good response to his PSA thus far," a doctor noted in July. "We expect this to continue to drop over the next six to twelve months."

Since he apparently had survived, he resolved not to waste any more time. He told his newest case manager he wanted any behavioral course at all that Mountain View would let him into, as long as it didn't require him to admit to a crime, so that finally he could qualify for something called a MAPP contract—the Mutual Agreement Parole Program, a stepladder of privileges leading eventually to parole. When he learned the parole commission planned to consider him in October, he wrote to

Chris Mumma: "I think they will try to get me to sign papers saying I'm guilty but I'm not. I don't think they want to let me out."

Chris, in reply, offered to write a letter to the parole board on Willie's behalf, in case it would help him in October. "We believe in your innocence, Willie," she wrote. "I'm sorry we are unable to do more in your case. I would do anything to have been able to find the evidence for testing."

He enrolled in Napoleon Hill, an eight-week course designed to teach "positive mental attitudes." Then he asked to enroll in Anger Management. In early October he wrote impatiently to the parole commission, to learn the outcome of his review, but two more months passed without news. When in early December prison loudspeakers summoned him to the sergeant's office, he guessed it had to do with his custody. Instead, it was because another sibling had died. This time it was Robert Lee, his last remaining brother.

The same law that had prohibited armed guards at Cliff Jr.'s funeral kept him from this one, also. Out there at the ceremony he imagined nieces and nephews whom he knew only barely, since they'd been toddlers when he was convicted. Besides those young strangers, now he was the only man he knew who remained a Vinson or Grimes. Just he and Gladys were left.

Four days later he learned he'd been denied a custody promotion. "This decision is based on severe nature of crime," read his file, and on "inmate's need to address crime related issues."

"Needs to participate in self-enrichment programs," read an additional note. "Poor judgment and influence of substance led to commission of crime."

After Anger Management, he enrolled in Thinking for a Change, a class designed to foster social skills, self-awareness, and problem solving. ("Lesson 15," read the syllabus: "Dealing with an Accusation.")

"He was very upset he didn't get minimum custody," his case manager noted. Still, he didn't intend to give up. He'd waited twenty years to become eligible for parole, and, unless Chris Mumma somehow achieved a miracle, he didn't see what else there was for him. He wrote her again to ask whether any state law required physical evidence be preserved for some period following crimes; it seemed logical that such a law would exist, and, if it did, he realized, clerks or police had almost certainly violated it. Was he right?

Partly, Chris replied a few days later. Such a statute existed, but it hadn't become law until 2001, a decade too late to help him, and it wasn't retroactive. "I'm sorry."

Blood tests showed his PSA had declined to zero, where it stayed. He wrote again to the parole commission, insisting he had enrolled in every course the prison staff had suggested, and had even tried to enroll in SOAR, "but they wouldn't let me because I am innocence." When he didn't hear back he wrote again. He asked for a transfer to Lincoln. He took up sudoku to occupy his afternoons and distract him, in addition to walking his loops around the camp perimeter.

Four months after he'd asked, his case manager told him he couldn't be transferred to Lincoln—since the last time he'd been there, Lincoln had been redesignated minimum security, so Willie was no longer allowed. He asked instead for Piedmont. It wasn't as near to Lawndale, but he'd heard that today an inmate at Piedmont got his own cell, and imagined some privacy there.

Regardless of where he shipped next, and even if he was granted parole, his case manager warned, things wouldn't suddenly become easier for him. Parole would mean finding a place to live on the outside, which was difficult enough for most inmates. It would be worse for a registered sex offender. She handed him a list of homeless shelters and halfway houses to begin looking into.

28

The Last Avenue I Can Think Of to Pursue

When nothing came of the *Denver Post* series, Chris instructed a staffer at the center to compile a list of every person who'd been convicted of first-degree rape in Catawba County between 1984 and 1990, a period that included three years on either side of Carrie Elliott's assault, to see whether any clue would emerge suggesting that one of those men was also Elliott's real rapist, rather than Willie. The staffer phoned the Department of Correction to ask for a search matching this criteria. Unfortunately, a search like this wasn't possible, the DOC answered. The best it could do was refer the staffer to the DOC website, where anyone could try an online search. So the staffer hung up and tried the DOC website, where, sure enough, she found a search function. But access was reserved for state agencies, which the center wasn't. She phoned the DOC again. This time someone referred her to an analyst in the research department, who told her a search like this *was* possible; he didn't know why anyone had said differently. Only two convictions matched the criteria Chris had asked for. One was Willie's. The other belonged to a man named Bernard Degree, who'd been convicted in July 1987 — meaning Degree had been in prison the following October, on the night of Carrie Elliott's rape, so couldn't possibly have assaulted her. Next the DOC analyst offered the staffer names from *every* Catawba County rape conviction, not just first degree, in the period the center had asked for. This turned out to include two additional inmates, neither of whose crimes shared anything conspicuous with Carrie Elliott's. If the DOC analyst expanded his search to include nearby Mecklenberg County, another twelve names popped up, but none of those offered any clues, either.

Aware that it was a long shot, since she or her staffers had already phoned both places and sent letters, Chris drove the two and a half hours out to Hickory to visit the clerk's office and sheriff's department personally. No one in either building would let her physically inside their evidence rooms, she knew, but she guessed that standing in the lobby would persuade them to search a little more rigorously. She waited with her arms crossed while they did this. Then she drove back to Durham and phoned Steve Hunt. Since his investigation—if Chris was going to call it that—into the Elliott assault, back in 1987, Hunt had left the Hickory force for a job at nearby Catawba Valley Community College, teaching basic law enforcement training. He had no recollection at all of collecting any apple core, he told Chris, but he was sure that Carrie Elliott's rape kit had been entered properly into evidence. There had been other supporting evidence, too, he was nearly certain, but he couldn't recall what it was.

Early the following week, Chris e-mailed Hunt to follow up:

Dear Mr. Hunt,

I spoke with you last week regarding the Willie Grimes case. As I mentioned, Mr. Grimes has maintained his innocence of the charges he was convicted of in 1988. Physical evidence collected in the case, specifically the rape kit, hair evidence collected from the bed sheets, fingerprints, and discarded fruit consumed by the perpetrator, could be DNA tested to answer questions in this case. The Catawba County clerk's office has indicated that the evidence has been destroyed. The North Carolina Center on Actual Innocence is following up with all other possible custodians of the evidence to ensure there is no evidence left.

Please let me know if you have any recollections regarding the evidence in the case or if your review of your files provides any insights regarding the disposition of the evidence.

Thank you very much for your assistance.

Chris Mumma

Hunt replied the next morning.

I have know evidence in this case, nor do I know where it is today. The last I saw any of the evidence was in court. Gene walker is the evidence person with the Hickory Police Dept. he might be able to assist your further.

At the bottom of Hunt's reply he had listed his current title at CVCC, "Director of Public Safety Training," as well as a strange e-mail signature: "Always be aware of your surroundings."

She drafted a clemency petition, twenty-six pages explaining the facts of Willie's case, including that he had maintained his innocence for twenty-one years now, despite the cost of earlier release and potentially even his chance at parole. Then she decided not to submit it. The current governor had never once granted clemency in a case where there hadn't already been a DNA exoneration. Chris was skeptical he'd suddenly begin now.

Instead she wrote to the state parole commission to support Willie's application for a MAPP contract. She'd been working on his case since 2003, she explained, and, of the more than one thousand claims that she and her center received annually from inmates, "Willie Grimes's case is one of the few where we are convinced of his innocence and the first for which I have ever written a letter in support of MAPP...The Center intends to file a clemency petition on Mr. Grimes's behalf. Whether through clemency, or through a MAPP contract and parole, Mr. Grimes should have his freedom."

* * *

She received an e-mail from a case manager on staff at Mountain View Correctional, who hoped to confirm that she was the same Christine Mumma who'd been corresponding with Willie Grimes. The case manager was e-mailing as a courtesy; she wanted Chris to know about Willie's upcoming parole review. Chris wrote back that, yes, she was the same Christine Mumma, and yes, she did know about the parole review. "I do want you to know that I have received thousands of claims of innocence from inmates, and I have rejected the majority of those claims," she added. "There are very few inmates I would put my reputation on the line for, but Willie Grimes is one of them. I completely believe in his innocence and if the evidence in his case had been preserved, I am confident his innocence would be scientifically proven."

She received another letter from Willie, insisting what he'd tried to tell her before: there *had* to have been some law, back when he was arrested, forbidding the destruction of evidence. He understood what she'd told him in a previous letter, that the current law hadn't been passed until 2001. But what about an earlier law, to the same effect? There *had* to be one. It made no sense for there not to be a law about something so obvious. Chris simply needed to look harder.

She had looked harder, Chris replied sadly. She knew it didn't make sense to him; it didn't make sense to her, either. Still, it was the truth.

She had more bad news, too. She knew Willie had been writing to innocence projects at law schools around the state, hoping someone else could help him. But all those projects—at Duke, Chapel Hill, Charlotte, Campbell, Elon, Wake Forest, and Central—were coordinated by the same center, meaning the various letters he'd written had all been forwarded to Chris. "I am sorry that those projects will all run into the same dead ends I have run into with regards to investigation of your case," she wrote.

"Willie just wants his name cleared," Chris scribbled in her notes. "He doesn't care about compensation, but thinks others might. He is willing to waive his right to compensation."

There was only one other option she could think of. She knew the IIC had recently won a federal grant, and she was considering forwarding Willie's case to the agency, so Kendra could conduct the same evidence search that she and others had, but with the authority of a court order. This could provide a final guarantee that the evidence in Willie's case was truly, fully gone. "This is the last avenue I can think of to pursue, although I will never stop trying to identify additional avenues to prove your innocence," she wrote him.

29

He Spoke About Going Through Changes

Chris Mumma wrote him again, to share that she'd spoken to the parole commission and learned his next review was scheduled for the end of November 2010. She'd also readied a clemency petition, though now she was concerned it might not matter; the new governor wasn't considering them, not even for inmates who were parole-eligible. "This Governor is clearly not going to be more inclined to consider clemency petitions than our last governor, regardless of how just the claims may be. I'm sorry the petition for clemency cannot help you, Willie, and we will have to put all our hopes and prayers into the Parole Commission. Please ask your case manager if there is anything else I can do to help with that process."

He was transferred briefly to Johnston Correctional, then in the same week back to Mountain View, where a psychiatrist conducted another community-risk assessment, identical to the one Willie had failed four years earlier.

CONFIDENTIAL

DEPARTMENT OF CORRECTION
COMMUNITY RISK ASSESSMENT

TO:	Mike Slagle, Assistant Superintendent for Programs	DATE:	3/30/2010
FROM:	Ken Yearick, PhD. Psychological Program Manager		

RE:	Willie Grimes	OPUS #:	0158046	LOCATION:	4855

*** This report is not to be shared with inmate ***

REFERRAL RATIONALE:

Willie Grimes is a 63 year old (DOB: 8/23/46) Black male serving a Life sentence for Rape First Degree (principal). This individual was referred for a Community Risk Assessment to aid in the determination of suitability for access to the community. The purpose of the assessment and the limits of confidentiality were explained to the inmate.

ASSESSMENT TECHNIQUES:

Record Review included BETA score, MMPI-2, Community Risk Worksheet, Static-99 and Official Crime Version.

HISTORY:

Willie Grimes was admitted to the prison system on 07/15/88 and has a maximum release date of Life. He was first arrested at age [41] by self-report. Prior to the current sentence this individual has been arrested [twice] and has served zero incarcerations for assaultive crimes. Also, on this sentence, this inmate has incurred zero infractions for serious institutional misconduct.

An inspection of this individual's background reveals a 12th grade education. Since leaving school, this inmate's work record has been fairly stable with employment in the Army and construction labor. The mental health history reveals past NC-DOC treatment and no treatment for a significant mental health disorder in respect to risk assessment parameters. Regarding substance abuse, the record shows frequent daily use of alcohol.

According to the Official Crime version, Mr. Grimes illegally entered the residence of a 69 year old female and forced the victim into vaginal intercourse. Her undergarments were ripped from her body. Mr. Grimes threatened the life of the victim while wielding a knife and holding his hands around the victim's neck. The victim had recently been widowed.

[…]

Conclusion: HIGH RISK FOR UNSUPERVISED ACCESS TO THE COMMUNITY
Ken Yearick, PhD   _3/30/10_
Ken Yearick, PhD   Date
Psychological Program Manager

To be determined a *high* risk rather than an *unacceptable* one was faint praise, but it was enough to leave the door ajar for the parole commission. The week after the assessment, Willie was sent one afternoon to Raleigh, to meet with a panel of DOC authorities. What changes had he made since he'd been incarcerated? they wanted to know. What classes had he enrolled in, and had those rehabilitated him? Did he think he posed a risk to the community?

He explained his baptism as a Witness and about Eddie and Virginia Moose. No, he wasn't any risk. In fact, he'd never been any risk in the first place.

After ten minutes he left the panel, certain they would deny him. Halfway through May, he learned instead they'd approved him for a MAPP contract.

The MAPP changed everything. This guaranteed that in two more years he'd be paroled, as long as he followed instructions, which he knew he could. Finally on the horizon he could imagine entire days beyond prison fences. It would mean reintegrating on the outside. This was crucial. Besides those first several years, when anger had disfigured him, the most damning fact of prison was not concrete or razor wire but the simple absence of anyone who recognized who he was. Except for Gladys, Eddie and Virginia, and a friend or two from Douglas High, for as long as he'd been on a camp, no one had known him as Woot, only as Inmate Grimes, #0158046. The MAPP contract would change this. On the outside, he would meet strangers who were not guards or inmates or administrators, and they would not all know of his conviction, meaning that, however rarely, he would be free of its associations — to them he would *not* be Inmate Grimes, he would be Woot, plain Woot, and shy as he was, he would meet a sponsor or employer or even people on the street, would meet social workers and more Witnesses, and all of them would see who he was, they would *have* to, they would listen and know he was innocent. On the outside, it would be impossible for someone to meet him and not see this. The more people who saw it, the more this most basic fact about him would travel, and the pressure it would bring on the prison would prove unbearable. Eventually they'd be forced to let him out for good.

There were things he needed to complete before this could begin. "The Mutual Agreement Parole Program (MAPP) is designed to prepare selected inmates for release through structured activities, scheduled progression in custody, participation in community based programs and established parole," read a form his case manager had him sign that spring. As long as he remained infraction-free, soon he would qualify for day passes; in July 2011, for work release; the following December, for home leave; and eventually for parole. He asked for a transfer to Gaston Correctional as soon as the DOC promoted him to minimum security, as he knew it would now be forced to. Gaston sat barely a dozen miles from Kings Mountain, where Gladys had moved, and less than thirty miles from Lawndale, and only thirty-five miles from Gaffney, just over the border in South Carolina, where Eddie and Virginia Moose now lived.

He was summoned to meet a classification committee: two case managers, a guard captain, and a coordinator, one of whom he recognized from his parole hearing. Why did he want minimum security, and would he be any threat there? Did he believe he deserved it? Had he taken any courses?

Yes, he deserved it; yes, he'd taken courses; no, he wasn't a threat to anyone.

After fifteen minutes they asked him to step outside the door, then called him back inside and told him to sign another form. "He spoke about going through changes," they noted in their subsequent committee report. "He also spoke about proving his innocence and the innocence project. It was the decision of the facility classification committee to recommend promotion for inmate Willie Grimes #0158046."

A nurse at Mountain View filled out a health-screening form on Willie's behalf, to update his records. Under Question 10—"Have you ever used alcohol and/or other drugs?"—she checked "Yes." Under "Date of last use," she wrote, "25 years ago." That same day he was transferred to Gaston Correctional, where promptly he signed up for Alcoholics Anonymous, a condition of his MAPP.

There were no reinforced perimeter walls at Gaston, no turreted guard towers or severe, hulking stone cubes. Only an aging, tree-lined campus of brick and white buildings with road names like Life Skills Lane and Safety Officers Drive, hemmed in by a single layer of fence. Unlike most camps he'd been at, which were isolated from the surrounding town, Gaston sat on the same unremarkable street as a community park and a strip mall: Arby's, Walgreens, Wells Fargo, a gas station. At the clothes house, he exchanged his brown prison uniform for a green one, the color of minimum custody. When he tried to shave the following morning, he learned he could purchase and keep his own razors, rather than sign one out from a guard.

"He said being housed at Gaston was a great help," his new case manager wrote in his file. "We went over his ability to work at a job like dorm janitor. He said he felt he could do that type of work and would try what ever he was told to do...He wants to do what ever is needed to remain in compliance and at the same time he knows it will be hard to find a work release job due to his crime."

He checked the activities board, found no announcement for a Jehovah's Witnesses meeting, so asked around and learned that no Witnesses visited Gaston regularly. One congregation had tried a while back, but when no inmates attended they'd stopped coming, and when they'd tried to start up again, administrators denied them permission. But Thursday afternoon a stranger named Bryan Stewart showed up, with news that Eddie Moose had called him. Stewart was a round man with wispy cotton hair and a habit of quizzing those he met on biblical trivia—he was an elder in the local congregation, he explained, and Gaston had given him a hard time about visiting Willie for Bible study, but he was allowed to come on Sundays, during regular visiting hours, as a normal guest. This was what he planned to do, as long as Willie would like him to. Today Bryan had argued with Gaston for just fifteen minutes to welcome Willie as a new arrival, but he promised to return over the weekend for longer. Willie agreed to add him to his list of approved visitors. "I'll see you Sunday," Bryan told him before leaving.

On Sunday, Bryan arrived at noon. Only a couple years shy of eighty, he was so effusive he seemed a decade younger. He owned a company in nearby Gaston, Pioneer Utilities and Plumbing, he told Willie, but really his calling was to spread the Truth as far and as loud as he could. Since he'd married, at twenty-one, and found Jehovah, he estimated he'd read the Bible more than thirty times, cover to cover, and in his own life he had seen miracles. A few years earlier he'd decided to erect a Kingdom Hall on the same grounds as his utilities company. When the authorities had told him he couldn't, due to zoning restrictions, Bryan began a petition, and soon enough the zoning prohibition was lifted. Still, he couldn't build there, authorities told him, since his driveway was too narrow. A few days later, a neighbor approached Bryan with a problem: He needed to sell off some of his property. So Bryan bought sixty feet and used it to widen his driveway. Still, he couldn't build there, authorities told him, since no fire hydrant was near enough. So Bryan planned to bore under a service road, beneath a highway, and tap into a water main, at a cost of thirty thousand dollars. Around then, however, he noticed for the first time a small, dilapidated house, visible from his office through an unkempt copse of trees. He could barely read its FOR SALE sign through the weeds. He scraped dirt from the phone number on the sign, called it, and made an offer, which the real estate agent accepted immediately. Then he walked the lot to take a closer look around. There on the corner, he told Willie, you could guess what he found: a fire hydrant. All he needed to do was give his congregation rights to use that hydrant through his property, which he happily signed over. Building the actual Kingdom Hall had taken less time than getting all the permits. "Why'd it work?" he asked. "Jehovah makes things work, if it's according to His will. Jehovah will provide."

Bryan had first visited Gaston after learning its warden had a brother who was a Witness, but that warden had since retired, and his successor was less accommodating—like its chaplain, to whom Bryan had tried explaining that all he wanted was to hold a simple Bible study. "What's a Bible study?" the chaplain had asked him.

"You know, where we read chapters," Bryan had replied, dumbfounded. "Ain't you a minister? You don't know what a Bible study is?"

The chaplain had not taken this well. Bryan was not always so tactful, he knew—this was one of his flaws, along with his belly—but it was a *Bible study*, after all. How could a chaplain be confused about that? Anyway, this was why, when Eddie Moose phoned to ask whether he would visit Willie at Gaston, Bryan answered that he was happy to, but could do it only on Sundays, because otherwise he wasn't welcome.

From then on, Bryan and Willie spent each Sunday afternoon together at a picnic table out on the yard, near the Gaston basketball courts. Every week Bryan clipped a Scripture lesson from *Watchtower* magazine, a Jehovah's Witness publication, for himself and Willie to study together. His open Bible lying flat atop the picnic table, Bryan followed lines of the text with his finger, his chin slumped to his chest, periodically looking up wide-eyed to emphasize a certain passage. Willie, seated placidly across from him, followed along in a Bible of his own, one hand neatly in his lap, the other pinching a page corner. He told Bryan what he had waited longer to tell Eddie: he was innocent, and could have been freed already if he'd only confessed, even though it wasn't the truth. Soon after, Eddie called Bryan at home, to tell him the same thing.

Bryan believed them. Already he'd noticed how different Willie seemed from other inmates he'd visited—so mild, so private, so polite. A typical inmate was not this way. Up at Avery County, he'd once studied with an inmate in the warden's own office, where every so often the inmate would leap up from his Bible to steal things. "Let me show you, I can open this safe," he would say, and Bryan would try to talk him out of it. Later, when Bryan rose to leave, the inmate would begin cackling. "Before you go, do you want your billfold?" he would ask, and suddenly he'd be holding Bryan's wallet. Bryan had tried his best, but Scripture hadn't taken. Not every inmate he'd met was so skilled, or so gleeful about it, but they were nearer to that than they were to Willie, whom Bryan couldn't imagine stealing anything. If he himself had spent two decades in prison, Bryan imagined, he wouldn't be so serene. But here Willie was. Another miracle.

On weekdays between Bryan's visits, meanwhile, Willie continued attending Alcoholics Anonymous meetings in the Gaston library. Next he enrolled in a class called Guides for Living, and another called Hard Focus on Freedom. Then he joined Narcotics Anonymous, though he'd never tried drugs, and a parenting class called Father Accountability, though he didn't have children and didn't plan to. Then, in autumn, a questionnaire arrived in the mail from something called the Innocence Inquiry Commission.

30

Send Him a Questionnaire

A grant from the National Institute of Justice allowed Kendra to increase her IIC staff to eight, including two investigators, a staff attorney, and a case coordinator. Now when one of them phoned a state office, the office had usually heard of the commission, and when a staffer asked an office for evidence, the office usually looked—without threats, without court orders, though the IIC could leverage either if it needed. Once or twice Kendra or one of her lawyers had even managed to track down some file or other that police or clerks had misplaced. This got her thinking. She knew the IIC was better equipped today than it had been in its infancy, meaning cases that had stymied them in the beginning they might now have solutions for. To see if this was true, she wanted to try an audit: to revisit certain cases they'd closed, find whatever obstacle they'd encountered, and see whether they'd since learned a way around it.

The IIC had never opened a file on Willie Grimes, but from the documents Chris had shown her, and the mock brief she'd prepared, Kendra had never forgotten about him. She recalled that Chris and the center had spent years looking unproductively for Carrie Elliott's rape kit, and for the hair recovered from her bedspread. Almost certainly this meant both those things had been destroyed. But who knew? Kendra had thought that before and been wrong. A nonprofit like Chris's, state offices might ignore. A subpoena from the IIC, they couldn't. By statute, anyone at all could refer a claim to the IIC: a lawyer, a family member, another agency. Or, theoretically, even Kendra herself. She'd never done this before, but no rule forbade it. Midway through her audit, she found Grimes's DOC record, printed it, and handed it to her case coordinator.

She thought she recalled Chris having told her that she didn't expect Grimes to apply to the IIC on his own, since the man had more or less resigned himself to prison or, if he got lucky, parole, so Kendra wasn't sure he would even fill out the paperwork. But she wasn't positive she was remembering this correctly, and, even if she was, Grimes could always change his mind. *You never know,* she thought.

"Send him a questionnaire," she instructed her case coordinator. "If he applies, then we'll look for evidence."

In September the coordinator mailed a questionnaire to Grimes at Gaston Correctional, where she knew he'd been transferred as soon as he was promoted to minimum security.

31

If They Had Anything, It Can't Match
Nothing from Me

He took the job he'd spoken with his case manager about, as a jan-itor, but there were problems with the next step of his MAPP contract, the community volunteer program, whereby a chaperone might bring him for a few hours each week outside the Gaston walls. Because he was a sex offender who'd never taken responsibility, the prospect of Willie out on a CV pass, even briefly, alarmed prison administrators. "I feel reluctant to recommend participation," a super-intendent wrote in Willie's file. "But due to his MAPP and its pre-planned promotions the facility must abide." Willie found a chaperone in his weekly AA meetings, a man from the outside who volunteered to drive him into town, for lunch at a farmers' market or at Golden Cor-ral. "You'll get used to it," the man told him. "Just need to adjust."

He *wasn't* used to it. He hadn't ridden in a car like this for more than twenty years, not since Brenda's, since that drive from their apartment to the Hickory police station. Not the Gray Goose, or a police cruiser—just a regular car, with a regular seat belt and win-dows, no guard in view and Willie right there in the passenger seat, his hands unshackled so he could turn the radio knob if he wanted. Bound not for a hospital or a distant camp but for lunch twice a month at the Sonic Drive-In, before AA in the rear of a church across the street. Otherwise there were few places he could go. Because they'd labeled him a sex offender, he was permanently forbidden to go anywhere "intended primarily for the use, care, or supervision of minors," including schools or nurseries, or any place minors might gather for "regularly scheduled educational, recreational, or social programs," like museums or playgrounds, or within three hundred feet of any mall or shopping center. "Said it was hard to find a place for his sponsor to take him," his case manager wrote in his file. "He is looking forward to completing his MAPP and going home."

The staffer whom Kendra assigned to Willie's claim was a recent hire to the IIC named Jamie Lau, a thin, pensive, dark-eyed man who liked to joke that he was a postconviction attorney only accidentally. At Duke, where he'd studied law, he'd never envisioned doing this sort of work, had never volunteered for the Innocence Project, barely felt interested in criminal law, planned instead to move to the Northeast and work in consumer protection. But then Lau's wife, a schoolteacher, found a job she liked there in Durham and decided to stay, even after Lau graduated. Lau noticed a position open at the IIC. A friend introduced him to Theresa Newman, who introduced him to Kendra. He began the following January. Three months later, Kendra strode into his office, a thin purple folder in one hand. "Here's a case where all the evidence is supposed to be gone," she told him. "I want you to take a look."

Inside that purple folder lay the questionnaire Grimes had returned. Under "Please explain why you are innocent," Lau noticed, the man had written: "Because I was not there and did not rape anyone." Under "Are you willing to have your DNA and fingerprints run against the databank?," he had written, "Yes."

Lau e-mailed the Catawba County clerk's office, whose evidence logs went no further back than 1991, and then the SBI, who forwarded him two laboratory reports—one it had conducted on Carrie Elliott's rape kit, from November 1987, another on hair samples from the following June. Neither showed anything Lau didn't know already. He drove to the SBI lab himself; maybe staffers there had missed something. They hadn't. He e-mailed the county sheriff, whose search, too, came up empty. He e-mailed the chief of the Hickory Police Department, who forwarded his request to a captain, who replied a week later: a search there had turned up only three pages of old forms showing that, after trial, all Grimes's evidence had been transferred to the clerk's office, except for film negatives and a pair of fingerprints recovered from the victim's apartment. To prove he was telling the truth, the captain scanned these pages and included them as an attachment.

Wait a minute, Lau thought. He e-mailed back. Was the captain saying those fingerprints, too, had been transferred, and simply weren't mentioned on the forms? Or rather that they were never transferred—that the fingerprints were still there at HPD, literally in custody?

Two hours later, the captain e-mailed again. Yes, he replied. There at the department, he'd found a card with two fingerprints on it. According to the accompanying notes, they'd been lifted from a fruit basket on the victim's kitchen table.

Get it in custody, Lau thought. *We'll suss out what it means later.* He reached for his phone, dialed the DA's office.

Lau drove west the 290 miles to Gaston Correctional, where guards led him inside a permanent trailer, barely yards over the fence from where he'd parked. Moments later the door opened again and Grimes appeared, taller than Lau had expected; Lau had seen a mug shot, but he realized now he hadn't considered Grimes's height. He clicked his tape recorder on. "We don't represent you," he cautioned, as Kendra had taught him to begin. He and his agency were investigating Grimes's case only to determine what had happened. This didn't mean they were on Grimes's side, exactly, since they weren't out to prove him innocent. "But if you *are* indeed innocent," and if Lau or his colleagues could prove it, there was a process theoretically Grimes could go through. Did he understand that? All right. Then Lau wanted to hear how Grimes had ended up here.

So Willie led Lau through the October day in question: He'd woken and visited the post office, returned home to shower and shave; he and his girlfriend, Brenda, had stopped into a supermarket, for food to bring to a friend's house party; he'd gone to that house party, and slept on Betty's couch; he and Brenda had driven down to Shelby the following morning with tax money for his cousins. Then he'd returned home from work two days later to learn from Brenda the police had come looking for him, so asked her to drive him to the Hickory station, to find what they wanted, where Steve Hunt arrested him. "He said, 'You know what you here for?' " Willie recalled. "And I said, 'No, I ain't did nothing.' He said, 'Well, you in big trouble.' I said, 'What for?' He said, 'If I was you I'd just be quiet.' I told him, 'I ain't did nothing. I'll take a lie detector test or anything.' He said, 'Best that you be quiet right now, and don't say nothing else.' " Here Grimes paused. "They went and locked me up. I been locked up ever since then."

Lau considered this. "I want you to know," he warned, "this has happened to me before." He'd visited inmates just like Willie who insisted they were innocent. One in particular, around Willie's age, also convicted of rape. "And he told me, 'I didn't do it,' " Lau recalled. "He said, over and over, 'I didn't do it.' " But Lau had investigated, and discovered the rape kit, which had matched. "He did it. There's no *doubt* he did it." Dutifully Lau had relayed this to the district attorney, and the inmate had stayed in prison, now technically also liable for perjury. "So, with that said, I want to make sure you want me to go look for these hairs," Lau finished. "And that you want me to have them compared to you, if I find them."

"Yes, sir," Willie answered.

Then Lau wanted a DNA sample. He offered two swabs to rub against the inside of Willie's cheeks. "We will make every effort to locate this evidence," he promised. "If it's out there."

"I know I'm innocent," Willie repeated. "If they had anything, it can't match nothing from me, because I know I'm innocent."

When Lau had left, Willie met again with his case manager, who decided CV passes had gone so smoothly he was ready to be promoted again, to work release. This required finding an employer, however, and Willie was a sex offender. An old man like him, and a convict? Who would possibly give him a job?

"*I'll* give you a job," Bryan Stewart declared one Sunday visit, waving his hand dismissively. What use was owning a company, if he couldn't do what he wanted with it?

So Willie relayed the offer to his case manager, who looked up the address for Pioneer Utilities and Plumbing, to see whether it neighbored any schools or day-care centers. It didn't. Mr. Stewart would need to come in, pass an inspection, she told Willie. But on a map, this looked like it might work. She gave him a form to sign, invited Bryan in for a meeting. He would supervise Willie personally on the job site, start him at eight dollars an hour, Bryan promised.

The case manager gave him a thick packet of forms. Then she drove Willie to Pioneer Utilities, to inspect the grounds—low office buildings, the Kingdom Hall that Bryan had built, a thirteen-acre field strewn with Caterpillar equipment. This looked like it might work, she said again.

That November, at an SBI laboratory in Asheville, a Special Agent Brian Delmas compared both fingerprints the HPD had forwarded him to those of Willie Grimes. They didn't match. So Delmas uploaded the first mystery print to AFIS—the Automated Fingerprint Identification System, the statewide criminal database—whose software compared it digitally against the constellation in its records. AFIS worked by returning its ten nearest statistical entries, each corresponding to an arrest number. On its own this list meant nothing, since *nearest* was relative, Delmas knew; AFIS had been programmed to *always* return a list of ten, even if none were exact matches. To find out, Delmas needed to look up each arrest number, find the name it corresponded to, then compare each print manually. Partway through this, he noticed something curious. AFIS's first hit, its nearest statistical entry, belonged to a man named Albert Turner. Its second hit *also* belonged to a man named Albert Turner. So did its third. So did its fourth. Turner had been arrested multiple times, so multiple sets of his fingerprints appeared in the database. All four nearest AFIS entries were his. One at a time, Delmas compared them manually. Each confirmed the same thing. The first mystery print matched Turner's left index finger. Not *nearly*. Exactly. Delmas reached for the second mystery print. This matched, too. Turner's left *middle* finger. To make certain, Delmas showed every relevant print to a colleague. He was right, she told him. Both prints were Albert Turner's.

Delmas mailed his conclusions to the district attorney, who forwarded them along to Lau, at the IIC: a 141-page report, including Delmas's notes and a screenshot of Turner's fingerprints on the AFIS interface, taken at 1:54 p.m. on November 7, 2011.

Early Monday morning Willie caught a bus from Gaston Correctional, stepped off at Pioneer Utilities by eight, and spent the day "piddling around," as Bryan called it: plucking weeds, replacing floorboards, soaping office windows. At four p.m. the bus returned to deposit him back at Gaston. One hundred and fifty dollars of his new salary he owed each month to the prison, for room and board, but the rest was his. "He was very pleased with the job," his case manager noted when she saw him next. But the arrangement had limits: for as long as his workday lasted, he was forbidden to leave the Pioneer grounds, and when he did—Bryan gave him a company credit card, and sometimes he used it to buy gas for the lawn mower—he worried over what might happen. What if, when he was out buying gas, another driver pulled up with a child in the backseat? What if, even if that *didn't* happen, someone *said* it did? No one besides Bryan would believe him, and they'd send him right back to Gaston for good. What if a crime happened somewhere in the town, Gastonia, on a day he was on work release? Who police would blame was no mystery. He felt permanently nervous, as jumpy as a fugitive. He could barely keep track of all the restrictions. Sometimes, while he was replacing linens, a visitor knocked at the door and he flinched, filled instantly with dread.

Back at Gaston he got a letter from Jamie Lau, saying his case had been accepted for formal inquiry, whatever that meant. Enclosed were a waiver and an affidavit. He could hire a lawyer if he wanted. He wrote to Chris Mumma. Would she represent him?

Her reply arrived three days later. "I would definitely want to represent you, and would do it without charging anything." But Chris didn't know, either, why the IIC had suddenly decided he needed a lawyer. She would find out, she promised. She would be in touch soon.

From her office, Chris e-mailed Kendra to ask what was happening. When several hours passed without reply, she phoned impatiently and left a message, then phoned another IIC staffer she knew, left a message there, too. Why did Willie need a lawyer?

Jamie Lau drove with Kendra to Hickory, where in a conference room at HPD the pair met with the town's police chief, sergeant, and the captain Lau had been e-mailing, who agreed to assign one of their officers, whose territory included Little Berlin, to assist the IIC's investigation—not to reopen any cases, from HPD's perspective, but to help with anything Kendra or Lau needed. Before the meeting Kendra had silenced her phone, but now, leaving Hickory, she turned it on again. Checked her voice mail. A message from Chris Mumma.

In Durham, Chris's phone rang. It was Kendra.

As soon as she hung up, she found the number for Gaston Correctional, phoned, explained she was Willie Grimes's attorney, she needed to speak with him. It was urgent, it was a legal matter. Willie was out on work release, a voice told her. Call after four forty-five.

She phoned again. This time Willie was there. Breathlessly she relayed what had happened.

Chris drove out to Gaston, more forms in her backseat. Privately she felt ambivalent. The call from Kendra had exhilarated her—and also made her furious. Obviously the fingerprints had been there, at HPD, this whole time. She still remembered asking them for evidence, them answering they had none. Four years since then Willie had spent in a cell, and she'd done nothing about it. *Goddamn it,* she thought. *Why does it always take this long? Why are the most obvious tasks so difficult?*

Would the fingerprints be enough? Still, they'd found those—who knew what else they'd find? Really what she wanted was the rape kit, the holy grail in a case like this, since it held DNA. If not that, then any of the clothing Carrie Elliott had worn, or even those hairs from the bedspread.

At Gaston she hugged Willie tightly. It was important not to expect too much, or look too far ahead, she warned him. No one knew what anything meant yet, and there was no use speculating. All Willie could do was keep the news to himself, concentrate on work release.

Willie didn't care about any rape kit. *They found the fingerprints.* Whatever else the lawyers were searching for, it was the fingerprints he'd always wanted, and now he had them. They *weren't* destroyed. He *knew* it.

He also knew that lawyers had held these once before, and found a way to convict him regardless. He would say nothing to Bryan or Eddie or even Gladys. If they learned the news, they would only get their hopes up, and then if his case went nowhere, it would devastate them. He'd been through that enough times himself. He couldn't put others through it, too.

Jamie Lau and a second investigator whom Kendra assigned to the case, Sharon Stellato, drove to the Catawba County clerk's office, to search personally for the rape kit, bedspread, anything at all they might test for DNA. In a basement near the Newton courthouse, the pair lifted one evidence box after another, read the label, put it down again. Nothing related to Grimes. Back in Raleigh, they wrote to the governor, then to the sheriff's office, the HPD, and the SBI, with orders for Willie's clemency file as well as criminal records for this

Albert Turner. Kendra wrote to Prisoner Legal Services, then to the parole commission, for more records on Willie; they wrote to the DOC for records on both men. For Willie alone, this represented six volumes, spanning more than two thousand pages. They read every one. They wrote to the Catawba Valley Medical Center, which had kept a two-page record from Carrie's emergency department visit, in 1987—but the hospital had forwarded this already to the HPD, so IIC staffers had already seen it. They wrote to the DA's office, which held nothing more than a trial transcript. The prosecutors who'd originally handled Willie's case, back in 1988, both were assistant DAs, and one had died since then; the other's law license had lapsed in the early 2000s. Lau and Stellato phoned him anyway. They phoned Noell Tin, in Charlotte. Tin had kept a file, but all it held was a trial transcript and a letter to Eddie Moose. He e-mailed these along.

Together Lau and Stellato drove to visit Steve Hunt. Four years earlier, when Chris Mumma had tried him, Hunt had had little to say, but Lau and Stellato held something Chris hadn't. A subpoena. Today Hunt was a tall, loose-limbed, bald-headed man with eyeglasses and a neat mustache; he'd retired from the police but still worked in Hickory, directing the Office of Multicultural Affairs at a local community college. Did he remember a case involving Willie Grimes? Lau asked him, sitting in his office.

"I don't remember much at all about it," Hunt replied.

"Okay," Lau said politely.

"I'm kidding, I'm kidding," Hunt said, and grinned. In fact Hunt remembered the case vividly. He personally had grown up in that area, even lived for a few years in the same public-housing complex, Hillside Gardens. Today, when he taught classes on crime scene investigation, there at the community college, he actually used the Grimes case as a model. "The point in doing that is just to show them how important the smallest piece of evidence can be," he explained. For Grimes, this was the hair; without that, Carrie Elliott's rape might never have been solved.

What about the fruit? Lau asked. Did Hunt remember anything about that?

He did. He'd seen that apple core, and those banana peels, lying behind Carrie's apartment, a sight that struck him as "bizarre," and inside had noticed more fruit on her kitchen table. So he'd pieced together that her assailant must have taken some of it. He even remembered in which direction the discarded peels suggested the man had fled: south, from Carrie's front door.

Did Hunt know why no one had collected them?

He didn't. Neither did he recall Grimes turning himself in — Grimes had turned himself in? — or Grimes ever claiming he was innocent, or anything about an alibi. While Hunt had worked at HPD, though, he'd often taken files home with him, and even in retirement had kept his file on Willie Grimes, to use when he taught. He spread this on his desk for Lau and Stellato to see.

Lau pointed to a particular page. This looked like a lineup, but Lau didn't recognize it. Now Stellato noticed, too. "May I see those photographs right there?"

"Oh, absolutely." Hunt slid the page over.

Stellato scrutinized it: a typical six-person lineup, with photographs arranged in two horizontal rows. But something different. She spun the page toward Hunt, pointed to a particular photograph that hadn't appeared in any lineup before this one. "Can I ask you a question? Do you remember this guy?"

"Oh, yeah," Hunt answered. That was Albert Turner.

Lau pulled the lineup from Stellato and squinted at it. Turned it over. On the reverse of each photograph, a number was listed — from the HPD filing system, Lau guessed. Except for Turner, who had no number. Instead, his full name was written out. Lau flipped the page over again. That was him, Albert Turner, in position number two, center photograph of the top row. He peered back at Hunt's file. Flipped two more pages. There. Another lineup. This one he'd seen before. This was the lineup officers had shown Carrie Elliott two days after the crime, after Linda McDowell's visit to headquarters.

Now Turner's photograph was gone. In its place, in the same position—number two—was Willie Grimes.

"Let me ask you a question," Lau said. He pointed to Turner's handwritten name. No one else's name was written out; did this imply Turner had been a suspect at one point?

Hunt wasn't sure. It wasn't him who'd put either lineup together. This one was only a copy; he didn't recall who he'd gotten it from. He had no memory of Turner ever being a suspect—although, now that he thought about it, it didn't surprise him that Turner might be included in a lineup, especially near Little Berlin, in those years, since the man was an often-violent criminal. Come to think of it, Turner also fit the profile, Hunt realized aloud. "Albert's about six one, six two, pretty close to the physical description of the suspect."

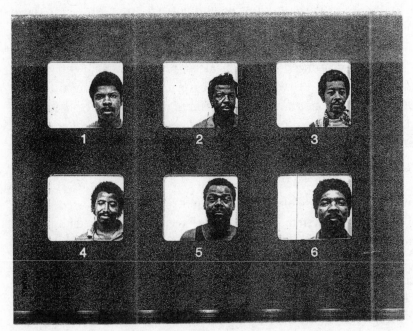

Courtesy of the Hickory Police Department

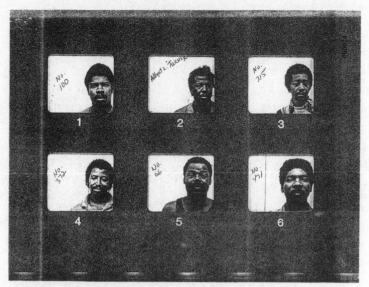

Courtesy of the Hickory Police Department

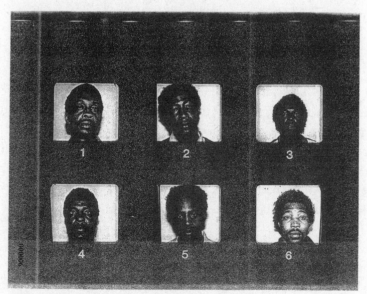

Courtesy of the Hickory Police Department

* * *

The officer whom Linda McDowell had phoned two days after the crime, to say she thought her neighbor's assailant sounded an awful lot like Willie Grimes, was Hunt's former sergeant Steve Bryant, who that same evening had driven out to Claremont, to show Carrie a second lineup, with Willie included. Today Bryant remembered nothing of the case, however, even after Lau phoned him in Massachusetts, where he lived now, and faxed him his original police file. Neither did Bryant follow who Lau was, or what this IIC was, or what they were doing, asking him about a case so old. "Did he all of a sudden, twenty-five years later, decide that he's—'cause I know a lot of people claim they're innocent," Bryant told Lau over the phone. "And actually they're not."

"Well, he's been asserting his innocence for twenty-five years," Lau replied.

"Oh." Bryant paused to consider the police file again. Was Lau certain he'd faxed the entire thing? He noticed it seemed a little thin. "I was saying that to my wife last night," he told Lau. "There has to be more than this."

The crime scene technician who had processed Carrie's apartment, Jack Holsclaw, still lived in North Carolina, so Lau and Stellato visited him for lunch, bringing along photographs Holsclaw had once taken and a transcript of his testimony at trial, to jog his memory. Despite those, Holsclaw didn't recall the case. "I wish I could do more," he told them. He'd spent thirteen years as a technician: "After you've been to hundreds of crime scenes, they all just kind of run together." No, he hadn't kept any files from his days with HPD. But he did remember Albert Turner. A local troublemaker.

The officer who had interviewed Carrie Elliott on the night of the crime, and shown her the HPD's first lineup—the one Lau and Stellato had discovered only recently, in Hunt's file—was Jeff Blackburn, who today owned a cleaning business in Columbia, South Carolina. Vaguely he recalled standing inside Carrie's apartment, but not showing her any lineup, or why Albert Turner's photograph appeared in it, or whose decision it was to include him.

Lau revealed another fact he and Stellato had noticed: this photograph of Albert Turner had been outdated even then. Carrie Elliott was assaulted in 1987. But this photograph of Turner was from 1985. Those two intervening years might not have mattered, had Turner kept the same hairstyle. But he hadn't. In 1985, and therefore in the photograph, he was wearing unkempt dreadlocks. By October 1987 he'd grown a short Afro. Carrie had described her assailant as having bushy hair. Still the HPD had chosen a photograph from two years earlier, showing him in dreadlocks.

Blackburn couldn't explain this. Typically an officer assembling a lineup would begin with a particular suspect in mind, then pull photographs of others who looked similar to him from a cabinet just outside the lieutenant's office. Assuming Turner's photograph was pulled from that cabinet, it should have been current, since any time someone was re-arrested, his newest mug shot replaced his previous one.

Lau flipped the lineup over, and showed Blackburn the name on its reverse. Was that Blackburn's handwriting?

No. Blackburn didn't recognize it. Maybe it was Susan Moore's?

The handwriting wasn't hers, Moore told them.

Did she recognize whose it was?

"Not a clue," Moore said. Back in the 1980s, she'd been one of the only HPD investigators who also happened to be a woman. This meant she often was asked to sit in on interviews with rape victims, hoping to put them at ease. Twenty-odd years later, she couldn't recall every single one distinctly. She didn't remember Carrie Elliott or Willie Grimes at all.

Like Steve Hunt, Linda McDowell had had nothing to say to Chris Mumma, but now, under subpoena, she remembered that, days after the assault, her neighbor Carrie had told her what happened, and Linda noticed the description of her attacker sounded familiar. "I said that sounded like Woot," she told Stellato. " 'Cause of the mole she said was on his face."

Stellato had read through the HPD reports, she pointed out gently, and it turned out that, in Carrie's initial description to police, she hadn't mentioned a mole at all. "It's not until after she talks to you that she mentions the mole. And we're just trying to figure out why." Might Linda have suggested the mole first, even inadvertently, and Carrie had accommodated it?

No. Carrie had said it first.

Did Linda believe it was Willie Grimes who had raped Carrie Elliott?

"Well, that's who she described to me," Linda answered. All she knew was what Carrie had told her, which sounded an awful lot like Woot.

At the IIC offices in Raleigh, Albert Turner's criminal history arrived: three densely printed, single-spaced pages, listing ninety-odd charges, including twenty-three for assault, several with a deadly weapon, one against an officer. Back in November 1985, Turner had begun a three-year prison sentence, but he'd been paroled at the end of April 1986. Meaning he'd been out of custody the following October, on the night Carrie Elliott was assaulted.

Then, eleven months later, after Willie was arrested, Turner had assaulted someone else. Three months later, someone else. Three months after that, someone else, plus larceny and resisting arrest. Two months after *that* he'd trespassed into housing projects, twice in the same week.

March 1990, assault. July and November, more trespassing. January 1994, May and June 1995, February 1997, January 1999— assault, assault on a female, assault with a deadly weapon, assault on a female, assault on a female. September 2001, June 2002, March 2003, more trespassing. April 2006, assault on a female with a deadly weapon. August 2007, disorderly conduct. April and September 2008, assault on a female, assault on a female. For a few of these he'd served time, but only briefly.

As Willie, meanwhile, was in prison.

From Turner's records, Lau pulled street addresses that various agencies had listed for him, and placed these onto a map. Five sat within a half mile of Carrie's apartment. Including the address listed most frequently, which was just around the block. And to the south. The direction Hunt believed her assailant had fled.

For weeks Kendra, Lau, and Stellato struggled to locate where Turner had gone, but finally the HPD officer assigned to help with their investigation heard on the street that Turner's health was bad, so they phoned around and found him in a nursing home up in Lenoir, a half hour west of Hickory by Route 21. Lau and Stellato drove out. Turner looked terrible; his short Afro was graying, and his shoulders sagged so badly that his features looked uneven. His posture was like melting candlewax. But he remembered Carrie Elliott. That was a white lady who lived in Hillside Gardens, he told Stellato, while seated with the pair at a dining table. She'd been raped? He remembered that now. Personally he'd never talked with the lady.

Did Turner know anything about the rape?

"No, I didn't hear nothing." But now he remembered he *had* talked with Carrie Elliott; often she'd invited him inside her apartment, to use her telephone. He even remembered Woot being arrested. Turner had barely known Woot, only that he was quiet and from Shelby. But in fact Turner and Woot had been together when the cops showed up and took him.

The police hadn't shown up anywhere, Stellato pointed out. Willie had turned himself in.

Oh.

"Do you have anything you think we should know?"

"No," Turner said. He guessed he *hadn't* been with Woot that night, even though he remembered it, the cops showing up, taking Woot away. He was willing to bet money. No? Woot had turned himself in? What night were they talking about, again?

"I'm gonna tell you something, okay? Are you listening? We found some physical evidence that matches you." Could Turner explain his fingerprints on fruit inside Carrie Elliott's kitchen?

"I ain't never ate no fruit at her house," Turner argued. He'd never been inside her kitchen at all. "So I don't know." Now he remembered something. He had brought Carrie fruit that one time, as a gift. Put it in her fruit basket himself.

From Turner's police records, IIC staffers created a timeline of his every offense, each listed alongside a date and the name of a victim, whom Lau and Stellato set about finding. First was Cookie Walton, a former girlfriend of Turner's whom court records showed he'd struck over the head with a liquor bottle. That was true, Walton confirmed, when the pair knocked at her door. She and Turner had dated for six or seven years, but the relationship ended when Turner stabbed her. There was no use estimating the number of times Turner had grown violent, she replied, in answer to Stellato's next question, since it was too many to count. Yes, sometimes he'd forced her into sex. She didn't want to estimate that number, either. "I just don't even want to think about it."

"Is your brother Albert Turner?" Lau and Stellato asked Martha Ferris.

"Oh Lord," Ferris answered, and swung open her door. "Come on in." No, Albert no longer stayed with her. In fact, he wasn't allowed, since that altercation with the housing authority. No, Albert wasn't violent—although, well, yes, he'd hit her before.

"Lord, no," Leroy Jenkins told them, when Lau and Stellato shared they'd heard he once ran with Albert Turner. Jenkins had only gone to school with Albert's brother. "He's totally different," Jenkins promised. He'd heard Albert was violent, and a drunk.

"Don't look at me," Jenkins's wife added.

"Lord have mercy," Jenkins said. He'd never wanted anything to do with Albert.

* * *

Wade Hefner had died in 1993, his widow, Shirley, told them. Before then, yes, he'd often hung with Albert Turner. In fact it had provoked arguments, since Shirley had never liked him. "Nothing but a drunk," she recalled. Would Lau and Stellato do her a favor, and not tell Turner where she lived? "I don't trust him with a ten-foot pole."

Juanita Probst had known Turner nearly her entire life, she agreed, so Stellato explained why she and Lau had come: they'd seen her name on a police report, were curious for details.

Probst thought she knew which crime they meant. "Him raping me?"

Stellato hesitated, startled. The police report she meant had listed only an assault charge.

"I wasn't but nine years old," Probst continued. She'd been babysitting some smaller children, left with Turner for a walk through the woods, where under cover of trees he'd pulled her clothes off. Afterward she had tried telling her parents, but they'd only smacked her for it, so she'd never said a word to police. She was glad these investigators had finally learned of it, however they had. "He's a very cruel person," she told Stellato.

They drove back to Lenoir, to see Turner again, who recalled now that he had known Carrie Elliott "real good," in fact had visited her nearly every weekend. "We'd use her telephone."

Had Turner ever been charged with assault?

One girlfriend he'd hit "a couple times," Turner admitted. Nothing otherwise.

What about his sister?

Oh, sure. He'd gotten in fights with his sister. But that was all. That one girlfriend, his sister.

"You know I know every woman you've assaulted, right?" Lau asked. He lifted the pages of Turner's criminal record. "So why are you not telling me everyone?"

"That's all I know," Turner insisted.

"You didn't assault Juanita?"

"Oh. I forgot all about Juanita," Turner said.

Had he and Juanita ever had sex?

"Yeah," Turner replied. "But I didn't rape her."

LAU: But—she had sex with you when she was twelve?

TURNER: Yeah.

STELLATO: How old were you?

TURNER: I was about fourteen, fifteen.

STELLATO: How old are you now?

TURNER: Sixty-five.

STELLATO: So, Juanita's forty-seven now.

TURNER: Yeah.

STELLATO: So you probably weren't fourteen or fifteen when she was twelve, right?

TURNER: I don't know.

STELLATO: You would have been thirty.

Thirty, Turner repeated, yeah, that sounded right. But Juanita had wanted it. "She was a hot little girl."

"This record doesn't look good," Lau told him, waving the pages again. "So why should I believe you, when you say you didn't assault Carrie Elliott?"

"Cross my heart," Turner said. Wait—were they talking about Carrie Elliott now? Or Juanita? Juanita, that was different. But he hadn't done anything to Carrie Elliott.

How had his fingerprints gotten on those bananas in Carrie's apartment, then?

That was because he'd brought her those bananas as a gift, put them in that bowl by her front door. That glass one, a green and white bowl. Bananas, that's right. And sometimes grapes.

"That's not at all what the bowl looked like," Lau told him. Carrie's fruit bowl had been plastic, and she'd kept it in the kitchen. Turner had told them he'd never been inside her kitchen.

"I didn't do nothing," Turner repeated. "I ain't no violent person. I was a nice guy."

"Would Carrie Elliott say you're a nice guy?" Lau asked.

"Who?"

"Carrie Elliott," Lau repeated.

"Who?"

They drove to Gaston Correctional again, to meet with Willie, whose case manager held him back from the bus to work release. Again Willie led the pair through that October Saturday, listed everyone he recalled seeing at that house party.

What about others he'd known before his arrest? Was he still in touch with Brenda Smith, or Betty, his former girlfriends?

Brenda had died way back in '91, Willie told them. As far as he knew, Betty was still living, though she'd long ago stopped answering his letters. So had her son, Christopher. Back when Betty had come to share his apartment, before all this had happened, Willie had often looked after Christopher, who'd been a small boy then, had even called Willie Dad.

By chance it was Christopher who answered the following morning, when Lau and Stellato knocked on the door to Betty's apartment.

"You're Chris?" Stellato asked, surprised. "Willie Grimes was talking to us the other day about you." That Willie had been trying to get in touch?

That was true, Christopher admitted. He just hadn't written Willie back. "Tell him I said I ain't had time. I've been working. I'm trying to do it, though. I'll get to it."

"He said he was raising you till you were about five?" Lau asked.

That was true, too. Christopher paused to consider this. "He's been gone that long? I'll be thirty this year." He tilted his head. "I remember him. He sent me a picture. I remember he used to buy me about everything, guitars and all that type of stuff. Stayed with him when my mama go to work. He used to watch me, keep me all the time. I thought he was my daddy." But Christopher had lost track even of which prison Willie was being held at. His eyes widened when Stellato told him it was Gaston Correctional, only a forty-five-minute drive.

"We're gonna tell him we saw you, okay?" she said.

Christopher nodded. "Tell him I miss him. I just haven't wrote him back."

Betty emerged then from another room, so Lau and Stellato explained why they'd come. "Woot was a good man," Betty told them immediately. "He was nice."

Had Willie ever hit her, or forced her to have sex? Had she ever heard of him doing either to anyone else?

Not once.

Had she ever spoken about the case with her sister, Linda McDowell?

Hardly. She'd only learned afterward, and from others, that it was Linda who'd given Woot's name to police. Betty and the others had tried telling Linda it was impossible—Woot had been at that house party, had slept on Betty's own couch—but Linda hadn't listened. To this day Betty had no idea why Linda had accused him. "She's *still* lying," Betty said. "If she gets caught in a lie, what happens to her?"

"She didn't testify," Stellato explained. Linda had never been called at trial. Since she'd never been under oath, she'd never committed perjury.

"Oh," Betty said.

Lib King had attended that same house party, still recalled seeing Woot there, even recalled—accurately—that he'd been arrested on a Tuesday. "Just knowing him, I don't believe it," she told Lau and Stellato.

Did King know a woman named Linda McDowell?

A little. King had always felt closer with Linda's sisters, Betty and Rachel and Carolyn, the latter two of whom had passed away since then. That was where she'd learned it was Linda who'd accused Woot; Linda's sisters had told her.

"What did they say about that?" Stellato asked.

"They thought she was just doing it for the money."

Richard Wilson, who'd held Willie's tax money that night, and happened to live across the street from that house party, remembered the same thing: Woot had crossed over to his house, retrieved his tax money, then crossed right back to the party. "So he couldn't have done that," he told Lau, meaning the rape. "He wouldn't have done it anyway. Woot wouldn't have done that. I'd stake my life on it. That's the wrong man."

Les Robinson remembered it, too. He'd dropped into that house party to borrow a pot for his wife, seen Woot there, returned later to watch television. Today Les and his wife, Turnell, were still married; she remembered the same sequence of events, though the couple couldn't agree on what exact time it had been. Before sunset, Turnell thought, since she'd needed that pot for dinner.

So both Robinsons believed Willie had never raped anyone?

"I'm sure he didn't," Turnell said. "I *know* he didn't. He was the most gentle person."

"I was sorry what had happened to the lady," Les added. "But get the right person."

Lau and Stellato offered their business cards, in case either Robinson recalled anything else. Before they could leave, however, Les spoke up again. Could he ask something he was curious about?

Of course, Lau told him.

"I'm just very curious about it," Les said. "We don't even see the young man no more. If he went to prison and spent all that time for nothing, why y'all wait so long to investigate on it, again?"

Ed de Torres still practiced law in Newton, still remembered those banana peels that police had neglected outside Carrie Elliott's apartment, still felt incredulous about it. "He's been the one client I've had that I really felt should not ever have gone to the Department of Corrections," he told Lau.

"So you do, in fact, believe he's innocent?"

"I do," de Torres said. "That's the reason I've assisted him throughout the years. Obviously, you know, I believe the woman was raped. It's obviously a terrible experience. But she was older and was just, I think, overwhelmed."

Lau peered at de Torres's desk, where he noticed an unfamiliar sheet of paper, and asked de Torres what it was. That was his original timesheet, and handwritten notes, from his work on Willie's case, de Torres answered. He slid this over to Lau and Stellato. They were welcome to see or photocopy it, or anything else from his files.

Stellato examined the page, pointed to a particular line. "Can you tell me what that says?"

"Sure," de Torres agreed. He leaned forward and squinted. It had to do with the party that night at Rachel Wilson's house and the affidavits he'd gotten, de Torres explained, which seemingly no one had read. "It says, 'Other people saw him there.'"

A third time, Lau and Stellato drove out to Gaston Correctional. "You're completely innocent of this crime?" Lau pressed.

"Yes, sir," Willie told him.

State law required that the IIC contact a victim's family to share what was unfolding, though the truth was Kendra would have done this anyway. She, Lau, and Stellato had all worked personally with crime victims, and knew what a trial verdict could mean to a family, as well as news that verdict was being investigated. They deserved to know what the IIC was doing. So Stellato phoned funeral homes around Hickory until she found the one that had handled Carrie Elliott's service, and asked an employee to fax her whatever it had kept. Carrie, a Baptist, had died on a winter evening in 1989, after a "brief illness," according to the death record that arrived. She'd been seventy-one. Before retiring, she'd worked as an aide at the Brian Center, a local nursing home and rehabilitation center.

Listed as Carrie's next of kin was Bobby Elliott. Her son. A search revealed he still lived in Hickory.

Stellato phoned and introduced herself, and together she and Lau drove out to meet Bobby and his daughter Tamera, Carrie's granddaughter. Out of concern for the family's privacy, neither Lau nor Stellato recorded the meeting, as they usually did, and even afterward declined to share anything about it with anyone but Kendra — except for Stellato's impression that Tamera, who'd done most of the talking, had struck her as a sweet, receptive woman, an attentive listener, and that everyone at the IIC hoped she and Bobby felt they'd been treated as kindly as possible. It required no imagination at all to appreciate what Bobby and Tamera might be feeling. It was Bobby whom Carrie had phoned that awful October night in 1987, when she couldn't remember the number for police.

Lau diagrammed a second map of Hickory, with pins dropped for Brenda Smith's house, where Willie had lived; for Rachel Wilson's house, where he'd reportedly been on the night of the rape; for Betty Shuford's house, where he'd reportedly slept on the couch; and, a few miles west, for Carrie Elliott's apartment in Hillside Gardens, surrounded by clusters of pins representing addresses for Albert Turner. This final map Kendra assembled with everything she or her investigators had discovered into a brief that ran 463 pages. Printed out, it weighed three and a half pounds. She mailed copies to all eight of her commissioners, drove again to Hickory for one final meeting with the HPD and the district attorney, then phoned Chris Mumma, to let everyone know she had called a hearing for the first week of April.

32

What She Said Happened, Happened

At a few minutes past ten in the morning on Monday, April 2, 2012, Kendra rose to a lectern in a windowless, carpeted room in the North Carolina Judicial Center, a stack of brick and glass rectangles nestled in a complex a few miles west of downtown Raleigh. Facing her sat eight commissioners at a horseshoe of tables already littered with neon highlighters, disposable coffee cups, and foot-tall stacks of paper. A row of plastic bins, stuffed with more files, ran the length of an entire wall. To begin, Kendra called Lau, then Stellato, to walk commissioners through portions of their investigation. Then she began calling witnesses.

For nearly an hour, Linda McDowell slumped in the witness chair, lips pursed, looking unhappy she'd been subpoenaed. Yes, she'd received a thousand-dollar reward for tipping police about Willie, but that wasn't why she'd done it. Her neighbor Carrie had described her assailant as "that tall guy with the mole on his face," and Linda had replied, "I know you're not talking about Woot," and Carrie had said, yes, it was Woot she was talking about. This was a week or so after the rape.

When Lau and Stellato visited her, three months ago, Linda had told them this conversation was the very day after Carrie's rape, Kendra reminded gently. Was she certain now it was a week later?

Linda didn't know.

From a folder Kendra withdrew the 1987 Hickory police report, and read aloud. "It says, 'Ms. Elliott advised that McDowell told her that she would give the name to the police only and no one else.'" She turned to Linda. Was she certain she'd told Willie's name immediately?

"Maybe," Linda said.

At trial, Kendra continued, Linda's own mother, plus three of her sisters, had testified that it was impossible Willie had committed this crime. Did Linda have any thoughts about why her entire family had gone to court and said this?

"I have no idea," Linda said.

"Ms. McDowell, I think I got confused in your testimony," one commissioner, a DA, admitted, once Kendra had opened the hearing to their questions. He asked Linda to lead him again through how she'd learned of Carrie's assault. Linda tried. She'd returned from the movies that night to a silent, still apartment, gone straight to bed. But also, Carrie's children had phoned that night, to tell Linda the news, so Linda had rushed to the hospital. But also, no one had phoned—Linda didn't *own* a phone—and Linda had never visited the hospital at all. She'd only seen Carrie back at the apartment once Carrie was discharged.

"How certain are you that Woot is the one who raped Ms. Elliott?" another commissioner asked.

"I don't know," Linda said.

"Do you think it's possible that he is not the one that did it?"

"I just—" Linda began, then stumbled. "The only thing I'm—" Stumbled again. "That's the only person I know with that mole on his face."

Steve Hunt, wearing a suit and a red tie, described for commissioners the apple core and banana peels he'd noticed on Carrie Elliott's lawn. On a map Kendra offered, he pointed to where he'd seen them, then repeated what he'd told Lau and Stellato: today he used this case as a model when he taught criminal investigation at his community college. "The point I wanted to make to students was, make sure you leave no stones unturned when you are doing a crime scene. Because what you do on the crime scene can determine whether people get brought to trial for crimes they commit, or turned loose for things they didn't do."

"About the no-stones-unturned aspect of this investigation," Kendra prompted.

"Sure," Hunt said.

"Do you think that collecting the banana peels, and the apple core, would have also been an essential part of the no-stone-unturned investigation?"

"Sure," Hunt agreed. "I—yes, I would've thought that."

"Okay," Kendra said.

"And if I may just elaborate on that just for a second."

"Please do."

"I would've thought that—my evidence technician had been an eight- or ten-year police officer. And when I left him on the scene, I—I thought he would have got that." Yes, Hunt was lead investigator, but that didn't mean he controlled anything. "Most of the investigation was done by folks other than me."

If Hunt, as lead investigator, hadn't directed the investigation, then who had told officers what to do?

"Well, no one," Hunt said. Mostly investigators had directed themselves, then reported back to him. "I was receiving the information once—you know, the lineup was shown, I got a yellow sheet saying that the lineup was shown. All of those type things."

"There was nothing you directed people to do in this case?"

"No," Hunt said. "This case came together fairly quickly."

The hairs HPD had collected from Carrie Elliott's bedspread, then submitted to a state laboratory, had been examined there by an SBI analyst named Troy Hamlin, who today still worked in the field. Hair comparison, he explained to commissioners, simply meant aligning two hairs under a microscope, then peering at a side-by-side comparison. There was no particular checklist for how this comparison worked. An analyst simply offered his subjective opinion. Few conclusions could be drawn this way, so really it was useful only in combination with other evidence. Or at least it was today. "But in the eighties," Hamlin admitted, "there were a lot of—not disagreement, but there wasn't—what I'm saying is, there wasn't a lot of guidelines to what your conclusions could be." Only since then had experts discovered that hairs could look similar without actually belonging to the same person. After one study of 268 criminal trials in which an FBI agent or analyst had testified about hair comparison, the Bureau now acknowledged that, in retrospect, 257 of those trials—or 96 percent—included "erroneous statements" during testimony. For defendants in nine of those cases, the study came too late. They'd already been executed.

Hamlin had no recollection of working the Grimes case specifically, but Kendra handed him his laboratory report and case notes, and Hamlin led commissioners through it. According to his own report, only a single hair from Carrie Elliott's apartment had been long enough for comparison, so Hamlin had measured it against sixty or so of Willie's hairs. Some of those had looked similar. Others hadn't. At trial, he'd testified that such resemblance was "rare," and therefore, the hair recovered from Carrie's bedspread "could have originated from Mr. Grimes." Both these conclusions Hamlin still stood by, he told Kendra, since personally he felt it *was* rare—that was simply his opinion, not a scientific claim—and, if two hairs looked similar, then technically it was true they *could have* originated from the same person. Aside from his own testimony, however, Hamlin had attended nothing else of Willie's trial, so he hadn't been in the courtroom during closing arguments, when prosecutors had told jurors, under the guise of a reminder, that an SBI agent— meaning Hamlin—had said, "The only place this hair could have come from is the defendant, from his head, and it came from him when he was assaulting this lady." Hamlin had never said *that*.

Kendra was curious—had Hamlin ever personally observed two similar-looking hairs, only to discover later they were from different people?

Yes, Hamlin replied. Well, maybe. Certain cases he'd worked on had been subjected afterward to DNA testing. Hamlin had never followed up on those results, though, so he didn't know what the DNA had proved.

"You do not know?" Kendra repeated, startled.

"I do not know," Hamlin agreed.

"Do you think it would be important that you..." Kendra paused. "Find that out?"

"No," Hamlin remarked offhandedly. "There's probably been others."

"But you didn't...you know that some work you did was later subjected to DNA. And you didn't want to find out whether the DNA said, 'Yes, it was this person,' or 'No, it's not'?"

Hamlin considered this. He swung his eyes toward the ceiling. "No, not particularly."

"When I think of cases I've handled, this is probably the one that haunts me still today," Ed de Torres told commissioners. He still remembered motioning for further testing at trial, the judge never ruling on it. "I did not follow up," de Torres admitted, which now he regretted. "I should have followed up." He didn't blame Carrie Elliott, since the poor woman *had* been raped. It wasn't *her* job to do an investigation. He shrugged sadly. "It's the kind of crime that, if you have a bad identification, it will go down the wrong way."

Early Tuesday morning, Willie woke at Gaston Correctional and met with guards who put him in a cruiser, drove him three hours to the Wake County sheriff's office, then handed him over to unfamiliar deputies, who put him in the rear of a second cruiser, drove to another building, and ushered him into a holding room, where he waited. Before long, a door opened and deputies led him into a larger room filled with strangers: men in suits and ties, women in knee-length wool skirts with matching blazers, all staring at him. *Degrees*, he thought, imagining the stacks of diplomas all these strangers must have earned, to dress like that. *So many different degrees*. He wore chinos and an oversize T-shirt that Gladys had bought him and he'd slipped on in the predawn gloom of his cell.

One of the strangers ordered him to place his left hand on the Bible, raise his right in the air, but deputies had shackled his wrists, so he couldn't separate them widely enough to do this. For a few moments he struggled against the chain. Finally he just tilted his palms in two different directions and promised he would tell the truth. At the far end of the room he recognized Chris Mumma, who smiled at him reassuringly. He remembered she had told him to speak loudly, so all these strangers could hear him, but also to show he wasn't hiding anything. So he explained where he'd worked and what he'd looked like, back in October of 1987—how tall he was, how much he weighed, that he had a mole on his face and a scar on his chest. Once more he recounted the day in question: the post office, the supermarket, the tax money, the house party. Returning home from work that Tuesday to learn the police had come looking for him.

What had he thought that was about? another stranger asked him.

"I didn't have no idea," he told her. "Because I knew I hadn't did anything. That's the reason I went up there, to find out." Instead, Steve Hunt had arrested him. When Willie complained, Hunt had told him not to say anything more, since he was in a lot of trouble.

"Did Investigator Hunt ever come back and try to talk to you later on about the case?" the woman asked.

"No, ma'am," he answered.

KENDRA: Would you have talked to him if he had?
WILLIE: Yes, ma'am.
KENDRA: Did any other officers ever try to talk to you about the case?
WILLIE: No, ma'am.
KENDRA: Would you have talked to them if they had?
WILLIE: Yes.

Since then, Kendra pointed out, Willie had written letters to a number of attorneys, in addition to Ed de Torres. Why had he done that?

"Because I knew I was innocent," he said. "I wasn't going to give up, just do the time, for something I didn't do."

A different stranger asked about his chest scar, so Willie pulled down the loose collar of his T-shirt to show it. He seemed to remember the details of that October night quite well, given that it had been so many years ago, another suggested. How?

Because of the tax money, Willie explained. He'd planned that day around bringing his tax money down to cousins in Shelby, so he knew every place he'd visited. Besides that, he'd had so much time in the years since to review those hours in his head. "I've always thought about it. Because I know where I was and I know what I did. And I know I wasn't into no crime that night." He shook his head. "It bugged me for years. Almost ran me crazy when I first went to prison." He laughed softly, shook his head again. "Eventually I got over it, and I saw that I wasn't going to get no help or anything. But I kept on trying, every way I thought to try."

The SBI agent who'd run the HPD's recovered fingerprints through AFIS, and matched them not to Willie but to Albert Turner, explained his method for commissioners. On an overhead television, Kendra flashed a screenshot of the AFIS software, so commissioners could see for themselves: two magnified fingerprints, side by side.

"I assume, then, the commission can feel pretty comfortable this absolutely is not Willie Grimes's fingerprint?" one commissioner asked.

The agent nodded. "Yes. Without a doubt."

"You may not be able to do this," the commissioner continued, "but in your opinion, is this absolutely Albert Turner's print?"

The agent didn't hesitate. "Yes."

"There's no doubt in your mind it's Albert Turner's print?"

"I have no doubt," the agent said. "Both of those prints."

News cameras from WRAL had rolled during all three days of the hearing, but now Kendra ordered them shut off, and asked everyone who wasn't a commissioner to leave the room. When the door was closed behind them, she called Tamera Elliott.

Back in 1987 she'd been twenty-eight, and living with her parents, Tamera explained privately to commissioners. She still remembered their phone ringing that October night, her mother picking it up, shouting at Tamera's father, who'd already gone to bed: *Get up! We have to go to your mother's house! She's been attacked.*

Tamera's grandmother had lived in Hillside Gardens three years or so by then, though she'd never felt comfortable there, since everyone knew it was a high-crime area. It was bad enough when Carrie's husband, John, had been around, but John had died of complications from a heart attack just before Thanksgiving 1986, so Carrie had been left there alone, looking for somewhere better. There weren't many apartments she could afford. That was why they'd ended up in Hillside Gardens in the first place. Before all this, she and John had regularly gone out dancing—scooter-pootin', Carrie called it. Later, once Carrie had given up driving, Tamera and her father had brought her on errands two or three times a week, but even this Carrie preferred to do during the day, since she avoided leaving her apartment at night. It was the same reason she attended church only on Sunday mornings. Weekday services were held in the evening, and traveling past dusk made her nervous.

From all her visits to her grandmother's apartment, Tamera knew who Linda McDowell was, but no one had spoken to her in the days following the assault about any identification, so Tamera didn't have a clue about Linda's role in the whole thing. Her grandmother had spoken of the incident only once, when she told Tamera a man had "hurt her really bad." Otherwise they'd never acknowledged it. Carrie died of pneumonia just two years later. "She was a good person," Tamera said, about her grandmother. "She was a kind person. I never heard her say anything bad about anybody. And I trust her judgment. You know, what she said happened, happened. I don't think she would have said it was someone else, if it was not. I cannot see my grandmother saying it was another person when it was not that person. I just trust my grandmother's judgment."

33

A Lawyer I've Never Met

He woke Thursday morning at Gaston Correctional, showered, dressed for work release, and walked toward the mess hall for his oatmeal and banana. In the dayroom he passed a mounted television screen, heard his own name, turned, and realized he was looking at his own photograph. Then a brief video of himself testifying in that room in Raleigh. "All eight judges," he heard.

In the mess hall, inmates were whooping and clapping their trays. He ate silently. When he stepped off the bus an hour later at Pioneer Utilities, a secretary was holding a telephone out to him. It was Chris. Once he'd left Raleigh yesterday, she told him, commissioners had voted unanimously to send his case on to a three-judge panel.

He knew, he said. He saw it on TV.

When he hung up, the secretary led him into an office where she'd set a laptop on a desk. She sat him in a chair and pressed Play. The whole hearing had been videotaped, she said excitedly. She wanted him to see what everyone had said, when he wasn't in the room.

In Raleigh, Kendra wrote to Chris Mumma and the Catawba County district attorney's office to let them know that, by statute, the chief justice of the North Carolina Supreme Court now had twenty days to appoint three judges for Willie's panel. Once that happened, the IIC's work on the case would be complete, and Kendra would step back and assist only as requested. The rest was up to Chris and the

DA. Into each envelope she dropped a flash drive containing transcripts of every interview Lau and Stellato had conducted and documents from every agency she'd subpoenaed.

From attending each day of Willie's hearing, Chris already knew, at least broadly, what the IIC had uncovered, but now she and her center staffers pored through the agency's entire file, encountering police and laboratory reports, interviews with victims they'd never heard of, and more documents they'd never seen. Finally, Chris arrived at Steve Hunt's personal file. It wasn't unusual that Hunt had kept one, she knew—many officers did—but now she realized something else. HPD policy back in 1988 had required that officers turn their formal reports over to the district attorney's office, where subsequently these became available for defense attorneys in preparation for trial, during discovery. This included incident, arrest, medical, and forensic reports. But no policy governed officers' *informal* reports, meaning handwritten notes or memos or even test results shared verbally rather than typewritten. And any folder an officer kept personally, separate from its counterpart at HPD, should have been synchronized, so that neither file held something the other didn't. No one monitored this closely, however, so often one did.

All this meant that the original lineup shown to Carrie Elliott— the one in which Albert Turner appeared, with his name written on the reverse, so anyone who saw it might conclude he was a suspect— had never made it out of Steve Hunt's personal folder. When Ed de Torres phoned Hunt before trial, asking for evidence, and Hunt referred him to the district attorneys, technically Hunt had been telling the truth: it wasn't *his* job to provide de Torres anything directly. That was the DA's job. But Hunt had neglected to mention the most important fact. His personal file included pages he'd never turned over. So when de Torres *did* write the DA's office, they, too, had told him the truth: the office held nothing more to give him. But the DA hadn't mentioned, and possibly hadn't known, what lay in Hunt's personal folder. This explained how de Torres had made it to trial without ever learning fingerprints had been recovered from Carrie

Elliott's apartment, and why no one outside the HPD had known at all about Albert Turner—until the IIC subpoenaed Hunt's file. Meanwhile, when Chris had phoned and e-mailed Hunt personally, in October 2007, asking if he knew where Willie's evidence had vanished to, Hunt had written back that he had no idea. But this was only partially true. He didn't hold the nightgown, or rape kit, or discarded fruit. But he *did* still hold his personal folder, with that original lineup. He'd been using it to teach courses at the community college. When Lau and Stellato visited him, it lay there on his office desk. And he hadn't said a word about it to Chris.

All that, plus commissioners' agreement it merited judicial review, left only one logical path forward, Chris knew. Technically, by IIC statute, no three-judge panel needed to be held at all. As long as the DA's office agreed this new evidence proved clearly and convincingly that Willie was innocent, then both sides could file a joint motion to dismiss, alongside a plea for declaration of innocence, thereby vacating Willie's convictions and freeing him. Obviously, the evidence proved this. Chris phoned the DA's office, drafted the relevant motions, and mailed them along.

A reply arrived in early autumn. This *was* new evidence, the DA agreed. None of it proved Grimes innocent, however, or that anyone but him was the true rapist. "At most," the response read, this new evidence suggested "residual doubt," which depended on "supposition and conjecture." Willie's plea of innocence, therefore, "should be denied."

To a local news station, the DA elaborated. If Grimes truly was innocent, then he needed "compelling physical evidence" that showed he was elsewhere at the time of the crime, or that implicated a third party. "And we just don't have that," he said.

Chris felt stunned. Five months since Willie's hearing she'd passed expecting to avoid a three-judge panel, and now it was scheduled for October 1. Quickly she filed an order for appointment of counsel. Willie was entitled to a court-appointed attorney, and Chris intended to get him one, regardless of her own involvement. This way he would have two attorneys, one local, both free—Chris because she worked pro bono, another through Indigent Defense Services.

A phone rang in an office up in Taylorsville, twenty miles northwest of Hickory, on the desk of Robert Campbell, a defense attorney. Campbell reached for the receiver. It was the assistant director at Indigent Defense Services. She had a proposal for him, she said.

Campbell glanced at his calendar. Late August. "Let me get this straight," he said into the phone. "You want me to jump into the middle of a case, trial date a month from now. With a lawyer I've never met. For a type of panel I've never seen?"

"Yes," the voice told him.

Ordinarily, Campbell didn't take postconviction work. On the other hand, he recalled hearing of the IIC, feeling intrigued by it. Here was somebody who needed his help. Hadn't he become a lawyer to help people? "Well, okay," he said. "As long as I have that straight."

The following day Chris Mumma phoned, promising to share her files. Campbell began reading.

Within the week, the pair were working twelve- and fifteen-hour days, phoning and e-mailing daily, sometimes hourly. Every so often Campbell drove the two hours east, to collapse into a chair in Chris's office and go over what he'd read. Until the phone call from IDS, he'd been preparing other cases, but now he put them all aside. Together he and Chris mapped every question they planned to ask of every witness they planned to call. They assembled a list of every documented instance over Willie's long incarceration that he'd insisted to his case manager or psychologist, or in a letter to the clemency office, parole commission, or Prisoner Legal Services, that he was innocent. They drove to Gastonia, so Campbell could meet Willie personally. They prepared to visit Albert Turner but discovered a problem. Turner had left his room in the nursing home. There was no forwarding address. Campbell phoned a private investigator he knew, who managed to find where Turner had gone. Catawba County jail. He'd gotten arrested again. Chris and Campbell drove there to see him. From an initial description, Chris thought she remembered Carrie's assailant without much hair on his chest, so now she leaned close and peered down the loose collar of Turner's jail uniform. No luck. She tried again. Too close. Turner reeked; liquor, sweat, something rancid. She recoiled. "Don't touch him," Campbell scolded.

Was there anything Turner wanted to tell them, about Carrie Elliott or Willie Grimes?

No. Turner didn't know anything about that.

They visited Bobby and Tamera Elliott, up in Conover. Turner was claiming he often visited Carrie's apartment, to chat or bring groceries or use her telephone, Chris confided to them. Was that possible?

No, Tamera answered flatly. If her grandmother had befriended someone, Tamera and Bobby would have known about it. Neither had heard the name Albert Turner.

Chris drove to Office Depot, to print a poster she and Campbell planned to introduce as an exhibit: the booking photograph from Willie's arrest, arranged below Albert Turner's, both magnified nearly to actual size. Not the outdated photograph of Turner, of him in dreadlocks, but the one police *should* have used, showing Turner's true appearance in the month of Carrie's assault. The resemblance was startling. Since then each man had aged differently, so today they looked nothing alike. But in their early forties? Similar mustaches and short Afros. Similar long, wide noses. Similar pairs of deeply set eyes. To a stranger, and after dusk? It would be no difficulty at all to confuse one for the other.

In her notebook, Chris scribbled a reminder for her opening and closing remarks. *Tell story from Willie's point of view. Put judges in his shoes.* Onto her finger she slipped a ring she considered good luck: six thin, interlocking gold strands, shaped vaguely like the double helix of DNA. A gift from the first client she'd ever helped free. Around her neck she normally wore a small cross; this didn't match

Albert Lindsey Turner, in unkempt dreadlocks. *Courtesy of the Hickory Police Department.*

Chris's poster. Top row: Albert Lindsey Turner. Bottom row: Willie James Grimes. *Courtesy of the Hickory Police Department*

her outfits for trial, but she refused to take it off. Instead she pulled it to the side and clasped it to the strap of her bra, where no one would see it. Then she remembered Bryan Stewart, meeting him on that visit to Willie at work release—how frequently he'd spoken of the Bible, the Kingdom Hall he'd built. She sent him an e-mail. "You have connections with upstairs," she wrote. "See what you can do about this."

34

A Type of Panel I've Never Seen

The Catawba County Justice Center looked much the same as it had so many years earlier, an ample courtroom whose walls were wainscoted from carpet to ceiling, hung with crimson drapes and portraits of aged white men in suits. This time, on the bench at one end, in place of a single robed judge there sat three: a graying white woman in eyeglasses, her fingertips pressed together in concentration; a black man with clipped hair, sitting as still as a sculpture; and a slope-shouldered white man with the air of a country doctor. To their right sat a pair of Catawba County district attorneys. To their left, Chris Mumma and Robert Campbell. Across an ornamented banister lined nearly a dozen rows of fixed auditorium chairs, holding Kendra and Lau and Stellato, from the IIC, and, a few empty seats away, Willie, who wore a dark suit now, and Gladys and two of his nieces. Beside and behind them, filling the courtroom halfway, sat Bryan Stewart, Eddie Moose, and more than a dozen other friends and Witnesses.

After her opening remarks, Chris summoned Sharon Stellato to the stand, to relate the discoveries of her and Lau's investigation—which amounted to little more than fingerprints from an old banana, an assistant DA, Eric Bellas, pointed out on cross-examination. Bellas's office had looked into it; just two grocery stores had operated in Hickory in 1987, and the one nearest Carrie's apartment was also nearest Albert Turner's. Was it so hard to believe that one of their fingerprints might turn up on the other's groceries? Anyway, hadn't Turner said he periodically brought Carrie fruit?

It was this assistant, Eric Bellas, whom the DA, Jay Gaither, had assigned to handle most of the questioning. Of everyone on his staff, he considered Bellas most capable, likely a better cross-examiner than he himself was, and Gaither preferred to concentrate elsewhere. He liked to watch a trial unfold, to observe the defendant and judges and opposing attorneys all in real time, since it helped him get a sense of things, to determine what and whom he believed. He couldn't do all that if he was also the one asking questions.

Gaither was nearly fifty, with a considerable chin and forehead and the gait, handshake, and meaty shoulders of a linebacker, which in fact he had once been, in high school right there in Newton. His family had lived in Catawba County for nearly as long as white folks had lived there at all; he liked to boast that ancestors of his had signed the Mayflower Compact and fought for the Confederacy. In social conversation, Gaither often spoke so much, and so rapidly, that after ten or fifteen minutes he would confess to having forgotten what the question was. He'd been elected district attorney in 2002 and reelected twice since.

The phone call he'd gotten a year earlier from Jamie Lau, explaining who Willie Grimes was, had surprised him, since he'd thought the IIC only took on cases in big cities. He knew the agency had never been popular with fellow DAs around the state, still recalled their grumblings when it had been up in the legislature, and a warning he'd heard from a colleague about how bad it might be. Personally he didn't feel strongly either way, though he *did* get nervous at the prospect of overturning a jury verdict, especially years afterward, once time had diminished everyone's recollection. A DA's office had only so many dollars and hours to spend, and Gaither didn't want to drain them by revisiting cases that were already settled. On the other hand, if somehow a man had ended up in prison who really *was* innocent, Gaither agreed they'd damn well better have some way to get him out. He wasn't the sort of person to toss up his hands: *Oh, well, over and done with, can't fix it now.* No! When Gaither's own father had become a doctor, the first thing he'd learned was Do No Harm. The equivalent for a lawyer was obvious. Do Not Convict an Innocent Person.

But there was more to this than people knew. One of the most difficult things for a DA, Gaither believed, was to proceed on a case—to examine the facts, reach a conclusion, prosecute aggressively, sometimes over months—all the while remaining available to alternatives, to the chance you'd missed something. Study a case long enough and all you saw were the same facts in the same order. It became easy not to notice, or not to take seriously, one that didn't fit—not deliberately, but because a DA was human, too, and his job was to make decisions. Assigning his smartest assistant, Bellas, to examine witnesses was partly Gaither's solution to this. Now he could observe the case fresh, and as a bystander. The IIC's unusual procedure also meant the burden of proof fell not on him this time but on Grimes, so a certain pressure had been lifted. Gaither would sit back and listen, then speak up during closing arguments.

Ed de Torres led Chris through his initial work on Willie's case: the alibi witnesses, the affidavits he'd gotten them to sign. "To your knowledge, did the district attorney's office, or the Hickory Police Department, ever interview any of those six alibi witnesses?" one of Chris's colleagues, a staffer from the center, asked him.

"They did not," de Torres replied.

The staffer waved a sheet of paper: a letter de Torres had written the DA, in March of 1988. "You specifically requested, quote, 'Any fingerprints and any other physical evidence obtained at the crime scene.' Is that correct?"

"Correct," de Torres said.

"Prior to trial, did the district attorney's office, the Hickory Police Department, the SBI, ever disclose any fingerprint reports to you?"

"No."

When de Torres *did* learn of the fingerprints, at trial, that they hadn't matched Willie's but that the HPD had compared them to no one else's, he'd asked the judge for—the staffer read aloud again from a transcript—" 'Cooperation of the State in sending copies of the prints to the FBI for comparison, to see if they have a match in their records.' " Had this ever happened? Had anyone run the fingerprints through any database?

"Not until this year," de Torres said, when the IIC had ordered it done.

"So—for twenty-five years, that request was never fulfilled?"

"That's correct," de Torres said.

Fingerprints or no, Eric Bellas proposed on cross-examination, wasn't it true Carrie Elliott had identified his client? Hadn't de Torres had an opportunity, at trial, to cross-examine Ms. Elliott, specifically about that identification? Hadn't he brought to jurors' attention then everything he felt was important, in terms of the possibility she might have made some mistake?

He had.

"No further questions," Bellas said.

Jennifer Dysart, a psychologist who specialized in the science of witness identification, reported at Chris's invitation that, by recent count, three hundred men and women in the United States had been exonerated by DNA, and, of those cases, 75 percent had included at least one eyewitness whose testimony turned out to be mistaken. Fully 30 percent had included *multiple* mistaken eyewitnesses. Those numbers represented DNA cases exclusively, Dysart clarified—they didn't include anyone who'd been exonerated by other means, counting which, obviously, there had been even more.

All those witnesses, Chris speculated. "Were they lying?"

"No, they were mistaken," Dysart corrected. This was the subject of her research exactly. Had Chris ever heard a joke, liked it, repeated it to others, then one day turned to a friend and said, "Oh, I've got this great joke to tell you," and the friend replied, "I know, I'm the one who told it to you"? "And all of a sudden you remember, *Oh, that's right*," Dysart said. This sort of thing happened all the time, to everyone. People naturally integrated new information into their memories, then overlooked where they'd learned what. With a joke among friends, this didn't much matter. When a crime was involved? The science was identical, but now the stakes were so much higher.

Eric Bellas wanted to know whether Dysart had personally read the HPD's every file on Carrie Elliott. When Dysart acknowledged she'd read only a portion, Bellas wondered aloud whether she was familiar with the problem of generalizing. Wasn't it impossible to include, just because research showed an overall trend, that it applied to any single, particular case?

Well, yes, Dysart agreed. She was familiar with this; she taught graduate courses in research methodology. "Correlation is in generalities. You're correct. It does not allow to give specific conclusions about a particular person."

So Dysart's research really only allowed her to "look overall at a population," Bellas suggested. "It does not give you the ability to form any opinions at all about the victim in *this* case, and whether *her* identification was accurate or not, does it?"

"That's correct. I do not know if the witness in this particular case was correct or incorrect."

"Nothing further," Bellas said.

"One question," Chris said, standing again and turning toward Dysart. "Was your testimony here today that you know the victim made a misidentification in this case?"

"No, it's not."

"Was your testimony that, based on various factors, a misidentification could have been made?"

"Yes."

"Thank you," Chris said, and sat down.

Linda McDowell recalled for Chris what her neighbor Carrie Elliott had told her that long-ago weekend. Again this recollection differed from what she'd told Kendra and commissioners, six months earlier, and Lau and Stellato, three months before that, and the Hickory police, back in 1987.

"Do you really remember any of this, Ms. McDowell?" Chris asked her.

"Not really, no," Linda admitted.

" 'Hair is very specific to one individual,' " Troy Hamlin, the forensic analyst, read aloud from a transcript of his own testimony. " 'It is rare that I see two individuals whose hair is the same under the microscope.' "

That word *rare* was interesting. On what statistics, exactly, had Hamlin based that conclusion?

"It's one of those things you cannot quantitate," Hamlin answered.

But it *was* possible, wasn't it, for two hairs to look similar, and still belong to different people? Not that Hamlin had deliberately misled anyone—that word *rare* might have been an honest mistake.

"I wouldn't term it as a mistake," Hamlin said. "I would term it as the science at that time."

Steve Hunt recalled arriving to Carrie Elliott's apartment that October evening to find Jack Holsclaw, the HPD's evidence technician, processing the crime scene, so Hunt had told Holsclaw about the banana peels on Carrie's lawn. A few days after that, Hunt recalled, Mr. Turner had walked into the police station, where Hunt, who'd been appointed lead investigator by then, arrested him.

"You're saying Turner," one of the judges interrupted. "Do you—"

"I'm sorry, Mr. Grimes," Hunt corrected. It was *Grimes* who'd walked into the police station, *Grimes* he'd arrested. He'd simply gotten their names mixed up just now.

Robert Campbell waved a transcript of Hunt's 1988 testimony, then read aloud a passage where Hunt had described his arrival to Carrie Elliott's apartment. " 'I just observed the outside of the apartment and the area, and there was nobody at the residence.' " Campbell lowered the transcript. Did Hunt recall saying that? Had Holsclaw been there, or not?

Hunt wasn't sure.

"So you could be mistaken here today, under oath, when you say you remember speaking with Officer Holsclaw about the bananas?"

"Yes," Hunt conceded.

Hunt had assumed, when he noticed those peels and apple core, that Carrie's assailant had dropped them, right? Since he'd heard something about fruit over his radio?

"That was the radio traffic, yes," Hunt agreed.

According to his own trial testimony, though, and despite what he'd just claimed, Hunt had never actually mentioned them to Holsclaw. Nor had he acted at all on the fingerprints lifted from Carrie's kitchen. He hadn't *known* Holsclaw lifted any fingerprints? How could he have managed not to know this? Hunt was lead investigator, wasn't he? Wouldn't Holsclaw have filled out a report and submitted it to him? He had seen no report like this, saying the fingerprints didn't match Grimes? From a binder, Campbell withdrew another sheet of paper, walked it over to Hunt. This was the report they were talking about, wasn't it?

It was, Hunt agreed.

CAMPBELL: And whose name is on the top of it?
HUNT: Willie Grimes.
CAMPBELL: Whose name shows as the officer on top?
HUNT: Holsclaw.
CAMPBELL: And is that the form that would have been in the Hickory Police Department file?
HUNT: Yes, it should have been.
CAMPBELL: Okay. What's the first item of evidence that shows being collected at the scene?
HUNT: One card of latent prints.
CAMPBELL: What is a card of latent prints?
HUNT: They are prints that are lifted at a crime scene.

And still Hunt was comfortable testifying he had no knowledge of any fingerprints until he'd heard about them at trial?

"Yes," Hunt said. "Right." Now he paused. "Wait a minute. Let me back up." Of course he *had* seen this evidence control form, back in 1987. What he'd meant before, about not knowing there were fingerprints—he'd only meant he didn't know they came from a *banana*. That was the part he hadn't known until trial.

"So you *did* have knowledge there were fingerprints."

Hunt wasn't sure. He couldn't recall. "But I'm sure I would have looked at this," he said, gesturing toward the form. "It's just routine."

"Would you also have looked at the actual latent lift card?" Now Campbell raised another sheet of paper. Hunt didn't recognize this one, either. "Does it appear to be a copy of a latent lift card?" Campbell pressed.

HUNT: Yes.
CAMPBELL: And does it have in big, bold print on it, "From banana on kitchen table"?
HUNT: Yes.
CAMPBELL: And does it bear Mr. Holsclaw's initials?
HUNT: Yes.
CAMPBELL: And does it bear the date of 10/24/87?
HUNT: Yes.
CAMPBELL: And those things are routinely kept in the Hickory Police Department files?
HUNT: Sure.

Campbell changed course. "You've used this case to teach about?"

"In crime scene investigations classes," Hunt agreed.

Could Hunt explain what he tried to teach?

"Sure. When you go to a crime scene, the crime scene speaks to you, as a criminal investigator. If there's anything that looks out of place, appears to be evidence, then you collect it. No stones unturned. Locate, photograph, collect, and process."

"And this crime scene spoke to you," Campbell suggested. "The perpetrator, you believed, had eaten those bananas."

"Yes."

"Yet you didn't ensure that they were collected?"

"Right."

"And you threw the apple core away."

"Yes, sir," Hunt said.

Eric Bellas invited Hunt to defend certain record-keeping practices—that, as far as Hunt knew, everything inside his personal folder should have also appeared in the departmental file, at headquarters. He had no idea why the initial lineup, containing Albert Turner, wasn't there. Obviously something had slipped through the cracks between HPD and the DA's office. That wasn't unheard of, and certainly it wasn't Hunt's fault, since Hunt had made sure to relay the most important evidence, the hair and Carrie's description, to the DAs.

"What specifically about the description did you find important?" Bellas asked.

"Well, the height, the weight," Hunt answered.

Campbell rose again. Carrie Elliott had described her assailant as weighing between two hundred and two hundred and twenty-five pounds, with a face scratched from her fingernails. Paperwork from Willie Grimes's arrest showed he weighed a hundred and sixty-five, and had no scratches. How was it possible Hunt had believed Carrie's description, especially height and weight, was the most important piece of evidence, then arrested someone who didn't match that description at all?

"Mr. Campbell, I've investigated a lot of cases in the years, and people who are in that moment, they don't give you accurate description of suspects," Hunt answered impatiently.

"They don't always get it right?"

"Right," Hunt said. "That's correct."

"I don't have any further questions," Campbell said.

One final time, Willie recounted for Chris where he'd been that October evening in 1987. He lifted his right hand to show the two missing fingers Miss Elliott had never described. He recalled he had shaved that morning, though Miss Elliott had felt stubble.

Could Willie please explain what SOAR was, and why he'd refused it for a decade? Chris asked.

"I would have to sign papers saying I was guilty," he answered. "I told them I would stay in there the rest of my life before I signed papers saying I was guilty of something I didn't do."

Nine years ago, he'd filed an application with the Center on Actual Innocence, and seven years after that he'd filed another with the IIC, Chris pointed out. Why had he filed those?

"Because I knew I was innocent," he said. "And I thought you all would be the only one that can help me."

Eric Bellas, on cross-examination, wanted simply to clarify a few things. Willie had spent two years in the army? He'd told Ed de Torres, immediately after his arrest, that he was innocent? He'd been baptized in prison as a Jehovah's Witness? All those were true, Willie confirmed. "It went to changing my life," he added, about his baptism. Before then he'd felt so angry and depressed. "Made me feel like a whole different person."

This was all Bellas had.

Immediately Chris stood. Those first years in prison, why had Willie felt so angry and depressed?

"Because I knew I was in prison for something I didn't do, and I couldn't get no one that would help me," he said. "Didn't seem like I was ever going to get no help."

Les Robinson testified again: he had seen Willie that night, at the house party. Betty Shuford testified again: it was her couch Willie had slept on. Richard Wilson testified again: it was he who'd held Willie's tax money. No one from the district attorney's office, or from the Hickory Police Department, had ever phoned or visited any of them to ask about the case.

Brian Delmas, the SBI agent, shared the comparison he'd run on the two recovered fingerprints. "They do not belong to Willie Grimes," Delmas confirmed. He showed judges the list AFIS had returned of matches, which he'd then inspected manually.

The first four names on that list—would Delmas please read who they belonged to?

"The first four all belong to Albert Turner."

Jay Gaither, the DA, offered Albert Turner an immunity deal, hoping to encourage him to testify; nothing Turner divulged today would Gaither use to prosecute him. So Turner slumped toward the witness stand, his yellow DOC jumpsuit, its collar open, hanging on him loosely. "What we're trying to do is get to the truth of the matter," Gaither told him. "We'd like to question you about that. Do you mind if we do so?"

"At this time we're going to invoke our right against self-incrimination," Turner's attorney interjected.

"Yeah," Turner agreed, lurching to and fro in the witness chair as if he were on an invisible rocker.

One of the judges spoke up. Turner held immunity—he wanted to invoke this right anyway?

"Yes," Turner's attorney confirmed. "It's a continuing objection."

"Yeah," Turner repeated.

"You're excused," the judge told him.

Tamera Elliott rose to the witness stand, so Campbell approached tenderly. He personally had heard Tamera complain, at least privately, to him and Chris, about the investigation into her grandmother's case, he hinted. Might Tamera confirm for the judges this was true? Might she also share what bothered her about it?

"We didn't know about the fingerprints," Tamera answered. Neither had her family known that Linda had collected any reward. Both these facts Tamera and her siblings had learned only recently, from the IIC, at its April hearing, and after much thought Tamera couldn't reconcile with the original trial verdict, the fingerprints especially. She could imagine no reason, save one, that Albert Turner's prints would appear inside her grandmother's apartment. There was no chance the two had been friendly, or that Carrie had invited him in, as Turner was claiming. Nor had Tamera felt any drop of reassurance listening to Steve Hunt testify. "We didn't know Mr. Grimes's witnesses were not contacted by the district attorney," she protested. "We didn't know any of that."

Personally Tamera no longer knew whether Willie Grimes was the man who'd attacked her grandmother. "If he didn't, and my grandmother was mistaken, she would be the first to apologize," Tamera said. She had brought with her today a family portrait to show the courtroom: her grandmother Carrie in the spring of 1986, in a powder-blue button-up sweater and gleaming white necklace, wearing rose lipstick, heart-shaped gold earrings, and huge, tortoiseshell eyeglasses, their lenses as wide as her cheeks. Behind her stood her husband, John, with a round nose and diminishing hairline and twice as broad as Carrie across the shoulders, his hand resting lightly on her arm.

Eric Bellas didn't have any questions.

On Thursday, the final evening of the panel, Chris's staffers from the center found a restaurant in town for dinner while Robert Campbell sped toward Chapel Hill to watch his daughter play trumpet in a university concert. Chris stayed alone in her hotel room, finishing her closing argument. She felt exhausted. Her vision had gone blurry and her legs wobbled when she stood. Her hotel bed was hardly visible beneath overstuffed banker's boxes, loose folders, and a printer. Before Campbell left for his daughter's concert, he'd told her *he* wanted to make their closing, and they'd argued about it, until finally Chris had prevailed. She'd let Campbell cross-examine Hunt. The closing argument was hers.

* * *

When court reconvened the following morning, however, it was Jay Gaither who went first. He'd run for district attorney in the first place because he wanted a job with purpose, where he could feel like he was doing the right thing, he remarked, standing at the courtroom lectern. When he and Eric Bellas retreated to his office the previous evening to consider their closing argument, they'd had a difficult time of it. Together the pair had reexamined every piece of evidence, listing as they went any detail they felt was problematic. When they'd finished, they tallied these. Thirty-five. Finally Bellas had looked up from the pages strewn across his desk, thrown his arms wide, and asked Gaither directly: "Where do you stand on this? What do you think?" And the answer had been, honestly, he believed Willie Grimes was innocent.

So what the hell were they doing?

"The State cannot argue any closing that does not support a finding of innocence for Willie Grimes," Gaither announced. He wasn't going to list all thirty-five problems he and Bellas had counted. He would keep this brief. "On behalf of the district attorney's office, and the State of North Carolina, we offer an apology to Mr. Grimes. That's all." He sat down.

Unsteadily Chris rose to replace him at the lectern. "I'm tempted to leave it right there," she admitted. Nonetheless she wanted to say a few words, if only to mention Carrie Elliott—who, from all Chris had learned, had been a kind, generous person—and to lament what Chris regarded as the disgraceful investigation into her assault. A case like Carrie's was precisely why the IIC, this three-judge panel, had been created. For a quarter of a century, Willie had begged every other court for justice. Finally this one had the chance to provide it. "Not just for Willie Grimes, but for the victims."

She sat down.

The judges recessed. They returned. They had been gone only seven minutes. Before he announced their verdict, their chairman, Judge Lee, swiveled toward his two colleagues. Was there anything either wanted to say?

"There is," Judge Barrett answered. She wanted to mention that, before Monday, when this panel had begun, she'd never served on anything like it, and she'd heard concerns that it undermined public trust in her courts. "I think just the opposite is true. It speaks to the *integrity* of our system that this kind of commission would exist. I feel that all the more strongly, having had the opportunity to serve on this panel."

Next Judge Fox cleared his throat. Before becoming a judge, he'd been a district attorney, he reflected, so he foresaw that Gaither and Bellas might face criticism for how they'd closed the state's case. Fox thought the choice had demanded courage. He wanted to thank them for it, and also to thank the state legislature, if it was listening, for creating the IIC in the first place. "This is perhaps one of the best changes in the judicial system in North Carolina in the last hundred years." He felt disappointed only that it hadn't existed sooner.

"In terms of the matters that have all brought us together to this moment," Judge Lee said. He listed the legal terms of Willie's conviction and the unusual statute that empowered him today. "It is *unquestionably* the unanimous decision of this three-judge panel that the defendant, Willie James Grimes, a convicted person, *has* proved by clear and convincing evidence that he is innocent. It is therefore ordered that the relief sought by Willie James Grimes is granted. The charges of rape and kidnapping of Ms. Carrie Lee Elliott, against Willie James Grimes, are dismissed."

Lee opened his mouth to say something else, but applause interrupted him. *"Yeah!"* a woman cried, as if she were at church. When the courtroom had quieted, Lee resumed. "It is further ordered that Willie James Grimes be removed *immediately* from the Sex Offender and Public Protection Registration program." He recited his own name, the names of his two fellow judges, then paused again, removed his reading glasses, and considered Willie directly.

"Mr. Grimes, you're a little bit older than I am," Lee observed. So he expected that Willie must remember, as Lee himself did, that August of 1963, the image of those steps to the Lincoln Memorial at the close of that famous speech that still echoed. "And I'm going to paraphrase it as we conclude this proceeding," he decided aloud, as Judges Barrett and Fox beamed beside him. "Free at last, free at last. Thank God almighty—thank *Jehovah*—Willie J. Grimes is free at last."

Lee thanked everyone and stood. At 10:29 a.m., his courtroom bailiff clapped a gavel.

35

A Long Time Coming

Free at last.

After all that time, *free at last.*

What did it feel like?

What did it *feel like?*

He felt as if his every vein was filled with helium. He felt weightless, he felt afloat. He felt the tallest he'd ever been. His every muscle and tendon seemed to slacken; he could hear his blood billowing in his ears. His chest was thrumming and his heart rattled in his fingertips.

Free at last.

He needed to find his case manager. Needed to find his case manager, tell her what had happened, tell her he wouldn't be checking in anymore. Fleetingly he thought of a meeting he had tried to attend some weeks earlier, in nearby Gastonia—what was it called? Not AA, something else—but they'd refused him, said they couldn't accept sex offenders. He would go there. He would go to Hickory, stride through the front doors of the police department, stand in the lobby, and watch the officers' faces. He would shout that he was innocent, he'd been telling them the truth, he no longer needed their help. He could do this. He could do *anything.* He was never going back to Gaston Correctional, never going back to any prison at all, except to tell his case manager this, that he was never going back to Gaston Correctional, never going back to any prison at all. He felt an urge to leap and shriek and pump his arms, just as quickly suppressed it. He wasn't going to let these people see him like that.

Gladys stood and slung her arms around him, he could feel her trembling, her tears soaking his suit jacket. A hand clapped his shoulder and he knew without looking it belonged to Bryan Stewart. Another hand. Eddie Moose. There was a sound he couldn't place, then he realized it was applause. The entire courtroom was applauding. Chris appeared beside him, her eyes glistening. He hugged her tightly. "Thank you," he tried to say, but it wasn't coming out right, he couldn't speak normally, he wasn't sure she understood him. Robert Campbell was there. Those two men from the DA's office whose names he couldn't remember. The three judges. Strangers. They were hugging him, shaking his hand. What did it feel like? they were asking him. Congratulations, they were saying. Had he seen all this coming? They were handing him business cards. He should call them, if he ever needed help. He should call them, if he wanted to talk. "My brother is free!" Gladys was wailing.

At the close of her first three-judge panel, for Greg Taylor, Chris had felt so overwhelmed, and so suddenly, that she had made a noise that was more than a gasp, that approached a scream, then cried uncontrollably. Colleagues had chastised her for it afterward, for not behaving professionally enough. Next time she would be more composed, she'd resolved. Now she hugged Robert Campbell, thanked him, hugged her center staffers, walked through the gap in the ornamented courtroom banister, hugged Gladys and Willie. "You're free," she told him.

"Oh, yes," Willie said. He was beaming wondrously, unlike she'd ever seen him, seemingly lit from within. "Oh, yes."

People with cameras were calling for their attention.

* * *

Bryan Stewart felt thrilled the judges had mentioned Jehovah. His wife was in tears. Had she heard that? he asked. They'd mentioned Jehovah.

Eddie Moose was drying his eyes on his sleeve. He'd assumed he was prepared for this, but he wasn't.

Greg Taylor was there. He'd come to support Chris and her latest client. He watched Willie, flushed and radiant, recalled vividly what this had felt like. A moment of uncertainty, of confusion—had he heard correctly?—before an upswell beyond anything he had imagined. All those years of doubt and frustration, each time he'd felt angry or sick or embarrassed, evaporating just like *that*. He still couldn't believe, at his own three-judge panel, he hadn't blasted through the courtroom ceiling.

He heard Chris calling his name now, saw her beckoning. She wanted a photograph: her and him and Willie.

They were inside a steak house, fourteen of them at one long table. Willie was tasting the best shrimp and steak of his life.

Chris wasn't. She couldn't eat. For her nerves, she ordered a glass of pinot grigio, immediately felt guilty about it, drinking in front of Willie and Bryan and a bunch of Jehovah's Witnesses.

From the steak house she drove Willie to the sheriff's office, a copy of the court order in her hand. Take his name off the registry, she demanded. Do it today.

Local news that evening showed a moment from the panel: Willie, his hands clasped against his chest, rocking forward in a courtroom chair, mouthing *Thank you* again and again. Gladys seated beside him, her face upturned, dabbing her eyes with a tissue.

A second shot. Willie and Gladys standing. How did it feel? a reporter was asking him.

"It's been a long time coming," Willie replied. He was nodding and smiling widely. "But I knew it would come, sooner or later."

A reporter was asking Jay Gaither about his closing argument. "My office is about seeking the truth," Gaither answered. "We never play 'hide the ball' for anybody, or any reason."

"Even after being exonerated, Willie Grimes did not have a bad word to say about the people who put him in prison," a news anchor was saying.

"And now evidence shows those people may have had information that could've cleared him," her co-anchor added. Producers cut to footage in Newton, then to the inside of the courtroom, where cameras had caught Tamera Elliott approaching Willie after the verdict. "These were things we didn't know until they all came out at the end," Tamera was saying to him, as Willie, at least a foot taller, nodded politely. Now one of Tamera's sisters spoke directly into the camera, looking stricken, shaking her head in disbelief. "The police officers, they didn't do their job," she exclaimed. "They got the ball rolling the wrong way."

On another network, Tamera standing on the courthouse steps. "We found out a lot of things we didn't know about the evidence," she was explaining into a microphone. "We as a family have all talked, and we feel like if he was not the one who did it, we need to make it right."

He stayed that night in an empty house Bryan Stewart owned, yards from Pioneer Utilities and the Kingdom Hall. It was the first time all day he'd been alone. He walked a short hallway and looked around. The lights were off but he saw everything clearly. The house was silent but he thought it might be glowing. His mind teemed with— nothing. Everything. He felt wetness on his cheeks before he realized he was sobbing. Then something loosed inside him and all at once he was kneeling there in the hallway, his body quivering. "Thank you," he whispered, to the empty house. His chest and skull throbbed. He stood. He was leaping, hurling his arms out wildly. "Thank you!" he shouted. "Thank you!"

When he finally slept he had no idea what time it was, how many minutes or hours he had passed howling and weeping in the hallway. It didn't matter. Time belonged to him now. He could spend it however he liked.

Willie and his legal team, Robert Campbell and Chris Mumma. *Courtesy of the NC Center on Actual Innocence.*

Judge David Lee congratulates Willie after his exoneration. Off to left stands Judge Sharon Barrett. *Courtesy of the NC Center on Actual Innocence.*

Willie with Chris Mumma and Greg Taylor. *Courtesy of the* Hickory Daily Record.

36

Cases of Innocence Still Open

M ore reporters phoned. From the *Hickory Daily Record*, the *Shelby Star*, the *Charlotte Observer*. The news division at Time Warner Cable. Was he angry? Did he plan to sue? What did he think of Albert Turner?

What *was* there to think of Turner? He'd known who Turner was, back before all this had happened—Hickory was a small town, Turner was his age—and even then had wanted nothing to do with him.

On the subject of a lawsuit he kept silent. He'd barely considered it, and, until he had, Chris warned him not to speak about it. But he didn't feel angry. He wanted reporters to know this. He was a different man than he'd been twenty-four years earlier, no longer carried that sort of bitterness. It disappointed him, what had happened. He missed his siblings, all that time they might have had together. He still didn't understand Steve Hunt, or Linda McDowell. "I *would* like to know why he really didn't take initiative to do his job, because I wouldn't have been in prison," he admitted to WRAL, about Hunt. But he didn't feel angry, at Hunt or anyone else. "It really feels great to be free," he told the *Gaston Gazette*. "I'll just be thankful to do what I want to do and go where I want to go. That's a privilege I haven't had in a long time."

No reporter understood this. How could he feel this way? He ought to feel angry, they told him. Even his friends hardly understood it, even Gladys, who would never stop feeling upset about what they'd done to her brother.

To one after another, he tried to explain. There was no question others had wronged him. But for every person who had done him harm, there was someone else who had loved him. For Steve Hunt, there was Eddie Moose. For Linda McDowell, there was Bryan Stewart. For those hardheaded prison guards, for Sergeant Orsky and Officer Mull, for that programmer at Craggy, there were Chris Mumma and Louie Ross and Thomas Hill. And there was Gladys—always. He repeated this all weekend long, each time his phone rang or someone knocked at his door, to strangers with microphones who he could tell did not understand him. But wasn't he angry? they asked. Finally he pulled his shades and stopped answering.

On Monday, October 8, reporters from WSOC-TV checked the North Carolina Sex Offenders Registry. The name Willie Grimes had been removed.

Chris bought him a prepaid cell phone, then drove him to the DMV, to get his driver's license back. This required a hearing and a hundred and fifty dollars in fines, since he hadn't held a license in so long, and technically that DWI, from 1982, had never been resolved. But a receptionist at the counter recognized him from her newspaper and promised to expedite things. She handed him a form. "Outline drug/alcohol use including date of last use and pattern of use in the past twelve months," read item 1. That was easy. He hadn't tried alcohol in two decades. "Give brief psychosocial history including family, work, legal history, abbreviated mental status and treatment history," read item 2.

With the phone Chris had bought him, he called Louie Ross, who'd attended his hearing in Raleigh but was unable to drive to Newton for the three-judge panel. Louie had asked that he phone as soon as he could. "It's over," Willie told him now.

Our prayers are answered, Louie thought. He felt so—just so—well, it was hard for him to describe. The fact of the verdict crystallized his anger. It clarified what had happened. His friend had told the truth; they'd imprisoned him anyway. At the same time, Louie felt jubilant. Woot was *free*. The first chance he got, he drove to see Willie in Gastonia, where, talking about something else, Woot confessed that he'd never seen the ocean. Louie was astonished. Could that be right? Woot had never seen the coast? Of course, he realized. Both men had grown up too poor for vacations, two hundred and fifty miles from the Atlantic, an untraversable distance, and when Louie moved away, Woot had stayed back, and then they'd arrested him. Of *course* he'd never seen the coast. Louie cleared a long weekend and drove his friend east to Wilmington, then south to Myrtle Beach, just Louie, his wife, Woot, and one other friend. Louie bought them all lunch at a sun-drenched restaurant right there on the boardwalk, its foundation flush against the sand, its second floor a wall of glass to an endless sheet of blue. Willie ate shrimp and stared.

When Thomas Hill heard the news, he drove to Woot's nephew's house and there he was, Woot, sitting on the couch, the first Thomas had seen him since JT's funeral, where Woot had worn handcuffs. Thomas fetched a camera. On a mantel in his own small house in Lawndale, he kept photographs he'd captured from annual reunions: Thomas and his classmates, Douglas High, class of '64. Woot was missing from all of them. "C'mon!" he urged now. "Let's take some pictures!" He snapped a few, disappeared, returned with more classmates from next door, arranged them all around Woot. He would frame these, add them to his mantel.

Chris brought him more forms to sign, drove him to Raleigh for another hearing, returned with him weeks later to collect an envelope. Compensation from the state, for having wrongly imprisoned him. Now that his innocence was a proven fact, laws in North Carolina entitled him to $50,000 a year for up to fifteen years, or a maximum of $750,000. Willie had spent twenty-four years and 208 days in prison. Inside the envelope was a check. Chris helped him arrange a trust with a bank in Raleigh. Most of the money went there, with a fraction deposited to him each month.

The language around the money was bizarre. Even its name seemed wrong, *compensation*. It made no sense as recompense. It righted no wrong. It could not restore anything. Even exonerating him hadn't. There was no sum that might accomplish this, no number that corresponded to any logic. The envelope was not an apology. It made sense only because it prevented a compounded injustice. Without it, he would return to the outside even poorer than he'd left it, an inexplicable gap on his résumé and renter's history, his bank account empty but for interest he'd accumulated from loans to fellow inmates inside prison, plus the little he'd earned from work release. He was sixty-six years old and if not for Bryan Stewart he would be homeless and unemployed. The envelope prevented this. It did in North Carolina, at least. Twenty-one other states offered no compensation at all.

Besides what he needed to live on, the money meant nothing to him. He expected he would save the rest, give it eventually to Gladys or the Witnesses. He kept his job at Pioneer Utilities, though Bryan ordered him to take a week off—paid, Bryan insisted, just like Willie was taking vacation. Soon after he returned, the economy faltered, and business at Pioneer slowed. Rather than stand around the office from nine to five, he trimmed his schedule to three or four hours a day, until he stopped entirely.

Every few nights he drove the bending road to Thomas Hill's house to play checkers. Thomas's new photographs overlooked them from the mantel, a few feet from where Willie sat with his hands in his lap, studying the board, as Thomas rubbed his forehead and groused about a losing streak. If not for their graying, thinning hair, their wrinkled faces, the fact that Willie had driven rather than walked, they might have been kids again, home in the evening from Douglas High, finished with cotton season. If not for everything else, they might never have missed a game. In another chair JT might have sat, or Cliff Jr., or Robert Lee, who might have brought chitlins. Would Brenda have come? Willie doubted it. He didn't think he and Brenda would have married. But he'd never had the chance to find out. Instead in the house sat only the pair of them, two men of nearly seventy, relearning how the other liked to play. If it wasn't checkers they played cards, gin rummy or spades. Or they went to lunch. Or Thomas was thinking about bowling.

Midday he went with Bryan Stewart to a pasture a few miles south, to feed the cows. Out of sheer habit he found an AA meeting nearby, attended weekly. On Thursday and Sunday evenings he drove to Kingdom Hall to worship. But he could feel a distance growing between himself and the congregation; the Witnesses wanted him married, and to another Witness, and he wasn't interested. He thought he might prefer worshipping alone, or just with Eddie or Bryan. He phoned congregations in DC, even drove up once, searching for Bryan Garner, that inmate from the benches at Harnett, the very first Witness he'd met. Last he'd heard, Garner had moved north, and Willie wanted to tell him what had happened, what Jehovah had come to mean to him, what Jehovah had accomplished in his case. But DC was so big. In the phone book he found men named Bryan Garner, but never the one he was looking for.

There was such a thing as the post-exoneration blues. A full week after Willie's panel, Chris still awoke numbly, feeling listless, as rootless and adrift as a mariner. For so many weeks she had surfed endorphins, the pressure had draped over her palpably, her purpose shone as clearly as a lighthouse, and now—what? Selfishly she had wanted that final day of the panel never to end—that lunch at the steak house, then marching into the sheriff's office with her shoulders back, order in hand. She could've stayed there forever. Now it was over. Willie was free, his name was off the sex-offender registry. He held a driver's license and a cell phone, had moved full-time to Gastonia. He didn't need her anymore.

How close she kept with an exoneree depended on the man. Greg Taylor lived right there in Durham. The pair still got coffee every so often. But Willie lived out west. Chris worried about him, out there on his own, which was mostly irrational, she knew. He had Gladys and his congregation. After a week of wandering, exhausted and nostalgic, she pulled that old notepad from her purse: *Cases of Innocence Still Open, Cases with No Avenues to Pursue*. Scratched out Willie's name entirely. Chose another name. Larry Lamb. There was work to do.

At the close of Willie's panel, Kendra had approached him and shaken his hand, still uncertain if he knew who she was. She had never explained her agency's work on his case, and didn't know how much Chris had told him. That was fine. It was the point. Grimes didn't owe her a thing. She, Lau, Stellato, her other staffers, had only done their jobs. They'd never worked on Grimes's behalf. Only on behalf of the truth. No headline she'd seen in the past two weeks read "Kendra Montgomery-Blinn Frees Man," and this was how she preferred it. It was what made her job different, made it special, she felt. She was in it for the right reasons. She had moved on to other cases she couldn't speak about.

It surprised her that no other state had followed with an IIC of its own, six full years after North Carolina's. Not yet, at least. Early on, after creating the new agency's rules and procedures, she'd also built a website, nearly chose innocencecommission.gov for its address, then realized she shouldn't, since when other states learned what North Carolina had achieved, they would follow with IICs of their own, and would need websites, too. So she appended -nc to the address. This left space for innocencecommission-ny.gov, -ca.gov, -fl .gov. None of those had happened. How come? Obviously there was a need. By now she or her staffers had discovered evidence in a dozen or so cases after being told no evidence existed. That was a frightening number, for everyone involved.

More frightening to Kendra was this: there was no reason to suspect that North Carolina was unique. It was simply that no one else was doing these investigations. An agency like hers wasn't the only model—a few states held conviction integrity units within their DA offices, those did good work, too, though they cost more to run. Most states had nothing at all, no one to run neutral, postconviction fact-finding, or to issue subpoenas and conduct searches. All that was a lot of work. Was it worth it? people sometimes asked her. She told them: "Why don't you go ask Greg Taylor if it was worth it?"

Kendra was right. That June, four months before Chris's closing argument at the Newton courthouse, the National Registry of Exonerations, a joint project of the law schools at Northwestern and the University of Michigan, issued its first report of known wrongful convictions in the United States, case after case summarized in compact, half-page paragraphs, alongside a notice that these were only the beginning—873 of them, between 11 and 66 in each year for more than two decades. Certainly more existed, going back further. But DNA testing had come into use only in 1989, and the registry had to begin somewhere. Its authors had chosen there.

Most of the 873 had been convicted of rape or homicide, only because these were the crimes where postconviction resources were concentrated. If you were a lawyer who recognized that trial verdicts could be mistakes, and felt moved to act, naturally you prioritized those assigned the longest sentences, or the death penalty, since it was where you felt most needed. Obviously those verdicts followed the most heinous crimes. This explained why most exonerations one saw in the news were for murders or rapes—not because those were the only verdicts reached in error, but because they received the most postconviction scrutiny. It stood to reason that innocent people were also being convicted of theft, or assault, or drug sales, or tax fraud, at roughly the same rate. It was just that no one was investigating those. "The procedure for convicting a defendant of a crime is set by law," the registry reported, to explain why it could be so difficult to identify mistakes. "There is no parallel procedure for deciding that a convicted defendant is innocent." In fact, this last sentence was false—of course there *was* such a procedure, here in North Carolina. Chris had seen to it personally.

The 873 exonerations had been discovered in forty-three different states, plus Puerto Rico and Washington, DC. The state with the most was Illinois, followed by New York, Texas, and California. It could be tempting to think, momentarily, that these were the states doing the worst job, wrongly convicting the most people. More likely the reverse was true; these were the states doing the *best* job, searching most responsibly for errors and overturning them. Two of the oldest, best-funded innocence projects in the country stood in Chicago and in New York City. Another was in Northern California. Well-run conviction integrity units were housed inside the DA's offices of Dallas and Houston. Coincidence? Chris doubted it. The prospect that kept her awake at night was that courtrooms in the other forty-six states across the country convicted just as many innocent people, proportionally to their populations, and simply hadn't noticed yet. Not a single exoneration, as far as the registry could find, had ever occurred in Maine or Vermont, in Delaware or New Mexico, in Wyoming or either of the Dakotas. Did that mean no innocent person had ever been convicted in those places? No. Men and women just like Willie, with siblings just like Gladys, with friends like Thomas Hill and Louie Ross, were languishing in those states at this very moment, wandering hopelessly in loops around a prison yard, or tossing on a thin, state-issue mattress, while Chris, sleepless at three o'clock in the morning, stared at her ceiling in Durham.

She wasn't surprised when, hardly ten months after its initial report, the registry published an update. Since listing those 873, researchers already had found 198 more. In 2012 alone, 97 people besides Willie had been exonerated—a new American record, though it would stand only briefly. Two years later would come 140 more exonerations. Which would stand even *more* briefly. The following year, 2015, would add another 151. The full tally by then would exceed 1,700, with at least one in each state in the country.

In its final pages, the registry's 2015 report would also mention, at last, a peculiar state agency. "In nine years of operation, the NCIIC has been responsible for nine exonerations. There's a lot to be said for agencies like the NCIIC—but there are no other agencies *like* the NCIIC in the United States. To create one would require legislative action and…funding by a legislature and a governor. Outside North Carolina, no state has been interested."

In 2016, 166 more men and women would be exonerated. Another record. "Since 2011," the registry would explain, "the annual number of exonerations has more than doubled."

On March 1, 2017, the number of exonerations would surpass two thousand.

Today the registry is adding exonerations weekly.

21,730 days—the total number of days that Dwayne, Willie, and Greg were incarcerated. Left to right: Dwayne Dail, Willie Grimes, Chris Mumma, Greg Taylor. *Courtesy of Christer Berg.*

A year or so after the three-judge panel, Teresa, the granddaughter of Carrie Elliott and sister of Tamera, who'd told reporters in Newton that obviously the Hickory Police Department had "got the ball rolling the wrong way," received a letter in the mail from Catawba County. A summons for jury duty. Unhappily she drove to the courthouse, asked a receptionist for the correct room, and took her seat to wait. Later, as lawyers spoke, the substance of the case hardly registered, only that it involved the Hickory Police Department, some crime they'd investigated. Teresa didn't need to hear anything more. When her number was called, an unfamiliar attorney approached. Could she think of any reason preventing her from being impartial?

"I wouldn't trust anything they do or say," Teresa answered, pointing toward the policemen. Neither she nor her siblings had attended their grandmother's trial, so they'd always just assumed it had gone properly; it shocked them, twenty-three years later, when the IIC reached out with news of a reinvestigation. What they'd learned about Willie Grimes, his fingerprints and hair and alibi, dumbfounded them. *How did they find him guilty in the first place?* Teresa had wondered, sitting beside her sister in Newton.

Today, a year later, she still felt grateful for the IIC, whom she'd never heard of before that. No one from the agency had ever whispered a single harsh word to her family, or about her grandmother, and it was obvious how much legwork they'd done. Without them, Teresa and her family would still believe a lie. She had not stopped feeling betrayed by the Hickory police. Her grandmother would never, *ever,* have chosen the wrong person on purpose, but it wasn't impossible to imagine what had happened: A friend whom Carrie trusted had told her something, and Carrie, in her shock, had believed it. And the police never investigated! And they paid the friend a reward! It was a shame this man Willie Grimes had gotten caught up in anything, and then so much time passed, and the *real* criminal got away, and today she was supposed to listen to the HPD? She didn't believe them one bit.

"No more questions," the lawyer told her. She was dismissed from the jury before she even sat down.

He had no interest in a lawsuit. Given the choice, like Teresa, he preferred not to return to any courtroom at all. All he wanted was a promise from the Hickory police, and from Catawba County, that neither would do to anyone else what they'd done to him. Or if not a promise then some sort of penalty, some public reprimand, where police would admit they'd been wrong, promise to do better. Without this, he worried nothing would change. They would simply choose another man and arrest him—another man like Willie, black and penniless and with no way to get out of it.

A penalty like that did exist, everyone told him. It was called a lawsuit.

So Chris found him a firm she trusted in nearby Raleigh, the same one that had handled the lawsuit for Greg Taylor. A typical attorney's fee for something like this was 40 percent of however much they won, but this firm had taken on Greg's for less, and Chris thought she could persuade them to do the same for Willie. She preferred not to represent her own clients in lawsuits. It wasn't where her expertise lay, and, besides, she didn't like the optics: exonerating a man, then turning around and suing? It allowed for a wrong impression of her motives.

"Federal Lawsuit Targets Area Officials," the *Hickory Daily Record* announced in October 2014. Willie's new attorneys had filed against the town as well as two county sheriffs, three clerks of court, two chiefs of HPD, and a pair of former officers, including Steve Hunt, who together had "conducted a grossly inadequate investigation," the suit alleged, "then withheld exculpatory evidence" despite "repeated requests...from Grimes's attorney," amounting to "negligent, willful, wanton, reckless, and deliberately indifferent acts and omissions," and robbing Willie of his liberty "without due process of law, in violation of the Fourteenth Amendment to the United States Constitution." Under common law in North Carolina, it also amounted to obstruction of justice.

The lawsuit was settled in August 2016, for $3.25 million. According to the language of the settlement, Hickory and its officials "do not admit liability of any sort," and their agreement is only "a compromise to avoid expense and to terminate all controversies...of any nature whatsoever, known or unknown, connected with the allegations."

In 2006, Steve Hunt ran for sheriff of Catawba County. He lost. In 2012 he ran for commissioner of Catawba County. He lost.

* * *

Because Carrie Elliott died in 1989, meaning, of course, that she can no longer testify, and because the only remaining evidence linking Albert Turner to her assault is a pair of decades-old fingerprints, Turner is unlikely ever to be charged with her rape. However. Statute requires the IIC to share with law enforcement any criminal evidence it discovers over the course of an investigation, related to any crime at all. After Willie's hearing, therefore, the agency turned over to Jay Gaither and the SBI the transcripts from its interview with Juanita Probst, the woman who'd misunderstood why Lau and Stellato had come and confided that Turner had raped her as a child. (Ms. Probst's name has been published already, in public documents.) The agency also turned over Turner's confession that he'd had intercourse with Probst when mathematically she'd been too young to consent. Which Probst hadn't done, regardless. There was no statute of limitations on a felony, Jay Gaither remarked to the *Hickory Daily Record*. That September, a week before Willie's three-judge panel, Turner was arrested. A month later, a district court judge found probable cause to charge him. A grand jury indicted him the following spring. But he never made it to trial. Turner died in April 2016, while out on bond. Police found him alone in his apartment when they visited to ask him about a welfare check. An autopsy showed his heart had failed from chronic alcohol abuse.

How would his life have gone, if none of this had happened? If Linda McDowell had never offered his name, if Miss Elliott had never chosen him from a lineup, if Steve Hunt had never knocked on Brenda's door. Where, and who, would he be?

He wasn't certain he would be alive at all. So many of his siblings, others he'd grown up with, had found problems with their thyroids or livers, or gotten diabetes, and couldn't afford their doctors' bills. One childhood neighbor had had knee and hip replacements, followed by organ failure. Even Gladys had cataracts. If the prostate cancer had befallen him on the outside, there was no chance he could have paid for surgery, radiation, all those appointments. The jobs he'd worked back then, at the textile plant and furniture shop, had offered no health insurance. Almost certainly that would have been the end of him.

If he'd survived, somehow? He guessed he would own some apartment and car, hold some job making hardly any money. Those things didn't matter. They weren't what he wondered about. The question was not what objects he would own but what person he would be. He felt he had been too impatient as a young man, too short-tempered, too distracted by the wrong things. Would he have overcome those on the outside, if his survival had not depended on it? Would he have found Jehovah? It was impossible to know. He would be different, he assumed. He hoped not by much.

He drove north from Gastonia to Lawndale, chugging up the rural hillsides in search of FOR SALE signs. Found one just eight minutes from where Thomas lived, on a winding road barely five hundred yards from a middle school, atop the crest of a rise overlooking an expanse of emerald and oatmeal and rust, hay bales lined countlessly to the horizon. The house had three bedrooms and its own outdoor shed and a red tin roof like the one from his childhood, so that he could hear the shelling rain. An old lady lived there and she promised him it was quiet, his neighbors wouldn't disturb him. When he moved in he noticed she'd left a decorative stone on the front steps with the word HOPE carved smoothly into an oval. He decided to keep it there.

She was right, the neighbors didn't disturb him. But one morning he was out mowing his lawn—he loved this part of owning a house, the fenceless outdoor solitude, his progress recorded slowly in the grass—when he noticed a neighbor's yard growing unruly. It turned out this was because the man who lived there worked all day and didn't have time to care for it, and couldn't afford to hire someone else to do it for him. Willie volunteered to mow that lawn in addition to his own. A second neighbor noticed and asked if Willie would mow his, too, even tried to pay him. Willie turned the money down. No one he knew in Lawndale wasn't poor, and he had a bank account now that his neighbors didn't. Soon he was mowing a dozen lawns, all for free. He bought a new riding lawn mower, then an old Dodge truck to haul the mower around.

For himself he bought a two-year-old Ford Taurus with only nine thousand miles on it, fancier than anything he'd ever owned. The week he steered it home, blue and red lights flashed in his mirrors and a police cruiser nudged him toward the shoulder. A car like that, silver and shining, there in Lawndale? Officers wanted to know where a black man they didn't recognize had gotten it.

Willie didn't know where to begin.

Acknowledgments

The people I spoke with in reporting this book, including many who appear in its pages, generously gave me their time, expertise, recollections, or records. I'm grateful to every one of them. Their names appear in my notes. A few deserve additional mention here, especially Willie Grimes and Chris Mumma, without whom there would be no story at all. I've done my best to get it right. Specific thanks also to Kendra Montgomery-Blinn. As director of a state agency, Kendra faced stricter confidentiality prohibitions than either Willie or Chris, and never once wavered from them, usually to my disappointment. She refuses to answer questions more politely than anyone else I've met.

Thanks to Sabrina Butler, Dwayne Dail, and Greg Taylor. In addition to Willie, these three exonerees helped me to see and understand life inside prison, and to begin imagining what it feels like to be sent there wrongly. That Dwayne and Sabrina don't appear personally in the narrative is only a disappointment of space.

Thanks to Teresa Hamlett, who shared with me the person her grandmother was. I'm sorry to Teresa and all her siblings for the trauma visited upon their family, and that it took so long to learn the truth of it.

Thanks to Jin Auh, at the Wylie Agency, for taking a chance on me, and for her advocacy. To the kind and responsive Jessica Friedman, also at Wylie. To Ben George at Little, Brown, for making me better. To the entire team there, including Pam Brown, Julie Ertl, Liz Garriga, Sarah Haugen, Lena Little, Pamela Marshall, and Carol

Fein Ross. To Tracy Roe, for her keen eye. To Ed Klaris, for his expertise, and for his patience with someone who never went to law school.

Thanks to my teachers. In chronological order of their generosity and influence: Mike Phelps, Richard Ford, Margot Livesey, Anthony Walton, Philip Gerard, David Gessner, Clyde Edgerton, and Dave Monahan.

A number of undergraduates at UNCW helped me to transcribe interviews. Without them I'd likely still be typing. Thanks especially to Nicole Aronis, Paula Eames, Marissa Flanagan, and Morgan Lehman.

Thanks to my family—my parents, Allan and Vicki, my brothers, Noah and Luke—who told me that I could.

And *mahalo nui loa* to Jaclyn—for so many things, large and small, that to list every one would require another book.

Notes

I first learned of Willie Grimes in January 2013, three months after he was exonerated. At the time I was twenty-six, in my first year of an MFA program in North Carolina, learning to write magazine features. I'm the middle of three brothers, and the age gap between me and Luke, the youngest, is two years. So Luke was twenty-four. That was my first thought, when I read of Willie in a local newspaper. *He's spent Luke's entire lifetime in prison.* I understood exactly how long this was.

I drove out to Lawndale in March thinking that, if Willie gave his blessing, I might try to write a magazine feature about his case. But the more I read, and the more I spoke with him and others, the more obvious it became that Willie's story did not occur in a vacuum. His experience would not have been possible — I would never have read of him — if not for an agency called the Innocence Inquiry Commission. And there was nothing else *like* the IIC anywhere in the United States. I didn't feel I could tell one of these stories without the other.

This book occupied most of my next four years.

By North Carolina statute, a portion of Willie's legal file became public record in April 2012, when the IIC voted his case forward to a three-judge panel. A further portion joined it at that panel the following October. Much of this archive may be found on the IIC's website, under *State v. Grimes*, at www.innocencecommission-nc.gov/grimes.html.

In addition, Willie waived attorney-client privilege on my behalf, and volunteered many of the documents he'd accumulated over the twenty-four years of his case. (Including, for example, his records from inside the Department of Correction.) Soon I met more attorneys and staffers at agencies that Willie had contacted, and they shared records of their own. The most important of these unpublished documents I have listed below.

Because of the braided structure of the book, it makes little sense to distinguish notes for each chapter individually, as though every one were reported separately from its neighbors. Their distinction in the narrative is only a stylistic choice. As the content of certain chapters overlaps, so did their reporting. Instead I have grouped notes more logically, according to their subject matter.

Documents that are published—and thus available more widely—I have listed separately, and alphabetically, in my sources.

PROLOGUE AND CHAPTER 1

Interviews: Stephen G. Fischer, at the FBI; Willie Grimes; Samuel Gross, at the National Registry of Exonerations; Betty Shuford Hairston; Teresa Hamlett; Chris Mumma; and Kendra Montgomery-Blinn.

Unpublished documents: For details of Carrie Elliott's assault and its investigation by the Hickory Police Department, I relied on the emergency department record and patient progress notes for Carrie Elliott from Catawba Memorial Hospital, dated October 24, 1987. I also relied on the case file from the Hickory Police Department, including evidence-control forms, incident and supplemental investigation reports, requests for examination of physical evidence, photographs of the crime scene, booking photographs, informal officer notes, and the arrest warrant for Willie Grimes, variously dated October 24 through 28, 1987. The North Carolina State Bureau of Investigation maintained an additional file, including a rape evidence kit and two SBI laboratory reports dated November 25, 1987, and June 28, 1988, respectively. Steve Hunt kept his own personal file on the case even in retirement, and I relied on that, too.

For details of pretrial maneuvering by Ed de Torres and the Catawba County DA, I relied on correspondence between Ed de Torres, William Johnson, and John C. Hennigar, dated spring and summer 1988. The attorney file of Ed de Torres also included personal notes and memos, pretrial motions from April 1988, and the affidavits filed in Catawba County Superior Court for William "Les" Robinson, Betty and Carolyn Shuford, Brenda Smith, Rachel Wilson, and Richard Wilson in February and March 1988.

Details about that first national report on wrongful convictions in the United States, and the cases it included, are drawn from the National Registry of Exonerations. The registry is listed in my sources, but it is also available online at www.law.umich.edu/special/exoneration/Pages/about.aspx.

For Willie's initial trial, in July 1988, of course I relied on the transcript of the proceeding. Further details, including what Willie and Ed de Torres were personally thinking at various moments, come from each man's testimony years later at the IIC hearing and three-judge panel. Transcripts from all three of those proceedings may be found through the Catawba County courts.

Three of the witnesses called during Willie's trial (the ER doctor, the evidence technician, and Willie himself) I present in the narrative slightly out of the actual sequence they were called to testify. I've done this only for clarity, so that readers can follow the events described at trial chronologically, without the confusing out-of-order sequence in which lawyers presented their arguments.

CHAPTERS 2–18 (EVEN)

These chapters follow Chris Mumma, Beverly Lake, and the Actual Innocence Commission from July 1988 to August 2005.

Interviews: Jim Coleman; Kim Cook, at UNC Wilmington; Ben David; Gretchen Engel, at the Center for Death Penalty Litigation; Mike Gauldin; I. Beverly Lake Jr.; Kendra Montgomery-Blinn; Chris Mumma; Theresa Newman; Pat Norris; Bob Orr; Donna Pygott; Russell Rawlings, at the North Carolina Bar Association; Rich Rosen; Tom Ross; Don Stephens; Jennifer Thompson; and Pete Weitzel.

Unpublished documents: In 1998, while a law student at UNC Chapel Hill, Chris Mumma wrote an assignment on her juror experience in the James McDowell case, "Change in Perspective: A Juror's View Ten Years After a Capital Punishment Verdict." I relied on this unpublished paper as well as court records from the case.

For details of the meetings of the North Carolina Actual Innocence Commission, the study group created by Beverly Lake, I relied on the private notes and correspondence of Lake as well as the private notes, drafts, receipts, and correspondence of Chris Mumma. The AIC also recorded its own legislative drafts, working papers, meeting agendas and minutes, and survey and poll results. Rich Rosen's welcoming monologue at their first meeting at Chris Mumma's house, on November 22, 2002, is drawn from his prepared remarks for the occasion.

For more details on the career and perspective of Tom Ross, I relied on his remarks upon receiving the William H. Rehnquist Award in Washington, DC, on November 13, 2000, and on his later remarks to the North Carolina Supreme Court Historical Society on October 10, 2013.

The memorandum by the Winston-Salem Police Department in reply to the AIC's recommendations concerning eyewitness identification was titled "Response to Eyewitness Identification Procedure Recommendations by the North Carolina Actual Innocence Commission" and dated January 30, 2004.

CHAPTERS 3–29 (ODD)

These chapters follow Willie's experience in prison from July 1988, when he was convicted, to September 2010, when the IIC accepted his case.

Interviews: Herbert Berg, at UNC Wilmington; Sylvester Branch, at *Watchtower* magazine; Sabrina Butler; Kim Cook; Dwayne Dail; Mary Duquette, at the Hickory school board; Dr. Amy Feldman, at Allergy Partners of Coastal Carolina, to rule out environmental causes for Willie's poor health; J. Phillip Griffin Jr., now retired from Prisoner Legal Services; Willie Grimes; Thomas Hill; Peggy Mainness, at Patrick Beaver Memorial Library; Eddie Moose; Chris Mumma; Gladys Perkins; Louie Ross; Bryan Stewart; Anne Stalnaker, at Hickory High School; Greg Taylor; and Afton Turner.

Unpublished documents: For details of Willie's time in prison, I relied on his file at the North Carolina Department of Correction, including medical and mental-health records; cell and case manager assignments; case management notes; administrative segregation and offense and disciplinary reports; infraction, classification, and transfer and external movement records; job activity, programs activity, arrest, and visitation histories; temporary leave forms; judgment and commitment orders; employment/work skill/military detail; and general control information. The NC Post-Release Supervision and Parole Commission kept an additional file on Willie, including correspondence. I also found useful an online forum called Prison Talk, where the families and friends of inmates can share tips and impressions of various facilities, including, for example, a prison's visitation and mail policies. The forum specifically called North Carolina Prison Profiles is available at www.prisontalk.com/forums/forumdisplay.php?f=346.

For the chronology of Willie's failed appeals, and more letters he wrote from prison, I relied on Ed de Torres's attorney file on Willie, including private notes, correspondence, and billable hours, as well as Willie's file at North Carolina Prisoner Legal Services, including his application, statements, and correspondence with J. Phillip Griffin, Marvin Sparrow, and Charles E. Jones. The North Carolina Center on Actual Innocence, once Willie applied there in 2003, kept its own file on him, including correspondence, application questionnaires, and internal memos. So did the IIC, once Willie applied there in 2010, including transcripts of interviews that Jamie

Lau and Sharon Stellato conducted with Willie over the course of their investigation. Noell Tin's attorney file on Willie Grimes, though only a page or two, since Tin intersected with Willie's case only briefly, through Eddie Moose, was also helpful. So was the private correspondence of Willie Grimes, Gladys Perkins, and Louie Ross, including with attorneys Ed de Torres and Walter T. Johnson.

For histories of the towns of Lawndale and Hickory, the indispensable Peggy Mainness, at Patrick Beaver Memorial Library, led me through archives of newspaper clippings, regional tourism pamphlets, and yearbooks from Ridgeview High, home of the Untouchables. Ann Stalnaker, who later became the principal of Hickory High School, wrote her 2013 doctoral dissertation, at UNC Greensboro, on the history of desegregation in the school and region, and she graciously shared it with me. It is called "Desegregating Hickory High School, 1955–1975."

For the beliefs and practices of Jehovah's Witnesses, in addition to my interviews with several Witnesses, elders, and a religion scholar at UNCW, I relied on publications from the Watch Tower Bible and Tract Society, including the magazines *Watchtower* and *Awake!* and its preferred New World Translation of the Holy Scriptures. These resources and others are available in print and also on jw.org.

Central Prison has been renovated since Willie arrived there in 1988. Neither K nor O dorm exists today. Wherever possible I relied on historical photographs and interviews with inmates who were incarcerated there from the time in question; however, I also relied generally on what the prison looks like today.

CHAPTERS 20, 22, 23, 25, 26, 28, AND 30

These chapters follow Chris Mumma and the Center on Actual Innocence from June 2003 to September 2010, as it worked on Willie's case, as well as the earliest cases of the IIC during this same period.

Interviews: Dwayne Dail; Ben David; Willie Grimes; I. Beverly Lake Jr.; Kendra Montgomery-Blinn; Chris Mumma; Cheryl Sullivan, at the Center on Actual Innocence; Greg Taylor; and Pete Weitzel.

Unpublished documents: Details on the earliest cases to proceed to IIC hearings—*State v. Reeves, State v. McNeil,* and *State v. Taylor*—may be found on the IIC's website, www.innocencecommission-nc.gov. By legislative design, those cases that proceeded further along in the IIC process offer progressively more in the public record. Greg Taylor, as the first person in U.S. history exonerated this way, has been covered most widely, and a range of published documents about him and his case appear in my sources.

For details about its own work on Willie's case, I relied on the Center on Actual Innocence file on Willie Grimes, including memos, reports, and correspondence, from August 2006 to September 2010, and the personal notes, drafts, and correspondence of Chris Mumma. I also relied on Willie's own correspondence over the same period.

For details of the ongoing, final meetings of the Actual Innocence Commission, from November 2002 to October 2006, I relied on meeting minutes and working papers from the group itself.

CHAPTERS 31–32

Chapters 31 and 32 follow the IIC's investigation into Willie's case from September 2010, when it received his application, to April 2012, the close of his eight-member hearing.

Interviews: Willie Grimes, Betty Shuford Hairston, Teresa Hamlett, Jamie Lau, Kendra Montgomery-Blinn, Chris Mumma, Gladys Perkins, Sharon Stellato, and Bryan Stewart.

Unpublished documents: For details of Willie's time in prison, I relied again on his files from the North Carolina Department of Correction, the North Carolina Post-Release Supervision and Parole Commission, and the Center on Actual Innocence, and all they include, listed previously. I also relied again on Ed de Torres's attorney file and the personal correspondence of Chris Mumma and Willie Grimes.

For details of the IIC's investigation, in addition to my own interviews with IIC staffers, I relied on testimony given afterward by Kendra Montgomery-Blinn, Jamie Lau, Sharon Stellato, and Dustin Nowatka at the IIC's eight-member hearing in April 2012 and three-judge panel the following October. The Center on Actual Innocence file on Willie Grimes contains notes, memos, correspondence, progress reports, and summaries, including summaries of the interviews conducted by Jamie Lau and Sharon Stellato with friends, relatives, attorneys, acquaintances, or victims of Willie Grimes and Albert Turner. Turner's criminal history is drawn from records of the Hickory Police Department, the Catawba County sheriff's office, and the NC Department of Correction. Of course I also relied on the full record of Willie's IIC hearing. In addition to the transcript, a video recording of that proceeding is available through WRAL, at www.wral.com/news/local/asset_gallery/10937343.

For details of the various suspect lineups and which documents appeared in one police folder but not the other, I relied on the Hickory Police Department file on Willie Grimes as well as Steve Hunt's personal investigative file.

For details of the AFIS software and its search run on the fingerprints recovered from Carrie Elliott's apartment, I relied on the relevant AFIS match report and North Carolina State Crime Laboratory report, both dated November 2011.

For details of the passing of Carrie Lee Elliott, in addition to my interview with one of her surviving grandchildren, I also consulted Ms. Elliott's death record.

As with Willie's 1988 trial in Chapter 1, several of the witnesses called during Willie's hearing I present in the narrative out of the sequence they were actually called to testify. I've done this only for clarity, so that readers can follow events chronologically, without the confusing out-of-order sequence in which witnesses actually were called. I've done the same with some of the interviews conducted during the IIC's investigation, and for the same reason. I have changed no content from any of these interviews or testimonies, only their sequence, so that readers may follow them logically.

CHAPTERS 33–35

These chapters follow preparations for, and the event of, Willie's three-judge panel, from April to October 2012.

Interviews: Robert Campbell, Dwayne Dail, Jay Gaither, Willie Grimes, Teresa Hamlett, Jamie Lau, Kendra Montgomery-Blinn, Eddie Moose, Chris Mumma, Gladys Perkins, Louie Ross, Sharon Stellato, Bryan Stewart, Cheryl Sullivan, and Greg Taylor.

Unpublished documents: For details of Chris Mumma's and Robert Campbell's work to prepare for the three-judge panel, I relied on the Center on Actual Innocence file on Willie Grimes, including correspondence, notes, memos, press releases, CVs for Robert Drdak and Jennifer E. Dysart, and a polygraph examination of Willie Grimes from September 21, 2012. I also relied on the personal correspondence of Chris Mumma and notes and exhibits by Robert Campbell. For the panel itself, of course, I relied on its transcript. I also relied on video footage of the proceeding, recorded by Gregg Jamback at Swiftwater Media. Gregg was in the courtroom to film a documentary on a different case. He kindly shared his unused footage with me.

As with prior trials and hearings, several of the witnesses called during Willie's three-judge panel I present here out of the sequence they were actually called to testify. I've done this only for clarity, so that readers can follow events chronologically, without the confusing out-of-order sequence in which witnesses were actually called.

CHAPTER 36

Chapter 36 follows the events after Willie's exoneration, from October 2012 to 2016.

Interviews: Burton Craige, at Patterson Harkavy LLP; Willie Grimes; Betty Shuford Hairston; Teresa Hamlett; Thomas Hill; Eddie Moose; Chris Mumma; G. Chris Olson, at Martin and Jones PLLC; Gladys Perkins; Maurice Possley, at the National Registry of Exonerations; Louie Ross; Bryan Stewart; and Afton Turner.

Unpublished documents: For details on the legal processes of removing Willie's name from the sex-offender registry, regaining his license, and applying for compensation, I relied on the Center on Actual Innocence file on Willie Grimes. I also relied on correspondence from the North Carolina Industrial Commission, the North Carolina Post-Release Supervision and Parole Commission, and the North Carolina Department of Transportation, Division of Motor Vehicles. For details on Albert Turner's death, I relied on his autopsy report, available through the Office of the Chief Medical Examiner, North Carolina Department of Health and Human Services. For details of the outcome of Willie's civil lawsuit, I relied on the settlement agreement itself.

Several figures with meaningful roles in the story, though I reached out to them, declined to comment. These include Eric Bellas, Steve Hunt, Ed de Torres, Linda McDowell, and Colon Willoughby.

Sources

Alexander, Maggie. "Judge Rules in Cummings Hearing." WECT (Wilmington, North Carolina). January 27, 2005.

———. "Race, Politics Not a Factor in Murder Trial, Judge Rules." WECT (Wilmington, North Carolina). January 28, 2005.

Allen Mitchell Funeral Home. "Albert Lindsay Turner: January 15, 1947–March 7, 2016." March 2016.

American Bar Association. "Toward Greater Awareness: The American Bar Association Call for a Moratorium on Executions Gains Ground." August 2001.

Associated Press. "Inmates' Claims Could Get Review." *Charlotte Observer,* 2006.

———. "James Parker: Victims Recant, Accused 'Molester' Freed." November 30, 2004.

———. "Judge Charges New Man in Rape Case After Panel Clears Gaston Man." *Gaston Gazette,* October 17, 2012.

———. "Man Is Put to Death for Double Slaying During Crime Spree." *New York Times,* October 24, 1992.

———. "North Carolina Death Penalty Panel Urged to Halt Executions." News 14 Carolina, January 4, 2007.

———. "Police Hunt for Suspect in Murder Outside Church." *Wilmington Morning Star,* August 21, 1987.

———. "Taylor Will Have to Wait for Pardon." *News and Observer,* May 8, 2010.

Atkins v. Virginia, 536 U.S. 304 (2002).

Balko, Radley. "How the Flawed 'Science' of Bite Mark Analysis Has Sent Innocent People to Prison." *Washington Post,* February 13, 2015.

Barefoot v. Estelle, 463 U.S. 880 (1983).

Barrett, Michael. "Panel: Gaston Man Wrongly Convicted of 1987 Rape." *Gaston Gazette,* October 5, 2012.

Begley, Sharon. "Leaving Holmes in the Dust." *Newsweek,* October 26, 1987.

Bennett Place 2241, United Daughters of the Confederacy. "I. Beverly Lake Scholarship." http://bennettplace2241.webs.com/scholarship.htm.

Betts, Jack. "A Gain for Justice." *Charlotte Observer,* February 23, 2010.

Blackburn, Jim. "About Jim Blackburn." Jim Blackburn Seminars, LLC. http://www.blackburnseminars.com.

Blake, William. "Voices from Solitary: A Sentence Worse Than Death." *Solitary Watch,* March 11, 2013.

Blythe, Anne. "Former Wake District Attorney Colon Willoughby Looks Back on Career." *Raleigh News and Observer,* April 5, 2014.

———. "Police Reopen '91 Murder Case." *Raleigh News and Observer,* March 18, 2010.

———. "Taylor Case Brings Commission Renown." *Raleigh News and Observer,* February 22, 2010.

———. "Three Know Taylor's Ordeal All Too Well." *Raleigh News and Observer,* February 19, 2010.

———, and Lynn Bonner. "DNA Law Raises Questions." *Raleigh News and Observer,* July 29, 2010.

———, and Amy Dunn. "Innocence Commission Founder Calls for Big Changes." *Raleigh News and Observer,* June 5, 2010.

Borlik, Joe. "Hickory Man Convicted in 1987 Rape to Get Chance at Freedom." Fox 8, April 5, 2012.

Bradshaw, Kourtney A. "Charlotte, NC: Birthplace (and Place of Death) of Integration in Public Schools." North Carolina History Projects. http://carolinahistory.web.unc.edu/charlotte-nc-birthplace-and-place -of-death-of-integration-in-public-schools/.

Brady v. Maryland, 373 U.S. 83 (1963).

Brown, Robbie. "Judges Free Inmate on Recommendation of Special Innocence Panel." *New York Times,* February 18, 2010.

Brown v. Board of Education (II), the Oyez Project at IIT Chicago-Kent College of Law. http://www.oyez.org/cases/1950-1959/1954/1954_1/.

Brown v. Board of Education of Topeka, KS. 349 U.S. 294 (1955).

Bune, Karen. "When the Innocent Become Victims." Officer.com, August 4, 2008.

Bush, Jack, Barry Glick, and Juliana Taymans. "Thinking for a Change: Integrated Cognitive Behavior Change Program." National Institute of Corrections Academy, 1997. Revised February 2002.

Candler, Laura. "After Innocence: James Waller Speaks About What Exoneration Feels Like." WUNC North Carolina Public Radio. Chapel Hill, NC: June 13, 2013.

Carolina Journal Online. "Friday Interview: N.C. Actual Innocence Commission Revisited." June 1, 2012. http://www.carolinajournal.com/exclusives/display_exclusive.html?id=9114.

Catawba County Government. "Profile—About Catawba County, North Carolina." http://www.catawbacountync.gov/about.asp.

Chalfant, Claudine. "24 Years Wrongfully Imprisoned Shaped Grimes into Man He Is Today." *Time Warner Cable News: Charlotte,* April 29, 2015.

Charlotte Observer staff. "Getting It Right: If N.C. Courts Convict Wrong Persons, Criminals Go Free." *Charlotte Observer,* August 18, 2005.

———. "Hickory Man Arrested in 1973 Rape Case." *Charlotte Observer,* September 28, 2012.

———. "Righting Wrongs: Panel Would Help Make Sure Criminals Don't Run Free." *Charlotte Observer,* July 11, 2006.

CNN. "Rogue Justice." *CNN Presents,* January 30, 2011.

Committee on Identifying the Needs of the Forensic Sciences Community, National Research Council. *Strengthening Forensic Science in the United States: A Path Forward.* National Academy of Sciences report. August 2009.

Connors, Edward, et al. *Convicted by Juries, Exonerated by Science: Case Studies in the Use of DNA Evidence to Establish Innocence After Trial.* National Institute of Justice report. June 1996.

Crabtree, David, and Keith Baker. "Life on Death Row: 'Am I Going to Be Next?,'" WRAL, February 27, 2013.

Crosby, David. "An Expanding Economy: In Diversification Is Strength." *Hickory Area Report.* 1988.

———. "Introduction." *Hickory Area Report.* 1988.

———. "Teamwork and Foresight: An Award-winning Combination." *Hickory Area Report.* 1988.

———. "A Transport Center: Planes, Trains and Trucks." *Hickory Area Report.* 1988.

Daily Cynema. "Central Prison—Home of North Carolina's Death Row." *Daily Cynema,* April 24, 2010. https://dailycynema.wordpress.com/2010/04/24/central-prison-home-of-north-carolinas-death-row/.

David, Ben. "Community-Based Prosecution in North Carolina: An Inside-Out Approach to Public Service at the Courthouse, on the Street, and in the Classroom." *Wake Forest Law Review* 47 (2012): 373–411.

Davis, Patty. "Wrongly Convicted Take Center Stage at Death Penalty Forum." CNN, November 15, 1998.

Death Penalty Information Center. "Legislative Activity—North Carolina." Accessed September 6, 2013. http://www.deathpenaltyinfo.org/legislative-activity-north-carolina.

———. "List of Those Freed From Death Row." Accessed November 15, 2016. http://www.deathpenaltyinfo.org/innocence-list-those-freed-death-row.

DeVayne, Richard. "Panel to Review Hickory Rape Case." *Charlotte Observer*, September 27, 2012.

Diane Wilson et al. v. Hickory City Board of Education. D. Ct. 529 (1966).

Duggan, Paul. " 'Sheetrock Scandal' Hits Dallas Police." *Washington Post*, January 18, 2002.

Duke, Steven B., Ann Lee, and Chet K. Pager. "A Picture's Worth a Thousand Words: Conversational Versus Eyewitness Testimony in Criminal Convictions." *American Criminal Law Review* 44 (2007).

Duke Law News. "Kendra Montgomery-Blinn '03." *Duke Law News*, June 26, 2009.

Durose, Matthew R., and Patrick A. Langan. "Felony Sentences in State Courts, 2002." *Bureau of Justice Statistics Bulletin*, December 2004.

Ehlers, Matt. "Taylor's Exoneration Prompts Police to Reinvestigate Case." *Raleigh News and Observer*, March 17, 2010.

"Eighty-Fourth Congress: January 3, 1955, to January 3, 1957." S. Doc. Biographical directory.

Eisley, Matthew, Anne Saker, and Andrea Weigl. "Cocaine Found in Office of NC Courts Top Administrator." *Raleigh News and Observer*, August 18, 2004.

Eubanks, Georgann. "Overturning Wrongful Convictions." *Duke Magazine*. July–August 2002: 28–33.

Exum, James G., Jr. "Presentation of the Portrait of I. Beverly Lake., Sr., Associate Justice." Opening remarks and presentation acceptance. June 15, 1994.

"Facing Controversy: Struggling with Capital Punishment in North Carolina." Curated by Biff Hollingsworth and Tim West. Chapel Hill, NC: University of North Carolina at Chapel Hill. Online exhibition. http://exhibits.lib.unc.edu/exhibits/show/capital-punishment.

Federal Bureau of Investigation. "FBI Laboratory Announces Discontinuation of Bullet Lead Examinations." Press release, September 1, 2005.

———. "FBI Testimony on Microscopic Hair Analysis Contained Errors in at Least 90 Percent of Cases in Ongoing Review." Press release, April 20, 2015.

Gardner, Kelly. "Convicted Rapist Maintains Innocence in 1987 Case." WRAL, April 3, 2012.

———. "DA: Taylor Didn't Meet Burden to Prove Innocence." WRAL, February 17, 2010.

———. "Innocence Panel Takes Up 1988 Catawba Rape Conviction." WRAL, April 2, 2012.

———. "Innocence Panel Refers 1987 Hickory Rape Case for Judicial Review." WRAL, April 4, 2012.

Garner, Bryan E. "An Escaped Convict Turns Himself Back In." *Awake!* February 8, 1994.

Gaston Gazette staff. "We Can Learn Patience, Grace from Willie Grimes." *Gaston Gazette,* October 12, 2012.

Geary, Bob. "What of Those Who Can't Afford Expensive Defense Attorneys?," *Indy Week,* April 18, 2007.

Gideon v. Wainwright, 372 U.S. 335 (1963).

Goldberg, Eric. "Ridgeview Overcame Obstacles." *Hickory Daily Record,* 1975.

Greene, Susan. "Apple Tossed in Garbage May Have Cleared Man." *Denver Post,* July 25, 2007.

Gross, Samuel R., Kristen Jacoby, Daniel J. Matheson, and Nicholas Montgomery. "Exonerations in the United States, 1989 through 2003." *Journal of Criminal Law and Criminology* 95, no. 2 (2005).

Gross, Samuel R., and Michael Shaffer. "Exonerations in the United States, 1989–2012." National Registry of Exonerations, June 22, 2012.

Hampton, Kristen. "Man Cleared in '87 Rape Case Says Police Cost Him 25 Years of Life." WRAL, October 12, 2012.

Harris, Stephen. "Violent Crimes Increase 47% in County." *Newton Observer-News-Enterprise,* July 6, 1978.

Helton, Sarah. "Tips Will Aid Fight by Police." *Hickory Daily Record,* August 31, 1988.

Herrera v. Collins, 506 U.S. 390 (1993).

Hickory Daily Record reporters. Bobby Elliott obituary. *Hickory Daily Record,* January 31, 2013.

———. "Breaking News: Innocence Commission judges Determine Grimes Is Innocent Of 1987 Rape in Hickory." *Hickory Daily Record,* October 5, 2012.

———. "Few Know Historical Date." *Hickory Daily Record,* October 28, 1983.

———. "Grimes' Future Hangs in the Balance as Arguments Begin in Innocence Inquiry Commission Hearing." *Hickory Daily Record,* October 1, 2012.

———. "Hickory Man Charged with 1st-Degree Rape." *Hickory Daily Record,* undated.

———. "Hickory Man to Be Freed from Prison After 24 Years." *Hickory Daily Record,* May 21, 2012.

———. "His Dream Led Him Out of the Projects to His Life's Purpose." *Hickory Daily Record,* February 13, 2012.

———. "1973 Rape Suspect in Hickory Gets New Attorney." *Hickory Daily Record,* May 7, 2013.

———. "Old Fingerprints Give Hickory Man a Chance at Freedom." *Hickory Daily Record,* April 4, 2012.

———. "Ratio of Blacks to Whites in Unifour Complex 8.53%." *Hickory Daily Record,* March 1, 1971.

———. "Suspect Sought in Reported Rape." *Hickory Daily Record,* undated.

Houck, Max, and Bruce Budowle. "Correlation of Microscopic and Mitochondrial DNA Hair Comparisons." *Journal of Forensic Science* 47, no. 5 (September 2002).

Houck, Max, et al. "Located Exchange: The Science of Forensic Hair Comparisons and the Admissibility of Hair Comparison Evidence: Frye and Daubert Considered." *Modern Microscopy* (March 2, 2004).

Hunter, Tye, and Danielle Carman. "Implementing the Right to Counsel in Innocence Inquiry Commission Proceedings." Memorandum from the Office of Indigent Defense Services to Kendra Montgomery-Blinn at the Innocence Inquiry Commission and Chris Mumma at the Center on Actual Innocence, February 12, 2008.

Innocence Project. "DNA Exonerations Nationwide." February 7, 2007. http://www.innocenceproject.org/free-innocent/improve-the-law/fact-sheets/dna-exonerations-nationwide.

———. "Fact Sheet: Eyewitness Identification Reform." January 31, 2007. http://www.innocenceproject.org/free-innocent/improve-the-law/fact-sheets/eyewitness-identification-reform.

———. "Fact Sheet: Preservation of Evidence." January 31, 2007. http://www.innocenceproject.org/free-innocent/improve-the-law/fact-sheets/preservation-of-evidence.

Jarvis, Craig. "N.C. Prosecutors Want More Bill Concessions." *Raleigh News and Observer,* February 17, 2012.

Johnson, Ellis. "Buffalo Bills Strengthened by Famed Ex-Ridgeview QB." *Hickory Daily Record,* November 5, 1964.

———. "Ex-Ridgeview Grid Great, Now Playing with Redskins." *Hickory Daily Record*, 1964.

———. "Ridgeview, Central Clash Slated Here Friday Night." *Hickory Daily Record*, 1964.

JW.org. "Bible Words Index." http://www.jw.org/en/publications/bible/nwt/bible-words-index/##p2204.

———. "Books of the Bible." http://www.jw.org/en/publications/bible/nwt/books/.

———. "Frequently Asked Questions About Jehovah's Witnesses." http://www.jw.org/en/jehovahs-witnesses/faq/.

———. "Jehovah's Witnesses." http://www.jw.org/en.

Kenney, Andrew. "Judge Upholds SBI's Firing of Duane Deaver." *Durham News*, August 27, 2014.

Khanna, Samiha. "Christine Mumma—Tar Heel of the Year." *Raleigh News and Observer*, December 30, 2007.

———. "Judge Clears Assistant Durham DA of Intentionally Keeping Man in Prison; Calls for New DA's Office Police." *Indy Week* blog, August 13, 2010.

———. "A Prosecutorial Mistake Leaves a Durham Man in Prison." *Indy Week*, June 23, 2010.

Lake, Beverly I., Sr. Interview by Charles Dunn. *Documenting the American South: Interview C-0043, Southern Oral History Program Collection (#4007)*. September 8, 1987.

Lamb, Amanda, and Erin Hartness. "Rape Victim Apologizes to Wrongfully Convicted Man." WRAL, May 9, 2008.

Lamb, Amanda, and Adam Owns. "Taylor, Now Free: 'Truth Has Prevailed.'" WRAL, February 17, 2010.

Langley, Scott. "The Execution Facilities of North Carolina at Central Prison, Raleigh." Langley Creations Photography. http://www.langleycreations.com/photo/deathpenalty/central-prison/.

Latta, J. L. "History of Hickory's Public School System Traced by Maj. Latta." *Hickory Daily Record*, date unknown.

Leslie, Laura. "N.C. Sets Up Innocence Inquiry Panel." *All Things Considered*. WUNC North Carolina Public Radio, August 3, 2006.

Lewis, J. D. "I. Beverly Lake, Jr.: 26th Supreme Court Chief Justice." http://www.carolana.com/nc/courts/iblakejr.html.

Little, Ken. "Death Sentence Stands." *Wilmington Star News*, January 28, 2005.

Littlejohn, Yolanda. "He Didn't Do It." *Raleigh News and Observer*, January 21, 2010.

Locke, Mandy. "Agent Defends Tests for Blood." *Raleigh News and Observer*, February 13, 2010.

———. "Bittersweet Liberty: Dwayne Dail Struggles to Adapt to Life Outside Prison and Bond with His Son." *Raleigh News and Observer*, December 9, 2014.

———. "DA Is Urged to Free Taylor." *Raleigh News and Observer*, October 13, 2009.

———. "Dail Takes an Interest in Another's Fight to Be Free." *Raleigh News and Observer*, February 17, 2010.

———. "Discarded Evidence Costs Some NC Inmates a Chance at Freedom." *Raleigh News and Observer*, March 16, 2013.

———. "Ex-FBI Agent Calls Taylor Arrest a 'Rush to Judgment.'" *Raleigh News and Observer*, February 10, 2010.

———. "Family Pushes for Convict's Release." *Raleigh News and Observer*, September 19, 2009.

———. "Greg Taylor Pardoned by Governor." *Raleigh News and Observer*, May 21, 2010.

———. "Hearing Gives Man Chance at Exoneration." *Raleigh News and Observer*, February 10, 2010.

———. "Historic Steps Lead Taylor to Freedom." *Raleigh News and Observer*, February 18, 2010.

———. "In Taylor Case, Blood Is the Issue." *Raleigh News and Observer*, February 11, 2010.

———. "Innocence Panel Sets Greg Taylor Free." *Raleigh News and Observer*, February 17, 2010.

———. "Judge Won't Delay Taylor Case." *Raleigh News and Observer*, January 16, 2010.

———. "Lawyers Fault Taylor Case." *Raleigh News and Observer*, November 26, 2009.

———. "Prisoner Awaits Decision on Release." *Raleigh News and Observer*, September 24, 2009.

———. "Prosecutors Would Limit Access to N.C. Innocence Panel." *Raleigh News and Observer*, May 8, 2011.

———. "Taylor Gets His Shot at Release." *Raleigh News and Observer*, February 7, 2010.

———. "Taylor Prosecutor Weighs In Again." *Raleigh News and Observer*, February 9, 2010.

———. "The Truth Seeps Out at Last; a Man Is Freed." *Raleigh News and Observer*, August 10, 2010.

———. "Victim's Sister Works to Clear Convicted Man." *Raleigh News and Observer,* February 13, 2010.

———. "Wake District Attorney to Contest Cary Man's Innocence." *Raleigh News and Observer,* October 13, 2009.

Locke, Mandy, and Anne Blythe. "SBI to Review Old Lab Cases." *Raleigh News and Observer,* February 28, 2010.

Locke, Mandy, and Titan Marksdale. "Wrongly Convicted Man Ready to Live Life." *Raleigh News and Observer,* August 29, 2007.

Locke, Mandy, and Joseph Neff. "Innocence Panel to Examine Contempt Charge Against SBI Agent." *Raleigh News and Observer,* October 1, 2010.

———. "SBI Employee Resumes Work." *Raleigh News and Observer,* November 13, 2010.

———. "State Police Group Urges Criminal Probe of SBI." *Raleigh News and Observer,* August 19, 2010.

———. "Taylor Suit Seeks Money from SBI." *Raleigh News and Observer,* June 29, 2011.

Maiatico, Jerome M. "All Eyes on Us: A Comparative Critique of the North Carolina Innocence Inquiry Commission." *Duke Law Journal* 56 (2007): 1345–76.

Mann, Lisa Hammersly. "After 14 Years, Parker Now Free." *Charlotte Observer,* November 30, 2004.

Mapp v. Ohio, 367 U.S. 643 (1961).

Marquis, Joshua. "The Innocent and the Shammed." *New York Times,* January 26, 2006.

Marsden, Lawrence. "After 25 Years in Prison, Grimes New Day in Court Arrives in Front of Innocence Inquiry Panel." *Hickory Daily Record,* October 3, 2012.

———. " 'Free at Last': Innocence Commission Judges Determine Grimes Is Innocent of 1987 Rape in Hickory." *Hickory Daily Record,* October 5, 2012.

———. "Key Witness in Grimes' Hearing Won't Testify Before Innocence Inquiry Commission." *Hickory Daily Record,* October 4, 2012.

Marsden, Skip. "DA Pursuing Probe of Possible Perjury in Grimes Hearing." *Hickory Daily Record,* October 9, 2012.

———. "Hickory Man Indicted for 1980s Rape." *Hickory Daily Record,* March 8, 2013.

———. "Probable Cause Found in Case Against '73 Hickory Rape Case." *Hickory Daily Record,* October 17, 2012.

Marsh, Michelle. "Man Claiming Innocence in 1987 Rape Released on Parole." WRAL, May 21, 2012.

Martinez, Rick. "A Better Way to Fix Mistakes." *Raleigh News and Observer,* June 9, 2010.

Marusak, Joe, and April Bethea. "Man Exonerated After 24 Years in Prison." *Charlotte Observer,* October 5, 2012.

Marymount International School. "Spotlight On: Christine Cecchetti Mumma." http://www.marymountrome.org/base.php?code=587.

Matsumoto, Evan. "Catawba County Denies Willie Grimes Lawsuit." *Hickory Daily Record,* December 11, 2014.

———. "Federal Lawsuit Targets Area Officials: Exonerated Man Files Suit, Alleges 'Reckless Investigation.'" *Hickory Daily Record,* October 15, 2014.

McBrayer, Sharon. "Surprise Arrest in 1973 Hickory Sexual Assault Case." *Hickory Daily Record,* September 27, 2012.

McMurtrie, Jacqueline. "The Role of the Social Sciences in Preventing Wrongful Convictions." *American Criminal Law Review* 42 (2005).

Mecklenburg County Bar. "Resolution and Memorial Commemorating the Life and Service of the Honorable Kenneth A. Griffin." June 6, 2002.

Miller, John. "Experts Focus on Witness Testimony, Reliability at Innocence Inquiry Commission Hearing." *Hickory Daily Record,* October 3, 2012.

Mills, Steve, and Ken Armstrong. "Convicted by a Hair." *Chicago Tribune,* November 18, 1999.

Miranda v. Arizona, 384 U.S. 436 (1966).

Moffeit, Miles, and Susan Greene. "Trashing the Truth." *Denver Post,* July 2007.

Moore, Robert F. "Innocent, but He Did 14 Years in Prison." *New York Daily News,* November 30, 2004.

———. Interview with Gil Kerlikowske. Date unknown.

———. "Triumphs and Tragedies of DNA Exoneration: Dwayne Allen Dail." Video recording of presentation at Postconviction DNA Case Management Symposium, National Forensic Science Technology Center, January 22–23, 2009. http://projects.nfstc.org/postconviction/video/m4v/0201.htm.

Mumma, Christine C. "Guidelines for Counsel Appointed by Indigent Defense Services for Claims Investigated by the North Carolina Innocence Inquiry Commission." North Carolina Center on Actual Innocence, August 14, 2007, updated March 16, 2011.

———. "Guilty Until Proven Innocent? Greg Taylor's Long Fight for Freedom." Working paper.

————. *Interview with NC Political Review.* August 2003.

————. Letter to the editor. *Raleigh News and Observer,* August 9, 2006.

————. "The North Carolina Actual Innocence Commission: Uncommon Perspectives Joined by a Common Cause." *Drake Law Review* 52 (2004): 647–56.

————. "The North Carolina Innocence Inquiry Commission: Catching Cases that Fall Through the Cracks," in *Wrongful Conviction and Criminal Justice Reform: Making Justice,* ed. Marvin Zalman and Julia Carrano (New York: Routledge, 2014), 249.

————, and Robert Campbell. "*State v. Willie Grimes:* Obtaining Freedom Through the Innocence Inquiry Process." *North Carolina State Bar Journal* 18, no. 3 (Fall 2013): 8–12.

National Institute of Justice. *Eyewitness Evidence: A Guide for Law Enforcement.* October 1999.

————. National Commission on the Future of DNA Evidence. Last modified April 3, 2013. http://www.nij.gov/topics/forensics/evidence/dna/commission/pages/welcome.aspx#overview.

National Registry of Exonerations. https://www.law.umich.edu/special/exoneration/Pages/about.aspx.

————. "Exonerations in 2013." February 4, 2014.

————. "Exonerations in 2014." January 27, 2015.

————. "Exonerations in 2015." February 3, 2016.

————. "Exonerations in 2016." March 7, 2017.

————. "Update: 2012." April 3, 2013.

Neeley, Olivia. "Innocence Project Contends Wilson Man Wrongfully Imprisoned for 36 Years." *Wilson Times,* January 23, 2013.

————. "Innocence Project Seeks Murder Convict's Release." *Wilson Times,* January 30, 2013.

Neff, Joseph. "Ex-SBI Agent Cleared of Contempt Charge." *Hickory Daily Record,* September 15, 2011.

————. "Former SBI Agent Duane Deaver Will Challenge Firing at Hearing." *Hickory Daily Record,* April 2, 2014.

————. "Legal Tangle May Slow SBI Reforms." *Hickory Daily Record,* August 20, 2010.

————. "SBI Agent to Face Contempt Hearing." *Hickory Daily Record,* October 8, 2010.

————. "SBI Agents' Testimony Is Critical of Deaver." *Hickory Daily Record,* December 10, 2011.

————. "SBI Fires Much-Criticized Agent." *Hickory Daily Record,* January 11, 2011.

———. "SBI in Minority on Test Results." *Hickory Daily Record,* December 26, 2010.

———. "State Is Slow on Records Access." *Hickory Daily Record,* November 11, 2010.

———, and Mandy Locke. "Former SBI Employees at Center of Greg Taylor's Wrongful Conviction Still Defend Work." *Hickory Daily Record,* December 19, 2013.

Newton Observer-News-Enterprise staff. "County Population Toward 100,000." *Newton Observer-News-Enterprise,* June 21, 1977.

New World Translation of the Holy Scriptures (2013 revision).

North Carolina Actual Innocence Commission. "Recommendations for Eyewitness Identification." October 9, 2003.

North Carolina Center on Actual Innocence. "North Carolina Center on Actual Innocence." http://www.coai.org.

———. "Willie Grimes Officially Exonerated By Innocence Commission After Serving 25 Years In Prison." Press release. October 2012.

North Carolina Department of Correction. "Policy and Procedures: Community Based Programs for Sex Offenders." June 25, 2010.

———. "Policy and Procedures: Inmate Release Procedures." January 30, 2013.

———. "Policy and Procedure: Community Volunteer Program." July 1, 2010.

North Carolina Department of Correction, Division of Prisons. "Handbook for Family and Friends of Inmates." February 2006.

———. "Prison Program Description: Mutual Agreement Parole Program." April 15, 2009. http://www.doc.state.nc.us/DOP/Program/mapp.htm.

———. "Prison Program Description: Napoleon Hill Project." February 14, 1997. http://www.doc.state.nc.us/DOP/Program/napoleon.htm.

———. "Prison Program Description: A New Direction/DART Treatment Program." August 28, 2008. http://www.doc.state.nc.us/DOP/Program/dart.htm.

———. Prisons: Policy and Procedure Manual." http://www.doc.state.nc.us/dop/policy_procedure_manual/.

———. "SOAR Fact Sheet." April 5, 2000. http://www.doc.state.nc.us/dop/health/mhs/special/soardesc3.htm.

North Carolina Department of Correction, Post-Release Supervision and Parole Commission. "Report on the Status of the Mutual Agreement Parole Program." March 1, 2011. http://www.doc.state.nc.us/legislative/2011/Status_of_the_MAPP_Program.pdf.

North Carolina Department of Health and Human Services, Office of the Chief Medical Examiner. "Report of Investigation by Medical Examiner for decedent Albert L. Turner." May 20, 2016.

North Carolina Department of Justice. "The North Carolina Sex Offender and Public Protection Registration Programs." Revised January 2011.

North Carolina Department of Public Safety. "Correction Enterprises: Plant Information." https://www.correctionenterprises.com/about/plant-information/.

———. "Division of Adult Corrections and Juvenile Justice Officials." http://www.doc.state.nc.us/admin/Official.htm.

———. "Offender Public Information: Brian E Garner." http://webapps6.doc.state.nc.us/opi/viewoffender.do?method=view&offenderID=0141350&searchLastName=garner&searchFirstName=brian&listurl=pagelistoffendersearchresults&listpage=1.

———. "Parole Commission: Administration." April 4, 2013. https://www.ncdps.gov/Index2.cfm?a=000003,002210,002215.

———. "Prisons." https://www.ncdps.gov/Index2.cfm?a=000003,002240.

———. "Prisons: Policy and Procedure Manual." http://www.doc.state.nc.us/dop/policy_procedure_manual/.

North Carolina General Assembly. "An Act to Make Various Amendments to the Law Regarding the Innocence Inquiry Commission." S.B. 144, General Assembly Session 2009, Session Law 2010-171. August 2, 2010.

———. "An Act to Provide That the North Carolina Innocence Commission May Compel the Testimony of a Witness and the Commission Chair May Grant Limited Immunity to the Witness from Prosecution for Previous False Statements Made Under Oath in Prior Proceedings." H.B. 937, NC General Assembly Session 2009, Session Law 2009-360. July 27, 2009.

———. "HB 1323 / S.L. 2006-184: Establish NC Innocence Inquiry Commission." August 3, 2006.

———. "NC General Statutes: Chapter 15A Article 89, Motion for Appropriate Relief and Other Post-Trial Relief."

———. "NC General Statutes: Chapter 15A Article 92, "North Carolina Innocence Inquiry Commission."

———. "996 HB 1323: Establish NC Innocence Inquiry Commission." August 11, 2005.

North Carolina History Project. "Catawba County (1842)." http://www.northcarolinahistory.org/encyclopedia/581/entry/.

North Carolina House of Representatives. *Amend Innocence Inquiry Commission*. 1795 SB 144. Roll Call Legislative Session Day 150. July 9, 2010.

———. *Establish North Carolina Innocence Inquiry Commission.* 1758 HB 1323, Roll Call Legislative Session Day 171. July 25, 2006.

North Carolina Industrial Commission. "Petition for Compensation Pursuant To N.C. Gen. Stat. § 148-82 *ET SEQ*," claimant Willie James Grimes. November 8, 2012.

North Carolina Innocence Inquiry Commission. Brief for *State v. Gregory Flynt Taylor,* Wake County 91CRS71728. September 2009.

———. Brief for *State v. Henry Reeves.* December 2007.

———. Brief for *State v. Willie J. Grimes,* Catawba County 87CRS13541-42. December 2007.

———. "Innocence Commission Names Durham Assistant D.A. as Its Executive Director," News release, March 28, 2007.

———. "Innocence Inquiry Commission Receives Federal Grant." News release, September 30, 2009.

———. "Man's Conviction Upheld in Innocence Hearing." News release, September 3, 2008.

———. "Mock Brief: State of North Carolina v. Billy Times." August 2007.

———. "North Carolina Innocence Inquiry Commission." http://www.innocencecommission-nc.gov.

———. "The North Carolina Innocence Inquiry Commission Rules and Procedures." Adopted May 25, 2007; revised in 2007, 2008, 2009, 2010, 2011.

———. "North Carolina Makes Legal History: Innocence Commission Conducts First Hearing and Case Is Referred to Three-Judge Panel." News release, December 17, 2007.

———. "Opinion of the North Carolina Innocence Inquiry Commission, State of North Carolina v. Terry Lee McNeil." January 23, 2009.

———. "Report to the 2008 Session of the General Assembly of North Carolina." February 4, 2008.

———. "Report to the 2009–2010 Long Session of the General Assembly of North Carolina." March 12, 2009.

———. "Report to the 2009–2010 Short Session of the General Assembly of North Carolina." April 8, 2010.

———. "Report to the 2011–12 Long Session of the General Assembly of North Carolina and the State Judicial Council." March 1, 2011.

———. "Report to the 2011–12 Short Session of the General Assembly of North Carolina and the State Judicial Council." February 15, 2012.

———. "Report to the 2013–14 Regular Session of the General Assembly of North Carolina and the State Judicial Council." February 14, 2013.

North Carolina Senate. *Amend Innocence Inquiry Commission.* 1584 SB 144. Roll Call Legislative Session Day 147. July 9, 2010.

———. *Establish NC Innocence Inquiry Commission.* 1583 HB 1323. Roll Call Legislative Session Day 174. July 26, 2006.

North Carolina State Bar. Order of Disbarment in the Matter of the Tender of Surrender of License of James L. Blackburn, 93 BCS 3 (April 16, 1993).

———. Order of Discipline in the Matter of the Tender of Surrender of License of Timothy E. Oates, 99 BCS 6 (1988).

North Carolina Victim Assistance Network. "History of NCVAN." http://www.nc-van.org/history.html.

Northwestern University. "Bloom Legal Clinic Center on Wrongful Convictions." http://www.law.northwestern.edu/legalclinic/wrongfulconvictions/.

O'Malley, Gabriel. "The Execution of Carlos DeLuna: Preventing Wrongful Convictions." *Boston Review,* October 22, 2012.

O'Neill, Patrick. "Innocence Inquiry Commission Could Help Clear Man Facing Life Sentence." *Indy Week,* August 27, 2008.

———. "Judges Uphold Reeves' Conviction." *Indy Week,* September 4, 2008.

———. "Key Witnesses Testify at Unprecedented Trial." *Indy Week,* August 29, 2008.

Porter, Jane. "Bill Would Eliminate Actual Innocence Commission." *Indy Week,* May 28, 2014.

Quillin, Martha. "Ex-Agent Deaver Ordered into Talks with Innocence Panel." *Raleigh News and Observer,* August 6, 2011.

Raleigh News and Observer staff. "A Life Saved." *Raleigh News and Observer,* February 21, 2010.

———. "Blood-Hounded." *Raleigh News and Observer,* February 19, 2010.

———. "Case Closed." *Raleigh News and Observer,* May 25, 2010.

———. "'F' in Science." *Raleigh News and Observer,* August 11, 2010.

———. "Innocence Panel Gets Grant for Tests." *Raleigh News and Observer,* October 3, 2009.

———. "Innocent, Right?" *Raleigh News and Observer,* March 18, 2010.

———. "Just the Facts." *Raleigh News and Observer,* February 22, 2012.

———. "Lab Assignment." *Raleigh News and Observer,* March 13, 2010.

———. "Long Enough." *Raleigh News and Observer,* October 14, 2009.

———. "A Long Wait." *Raleigh News and Observer,* April 9, 2012.

———. "Taylor Found Innocent." *Raleigh News and Observer,* February 17, 2010.

————. "Testimony on Blood Test Changed." *Raleigh News and Observer,* August 19, 2010.

————. "Testing the Crime Lab." *Raleigh News and Observer,* March 3, 2010.

————. "Two Years Free After 6,149 Days In Prison, Greg Taylor Unsure of a Direction." *Raleigh News and Observer* blog, April 23, 2013.

————. "What the Agent Said." *Raleigh News and Observer,* October 6, 2010.

Ridgeview High School Annual. "Panthers Football: 1930–1965." 1966.

Rosen, Richard A. "Innocence and Death." *North Carolina Law Review* 82, no. 1 (December 2003).

————. "Reflections on Innocence." *Wisconsin Law Review* no. 2 (2006).

Ross, Tom. "Remarks of Thomas W. Ross on the Occasion of William H. Rehnquist Award Presentation." November 13, 2000.

Rutledge, John P. "They All Look Alike: The Inaccuracy of Cross-Racial Identifications." *American Journal of Criminal Law* 28 (2001).

Ryan, George H. "Governor Ryan Declares Moratorium on Executions, Will Appoint Commission to Review Capital Punishment System." Press release, January 31, 2000.

————. "Report of the Governor's Commission on Capital Punishment." Press release, April 15, 2002.

Saunders, Barry. "The Girl Her Sister Knew." *Raleigh News and Observer,* February 25, 2010.

————. "Relook, Don't Retread." *Raleigh News and Observer,* March 30, 2010.

Schwartzapfel, Beth. "Who Shot Valerie Finley? Why One Man's Innocence Is So Hard to Prove." *Boston Review* (March/April 2013).

Secret, Mosi. "Changes Urged in Legal System to Protect Poor Defendants." *Indy Week,* March 7, 2007.

————. "N.C. Innocence Inquiry Commission Begins Nov. 1." *Indy Week,* November 8, 2006.

————. "Questions Raised About Victims' Rights Advocate." *Indy Week,* November 8, 2006.

"The Seventeen-Year Saga of Greg Taylor." *Dateline.* NBC, May 31, 2013.

Sheehan, Ruth. "Did a Fox Guard the Hens?" *Raleigh News and Observer,* October 28, 2009.

————. "He Fought to Fix Wrongs; Now He Waits." *Raleigh News and Observer,* February 10, 2010.

————. "What Is the DA Thinking?" *Raleigh News and Observer,* February 17, 2010.

Shipp, E. R. "'Forgive,' Asks Woman in Rape Disavowal." *New York Times,* November 28, 1985.

6,149 days: The True Story of Greg Taylor. Directed and produced by Clay Johnson. Capital Broadcasting Company, 2012. Online at http://www.wral.com/news/local/documentaries/page/10942135/.

Smith, Clive, A. Stafford, and Patrick D. Goodman. "Forensic Hair Comparison Analysis: Nineteenth Century Science or Twentieth Century Snake Oil?" *Columbia Human Rights Law Review* 27, no. 227 (Winter 1996).

Smith, Ken. "Innocence Commission Is Lake's Legacy." WRAL, February 19, 2010.

Smith, Sharon. "Man in Prison for 24 Years on a Wrongful Conviction Files Federal Lawsuit." *Charlotte Observer,* October 13, 2014.

State of North Carolina v. Gregory Flint Taylor, 337 N.C. 597, 447 S.E.2d 360 (1993).

State of North Carolina v. Gregory Flynt Taylor, 91 CRS 71728. Innocence Inquiry Commission Evidentiary Hearing (Superior Crt. 2010).

State of North Carolina v. James Courtney McDowell, 329 N.C. 363, 407 S.E.2d 200 (1991).

State of North Carolina v. Willie J. Grimes, Innocence Inquiry Commission Evidentiary Hearing, 87 CRS 13541/42/44. (Superior Crt. 2012).

———. Innocence Inquiry Commission Evidentiary Hearing, Opinion, 87 CRS 13541/42/44 (April 4, 2012).

———. Three-Judge Panel Hearing, 87 CRS 13541/42 (Superior Crt. Special Session, October 1–5, 2012).

State of North Carolina v. Willie James Grimes. "Affidavit." May 21, 2012.

———. "Decision of the Three-Judge Panel Pursuant to N.C. Gen. Stat. § 15A-1469." October 5, 2012.

———. "Motion to Compel Discovery." August 13, 2012.

———. "Motion to Hold in Abeyance." May 2012.

———. "Plea for Declaration of Innocence." September 2012.

———. "State's Response to Commission Order." September 3, 2012.

———. "Stipulation of Facts." September 2012.

State of North Carolina vs. Willie James Grimes, 87 CrS 13540; 13541; 13542; 13544 (Superior Crt. July 1988).

———. 386 S.E.2d 214, 96 N.C. App. 489 (1989).

———. 397 S.E.2d 227, 327 N.C. 485 (1990), cert denied.

———. 923 F.2d 849, 1991 WL 5924 (4th Cir. (N.C.)), Unpublished Disposition, dismissed.

———. AOC-CR-350 (Rev. 10/83), 87CRS13542-44 (1988).

———. Brief for the State, No. 8925SC119 (1989).

————. COA-75 (Rev. 9/1/88), NC Ct. of Appeals No. 8925SC119 (1989).

————. Defendant appellant's brief, COA08-1597 No. 8925SC119 (1989).

————. Hearing, 87 CrS 13540; 13541; 13542; 13544 (Superior Crt. 1988).

————. Motion for Appropriate Relief, NO. 8925SC119 (1989).

————. N.C. 569A88 (1989), vacated and transferred to NC Court of Appeals.

————. No. 270P95, 342 N.C. 416 (1995), cert denied.

————. No. 8925SC119, Motion for Extension of Time (1989).

————. Order to Amend Judgment and Order of Commitment, 87 CRS 13544-42 (1991).

Stewart, Alva. "Hickory, N.C.—'Best-Balanced City.'" 1986.

Tate, Mary Kelly. "Commissioning Innocence and Restoring Confidence: The North Carolina Innocence Inquiry Commission and the Missing Deliberative Citizen." *Maine Law Review* 64, no. 2 (2012): 531–52.

Taylor, Cyndie. "Report Shows Crime Rate Soaring in Newton." *Newton Observer-News-Enterprise,* February 10, 1981.

Thompson, Estes. "James Blackburn: His Life as a Prosecutor, Convict and Waiter." *Lubbock Avalanche-Journal,* October 8, 2000.

Thompson, Jennifer. "Triumphs and Tragedies of DNA Exoneration: Ronald Cotton." Video recording of presentation at Postconviction DNA Case Management Symposium, National Forensic Science Technology Center, January 22–23, 2009. http://projects.nfstc.org/postconviction/video/m4v/0201.htm.

————, and Ronald Cotton. "Picking Cotton: Jennifer Thompson and Ronald Cotton's Story." YouTube book trailer video, Keppler Speakers, August 31, 2012. https://www.youtube.com/watch?v=XsBplRi1PfA.

Thompson-Cannino, Jennifer, and Ronald Cotton with Erin Torneo. *Picking Cotton: Our Memoir of Justice and Redemption.* New York: St. Martin's Press, 2009.

United States Department of Justice, Office for Victims of Crime. "Victim Service Award Nominees, 1995: Augustus A. 'Dick' Adams." http://www.ovc.gov/ncvrw/1995/awardees.htm.

University of Leicester. "Alec Jeffreys and Genetic Fingerprinting." http://www2.le.ac.uk/departments/genetics/jeffreys.

University of Michigan Law School. "The National Registry of Exonerations." https://www.law.umich.edu/special/exoneration/Pages/about.aspx.

U.S. Census Bureau. "Hickory, North Carolina." American Community Survey Estimate: 1990, 2000.

Wake County Board of Commissioners. "Growth Trends." PowerPoint presentation of the 2010 U.S. Census. http://www.wakegov.com/data/bythenumbers/Documents/Trends2012.pdf.

Watchtower Bible and Tract Society of New York. *What Does the Bible Really Teach?* Brooklyn: Watchtower Bible and Tract Society of New York, 2005.

WBTV. "State Clears Man Wrongly Convicted in 1987 Rape Case; a Witness Could Face Charges." October 4, 2012.

"Weidner Among First Settlers." Source unknown. Hickory, NC. 1988.

Weigl, Andrea. "Innocence Panel Closer to Reality After Senate Vote." *Raleigh News and Observer,* July 11, 2006.

———. "Lake Pushes Innocence Panel." *Raleigh News and Observer,* April 17, 2005.

———. "Panel Approves Innocence Plan." *Raleigh News and Observer,* March 8, 2005.

———. "Wrongful Conviction Spurs Quest." *Raleigh News and Observer,* October 31, 2005.

Weinstein, Henry. "North Carolina to Weigh Claims of Innocence." *Los Angeles Times,* August 4, 2006.

Wells, Gary L., and Elizabeth A. Olson. "Eyewitness Testimony." *Annual Review of Psychology* 54 (2003).

Westervelt, Saundra, and Kimberly Cook. *Life After Death Row: Exonerees' Search for Community and Identity.* New Brunswick, NJ: Rutgers University Press, 2012.

"What God Has Done for You." *Watchtower* 135, no. 5 (March 1, 2014).

"What Jennifer Saw." *Frontline.* PBS. http://www.pbs.org/wgbh/pages/frontline/shows/dna/interviews/thompson.html.

Whitener, Pamela. "Hickory Marks Anniversary: 1st City Election Held Jan. 3, 1870." *Hickory Daily Record,* January 3, 1970.

Wiggins, Norman A. "Presentation of the Portrait of I. Beverly Lake, Sr., Associate Justice." Presentation Address, June 15, 1994.

Wilgoren, Jodi. "Citing Issue of Fairness, Governor Clears Out Death Row in Illinois." *New York Times,* January 12, 2003.

Willie Grimes v. State of North Carolina, 5:96CV9-MU, W.D.N.C. 8925SC119 (1996), dismissed.

Willie James Grimes v. City of Hickory et al., Complaint, Case 5:14-cv-00160. Filed October 6, 2014.

Willie James Grimes v. G. G. Hayes et al., AO 241, W.D.N.C., ST-C-91-55 (1992).

Willie James Grimes v. G.G. Hayes et al., AO 450 (Rev. 5/85), W.D.N.C., ST-C-91-55 (1993).

Willie James Grimes v. Joseph Lafton et al., AO 241 (Rev. 5/851), 4th Circ., 8925SC119 (date unknown).

Willie James Grimes v. State of North Carolina, Defendant's pro se appellant brief, N.C. 569A88 (1989).

Woolverton, Paul. "Innocence Panel Advances." *Fayetteville Observer,* July 13, 2006.

WRAL. "Easley: Innocence Commission Will Help Wrongly Convicted." August 3, 2006.

———. "Lawmakers Reach Compromise on Innocence Commission." July 25, 2006.

———. "N.C. Innocence Commission Already Has Hefty Caseload." December 26, 2006.

———. "NC Wanted: Raleigh Family Seeks Answers in Unresolved Case." September 6, 2014.

———. "Senate Approves Innocence Commission." July 11, 2006.

———. "Willie Grimes Innocence Commission Hearing Video," Pts. 1–14. http://www.wral.com/news/local/asset_gallery/10937343/.

WSOC. "DA Grants Limited Immunity for Inmate Testimony in Grimes Case." October 3, 2012.

———. "Gaston County Man Fights to Clear His Name, 25 Years Later." October 3, 2012.

———. "Grimes' Name Removed from NC Sex Offender Registry." October 8, 2012.

———. "Grimes Testifies After 25 Years of Serving in Prison for Rape." October 2, 2012.

———. "Grimes Testifies on Tuesday Against 1987 Rape, Kidnapping Charges." October 2, 2012.

———. "Judge Finds Probable Cause to Charge Hickory Man with Decades Old Rape." October 17, 2012.

———. "Man Cleared of Rape Conviction After Spending Years in Prison." October 5, 2012.

———. "Man Fights to Clear Conviction After Spending Years in Prison." October 1, 2012.

———. "Man Refuses to Testify in Hearing About 1987 Rape Case." October 4, 2012.

Z. Smith Reynolds Foundation. "2009 Nancy Susan Reynolds Award Winners." July 1, 2009. http://www.zsr.org/announcements/2009-nancy-susan-reynolds-award-winners.

Zerwick, Phoebe. "Innocence Commission: N.C. Creates First in Nation to Backstop Courts." *Winston-Salem Journal,* August 20, 2006.

Index

Note: The abbreviation WG refers to Willie Grimes.

About the Author

Benjamin Rachlin grew up in New Hampshire. He studied English at Bowdoin College and writing at the University of North Carolina Wilmington. His nonfiction has appeared or is forthcoming in the *New York Times Magazine, Time,* and the *Virginia Quarterly Review,* among other publications. He lives in Boston.